Making Love Modern

Making Love Modern

The Intimate Public Worlds of New York's Literary Women

NINA MILLER

Oxford University Press

New York Oxford

1999

Oxford University Press

Oxford New York
Athens Auckland Bangkok Bogotá Buenos Aires Calcutta
Cape Town Chennai Dar es Salaam Delhi Florence Hong Kong Istanbul
Karachi Kuala Lumpur Madrid Melbourne Mexico City Mumbai
Nairobi Paris São Paulo Singapore Taipei Tokyo Toronto Warsaw

and associated companies in
Berlin Ibadan

Published by Oxford University Press, Inc.
198 Madison Avenue, New York, New York 10016

Oxford is a registered trademark of Oxford University Press.

Library of Congress Cataloging-in-Publication Data
Miller, Nina.
Making love modern : the intimate public worlds of
New York's literary women / Nina Miller.
p. cm.
Includes bibliographical references and index.
ISBN 0-19-511604-6; ISBN 0-19-511605-4 (pbk.)
1. American literature—New York (State)—New York—History and criticism. 2. Feminism and literature—New York (State)—New York—History—20th century. 3. Women and literature—New York (State)—New York—History—20th century. 4. Women authors, American—New York (State)—New York—Biography. 5. Love poetry, American—Women authors—History and criticism. 6. American literature—Women authors—History and criticism. 7. American literature—20th century—History and criticism. 8. Women—New York (State)—New York—Intellectual life. 9. Modernism (Literature)—New York (State)—New York. I. Title.
PS255.N5M55 1999
810.9'9287'097471—DC21 97-44487

Portions of chapters 2 and 3 first appeared as "The Bonds of Free Love: Constructing the Female Bohemian Self," *Genders* 11 (Fall 1991): 37–57 and are reprinted with permission from University of Texas Press.

Portions of chapters 4 and 5 first appeared as "Making Love Modern: Dorothy Parker and Her Public," *American Literature* 64 (December 1992): 763–784 and are reprinted with permission from Duke University Press.

Portions of chapters 6 and 7 first appeared as "Femininity, Publicity, and the Class Division of Cultural Labor," *African American Review* 30: 2 (Summer 1996): 205–220 and are reprinted with permission from Indiana State University Press.

1 3 5 7 9 8 6 4 2

Printed in the United States of America
on acid-free paper

To my parents

Kirsten Marie Jensen

and

Donald Gray Miller Jr.

Tusind Tak

Acknowledgments

When I think of how long it has taken me to write this book, I am doubly grateful to the many excellent colleagues, friends, and relations who have managed to stay interested in the outcome. The project began as my dissertation, and I would like, first of all, to thank my committee: Christine Froula, for good-natured support and salutary skepticism; Michael Warner, for being the first to think my "minor women" were worthy of critical attention, for teaching me so much, for unwavering enthusiasm, and for friendship; and John Brenkman, my director, who from my first day of graduate school provided me with the kind of intellectual guidance most people only dream of getting and the sense of why academic work is important and what responsibility it carries.

I had wonderful early readers in Nancy Ring and Glenn Hendler (the dissertation group), who comprised my first, best, intellectual community and without whom I would still be ABD. Doug Payne was an astute and enthusiastic reader of the early chapters. Ken Wissoker gave me critical feedback for what would be the final shape of the book. My father, Donald Miller Jr., read much of the material and kept me honest and moving toward clarity (at least, he tried); thanks for unfailing interest in all my endeavors. Kristen Mahlis and Brenda Daly gave useful feedback on key sections and very welcome support. Jackie Litt and Jim McGlew dropped everything to render me sage advice at a critical juncture. Fern Kupfer and Ruth Yasser answered my endless Yiddish translation questions with perfect good humor and generosity; I thank Ruth in particular for taking the time to read the Dorothy Parker material and encourage me in my efforts.

Al Clarke was a remarkably efficient research assistant, scrounging up last-minute citations on slim leads; for that and for genuine interest in the material, thanks. Thanks to Sheryl Kamps for last-minute typing; Courtney Peterson and Andy Swan for computer support; and thanks to my daughter,

Kendra Hejbøl Miller Scheuerlein, for typing, foraging, expert photo selection, and, mostly, putting up with it all, all through her young life.

I am grateful to the Northwestern University Alumnae Association for granting me a full year of fellowship support at an early, critical stage; to Iowa State University for a summer research grant and a faculty development grant; and to ISU's Women's Studies Program for financial support.

T. Susan Chang, literary acquisitions editor at Oxford University Press, had faith in this project from the very first and acted on that faith to see the book into print. Rahul Mehta and Susan Barba, Susan Chang's assistants, were always gracious and helpful; thanks to the anonymous manuscript readers for their generous and detailed responses.

Carla Kaplan has been an essential reader, particularly of the Harlem chapters, and an unfailingly supportive colleague.

My greatest debt is to Mathew Roberts, who read everything, many times, and gave me the benefit of his always-acute assessment (whether I wanted to hear it or not). Without his tireless engagement, lively intellect, and unfailing good judgment, it is hard for me to imagine how this book would ever have come into being.

"Day Dreams," "Finis," "Folk Tune" by Dorothy Parker, copyright 1926, renewed 1954 by Dorothy Parker. "The Far-Sighted Muse" by Dorothy Parker, copyright 1926, by Dorothy Parker, renewed. "For R.C.B." by Dorothy Parker, copyright 1928, renewed © 1956 by Dorothy Parker, from *Dorothy Parker: Complete Poems* by Dorothy Parker. Used by permission of Penguin, a division of Penguin Putnam Inc.

"Black Laughter," "The Desert Remembers Her Reasons," "Doomsday," "Elegy," "The Enamel Girl," "Epithalamium," "Galatea Again," "If You Are a Man," "Just Introduced," "Man in the Wind," Introduction from *May Days: An Anthology of Verse from Masses-Liberator,* "Poet Out of Pioneer," "Quarrel," "Truce," "Two Captives," "Two in a Dark Tower: No Child Roland," "Unacknowledged Dedication" by Genevieve Taggard, reprinted by permission of Marcia D. Liles.

Contents

Making Love Modern

Introduction

> The group, the movement, the circle, the tendency seem too marginal or too small or too ephemeral, to require historical and social analysis. Yet their importance, as a general social and cultural fact, especially in the last two centuries, is great: in what they achieved, and in what their modes of achievement can tell us about the larger societies to which they stand in such uncertain relations.
>
> Raymond Williams,
> "The Bloomsbury Fraction"

The aura surrounding the 1920s shows no sign of diminishing. Our postmodern attention to modernism has moved most recently and conspicuously into the movies, where in an eight-year span we have had no fewer than five major Hollywood events: *The Moderns* (director Allan Rudolph, 1988), *Henry and June* (director Phillip Kaufman, 1990), *Tom and Viv* (director Brian Gilbert, 1994), *Mrs. Parker and the Vicious Circle* (director Rudolph, 1995), and *Carrington* (director Christopher Hampton, 1996). Lavish of intellect and emotion, determinedly on the edge, the modernists are Beautiful People enlarged by consummate articulateness.[1] Critically speaking, they are ripe for literary gossip, as well as for the reconstruction of "background" for individual literary genius. But what of modernist self-consciousness itself? How does it go to shape the very nature of those "movements and circles" filling the scene? In exploring the work of modernist women love poets, I wanted to make self-consciousness—the aura of *being* a modern—part of the equation. Having once fixed my attention on it, I discovered my writers' "aura" to have more than one source: not just a local self-understanding (and a nostalgic projection from the present), aura also enwreathed a wider construction of womanhood in this period. What were the mechanisms and uses of such a seemingly intangible convergence? And what did they mean for women writers ranged at various intersections of racial identity, class status, and subcultural ethos on the larger map of modern New York?

Making Love Modern is a work of feminist criticism that uses cultural studies methodology to give material grounding and nuance to the question of women's literary strategy. The interest of my writers—Edna St. Vincent Millay, Genevieve Taggard, Dorothy Parker, Gwendolyn Bennett, and Helene Johnson—lies in the fact that each is clearly situated as simultaneously a subject, a producer, and (directly or indirectly) an icon of modern culture. Several interpenetrating contexts define the work of these writers: the geographical center of New York City in the late teens and twenties, the discursive "space" of particular modernist subcultures, the ideological force of local feminine icons, and the genre of love poetry. It goes without saying that I believe these writers deserve scholarly attention, yet my interest lies to one side of current debates about the modernist canon and literary value. While I am indebted to the tremendous revisionary work of recent modernist criticism, I find that issues of aesthetic definition and the canonical writers themselves are only tangentially related to my study.[2] For me, the real significance of my writers' work lies in their intense engagement with *modernity.*

Rita Felski offers the following distinctions in *The Gender of Modernity*: if "modernism" is "a specific form of artistic production . . . [c]haracterized by such features as aesthetic self-consciousness, stylistic fragmentation, and a questioning of representation," the French "modernité" captures the modern *experience*: "[C]oncerned with a distinctively modern sense of dislocation and ambiguity, [modernité] locates it in the more general experience of the aestheticization of everyday life, as exemplified in the ephemeral and transitory qualities of an urban culture shaped by the imperatives of fashion, consumerism, and constant innovation."[3] Felski's introduction also includes the following caution to scholars: "Rather than simply subsuming the history of gender relations within an overarching meta-theory of modernity articulated from the vantage point of the present, feminist critics need to take seriously past women's and men's own understandings of their positioning within historical and social processes" (8).[4] Following Felski's clear-sighted injunction and her equally useful definitions, the present study will take *subcultural self-understanding* as its central analytic framework for approaching modern women's love poetry.

As it has come to be defined by the Birmingham school of cultural studies, subculture grows out of working-class life.[5] Research in this mode has focused on the ways "members of subcultures collectively work through, contest or resolve issues related to their social station."[6] By contrast, Raymond Williams, writing of Bloomsbury and the Pre-Raphaelites, draws attention to what he calls the "fraction": a group who are *of* the bourgeoisie and yet distance themselves from it in an implicit or explicit posture of critique.[7] "It is[,] then," says Williams, "a revolt against the class but for the class," since the terms of revolt "really belong to a phase of that class itself" (159). Like the current cultural studies scholars, Williams sees the value in the (self-) marginal(ized) group to be what it reveals about historical interclass and intraclass dynamics, and the experience of class identity. I want to take seriously Williams's call for careful attention to the particularity of any group's internal formation and relation to the larger society of which it is a part. None of the groups under discussion in the present study emerges out of working class resistance, and none could, strictly speaking, be called a fraction, given that none derives from aristocratic privilege. They are, however, middle-class groups (mostly *petit*, with some *haute* bourgeois mixed in) with a critical stance toward the middle class. They are, furthermore, groups of artists with a well-developed sense of social marginality in relation to the world of respectable industry.[8] Hence, while I make use of Williams's rich paradigm for intraclass analysis, I use the term *subculture* in an effort to capture the groups' modern experience of distance from normative society, and for convenience, to refer unambiguously to the material reality of these groups as such.

So defined, subcultural affiliation is, in fact, a key mediating horizon for many writers of the modern period. The best known examples are European—Natalie Barney's lesbian salon and, of course, the Bloomsbury Group. The present study seeks to bring the same notion of (in Williams's phrase) "a cultural group which [has] in common a body of practice or a distinguishable ethos" to the study of Manhattan literati (148). My relevant social formations are Greenwich Village bohemia in lower Manhattan, the Algonquin Round Table in midtown, and the New Negro Renaissance in Harlem. Taken as discursive matrices, these artistic subcultures provide a set of concretely definable (and interrelated) local spheres of public discourse, the terms of which have significant impact on the poetics of the writers who were affiliated with them—even as those terms were significantly shaped by the writers themselves. This two-way flow registers the simplest way in which these writers were true subjects of their subcultures; the structural nature of the modern subculture suggests the more profound dimensions of this dynamic. An urban formation and, by definition, oppositional, artistic subculture sets itself apart from the dominant bourgeois order in a posture of critique, distance, or, at least, ambivalence. More than a position, the subcultural posture marks a certain kind of person—quintessentially modern, defining herself in the paradoxical space of insider (to the subculture)/ outsider (to the mainstream).

Accordingly, particularizing the terms of any given subcultural ethos—or local public sphere—depends partly on understanding the subculture's position vis-à-vis the mainstream culture. The nature of these relations varies according to the degree to which subcultural members feel themselves addressed and acknowledged by the national culture, the means and destination of their literary production, and the grounds of their oppositionality. Class is central to all these factors, as in Williams's model, but as a category interpenetrating with race and with gender.[9] As different as their respective relations to the dominant mainstream were, all three subcultures in this study partook of the cultural hegemony New York exerted over the country as a whole.[10] Village bohemianism, midtown urbanity, and New Negro aesthetics and pride were all critically important exports to the nation beyond New York, just as the sense of national influence was critical to the self-understanding of its producers.

New York, then, emerges in this schema as the engine of modernity in America (particularly implicated is the Round Table, with its close ties to the publishing giants). Through syndicated newspaper columns and mass circulation magazines, urbane New York (helped along by Hollywood) largely directed the new national culture and ushered in a specifically modern fantasy of classless, raceless homogeneity—a democracy of free, self-fashioning consumers. In Ann Douglas's phrase, it was "not an egalitarian society, but something like an egalitarian popular and mass culture" (8).

But this slick "utopian" face was countered by that other face of New York, "the past": the substantial immigrant populations crowding the city's less fashionable spaces and serving as a perpetual contradiction to the assertion of "modernness." New York in the teens and twenties was finally as ethnically diverse as it was assimilationist. This common urban matrix necessitated specific ethnic denials and identifications among the subcultures examined here, and while such dynamics consolidated self-definition, they served equally to root these ostensibly autonomous cultural groups in New York and, indirectly, in each other.

So, for example, the transcendent urbanity that defined the Algonquin Round Table took much of its force from the suppressed Jewish identity of a large proportion of its members. The most visible manifestation was a style of masculinity best described as parodic, which was most famously embodied in those Round Table fellow-travelers, the Marx Brothers. Parker had her own, feminine negotiations with (suppressed) Jewishness that helped her imagine what I call the "intimate public" on which her particular "modern love" depended. The midtown style of urbanity made its way uptown, where a certain wing of the Harlem Renaissance used it to structure and mark their oppositionality. Displacing racial identity with the modern transcendence of "madcap personality," the columnists of Harlem's *Messenger* waged rhetorical war on the project of the New Negro aesthetic. Meanwhile, among those Harlemites who would celebrate racial authenticity, it could be argued that Jews often appeared as a utopian ideal and point of identification—though never as themselves, those threateningly degraded neighbors from the Lower East Side. Instead, they entered as "Russians," safely distant and faintly exotic.[11] In a different register, bohemian writers suppress, to a significant degree, the Jewish and unmistakable Italian presence in the Village as they compete for the meaning of their common terrain. Most clearly at stake was the Bohemian ideal of poverty as a lyrical (and native) choice—rather than a grubby (and foreign) necessity.

With subcultural discourse so greatly overdetermined, the framework of subculture itself has particular advantages for the work of feminist literary analysis, providing a relatively fine-tuned instrument for detecting the "publicness" of women's writing and, hence, women's engagement with the public sphere. Subcultural study supplements the feminist work of recovering those women lost to historiography who were active in the political realm as well as the feminist revaluation of the private sphere as itself historically significant. Through the lens of subculture, we may see even love poetry, that most "feminine" and quietistic of genres, as actively invested in the sphere of public value, shaping and responding to public debate, and defining identity in relation to the terms of a public ethos.

The subcultural matrix brings out another crucial dimension of women's publicness as well: the modernist woman love poet's function as a public embodiment of femininity, specifically as a local redaction of the "New Woman." As Carroll Smith-Rosenberg and Rita Felski, among others, have argued, the modern period saw an escalation in the anxiety generated by the New Woman, a long-standing site of cultural contest in the West.[12] The term had its greatest currency in the late nineteenth century, but feminist historians, with justification, treat as its progeny the multitude of popular discourses on femininity that proliferated in the 1910s and 1920s. The continuity lies in their function as popular and institutional responses to symbolically important advances in women's social status, beginning in the United States with the founding of the first women's colleges in the 1860s. Though only a tiny population in real numbers, the scholars who were the original New Women drew vociferous condemnation from the scientific establishment, who saw in them the violent inversion of all established hierarchy. Breaching as they did that first principle of social order, the gendered dichotomy of (female) body and (male) spirit, women scholars were metonymically associated with the specter of social chaos attending immigrant incursions and economic upheaval.

Though the original discourse of the New Woman faded with the generation of women's settlement houses, the notion of "new" or unconventional women as an emblematic threat to the social order persisted. Highly visible social phenomena served to maintain the "newness" of women as a magnetic arena in and around which cultural anxieties gathered and were played out. At the broadest level, the social-symbolic order of "separate spheres" was giving way to a newly heterosocial and urban self-understanding—a world in which modern women were encroaching on the formerly all-male turf of college, office, and street (needless to say, the "mixing" of spheres all flowed in one direction). And among the more incendiary particulars of these new social arrangements was the ostensible sexual license of the "younger generation" of women.[13]

Equally important to her cultural meaning by the 1920s, however, was the promise with which the New Woman was infused: her forthright sexuality and sophistication lent her an aura of modernness highly desirable to an era significantly self-identified with the modern world of technological innovation, personal style, and fast-paced living. It was this desirability that partly motivated and sustained the mass media's ever-increasing commodification of the female image. Through such overdetermination, the public, commodified New Woman took on the ambivalent cultural charge of modernity itself. Felski's assessment of fin de siècle dynamics only gets truer in the subsequent decades: "The figure of woman pervades the culture . . . as a powerful symbol of both the dangers and the promises of the modern age."[14]

For the women poets who wrote in her shadow, the New Woman was both a symbolic and a subjective reality, as indeterminate as she was inescapable. An urgent imperative for this generation as a whole was to break (radically, if possible) with their predecessors, whose associations with women's colleges, settlement houses, and woman-identified lives rendered them "repressed" or, worse, "inverted" (lesbian) from the perspective of the new sexology. Whether romantic "free lover" or hard-bitten "modern lover," the New Woman of the 1920s had to be visibly and insistently heterosexual. But this imperative occurred in tension with the need to avoid the degradation of public sexual exposure, and the precise balance between the two was a matter of local (subcultural) possibilities and needs.

In producing love poetry, in asserting a public femininity, women like Millay, Taggard, Parker, Bennett, and Johnson gave concrete shape to a highly amorphous and contradictory ideal. Put differently, they were seen in its light, whether willingly or not. Importantly, that light was largely local: embedded in the complex ethos of each subculture studied here was a vision of modern femininity which harbored the subcultural ideal and its anti-ideal. Within bohemia, the iconic "woman" was as much the threat of bourgeois domesticity as she was Muse and Free Lover; for the Algonquinites, she stood for the degraded mass audience even as she personified elite sophistication. The case of Harlem was complicated by an iconic doubling reflective of the polarization within the renaissance itself: the dual ideals of the primitive African woman on the one hand and the cultured and genteel bourgeoise on the other (each with her own anti-ideal) served to bridge as well as divide Harlem's cultural establishment and its rebellious avant-garde fringe.

Whatever their local specificity, these feminine icons of the New York subcultures marked the border between the national and the subcultural, simultaneously linking and differentiating the two spheres. In their generality, they functioned as desirable commodities in serial relationship to the wider capitalist world of desirable feminine commodities; in so doing, they brought the subculture itself into the wider, national circuit of desire. As highly specific figures of femininity, they represented the subculture to the outside world—an essential audience to subcultural uniqueness, and even existence. But the most immediate function of the subcultural feminine icon was to organize the contradictory symbolic life of the subculture itself. As suggested by the "dangers and promises of modernity" suffusing Felski's general figure of womanhood, the symbolic figures under examination here were engines and products of ambivalence, as well as the best hope of reconciliation.

AS MAY BE PREDICTED from the foregoing discussion, the subcultural terrain which the feminine icon was to organize was itself defined by masculine subjectivity: the center of bohemian consciousness, of Round Table consciousness, and of New Negro consciousness was implicitly male. How does a woman writer position herself between the (invisibilizing) alternatives of being an icon and male masquerade? Perhaps it is worth asking the prior question—why would she want to?—to make the point that subcultural identity was clearly something the writers of this study were drawn to and found enabling. Creatively negotiating its terms, each inhabited her respective subcultural ethos to so full an extent that she made it manifestly her own. The proof finally is the modern self she was able to derive (or assert) through subculturally specific love poetry.

The neglect of love poetry in revisionist American literary criticism suggests that it is perceived as either fatally ephemeral or (ironically) as fatally lacking in historical interest.[15] This study attempts to show both discursive and generic reasons for attending to women's conventional love poetry as a significant literature of the modern period. The first reason is the widespread proliferation of love discourses. Built into the New Woman as a central fact of symbolic life in the teens and twenties was a widespread fixation on heterosexual love. In contrast to a long-standing emphasis on the reproductive family as the sober and responsible foundation of society, the heterosexual couple now took center stage, putting the values of romance, sexuality, and "companionship" in the forefront of general fantasies and expectations. This tendency in the national culture was highly overdetermined, and for every contributing medium—movies, sexology, marriage manuals, advertising, magazine fiction, celebrity tabloids, humorous journalism—there were constructions of gender relations and gender identity, some overlapping, some conflicting. But pervading the whole was a sense that gender identity and gender relations were a problem to be managed. This tension took different, partly complicitous and partly oppositional forms within each subculture, depending upon the specific ideals and contradictions it sustained. Whatever the particulars, writing love poetry under these circumstances became public cultural work. And while widespread commodification of femininity and love put the woman love poet at greater risk of becoming a public spectacle, it also presented her with increased capacity for shaping the terms of heterosexuality and feminine identity—for making both "modern."

Love poetry enters this study as a rhetorical social practice in synchronic relation to subcultural and national discursive milieux. I am interested in the ways women writers use this practice to define and assert a public identity rather than in what poetry may reveal about their private desires. By the same token, I take it for granted that the desires of my writers exceeded what was evident in their literary engagement with normative heterosexuality. But it is precisely the potentials of normativity that are at issue here. Given the tremendous pressures attendant on their speech, what were Millay, Taggard, Parker, Bennett, and Johnson able to say? How did each of them pull viably public femininity and modern(ized) love out of a highly overdetermined discourse?

To argue for the historical immediacy of love lyrics is not to deny their private character: love poetry *is* personal, and both public and private are necessary categories for its analysis. Much of the interest of women's love poetry in the modern period resides precisely in this duality: love poetry stages intimate self-Other dynamics and boundaries within a specific historical field of discourse. As such, it provides an arena for enacting a gendered identity through manipulation of cultural paradigms of gender; in the course of constructing a womanly speaker, a writer may to some extent designate what constitutes a woman. Beyond throwing into question the privatized nature of women's writing, then, love poetry intervenes in the very culture that constitutes women as private. Arguably, to the extent that women of the 1920s inhabited the world of mass culture, they, too, experienced their private selves—and, insofar as they were an extension of their femininity, their domestic spheres—as subject to a public gaze. In an era of advertising and social scientific expertise, woman's private domain was permeated by a public normativity, while her person constituted a paradoxically private public display. The contemporaneous woman love poet, with her public constructions of a private self (as lover) and a private sphere (of love), was positioned in an analogously contradictory space. In a culture where the self was both privatized and publicly adjudicated, the professional public woman was less a special case than an extreme one. By virtue of her gender, which, through a long history of objectification, was "saturated with sex,"[16] and her medium, which was saturated with her gender, the woman love poet was perpetually at risk of collapsing into hypostatized femininity and becoming pure display. What I hope this study will show is the remarkable range of creative response to social, symbolic, and psychic imperative embedded in modern women's poetic praxis.

THIS BOOK IS STRUCTURED to elaborate a relevant universe of values and possibilities for each of its writers before taking up a detailed analysis of that writer's specific poetic strategies. Chapter 1 serves as an emblematic rather than a strictly typical case, suggesting in schematic form the dynamic that the rest of the book will explore at length. "Edna St. Vincent Millay" offers a peculiarly stark example of the interplay between a modernist woman's literary praxis and the cultural dynamics out of which it emerges. Edna St. Vincent Millay was the personal embodiment of the Free Love ethos which grounded Greenwich Village bohemia's identity and distinguished it from the mainstream. By tracing a highly self-reflexive literary dialogue between the short fiction of Floyd Dell, bohemian writer and self-appointed spokesperson to the mainstream, and the early lyrics of Millay, the writer he would "exalt" to the status of Muse, we see Millay giving shape to her own iconicity as well as to bohemian poetics and values, particularly those of Free Love and art. Chapter 2, "Love in Greenwich Village: Genevieve Taggard and the Bohemian Ideal," further pursues the case of bohemia by first examining its radical utopia of Free Love, feminism, and art in the context of the popular and scholarly discourses of love and sexuality with which it was complicitous. Underwritten by the authority of sexology, Greenwich Village culture implicitly defined itself as a masculine bulwark of art and individualism in a feminized world of bourgeois domestic and economic responsibility. Villager Genevieve Taggard claimed bohemian artistic identity by taking up as her own the cause of the male artist persecuted by market imperatives, elaborating a poetics of the artist-lover couple in solidarity against a society unable and unwilling to reward art. Chapter

3, "Aestheticized Love and Sexual Violence," concludes the section on bohemian women by focusing on Taggard's moment of greatest ambivalence regarding her investment in bohemian ideals and her simultaneous critique of its denials and exclusions. Under scrutiny here is Taggard's intricate configuration of male violence, female sexuality, and the bohemian determination to aestheticize love.

Chapter 4, "The Algonquin Round Table and the Politics of Sophistication," describes the Round Table subculture in terms of the matrix out of which it emerged: publicity. First tracing how a wide range of Round Table work by men was shaped by the commodification of "personality" and the aesthetic of "sophistication," we come to the special place of Dorothy Parker, token and inoculatory woman of the circle. In the midst of high masculine anxiety and gender antagonism, Parker positioned herself as the epitome of Round Table sophistication—and the cynical flip side to Millay's lyrical New Womanhood. Chapter 5, " 'Oh, do sit down, I've got so much to tell you!': Dorothy Parker and Her Intimate Public," argues that Parker resolves the contradictory psychic and cultural imperatives of her situation by rupturing the self-enclosed emotional dyad of traditional poetic love to admit (rhetorically and affectively) the public. Taking self-definition through her imagined public rather than through the male Other releases Parker from the heterosexual hothouse into an enabling publicity in which she finds self-possession, sexual options, and even justice.

Chapter 6, " 'The New (and Newer) Negro(es)': Generational Conflict in the Harlem Renaissance," explores the ways class and gender organize highly fraught questions of racial and artistic self-definition in the public sphere of the renaissance as defined by its journals. Having identified the central tension between the Harlem cultural establishment and the core of "Younger Negro Artists" who resisted their influence, I describe the deeply conflicted position of the bourgeois woman writer. As the "face of the race," she must direct (white) public scrutiny to her own gentility in an ongoing public relations gesture; by the same token, she must bear the scorn of the young artists who target her as the emblem of bourgeois propriety. Chapter 7, " 'Exalting Negro Womanhood': Performance and Cultural Responsibility for the Middle-Class Heroine," explores more fully the imperative to "perform" bourgeois womanhood as it is expressed in several narrative works by renaissance women writers. I argue that performance itself constitutes a disabling assault on bourgeois identity, necessitating the presence of "primitive" or working-class women in the text to draw to themselves the danger and degradation that would otherwise befall the bourgeois heroine. My final chapter, " 'Our Younger Negro (Women) Artists': Gwendolyn Bennett and Helene Johnson," focuses on the poetry of Bennett and Johnson, tracing its difficult movement from the safety of middle-class feminine respectability to identification with the essential core of the New Negro Renaissance, the masculinist avant-garde elite. In preparation for this analysis, I read a representative series of lyrics by other women writers, identifying a collective tendency to use the lyric "moment" to assert a noncontingent feminine self, free from the performative imperative. Moving on to Bennett and Johnson, I argue that each of them marshals this lyric plenitude toward the goal of feminizing avant-garde poetics, claiming for herself a place within the essential renaissance.

ONE

Edna St. Vincent Millay

[John Peale Bishop and I] both, before very long, had fallen irretrievably in love with her. This latter was so common an experience [as to be an] almost inevitable consequence of knowing her in those days. . . . One cannot really write about Edna Millay without bringing into the foreground of the picture her intoxicating effect on people, because this so much created the atmosphere in which she lived and composed.

Edmund Wilson,
The Shores of Light

In the 1920s, Edna St. Vincent Millay was America's most read, most beloved poet.[1] Critical biographer Elizabeth Atkins gives some indication of Millay's nationally "intoxicating effect on people" in describing the reception of her second collection, *A Few Figs from Thistles*:

> To say it became popular conveys but a faint idea of the truth. Edna St. Vincent Millay became, in effect, the unrivaled embodiment of sex appeal, the It-girl of the hour, the Miss America of 1920. It seemed there was hardly a literate young person in all the English-speaking world who was not soon repeating [her verses].[2]

Such dramatic national success had tangible effects on Millay's status among New Yorkers, naturally enough. Yet in this fact we also glimpse the dynamic circuit in which New York took cues from the national culture even while dictating most of its terms. Millay had an enormous literary and personal influence among the New York literati. Greenwich Village regarded her "with awe" even before her arrival there, on the strength of one passionate poem;[3] John Peale Bishop and Edmund Wilson, young poets and literary editors at the middle-brow journal *Vanity Fair*, made it a personal mission to bring her work before a wide reading public;[4] Genevieve Taggard and the other editors of the high-art little magazine *Measure* took Millay as their unofficial poet laureate; Countee Cullen, favorite son of the Harlem Renaissance, wrote his undergraduate thesis on Millay and pursued his professional career along distinctly lyrical and traditional lines;[5] and even Dorothy Parker, embodiment of midtown urbanity, described her own significant (and significantly national) career as a matter of following Millay's example. In short, in the era literary criticism has taught us to see as dominated by

Photograph on preceding page: Peggy Bacon, "Frenzied Effort at the Whitney Studio Club," (1925). (Photograph © 1997 by the Whitney Museum of American Art)

avant-garde formalism, Millay's passionate sonnets were widely admired and imitated by writers of all kinds.[6]

But, as Atkins's comment suggests, Millay stood for more than lyricism and sentiment; she represented New Womanhood and the assertive female sexuality that gave focus to the culture's diffuse ambivalence about contemporary social change. Through a poetry that was equal parts transgressive and traditional, Millay provided symbolic access to modernity for her national audience. In the Village, she served to anchor bohemian identity in Free Love, the pursuit of authentic intimate relations without interference from artificial constraints, legal or social, or their psychological residue, jealousy. No mere hedonism, the personal transformation upon which this ideal depended was seen explicitly as part of wider cultural and political change.[7] For the period of its greatest prominence, Edna St. Vincent Millay was the exemplar of Free Love and Greenwich Village bohemia's emblem of self-understanding, its assurance of itself as a definable entity essentially different from the bourgeois mainstream it opposed. And for women writers of modernist subcultural New York—like those of this study—she was a powerful model for their own struggle to reconcile the competing demands of a simultaneously public, iconic, and literary femininity.

Many women who were writing in the late teens and twenties had to negotiate the cultural paradigm of the New Woman, but Edna St. Vincent Millay had somehow to *be* her. The nature of Millay's position in bohemia makes her subcultural affiliation uniquely accessible as a discrete determining force in her work. Widely represented in accounts of bohemian life, she could not but respond in the course of representing herself. The resulting dialogue between the subculture and its feminine icon makes a highly suggestive beginning for exploring women's public poetic strategy in modernist New York.

ONE COULD ARGUE THAT Millay's unique status in the Village was assured even before her arrival in 1917. According to Floyd Dell, chief chronicler of the Village in these years, Millay made her first appearance at an audition for one of the numerous storefront plays enlivening bohemian society in its "high" period (in fact, Millay had come to New York to act, not write).[8] Upon leaving her name after the reading, she was recognized as the author of "Renascence," a poem whose passionate romanticism had won her a place in the prestigious Lyric Year poetry contest several years before, as well as the general admiration of the Village literati.[9] Once in her presence, according to Dell, (male) bohemian admiration spilled over into worshipful love, as well as rivalry. The scenario suggested by both Dell and Edmund Wilson is that of a perpetual grand ball (or perhaps a Scarlett O'Hara barbecue) with Millay the irresistible belle doling out privileges to a swarm of disproportionately grateful suitors.[10] While it is true that Millay went on to act the part of the Free Lover to perfection, it seems equally apparent that the Village—as defined by its leading men—was so desirous of her presence that, had she not conveniently come along, they would have had to invent her. What, we might ask, propelled this powerful collective fantasy?

The answer lies in the economy of values by which the subculture maintained its oppositional self-understanding. It was primarily men, and particularly Dell, who generated the self-representation of bohemia and Millay's place within it. Yet this dominant view and the perceptions of female bohemians form no neat opposition: to the extent that women identified themselves with the subculture, they were invested in upholding its terms—and emboldened to make those terms fit their needs.

It was 1917 when Millay graduated from Vassar and made her way to the Village. This was the year Malcolm Cowley remembers as marking the generational divide between the original bohemians and "those who had just arrived from France or college."[11] Cowley describes the stark philosophical differences between the two groups:

> "They" had been rebels, full of proud illusions. They made demands on life itself, that it furnish them with beautiful adventures, honest friendships, love freely given and returned in an appropriate setting. Now, with illusions shattered, they were cynics. "We," on the contrary, were greatly humble and did not ask of Nature that she gild our happy moments or wildly re-echo our passions. . . . We had lost our ideals at a very early age, and painlessly. If any of them survived the war, they had disappeared in the midst of the bickerings at Versailles, or later with the steel strike, the Palmer Raids, the Centralia massacre. But they did not leave us bitter. . . . We were content to build our modest happiness in the wreck of "their" lost illusions, a cottage in the ruins of a palace. (72)

If 1917 is the cusp of these two ideological eras, Millay figures importantly for both: the older generation, who claimed her as the emblem of waning bohemian authenticity and the younger generation, who turned to bohemia as part of a national urge to do so (citing Cowley again: "Later we should be affected by Greenwich Village ideas, but only at second hand and only after they had begun to affect the rest of the country" [73]).

Bridging both groups was not, in fact, the stretch it seems to be from Cowley's account, for the evolving Village retained its idealism alongside its realism, its sense of authenticity along with its alienation. Indeed, it might be most accurate to say that Millay came into her status as the icon of bohemia just at the point when the Village took on a pronounced sense of *self-consciousness* as a subculture, with a concomitant loss of "innocence." The Village had existed as a bohemian sanctuary for decades with little internal fanfare, but the attention of the outside world in the late teens—an attention most crudely manifested in actual tour buses of gawkers winding their way through the hallowed streets—produced in its inhabitants a preoccupation with subcultural boundaries and self-definition. At stake was the integrity of its difference from the mainstream, and, in the wake of increasing commercialization (fueled in no little measure by enterprising artists like Dell himself), the authenticity of its existence as anything but the voyeuristic projection of outsiders.[12] If deliberate ideological opposition to the bourgeois world had afforded bohemia a sense of identity and autonomy, the reciprocal attention of a bourgeois audience threatened to reduce Village life to an empty, objectified spectacle. In her comprehensive 1935 study, sociologist Carolyn Ware attributes the nature of Village self-understanding precisely to the development of the Village itself as a cultural/media spectacle.[13] Cowley's more impressionistic firsthand account locates the relevant bourgeois audience in the *Saturday Evening Post*, which waged "a long campaign of invective beginning before the steel strike or the Palmer Raids and continuing through the jazz era, the boom and the depression. The burden of it was always the same: . . . the Village was dying, had died already, smelled to high heaven and Philadelphia" (53).

A fairly sensitive barometer of Village instability under this onslaught is its use of satire. One of the clearest early manifestations of Village self-consciousness, satire was the basis of many plays about Village life produced by the Liberal Club and, later, the Provincetown Players.[14] But satire *by* Villagers *for* Villagers—the production of, say, "Human Nature: A Very Short Morality Play" in the intimate setting of a MacDougal Street stable—reinforced rather than threatened Village identity. Dell's prefatory note to his own collection of early Village plays calls them "souvenirs of an intellectual play-time which, being dead"—as early as 1922—"deserves some not-too-solemn memorial."[15] As the Village became increasingly the target of satire by outsiders (and insiders writing for outsiders), the real and satiric Villages became difficult to distinguish.[16]

This relay effect between bohemia and the mainstream was complicated by the third party with whom the bohemians shared the space south of Fourteenth Street: the predominantly Italian immigrant community. Consistent with bohemia's romantic tradition, Village counterculture rejected the world of capitalist production to make a refuge in which individuality could flourish through creativity, personal discovery, and romantic love. The physical terrain of this idyll was a square mile of streets obligingly oppositional in its tangled defiance of New York's strict geometrical gridwork, and resistant (even after the 1917 implementation of the Westside subway) to the traffic and pace of the rest of the city. Its shabby quaintness and low-rent garrets served perfectly to express the bohemian contempt for bourgeois life. But confusing this primary dichotomy were the immigrants who dominated the physical space of the Village. Ware itemizes the significant cultural differences keeping the Italians and the Villagers at odds, especially differences over sexual mores (which may partly explain the very centrality of Free Love to bohemian self-understanding).[17] But one is struck equally in her account by the uncomfortable similarities lurking within those differences. Indeed, might not the often desperate necessity of immigrant poverty erode the confidence of bohemian poverty as a lyrical choice? Worse, might it not throw into doubt the degree to which one can ever "choose" one's way out of subjection to market forces? And might not the fervent Catholicism of their neighbors muddy the distinction between scorned "Puritan" constraint and exalted "Pagan" spirituality?

Peering determinedly past these uncomfortably proximate neighbors to gesture their contempt for the distant bourgeoisie, the Village bohemians appear nonetheless to have made certain necessary accommodations for the Italian presence at the level of their self-understanding. Implicitly, they came to distinguish themselves as white Americans, their poverty as genteel, their economic "idleness" as moral purity. Indeed, Ware identifies as foundational to Village culture a demographic element "drawn largely from cultivated families of old American stock" (245). By contrast, these Others were dark foreigners, grubby and grasping, unconcerned with higher values in their pursuit of capitalist success (while to the Italians, the Bohemians were contemptible "suckers" [Ware 110–111]). Though the Italian presence is relatively muted in Village representation, it does emerge at key moments—not, for the most part, in disinterested acknowledgment of immigrant reality but as a means of resolving certain gendered conflicts internal to the bohemian ethos.[18]

Representing Bohemia: Floyd Dell and *Love in Greenwich Village*

> All right,
>   Go ahead!
> What's in a name?
> I guess I'll be locked into
> As much as I'm locked out of!
>
> Millay, "The Prisoner"

Out of this precarious subcultural foundation, Floyd Dell wrote *Love in Greenwich Village* at the relatively advanced date of 1926. Autobiographical and mythologizing, intimate and satiric, conventionally sentimental and psychologically dark, this work was suggested by *Century* editor Carl Van Doren and sold piecemeal to a variety of journals (some of them mainstream) before it finally saw print as the definitive bohemian history—addressed equally to insiders, voyeurs, and the new generation of Villagers. Its strong implication is that, by 1926, the essential bohemia lay somewhere in the interstices of all these categories—or nowhere at all.[19] Perhaps the sense that the physical space of bohemia was evaporating under pressure from the tourists on the one hand and the immigrant descendants on the other led to the tendency in Village sketches to figure bohemia as a dreamspace, the romantic/psychological underside of bourgeois urban reality.[20] In any case, Dell's history of the true Village presents itself as capturing and crystallizing the (always-already) disappearing bohemia and as codifying its values. *Love,* then, has the unusual status of a metadiscourse on bohemian life rather than an aesthetic expression generated from within the bohemian ethos (such as we shall examine in the work of Genevieve Taggard and, more immediately, Millay herself).

But rendered as it is in the concrete world of narrative, *Love*'s bohemian rejection of the bustling world of capitalist production calls for the same complexly gendered compensations as would any other fantasmatic construction of the material world below Fourteenth Street. Chief among them was an association of artistic endeavor with male identity: (self-) excluded from conventional manly success, many bohemian men took up an identity of hypernormative masculinity. Novelist Max Bodenheim, for example, built up an impressive notoriety on the basis of his womanizing, which led in two cases to suicide attempts (one successful, both well publicized). With less drama but the same conscious cultivation, radical journalist Mike Gold made himself known as a cigar-smoking swaggerer, a personal style he saw as Whitmannian (Whitman being an important hero of the pagan, democratic Village). More generally, Village affinity with the "swashbuckling" Wobblies and the labor movement had given currency to a rough-and-tumble "working-class" style.[21]

For a man like Floyd Dell, however, who could trace a prominent bohemian career back to his youth in the artists' colony of southside Chicago,[22] masculine identity derived more directly from subcultural difference itself and even included a strong bohemian investment in the "Woman Question." To Dell, male identity and subcultural definition were mutually reinforcing: the very project of interpreting bohemia positioned him as the sentient male artist in relation to an elusive and aesthetically powerful object. In *Love in Greenwich Village*, Dell's primary opportunity for "speaking bohemia," he described that world as the product of unconscious female forces, a collective Muse to which he stood pleasurably enthralled.

> The story of the Village, [Dell tells us,] properly begins with Egeria [Henrietta Rodman]. . . . People laughed at her a good deal, and loved her very much indeed, and followed at her beck into the beautiful and absurd schemes she was forever inventing. She invented Greenwich Village. . . . It wasn't at all what she had meant it to be—for she was a very serious young woman, and it was incurably frivolous. But still—she did it! . . . She was like one of those catalytic agents in chemistry, that disintegrate and change and recombine whatever bodies they come in contact with.[23]

But if "Egeria" invented the Village, then "Grace"—the fictional Millay—propelled its ongoing life:

> [Bohemia's] true presiding spirit, its inspirer and guide and stimulus, was Grace. It would wrong her to say that she was its organizer. It would be truer to call her the flame at which its new life was kindled. She was wonderful, adorable, beautiful, restless, serene—but who can describe Grace? Not I. We were all in love with her; and we all still are.[24]

Thus does Millay take her place in Dell's design: she is the elusive spirit of bohemia, always to be defined and always escaping definition. Millay represents the possibility of the bohemian ideal and, simultaneously, the guarantor of Village identity—but not independent of Dell's inscription of her as such. In Dell's literary conception, Village life has the status of an artwork, requiring both the articulate male and the inspired female for its perpetuation. And yet even the consciously mythic *Love in Greenwich Village* reveals this division of labor to be unstable: Millay was paradoxically both the Muse of bohemia *and* its best-known writer. Though of a piece with her appropriation of male sexual freedom, her breach of the gendered artistic divide was potentially the more threatening to bohemian self-understanding.

In keeping with its status as a history, *Love in Greenwich Village* is fairly direct in its treatment of Millay's relation to the Village and of the crisis of instability within Village identity. Dell announces in his introduction that he will describe "the rise and fall" of the true Village,

> for it has fallen, like Troy, like Babylon. Its ruins—lived palely among the inhabitants of the Eighth [generation or "wave"] and present Village—are a shrine to which the golden youth of America still makes pilgrimages from prairie towns. But it is gone for ever, the Greenwich Village that I knew—and therefore I tell its story.

By contrast, the true, "seventh wave" Village was that

> of which all the world has heard—which has become a byword, which has been loved and feared and laughed at by millions of Americans who have never seen it—and which some clever folk have declared never existed at all outside the realm of fancy. (17)

Having established the ephemeral nature of this subcultural world, Dell presents a series of stories and poems that capture the life of its perhaps equally ephemeral denizens. Prominent, though embedded within the series, are two fictional portraits of Millay.

"The Gifts of the Fourth Goddess" is a fanciful myth of origins for Millay fans saturated in the characteristically playful irony Dell reserves for his coyly veiled celebrity pieces. Yet it unquestionably delivers a serious admonishment to Millay herself regarding her responsibility to Bohemian life in its time of trouble. In the story's final scene, "Pat," the Millay character (or, as Dell puts it, "the girl poet you all love and wonder about"), has her fortune told on the eve of her wedding. As soon as he discovers her identity as the great poet, the fortune-teller reveals himself to be a fake and retracts the prophecy of domestic bliss he had offered when he took her to be an ordinary bohemian woman. Then follows an explicit lesson in the responsibilities of public life. Speaking for her reading constituency—and most directly, for Dell, the self-appointed guardian and public relations director of Greenwich Village—the young man advises Pat of her unique and necessary position in American and bohemian culture.

> "I've worked on newspapers all over the country, and everywhere I've gone, people are reading you and talking about you. Young people, I mean."
>
> "What do they say about me?" she asked.
>
> "That's just it. They say awful things about you—or things that would be awful if they were said about anybody else. But—they love you for it."
>
> "That's curious," she said.
>
> "In Philistia [mainstream America],"[25] he said, "the pagan spirit has been pretty well stamped out. But still it's there—in the young people. They read your poetry. It means something to them. It's beauty, it's joy, it's freedom. And here you want to go and spoil it—by getting married! Why you *can't* get married! You're our pagan goddess, if you only knew it. All the beautiful things we want to do, and can't, because we live in Philistia, you do them for us, and write about them for us, and we worship you for them."
>
> "How do you know I do the things I write about?" she asked.
>
> "That makes no difference, so long as we believe it. But if you get married—why, everyone will think those love-poems are written to your *husband*! . . . You can't belong to just one person. You belong to us all—the boys and girls of the younger generation."
>
> "I see," said Pat. "I've a certain—you might call it social responsibility in this matter." (145–146)

Whereas the biographical Millay did finally get married in what Dell implies was a flagrant violation of public trust,[26] the fictional Pat Flower is persuaded to break her engagement to "poor John"—and go off to dinner with the phony fortune-teller (who "*was* rather handsome").

The notable feature of the fortune-teller/journalist's description of Flower's status is that she does not so much *represent* a way of life as *embody* one. Her necessary function is to serve as an emblem of possibility; there is no question of masses of women following her example. The young man never mentions bohemia as a geographical place and hence as an attainable escape from Philistia—even though such escape is clearly the organizing premise of most of *Love*'s stories. In effect, the young man locates bohemia exclusively in Pat Flower's pagan love poetry. Yet while Flower/Millay separates Greenwich Village from the bourgeois mainstream, she is also their paradoxical point of equivalence insofar as they are both in thrall to her. To the "boys and girls" of mainstream America, she is understandably a remote ideal, but the precise nature of her "social responsibility" to the Village itself is less clear.

To return to "The Gifts of the Fourth Goddess," the unreality of bohemia is here underscored in the young man's imposture of a cliché Village curiosity, the fortune-teller (and, we should note, a culturally "Italian" moment in the commercial Village). From the moment the man pulls off his beard, Dell has introduced to the story of bohemia's true Muse bohemia's anxiety and vertigo as a subculture. At its most extreme, the commercialized Village expressed itself in such sideshows as "Guido's Garret," where uptowners and out-of-towners alike could pay a fee to witness real "starving artists" acting eccentric in their natural habitat.[27] But more threatening than the extremes was the gray area where most Villagers dwelt. The young man of

"The Fourth Goddess" is not simply an enterprising Villager preying on gullible believers (among them, Pat Flower herself); he is simultaneously a voyeuristic journalist investigating Village life for an audience of curious outsiders *and*—incredibly—the defender of bohemian ideals. For her part, Pat Flower functions both as a dupe to the false Village and as the very core of bohemian authenticity (which, true to form, she can embody but not articulate).

Dell used "The Fourth Goddess" as an occasion for setting down the essential qualities that rendered Millay a fit Muse of bohemia. Like Sleeping Beauty, Pat Flower has been blessed at birth by ancient pagan goddesses who grant her certain personal powers, among them "the power of changing thine own shape, so that thou shalt be to any one [*sic*] whatever thou pleasest to seem."[28] The other gifts are similarly contrived to produce the ideal of restless and elusive bohemian womanhood: the perennial and unrequited search for "mortal love" and a "secret," which, "if any rash mortal lover learn it from thee, will bring a swift end to the mortal happiness you have shared." The titular fourth gift of social responsibility, though incongruous, keeps her to the duties of what is, indeed, a public life and a public trust. In the subcultural context, this fourth gift has a critical place in Millay's feminine persona, and surely gifts one through three are pretty clearly designated as feminine even on their own terms. Yet Dell's story makes a point of implying just the reverse: Pat was to have been a boy, and both her mother and the goddesses (her godmothers) had planned their reception of her accordingly, making no adjustments for the gender surprise which comes to pass. We are to conclude (all in the spirit of playful irony, of course) that a twist of fate has allowed Pat Flower/Edna Millay to abscond with the qualities of a masculine temperament and fate.[29]

Here the Free Lover shows her clear relation to the larger heterosocial cultural context: as an icon of femininity distanced from the mass of women, she must finally be "one of the boys" in her singular privilege. As we shall see, this dynamic produces a double standard within bohemian self-representation. Even when she is the heroine, the average fictional bohemian woman ends her search for personal fulfillment in marriage.[30] The iconic Free Lover, however, maintains her independent symbolic status; her romance narrative is necessarily nonteleological. Moreover, as a genuine Free Lover, she is also a true artist according to what will emerge as a highly exalted bohemian equation of love with art.[31] Her claims to artistic status, then, rival those of the male. Dell stages the resulting gender conflict most starkly in "The Kitten and the Masterpiece," the second of the *Love* stories to render Millay in the larger context of bohemian life. The trope by which this story articulates bohemian contradiction is that of *economy*—the literal management of money and the metaphoric circulation of persons and values. Definitive of bohemian expression, the trope of economy will prove just as critical for Millay's own *counter*representations.

Village Economies: "The Kitten and the Masterpiece"

> Cut if you will, with Sleep's dull knife,
> Each day to half its length, my friend—
> The years that Time takes off *my* life,
> He'll take from off the other end!
>
> Millay, "Midnight Oil"

The first story following the introduction to *Love in Greenwich Village* tells of a man in love with a woman we are given to assume is Edna Millay; like "The Gifts of the Fourth Goddess," then, "The Kitten and the Masterpiece" functions as a founding myth of bohemia. But what in particular it conveys is the curiously disruptive effect of bohemia's chief representative on bohemia's most cherished ideals: love and art.

Crucially, love and art can unfold only in a matrix of romantic poverty, for bohemian gaiety derives largely from the freedom which follows from breaking with bourgeois materialism. As Dell puts it in his introduction to the volume, "How otherwise, except by being very poor, should we ever have learned to make the most of those joys that are so cheap, or that cost nothing at all, the joys of comradeship and play and mere childlike fun?"[32] By contrast—and unstated—is the transcendent refusal to struggle against want, a struggle associated with that immigrant population against which the Village implicitly defined itself. And yet, bohemian writings evince as much preoccupation with scarcity as they do conviction that in poverty lies happiness.

The protagonist of "The Kitten and the Masterpiece" is Paul, a writer with a small nest egg he intends to put toward producing a novel. The writer worries at great length over the problem of resources. The problem is real enough, and yet Dell's narrator takes a distinctly ironic stance in presenting it. Indeed, aside from the worry itself, other significant details undercut Paul's status as a true Villager: he is there, first of all, not as a seeker, but for the cheap rent, and he secludes himself from Village conviviality in the $8-a-month room he occupies. Though we learn of his past life spent in protobohemian fashion (i.e., mooning around, reading, and talking), at the start of the narrative he has bent all his wayward desire toward producing a novel. Dell has an autobiographical pretext for the ironic tone he takes toward our hero—presenting him as an overly earnest youth he hints is himself—but irony serves as inoculation here, too, for in the course of things, this young writer comes perilously close to unmasking the contradictions at the heart of the bohemian idyll.

Paul figures his assets meticulously, and with perfect concentration on his artistic goal.

> Five hundred dollars a year is nine dollars and sixty-one cents a week,—or nine dollars and sixty-two cents, if you want to call the odd fraction a cent.

> But preferring to be always on the safe side in his finances, he thought of his weekly income as nine dollars and sixty-one cents.
>
> A novel contains anywhere from eighty thousand to a hundred and sixty thousand words. His would be a fairly long novel. But one can easily write fifteen hundred words a day, and at that rate his novel would be finished in a little over three months. However, he wanted to be conservative in his expectations; at the very least, then, he would write five hundred words a day, and have his novel finished in ten months, with plenty of time left to revise it in.
>
> Every dollar in his hoard meant seventeen-and-a-half hours of freedom, and a page done toward his novel. These were his plans. (49–50)

What emerges from this passage is that the problem is not simply (or really) one of money per se, but of bohemian economy as a whole. Money, the core of bourgeois and immigrant life, must be translated into the bohemian values of art and freedom from conventional work. What "Kitten" ultimately foregrounds, however, is a conflict *within* this more specialized economy: art, as it turns out, must compete with the other prime bohemian value, love. The hero meets a "girl" and, in no time at all, squanders his fortune on restaurant dinners and taxi rides in the park. Such is the power of his feeling for her that he resolves to give up his writerly ambitions for marriage. Moments before proposing, he reflects on the implications of his decision:

> If he married, he wouldn't be able to save up to write. He would have to think first of his wife always. And then there would be babies. He would have to give up his freedom.
>
> "But I don't mind," he thought. "That's the odd thing about it. As an artist, I ought to mind. When an artist marries, he is simply taking money that belongs to his art and spending it on a girl—and her babies. And yet my friends will congratulate me. They'll think I am doing a fine thing. If I were a bank cashier and betrayed my trust in order to spend money on a girl, they wouldn't congratulate me. They'd put me in jail. But *I* shall be considered a good citizen."(71)

The bitterness with which this line of thought culminates belies the positive worth of love in itself and certainly in its "natural" affinity with art. For the story—consistent with *Love in Greenwich Village* as a whole—is ostensibly a celebration of love as the quintessence of bohemian life.

The "girl's" answer, when she gives it, is a shock for our self-sacrificing hero.

> "You love me, don't you dear?"
>
> "Yes; but I don't want to be your wife. I don't want to be anybody's wife. I want to write poetry."
>
> "You want—"
>
> "Yes, of course. That must come first always. And so I mustn't try to be a wife to any one. It's terribly nice of you to want me to be, Paul. And what you say is true. It would be pleasant to be taken care of, and all that; but I'll have to take my chances. Oh, I know I would be happy, being your wife. It's just that I'm most afraid of! Don't you see?"

> "Oh!" he said.
>
> "I'm sorry, dear," she said, pressing his hand in hers. "It's been so lovely, all of it; but—I thought you understood!" (72–73)

"June Glory" has apparently turned out to be the *real* bohemian, and suddenly the earnest personal struggle that has so preoccupied Paul appears to have been nothing more than a delusion born of masculine self-importance.

Having arrived at this climax, we recall a scene midway through the narrative that perfectly anticipates Paul's foolishness. He has just reaffirmed his vow of poverty in the interest of his art when he is followed home by a kitten. Recognizing immediately the dire threat the creature poses to his artistry, he delivers the following stern speech (before capitulating utterly to its charms).

> "Cat," he said, "it is not true that I am poor; I'll be honest with you. I am rich. I have two hundred and eighty dollars right here on these premises. Think of all the milk I could buy for you with two hundred and eighty dollars! And fish—and liver—everything your little heart might desire! And if I were a regular human being, I'd go right out and buy you what you ask for. But that's where you've made your big mistake. I'm not a regular human being! I'm an artist. Do you know what an artist is like? Well, you'll find out if you stick around here. But I'm sorry for you, cat. A pint of milk costs only eight cents, but that eight cents will buy me time and freedom in which to write twenty-nine words of my novel. You wouldn't think I could possibly care more for twenty-nine words than for a pretty little thing like you. But that's what artists are like—when they are really artists." (61–62)

The kitten, as it turns out, shows no respect for Paul's artistic mission and, moreover, leaves him as soon as "there was no novel-writing to interfere with" (70). But by then, Paul has been thoroughly cured of his zeal and initiated into what we are to understand as a richer and nobler—and a more truly bohemian—mode of existence.

As a prelude to the story, Dell had set up the ethical implications of Paul's choice by relating an anecdote popular in Village circles: when H. G. Wells (a major intellectual hero of bohemia) was asked whether, were he in a burning building, he would save "a great masterpiece" or "a child he had never seen before," he was said to have replied, " 'I would save the child, or, if it were a kitten, the kitten' " (47). Paul, too, "saves the kitten," whom the story quite straightforwardly equates with June Glory. But like her feline predecessor, June apparently leaves Paul as soon as she has succeeded, however inadvertently, in breaking his artistic resolve; we may assume that, like the kitten, she, too, has "found a home in another house."

The implication in the prologue is that Wells was pronouncing judgment on a widely accepted construction of the "problem" of art within the artistic community. But what happens when the very dichotomy of artistic and worldly demands breaks down—that is, when the kitten/woman lays claim to her own artistic prerogative? How then shall the male artist conceive the imperatives of his artistic economy? Whereas the dilemma structuring "Kitten'' appears to be a conflict *between* art and ''life,'' the conclusion suggests that the tension lies within artistic life itself. For Paul, imagining himself as the subject of a difficult but finally straightforward choice between bourgeois and artistic duty, the surprise is June's refusal to serve as the pretext for his decision.

June and Paul need to be seen in light of the dominant narrative pattern of the collection as a whole, in which situations of Free Love repeatedly resolve themselves into a conventionally gendered model of male artist and supportive female other. At the close of ''Kitten,'' the narrator delivers an epilogue intended to supply the subcultural framework within which this love story's abrupt termination offers satisfying closure, despite appearances to the contrary.

> All this happened several years ago in Greenwich Village, when rents were low and artists and writers lived there happy in their poverty and youth, scornful of the great world, disdaining its wisdom, finding for themselves in kisses and tears a wisdom of their own. Here, and in such a manner, were begun two careers, the further developments of which are sufficiently set forth in the pages of Who's Who. (73)

Hence, we reconcile this true Free Love story with the rest of the volume of near misses with the knowledge that Paul and June are ''real'' and have all along been standing in for Dell and Millay.[33] The narrative outcome of ''The Kitten and the Masterpiece'' is necessarily exceptional. The mass of psychologically conventional women characters who inhabit bohemian writings are the enabling condition for the fictional Millay's paradoxically singular embodiment of the bohemian ethos: *they* renounce art and freedom, thereby upholding the gendered artistic economy, that *she* may serve as the elusive ideal, the iconic assurance of bohemia's radical difference from bourgeois society.

The insistent frivolity which attaches itself to Dell's fictional depictions of Millay may suggest that the ideal of Free Love is finally unimaginable as a serious proposition.[34] It may likewise suggest that, as artist and Free Lover, Millay commanded as much resentment as adoration. Beyond this rather emphatic use of tone, *Love* suggests more insidious possibilities for the ideological containment of Millay's personal power: the driving ambition that allows June Glory to sacrifice her lover to poetry (even as he himself is learning the folly of that very choice) carries the taint of the dubious ''immigrant values'' we have witnessed earlier in the book.

''Kitten'' recalls a prior narrative, the first in the sequence of the collection. Dell's introductory essay, ''The Rise of Greenwich Village,'' concludes with a love story intended to illustrate the elusive bohemian ethos he has until then been trying to set down abstractly. What happened to the lovers Paul and Rosika was, he says, ''in some respects . . . not an altogether everyday occurrence, but in its essence it was sufficiently characteristic of the Village'' (35). Love, then, is bohemia's central experiential framework, and the story of Paul and Rosika is somehow paradigmatic. ''Paul'' is, of course, the autobiographical hero who will appear throughout the volume; Rosika, however, is entirely singular. Neither a figure for Millay nor a representative domestic-bohemian, Rosika is identified as Hungarian, but the cumulative effect of her "queer," "barbaric" singing, her dancing that "seemed to bring the hot breath of the jungle into the room," the "half-Oriental gypsy-music" to which she dances, the "defiant" flash of nudity with which she concludes her dance, and her "temperament" is more the general "exotic" so fascinating to modernist culture at large. Under these circumstances, Rosika's dancing expresses less a commitment to art than a racial essence.

All action, Rosika has no hesitations about the future and nothing but contempt for those who do. We see her against the background of the cerebral Dirck, Paul's apartment-mate, "nearly thirty" and effectively paralyzed by the (bohemian) conjunction of cynicism and idealism that defines him. A "tragic-comic figure," "a writer who did not write," he "dreamed of a great novel, but he never could write a perfect first page: and until the first page was perfect, why go on to the second?" (36). As the elder bohemian, Dirck has initiated Paul into both his artistic philosophy and the "hack-work" of book reviewing. Paul, as a neophyte Villager, takes his cues from Dirck and yet is chagrined by Rosika's passionate condemnation of their idleness. One night, in demonstration of her superior artistic worth, she performs a spontaneous shawl dance, which excites Paul's admiration and romantic interest. Truly, Dirck and even Paul himself have nothing to match Rosika's art. And yet, Rosika clearly needs Paul: in the first moments of their first, inevitable embrace, she elicits from him both confirmation of her talent and a promise to teach her "words"—that is, English. In granting her requests, he remains the same befuddled and undistinguished character he has been and will continue to be throughout the story. The reader can conclude only that what someone like Paul has to offer someone like Rosika is nothing of his own, but merely the overflow of his social privilege as a real bohemian—which identity we now see in focus as white American (in the judgment and dissemination of culture) and as genteel (in staying above the fray of ambitious labor). Poor Paul devotes himself to Rosika, only to have her abandon him at the point when he "had something important to say to her"—a marriage proposal, presumably—but she "had begun to find the fame she coveted" (42). Here we see the link between Rosika and Millay/June Glory. But whereas the woman of "Kitten" wrought her damage with the charming thoughtlessness of light comedy, this foreigner takes Paul to the same end in the mode of tragedy, overtly using him, just as she uses everything within her reach—books, shawl, music—as a means to her single-minded end.

Whatever the irony that attaches to Dirck, Rosika has failed to return the love our hero feels for her, and, as readers, we cannot help but see her (and her artistry) in that light. Moreover, with Paul's education at the center of the story, the tension between artistic determination (Rosika) and artistic sensibility (Dirck) comes into focus as key to the bohemian ethos. Through Rosika's influence, Paul has ceased being blocked altogether—he *has* "set to work once more on his play'' and acquired ''a studio of his own.'' However, his primary emotional investment is so clearly in his relationship with this woman that we must also see him as clinging to *sensibility*—now in the form of romance—for his definition of bohemian identity.

Within this larger tension, left unresolved by the story, we must note the way in which Rosika locates certain qualities of the ''elusive'' Millay in the values of the ethnic Village. Caught between bohemia's twin ideals as the personal embodiment of one (love) and the supremely successful practitioner of the other (art), Millay must protect her writing from heterosexual gender hierarchy. On the face of it, Free Love, judiciously applied, would seem to serve this arrangement nicely. The trouble (vis-à-vis those for whom she serves as iconic ideal, like Dell) comes when her very success in juggling contradiction puts her under suspicion of bad faith. The ''free'' lover must stay free to fulfill her trust to bohemia; but she must also finally defeat the artist in herself—*lose* her freedom—to maintain the fragile gender arrangements of bohemian social life, not to mention masculine self-understanding. The suppressed accusation emanating from ''Rosika and Paul'' is that Millay walks a fine line between the Village and the anti-Village. Her status as ''pagan goddess'' is shadowed by identification with something less than bohemian, her assertive and purposeful womanhood verging on the foreign, the lower class, and the benighted.

Village Economies: ''My candle burns at both ends''

> Not a matter of wanton wastefulness but of almost methodical, tasking exhaustiveness, the Bohemian project is thus aptly figured in the seemingly opposite, straightlacing, vow-keeping, binding contract any sonnet must be.
>
> Debra Fried, ''Andromeda Unbound: Gender and Genre in Millay's Sonnets''[35]

Embodying bohemian ideality presented Millay with enormous pressures, social pressure not least among them. As Edmund Wilson wrote in his fictionalized rendition of the time: ''We [suitors] swarmed to her apartment, devoured her time and her force, and finally, at the period of which I write, had rendered her life intolerable.''[36] But it is also true that Millay participated actively in the construction of her own persona and significantly shaped the very subcultural ideals to which it answered. Insofar as her poems negotiated the imperatives of her authorial position, their principal task was the management of a public, unconventional, female sexuality—one capable of reflecting the self-image of a national as well as a bohemian readership. In this capacity Millay was most New Woman: on the one hand, representing a concrete and accessible modernity in the sexuality her poems expressed; on the other hand, in her lyricism, her traditional forms, and even in her poetry as such, representing the rejection of the ordinary mainstream world—including its fetishization of modernity. As the symbol of Free Love, she had to balance male prerogative and conventional femininity as well as control the meaning of her own universal desirability. The sexual circulation that set such desire in motion—as represented in her poems and as enacted in the buying and selling of her books—made her acutely vulnerable to denigration as a woman. It furthermore narrowed the crucial distance between herself as a Yankee-bred bohemian and the peddling, bartering, marketing women of the Italian Village. As we shall see, Millay tackled the intricacies of her predicament partly through a synthesis of female sexuality and the typically bohemian poetics of economy.

Millay's early collections contain some of the best-known articulations of the bohemian ethos. No stranger to scarcity, Millay had been raised in a spartan New England home, and as a young professional poet kept body and soul together by writing "bread-and-butter" pieces alongside her properly "artistic" endeavors. As it happened, she was also keenly attuned to the aesthetic dimension of garret life.

But even her most seemingly straightforward paeans to Village freedom are undergirded by perfect care and thrift. Written at the highpoint of her bohemian career, "Recuerdo" spins out scenes of lighthearted romance within a kind of blueprint for resource management.

We were very tired, we were very merry—
We had gone back and forth all night on the ferry.
It was bare and bright, and smelled like a stable—
But we looked into a fire, we leaned across a table,
We lay on the hill-top underneath the moon;
And the whistles kept blowing, and the dawn came soon.

We were very tired, we were very merry—
We had gone back and forth all night on the ferry;
And you ate an apple, and I ate a pear,
From a dozen of each we had bought somewhere;
And the sky went wan, and the wind came cold,
And the sun rose dripping, a bucketful of gold.

We were very tired, we were very merry,
We had gone back and forth all night on the ferry.
We hailed, "Good morrow, mother!" to a shawl-covered head,
And bought a morning paper, which neither of us read;
And she wept, "God bless you!" for the apples and the pears,
And we gave her all our money but our subway fares.[37]

The poem begins with an implicit refusal. Arranged contiguously, "We were very tired" and "we were very merry" are conspicuously *not* explained by a connecting "but." In fact, the ordering of the phrases implies that "we were merry" *because* "we were tired." Having suggested (or asserted) such an economy of plenitude, the speaker goes on to an image simultaneously suggestive of bohemian antiproductivity and a dynamic of pure circulation: "We had gone back and forth all night on the ferry." Each of the poem's three stanzas begins with a reiteration of this schema. If in the conventional world "merriness" produces "tiredness," in bohemia merriness is the *effect* of tiredness; the way to a bohemian temperament is through constant emotional expenditure. Yet the dynamic of merriment through tiredness comes back on itself: once merry, the bohemians engage in more tiring behavior (described in the ensuing stanza), which leads them back to the merriness of the subsequent refrain.

Within the poem, the display of plenitude is at least as important as the management of scarcity. While the one upholds bohemian identity, the other ensures the survival of the individual bohemian. Other details of the poem follow this basic pattern of thrift amid seeming profligacy. The speaker and her companion carelessly buy fruit ("somewhere") and give it away, along with their money, to an immigrant woman whose tearful gratitude only serves to highlight their own transcendence of material need—the difference of their bohemian poverty. But again, there is a careful, even meticulous economy at work here. The show of giving has an important ideological dimension but also serves as a refinement away from crude hoarding toward the precise measure of needs—a perfect economy of no waste. Hence, "you ate an apple and I ate a pear"—enough to sustain them and neatly designate their sexual difference and the "pagan" nature of their relationship. Again, money for such a pair has only the utility of gaining them access to further circulation, this time on the subway.

Yet this achieved synthesis of bohemian ideals and economic mastery suffers at least one moment of rupture. At the close of the poem, their distance from the world of needy, hoarding capitalism (immigrant *and* bourgeois) tidily established, the lovers look trustingly out over the rising sun, a scene belonging by rights to the realm of bohemian lyrical ideality. Yet here they find themselves confronted with a gaudy, "dripping . . . bucketful of gold." As an index to the speaker's psyche, the image registers an unconscious preoccupation with opulence beneath her willed frugality. As a commentary on the bohemian project the poem describes, it signals a certain fragility at the core.

Subliminal threats notwithstanding, "Recuerdo" is overwhelmingly successful as a classic bohemian idyll. The stakes get higher—and the balance more difficult—when Millay figures a more explicitly sexualized female speaker. "MacDougal Street," from the same high-bohemian period, enacts the failure of a specifically sexual economy. As with "Recuerdo," the poem begins with a bohemian rhythm of pure circulation: "As I went walking up and down to take the evening air." But while the "back and forth" of the ferry ride is reasserted with every new stanza, the systematic nature of this speaker's stroll—and her control of the situation she inhabits—is lost after the initial moment. Yet, though it fails to put her in charge, the pattern of circulation that the line sets in motion does generate bohemian desire.

As I went walking up and down to take the evening air,
  (Sweet to meet upon the street, why must I be so shy?)
I saw him lay his hand upon her torn black hair;
  ("Little dirty Latin child, let the lady by!")

The women squatting on the stoops were slovenly and fat,
  (Lay me out in organdie, lay me out in lawn!)
And everywhere I stepped there was a baby or a cat;
  (Lord, God in Heaven, will it never be dawn?)

The fruit-carts and clam-carts were ribald as a fair,
  (Pink nets and wet shells trodden under heel)
She had haggled from the fruit-man of his rotting ware;
  (I shall never get to sleep, the way I feel!)

He walked like a king through the filth and the clutter,
  (Sweet to meet upon the street, why did you glance me by?)
But he caught the quaint Italian quip she flung him from the gutter;
  (What can there be to cry about that I should lie and cry?)

He laid his darling hand upon her little black head,
  (I wish I were a ragged child with ear-rings in my ears!)
And he said she was a baggage to have said what she had said;
  (Truly I shall be ill unless I stop these tears!)[38]

Unlike "Recuerdo," whose title ("I remember") implies the speaker's narrative control, "MacDougal Street" places its speaker at the mercy of a defining urban context. She, too, is remembering, but tormentedly and against her will. The use of a double voice conveys the speaker's psychic oscillation from the bed where she lies to the details of the street, with the clear sense—which the title underscores—that this place has a magnetic hold on her. While an encounter with the object of her desire is a psychologically obvious fixation, the event is overwhelmingly defined by its setting. What is the significance of MacDougal Street?

The chaos which at first seems to emanate from the lovesick mind of the speaker is, on closer inspection, an objective chaos of the street itself. Dirty children, squatting women, babies, cats, pink nets, rotting fruit, filth, clutter—MacDougal Street is rank with sensuality. More specifically, it is an overflowing market of female sexuality. Not simply "slovenly and fat," the "squatting" women of the stoops are implicated in a grotesque fertility by virtue of the teeming babies and cats surrounding them. The central sexual figure is the child, appropriately called a "baggage," both saucy child and wanton woman. Apart from her seeming flirtation with the loved man, this child brings the market explicitly into play as she "haggl[es] from the fruit-man of his rotting ware." The sequence in this stanza suggests that she does so in response to the "ribald" allure of the carts. Yet given her poverty and her bartering skill, we must also assume that she is engaged in a routine struggle to feed herself. In a sense, the poem conflates poverty and explicit female sexuality, implying that it is ''dirty'' immigrant women who must inhabit the marketplace of physical need—of ''fruit-carts and clam-carts.''

And yet the distance between the women of MacDougal Street and the privileged bohemian speaker is tenuous. The poem works very hard to make the separation: she is ''shy'' and susceptible to nervous illness; her affective life is safely privatized within parentheses, just as her experience is itself recalled from within a domestic seclusion, and her fullest embodiment comes in the form of a wish to be a cool corpse, separated by death and rich fabrics from poverty and desire. But where the equally privileged man ''walked like a king'' through MacDougal Street, casual and condescending in his interactions, the female speaker moves in an agitated horror of contamination.

When the speaker expresses the direct wish to *be* ''a ragged child with ear-rings in [her] ears,'' it is with the assurance that such an identification is ridiculously far-fetched. And yet, the child is the speaker's most direct link to MacDougal Street; though a ''dirty, Latin child,'' she is clearly the speaker's sexual surrogate. Her multiple marks of class, ethnic, and generational difference serve to render the identification safe, but they also represent a fantasy—albeit a highly ambivalent one—of sexual freedom without sexual consequences. A child, she is more gamine than woman, whatever the content of her ''quips.'' Moreover, life on the market being a foregone conclusion, she can work it aggressively to her own advantage. Where the speaker is condemned to waiting for the loved man to do more than ''glance [her] by'' out of fear of her own descent into MacDougal Street sexuality, the girl's relation to him is uncomplicated by either implications for her identity or consequences for her actions.

As we have seen, the ''shawl-covered'' immigrant ''mother'' of ''Recuerdo'' served to enhance the transcendent status of that poem's lovers. But the sexualized women of ''MacDougal Street'' have only a precariously inoculatory effect for this speaker and the quality of her relation to her love object. Though the public Free Lover is ultimately saved by her middle-class ''American'' aesthetic sensibility, the poem is unsparing in its depiction of the dangers she perceives herself as negotiating. For the bohemian speaker, the women of MacDougal Street raise the specter that taking to the streets—parading her desire, writing Free Love poetry, being the very national icon of Free Love—will reduce her to the level of ''pink nets and wet shells trodden under heel.''

The Woman Lover in Nature

Long have I known a glory in it all,
  But never knew I this;
  Here such a passion is
As stretcheth me apart,—Lord, I do fear
Thou'st made the world too beautiful this year;

> My soul is all but out of me,—let fall
> No burning leaf; prithee, let no bird call.
>
> Millay, "God's World"

The management of Free Love, emblematic and otherwise, spills over into Millay's nature poetry, which has as important a place in her larger New Womanly strategy as the poetry of explicitly interpersonal content. While the love poems themselves focus predominantly on the outward shape of love, the nature poems enact various of its psychosexual dimensions. Millay's many love poems trace themes of sexual desire, ephemeral passion, and amorous adventure for its own sake. They issue from a voice which is sometimes suffering, sometimes haughty and heartless—yet, as critics from Edmund Wilson to contemporary feminist Jan Montefiore have pointed out, Millay's lover voice was nearly always suggestive of a perfectly integrated, self-possessed speaker. Even those poems that thematized despair and loss imparted the sense of love and its sorrows as a personal experience for the woman speaker, an enhancement of her individuality, rather than an event generated out of her interaction with a significant Other. The speaker's identity was that of a lover—more in spite of than because of the presence of a loved one. Montefiore makes this point, citing Wilson's remark that "when [Millay] came to write about her lovers, she gave them so little individuality that it was usually, in any given case, impossible to tell which man she was writing about" (apparently a sore point).[39]

Yet as the embodiment of Free Love and New Womanhood, Millay was bound to display not only sexual tough-mindedness but also psychological characteristics conventionally considered essential to femininity. The culturally new possibility of an actively desiring woman did not necessarily imply a radical conceptual revision of female sexuality as a whole. In fact, as we shall see in chapter 2, the scientific discovery of women as sexual beings was often presented alongside the discovery of a biological foundation for female passivity or for early marriage.[40] A woman might be a sexual adventurer, but her "nature" demanded that she experience intimacy as submersion in a powerful male Other. The contradictions of this modern sexuality intersect in complex and even widely divergent ways with Millay's other central imperative as a woman writer, that of attaining literary authority.

Millay's nature poetry frequently stages the threatened loss of self conventionally associated with the "woman in love." In the interest of achieving a tenable persona as Free Lover and New Woman, Millay superficially divorces the ideals which in general she and bohemian ideology strive to equate: *love* may be good or bad but it is an experience that reinforces individual identity; *beauty*, however, as it appears in Nature, is the intersubjective "Other" that threatens the self. And yet, even this threat is a nominal one. Working within the Romantic tradition of transcendence and the sublime, Millay transforms a classically feminine psychological posture of self-abnegation into an achievement of literary authority.

"Assault" (1921) is a nature poem with an especially sexualized—or, more accurately, gendered—framework. The speaker depicts herself as a vulnerable woman in a desolate place in fear of being "raped" by Beauty.

I

I had forgotten how the frogs must sound
After a year of silence, else I think
I should not so have ventured forth alone
At dusk upon this unfrequented road.

II

I am waylaid by Beauty. Who will walk
Between me and the crying of the frogs?
Oh, savage Beauty, suffer me to pass,
That am a timid woman, on her way
From one house to another![41]

What is remarkable about this poem is the contrast between the concreteness of the woman, her situation, and her sense of imperilment, on the one hand, and the abstractness of the threat itself as Beauty on the other. Of course, this threat is only sometimes abstract: in its alternate incarnation it is strikingly mundane and specific. While an aesthetic response to the croaking of frogs is arguably well within the bounds of poetic convention, the sense of acute physical imperilment expressed by the speaker seems jarringly disproportionate. But it would seem that this impression is rendered intentionally. To the extent that her responses diverge from the expected, the speaker has demonstrated the singular acuteness of her sensibility—and the singular personal risk to which it subjects her. The specifically womanly fear she experiences in passing through "savage Beauty" on her way from "one house to another" testifies simultaneously to her artistry and her femininity—with the remarkable outcome that artistry and femininity come to seem mutually interdependent.[42]

Millay was also able to imagine this conjunction in less overtly ambivalent terms. In fact, certain of her formulations suggest a utopian synthesis of sexuality and poetic vision. In "Journey," nature provides a framework for what emerges as the unconventional psychosexual dynamics of Free Love. From the same volume as "Assault," "Journey" is a study in threatened dissolution and reintegration. In the first lines, the speaker travels down a road, symbolic of her life, and yearns to enter the natural idyll to either side of her.

Ah, could I lay me down in this long grass
And close my eyes, and let the quiet wind
Blow over me,—I am so tired, so tired
Of passing pleasant places! All my life,

Following Care along the dusty road,
Have I looked back at loveliness and sighed;
Yet at my hand an unrelenting hand
Tugged ever, and I passed. All my life long
Over my shoulder have I looked at peace;
And now I fain would lie in this long grass
And close my eyes.[43]

In this passage, the "quiet wind," the "loveliness," and "peace" promise a relief from "Care," which is suggestive of death. The "unrelenting hand" of human obligation has "tugged ever" at the human drive—the "hand"—of the speaker, keeping her from her desire. At this point in the poem, the implied opposition is drawn fairly simply between dogged forward motion and its absence in tranquillity. The shape of the landscape changes in the subsequent passage, when the speaker has moved "Yet onward!" What had been merely soothing becomes particularized, provocative, and alluring.

Cat-birds call
Through the long afternoon, and creeks at dusk
Are guttural. Whip-poor-wills wake and cry,
Drawing the twilight close about their throats.
Only my heart makes answer. Eager vines
Go up the rocks and wait; flushed apple-trees
Pause in their dance and break the ring for me;
Dim, shady wood-roads, redolent of fern
And bayberry, that through sweet bevies thread
Of round-faced roses, pink and petulant,
Look back and beckon ere they disappear.

Here, nature has lost its former blandness, taking on color and sensual definition. Still bound to the road, the speaker now experiences the lure of the roadside as a direct erotic appeal—as, in fact, *multiple* erotic appeals. In the short space between the nature of death and the nature of sex, the dynamics of the scene have evolved considerably: the speaker's strong desire has evoked a like response in the passive landscape. In the process of becoming mutual, this exchange has likewise become erotic and dispersed, emanating from formerly hidden sites, which come into focus only in the act of desirous expression.

Still the speaker sticks to the road ("Only my heart, only my heart responds"): she knows the consequence of straying from this discrete and driven existence is the final "peace" of dissolution into nature. Yet by the conclusion, the basic opposition that has structured the poem throughout has broken down; the final lines assume no tension between road and roadside.

. . . blue hill, still silver lake,
Broad field, bright flower, and the long white road.

A gateless garden, and an open path:
My feet to follow, and my heart to hold.

Moreover, the character of the nature described has shifted for a third time. Not the balm of grass in the wind or the eroticism of "flushed apple-trees," the elements of this final landscape have the schematic quality of myth—of a *literary* landscape. What appears at first to be the speaker's reconciliation to a life divided between desire and duty emerges finally as erotic-aesthetic mastery.

Yet, ah, my path is sweet on either side
All through the dragging day,—sharp underfoot,
And hot, and like dead mist the dry dust hangs—
But far, oh, far as passionate eye can reach,
And long, ah, long as rapturous eye can cling,
The world is mine: blue hill, still silver lake,
Broad field, bright flower, and the long white road.
[emphasis added]

The speaker realizes a utopian vision of unrestrained and free-playing desire through her "rapturous," "passionate," "reach[ing]," "cling[ing]" "eye." Far from annihilating her, this sexuality gains her poetic control over the object of her desire, "the world."

By way of negotiating the problematic sexuality of the Free Lover, "Journey" achieves the ultimate bohemian ideal: the fusion of love and art. But whereas the literary authority of "Assault" depends directly on female vulnerability, the achievement of mastery depicted in "Journey" is at a distinct remove from conventional femininity. In fact, it resonates at key points with male transcendentalism: not only is the mastering "eye" itself strongly reminiscent of Emerson but also the "road" with which the speaker is all along associated puts her squarely in the tradition of Whitman. Moreover, in the most directly sexualized passage of the poem, femininity would seem to be deflected away from the speaker and onto nature, with its "wait[ing]" vines, "pink and petulant" roses, and coyly "beckon[ing]" wood-roads. Yet their invitation to her is not to dominate them as a masculine Other but to join them as the kindred being she is: the "apple-trees/Pause in their dance and break the ring for me." As we have seen, she declines to join them in fear for her life as a discrete being. But that is not to say that her survival requires a steady forward progress on "the open road." To the contrary, in the crucial last lines, the road is subsumed in the larger artistic landscape, a scene which is itself testimony to the speaker's aesthetic mastery. Moreover, the "eye" from which this mastery emanates represents not masculine transcendence but female "passion" and "rapture" as the very essence of poetic sensibility.

"Journey" suggests that Millay's professional economy depended on the convergence of these seemingly opposed terms. Whereas high-modernist contemporaries like Marianne Moore and H. D. found the possibility of self-protection and even transcendence of gender in a formalist aesthetics, Millay used traditional verse to turn her (inescapable) female sexuality to artistic authority.

Despite the ultimate synthesis that "Journey" achieves, the equation of mastery with masculinity has a strong pull for Millay, and in certain other works it finds clear expression. Most striking are those instances in which her speaker achieves aesthetic-erotic mastery by dominating an expressly feminized addressee. There are traces of this tendency in the "pink and petulant" roses of "Journey," but a starker example is Millay's poem to her youngest sister, Kathleen Millay, a woman who aspired to be a writer herself and, we can only guess, lived in acute consciousness of Edna's stellar example:[44]

Still must the poet as of old,
In barren attic bleak and cold,
Starve, freeze, and fashion verses to
Such things as flowers and song and you;
Still as of old his being give
In Beauty's name, while she may live,
Beauty that may not die as long
As there are flowers and you and song.[45]

"To Kathleen" implicitly counts its writer among the (male) "poets of old" while unambiguously declaring the ostensible object of its praise insentient (female) "Beauty." Millay has accorded herself a consciously classic, even cliché—and certainly bohemian—artistic posture, expressly at the expense of "Kathleen's" own claims to creative authority. By the same mechanism, she has aggressively defended her own iconic identity as the bohemian Muse against the taint of feminine objectification. Indeed, we may see this poetic exercise as an escalation of the protective persona of "Vincent," under (short-lived) cover of which Millay made her first splash in the Village as the poet of "Renascence." While she went on signing her family correspondence this way (playing the boy to her mother and sisters), fame as a New Woman so fixed her public femininity as perhaps to necessitate—or, at least, invite—a gesture like "To Kathleen."

Millay's negotiations of her singular subcultural status only rarely took such dubious form, but to the extent that Millay is an extreme case, she serves to highlight the thorny immediacy of a masculinist subcultural context for the production of a woman's poetry. By the same token, she suggests the resourcefulness with which a woman's poetry may manipulate the possibilities and imperatives of her subcultural milieu.

Indeed, the same milieu may produce vastly different poetic strategies in two women writers, as is evident in the comparison between Millay and Genevieve Taggard, the subject of the next two chapters. Obviously, Millay and Taggard were women with different personal histories and imperatives, but just as important was the structural difference of their respective positions within bohemia. Millay's almost literal equation with the symbolic life of the Village locked her in to a tight set of possibilities, as well as a significant investment in her own image. Taggard, by contrast, entered bohemia with the low profile of the feminine rank and file, which freed her to push at the contradictions of bohemian ideology as well to give herself over fully to its values. Less implicated in iconic bohemia, she had proportionately less to lose in testing the limits of its consciousness. Immediately evident to the reader will be the stark difference of her tone: where Millay has a certain (necessary) "lightness" we might associate with the thrust and parry of self-preservation, Taggard throws all of her considerable rhetorical force behind a bracing radicalism. If Millay is the Muse of bohemia, Taggard is its conscience.

T W O

Love in Greenwich Village

Genevieve Taggard and the Bohemian Ideal

> Marriage is the only profound experience; all other human angles are its mere rehearsal.
>
> Genevieve Taggard,
> "Poet out of Pioneer"

Examining the bohemian poetics of Floyd Dell and Edna St. Vincent Millay, we come to recognize the degree to which bohemia as such is a construction in flux, variously and temporarily fixed in the service of a particular identity or self-positioning. While Dell is the more-or-less official Village historian and Millay its universally acknowledged icon, and while each of them has a special place in the given "material" of bohemia, even the rank-and-file Village writer has a subcultural space to construct in the course of asserting a literary self. For a variety of personal and cultural reasons, Villager Genevieve Taggard made the theory and development of bohemia's utopian impulse her particular business. A public New Woman inasmuch as she published writing of contemporary gender relations, she was not, however, called upon to be a publicist for the Village. Perhaps as a consequence, her writing from this period is free to pursue a single-minded and highly personal exploration of the utopian possibilities of heterosexuality in the context of bohemian values. Specifically, the privileged status accorded to romantic love in the Village gave Taggard full rein to delve into the dynamics of her own marriage as a means of arriving at a theory of (in Max Eastman's famous phrase) "love and revolution."[1]

In his useful study of "first wave" women poets in America (and the only focused analysis of Taggard's life and work to date), literary historian William Drake notes that "Taggard's career unfolded in much the same way as that of other women poets of her generation—the early promise, the struggle against a restrictive background, the move to New York, the acceptance into a lively subculture of writers and artists."[2] What the following exploration should make clear is the particularity of any given rendition of such subcultural experience. Like Millay, Taggard came to the Village as a recent college graduate in the late teens and straddled the generational divide between those Malcolm Cowley called the "Old Villagers"—founders like Floyd Dell—and the "New Villagers," those who, like Cowley himself, came to the Village "after the War or college," and were distinguished from their predecessors by their pronounced lack of idealism. Taggard was strongly invested in bohemian ideals, so much so that in 1926, she took it upon herself to publish a work of tribute to and preservation of the old Village. Never nostalgic, her lengthy introduction to *May Days: An An-*

Photograph on preceding page: Bohemians en route to a costume ball (c. 1924). (Delaware Art Museum, Helen Farr Sloan Library Archives)

thology of Verse from Masses-Liberator nonetheless conveys the sense that it is in bohemia she finds her anchor as a poet in the world.[3] *The Masses* was a "little magazine" that ran under a Village editorial collective starting in 1912, becoming *The Liberator* in 1917 (after being shut down for sedition); for all those years and after, it stood for the exuberant and heterogeneous radicalism of the true bohemian era. Cofounder and artist Art Young called it "one magazine which we could gallop around in and be free."[4] *The Masses* was also emblematic of the fragility of those "free" years, and in her effort to capture that essence before it was gone, Taggard collected nearly three hundred pages of *Masses-Liberator* poetry.

Perhaps her commitment to bohemia is nowhere more evident than in the rather strained assertion that "*The Masses*, in spite of its readers [who were bourgeois], and the economic status of its editors [also bourgeois], in spite of its editorial background, in spite of almost everything—was revolutionary" (6). Perhaps it is true that this revolutionary quality resided in "the desire for a realistic grasp of [American] life as a whole" (6), or in the "combination of sophistication and naiveté" (8) with which "the *Masses* group" approached American life. But surely at least part of the affective charge for Taggard resided in the idea of "the *Masses* group" itself. At the center of her *May Days* analysis are three men "in [the] curious role of father-teacher-hero to that generation of young Americans": Max Eastman, whom she designated "realistic philosopher and poet"; Jack Reed, "man of action and human symbol for the time"; and Floyd Dell, "teacher and intimate psychologist" (6–8). "More than three people," Taggard declares, "in close contact . . . they drew to themselves a swarm of excellent artists and social satirists. . . . This was a living combination and the ideas that grew from it had kinetic energy." Heroes and the kinetic group—Taggard looks back as much as at anything on the luminous subcultural life itself. In this sense, her history is akin to Dell's own *Love in Greenwich Village*, published the same year. But Taggard is scrupulously undeferential to this generation she names as the "heroes" of her own, and where Dell is characteristically moony, Taggard is finally tough-minded. Praising the *Masses* political cartoons, she pronounces the poetry a failure by comparison:

> The poets tended either to a Tennysonian convention or to journalism. There are a few exceptions worth all the failures. If the *Masses* had continued another twenty years, this anthology might have preserved for English literature not four great poems, but forty.
>
> But it ceased, and the buds on the two trees wither for lack of each other. It is the artist's fault because he is afraid of revolution. It is the propagandist's fault for giving the artist a job he cannot perform. And it is nobody's fault, as well, but simply the effect of a world change. (14)

If this seems an oddly deflationary launch for the anthology itself, it is nevertheless consistent with Taggard's proprietary self-positioning vis-à-vis bohemia: guardian of its utopian potential, she was also the unsparing critic of its reality.

Immersed in Village life, Taggard is a "typical" bohemian and yet, as we see, typicality in a utopian subculture was hardly an unexamined state of being. Even more than in her relation to the "heroes" she names, Taggard actively worked through Millay's symbolic meaning for her own life. From her earliest days in the Village, working for B. W. Huebsch and running in core intellectual circles, Taggard had a powerful and articulate sense of the importance of Edna Millay's life and work for her own identity as a woman poet. This identification is the more remarkable given the stark differences between them, not least of which was the disparity in their visions of bohemia. But Taggard's vision *must* have included bohemia's womanly icon, almost by definition.

Taggard defended Millay in the most impassioned terms against what she unflinchingly named as a gender-based trivialization of her work. Reviewing *The Harp-Weaver* for *Measure*, a relatively prestigious poetry journal of which she was a founding editor, Taggard titled her essay, significantly, "Her Massive Sandal":

> This poetry magazine exists in an age that has undoubtedly produced one of the poets of all time—yet it has never been seen to rejoice in proportion of the fact nor even to realize very clearly its advent. . . . When Miss Millay is too sincere and simple for our age, she is called infantile; when she is brave and ironically wise, she is called flippant. The critics, usually dismayed gentlemen who are completely incapable of coping with both qualities, have said a good deal under each of these heads, while the world, meanwhile, rises with a roar to receive its poet.
>
> Most of our assayers of literature have still hiding deep in one rococo [*sic*] corner of their hearts, along with a shamed liking for plush and gilt, a horrified prejudice against any woman "naked of reticence and shorn of pride," ruthless and intense in her own genius. . . . Miss Millay with Emily Dickinson has sinned arrogantly and wilfully against much that is male and pontifical and she must be told that she is a clever child, merely—naughty, if not the less charming.[5]

In general, the *Measure* held Millay up as a beacon in the darkness of "free verse" and the "higher" modernism, but it was Taggard who found in Millay the assault on patriarchal propriety, identifying with her struggle both personally and professionally. Indeed, not long into her Village career, Taggard wrote to Josephine Herbst, close friend and fellow writer, that "she's the only girl that's at all like us."[6]

Into the context of what we might well deem a paradigmatic Village career came Taggard's marriage in 1921 to fellow Villager and writer Robert L. Wolf.[7] Dating from almost the time of her arrival on the bohemian scene—and followed in quick succession by a baby—this relationship is closely interwoven with Taggard's experience of bohemia itself and forms the matrix of her intellectual-affective struggle to make its utopian ideality her own. As documented in Taggard's letters to Herbst, the marriage was fraught with the tensions of gender-based inequity and the imposition of a grinding domesticity on what was to have been an artist-lovers' idyll.[8] In a 1922 letter, Taggard lamented, "If I didn't have this terrible financial burden I could be such an artist now. . . . But how can I when [the baby's] whole existence and Bob's single chance at self-realization depend on whether I work hard enough to earn $250 a month!"[9] Consistent with their bohemian self-understanding, Taggard and Wolf assigned a privileged status to artistic endeavor and identity, as well as to personal independence, yet the bohemian model of artistic life also provided the specific justification for a traditional division of labor within their marriage. Though herself a respected and accomplished poet, Taggard had primary responsibility for tending the child, keeping house, and generating income in order that the way might be clear for Robert to pursue his Muse. As we shall see, this arrangement represented more than simply the default of conventional gender hierarchy.

Notwithstanding the material reality of her own life, Taggard was able to write in a heartfelt essay of 1924 that

> it is hard to be an artist under any circumstance; it is harder in America than it has been at other stations in time and space; but hardest of all, multiplied by fractions, decimals, and whole numbers, to be an artist in this country *if you are a man.* [original italics]

Taggard briefly itemizes what she sees as the principal styles of masculine artistry and concludes, "All these groups give a sense of locked-up talent, denied and outcast desire—but almost never a poem." Masculine failure (which—in a pointed twist on the perennial debate about whether *women* can write at all—she merely asserts) is rooted in the peculiar relationship men have to economics.

> Those of us who know a large number of struggling men who have often it appears, much more talent than the women, but almost never a poem to be placed with their best, see for them one terrible problem in common: the problem of earning a living. Not merely a living for one, unless the man so determines to simplify matters. Bread and butter for an average three or four change the picture enormously.

The essay moves quickly from what is simply counterfactual to Taggard's own experience and recasts the problem of objective economic imperatives in terms of an existential struggle for the American male artist.

> The creative boy must purge himself of the slow poisons of middle-class morality before he can render himself pure for the work of an artist. And this is no small thing to do. It keeps him shadow-boxing and arguing eternally trying to convince himself that the white-collar slave is not really a better man than he.[10]

The use of "boy" to refer to the male artist is consistent with the implicitly maternalistic bent of the argument as a whole, not to mention the focus of the special issue in which it appears: "Men Poets," presumably Taggard's idea, since she was serving as editor for the month. One hears a further echo in Taggard's private remark to Herbst that "He's [Wolf's] really a boy you know Joe . . . and he has hallucinations he won't finish the novel."[11] In both her private and public writings, Taggard tends to assume the superior strength of women in their capacities as people and artists. And we have seen evidence of her sharp critique of literary gender politics.

But like many of the literary-intellectual men (and women) of her generation, Taggard sees female strength as coming at a direct cost to masculinity in men. Applying "If You Are a Man" to Taggard and Wolf, she and Marcia, their child, are the embodiment of the presumptive material burden which prevents Wolf from realizing his presumably superior talent. Simultaneously, Taggard attributes her own far better writing to, of all things, the luxury of her cultural and economic freedom. The ideological framework within which such contradiction may be seen as coherent is that of the bohemian opposition of artist and world, mapped onto the romantic opposition of transcendent male and immanent female.[12] As it functioned for Taggard and Wolf, questions of gender and power relations within their domestic arrangements could be refigured as questions of art (Wolf's novel) and the constraints on art (Taggard's baby and bills).

Yet Taggard and Wolf seem to have been regarded by at least some of their contemporaries as the embodiment of the bohemian literary-romantic ideal: lovers and writers in a relationship of equality. In her biography of Josephine Herbst, Elinor Langer states that Herbst was "comforted by their example." According to Langer, "As a couple [Taggard and Wolf] were romantic and modern. They wanted love and work, freedom and commitment, involvement with other people and absorption in themselves."[13] The sense of its importance for Taggard herself may be seen in the epigraph to this chapter, in her claim that "marriage is the only profound human experience." She was conscious of her relationship to Wolf as a paradigm for—or perhaps a test of—ideal love, for her poetry is simultaneously autobiographical and infused with a commitment to forging and theorizing two quintessentially bohemian relations: that between male and female as artist-lovers and that between society and the heterosexual couple who embody love and art. The oppositionality on which Village identity depended centered on the artist's struggle against the bourgeois world, which, as we have seen, Taggard identified as a male drama. Though herself a serious and independent artist, she gives this masculine agon a central place in her poetry, often within the terms of its most masculinist expression. Meanwhile, the impulse to account for the sense of her own strength—as against what she saw as its absence in men, specifically Wolf—is itself traceable to her internalization of a cultural paradigm of female power and especially, female sexuality, as inherently destructive.

Bohemia's constructions of gender and sexuality were complexly informed by those of the larger cultural context that it so emphatically rejected.[14] While Dell and Millay's poetics of lyrical poverty make us aware of the pressure of immigrant life on bohemian self-understanding, Taggard's concern with the nature of love brings into focus the power which mainstream sexology exerted over Bohemian ideals.

Sexology in Bohemia

The decade of the twenties was characterized by a general movement away from the civic and politicized sensibility of the previous decades toward one of privatization.[15] This shift was manifested not only in fundamentally conservative social elements but also in the forces of social rebellion, which had come to be organized around the notion of personal freedom as an end in itself. In this era of popular Freud, such freedom was identified with sexual fulfillment: it was primarily by their unrestrained sexual conduct (illusory by most accounts) that the "Younger Generation" defined itself and so threatened its elders. Even feminism, as it pertained specifically to white middle-class women's lives, had been largely reduced, in theory and practice, to the right to sexual expression.[16]

In the absence of a gender critique of the increasingly powerful medical establishment, many women, feminists among them, looked to the ostensibly neutral scientific authority of sexology for the terms of their liberation. What had begun in the late nineteenth century as an esoteric study had grown by the 1920s to be a widely popularized science that effectively promoted traditional gender relations in quintessentially "modern" terms. Within this discourse, women's liberation qua sexual fulfillment found its ironic culmination in monogamy and ultimately, motherhood. Having thus reasserted sexuality as the primary arena of female self-definition, sexology declared feminist activism and professional ambition to be evidence of sexual frustration or maladjustment.[17] Under this regime, Progressive Era feminists, with their woman-centered communities, were not merely marginalized but derided as examples of failed sexual "adjustment." For their part, younger feminists not only sought freedoms precluded by traditional feminism but also viewed their feminist forebears with condescension, if not contempt. To demonstrate (to themselves and the world) the success of their own "adjustments," they rejected a heritage through which they might have brought critical pressure to bear on their predominantly masculinist contemporary culture.[18] The women's movement seemed to have lost its unity and force just as a highly visible minority of women successfully penetrated certain formerly all-male professional and educational arenas, giving the lie, in the popular imagination, to the idea of institutionalized gender oppression.[19] Cut off from feminist discourse and having theoretically achieved parity with men, women of the twenties were left to negotiate their experience of gender oppression within the arena of the personal.[20]

The domain of "personal" life, meanwhile, was expanding as domesticity and leisure came to occupy more and more of individual and family existence for the middle class. But while the emergence of a youth culture opened up a whole new consumer market—and even depended on the consumption of style for group definition[21]—expanding middle-class consumerism faced the threat of women's refusal to consume full-time for the family. For the sake of corporate as well as broad conservative interest, advertising and sexology pushed hard to redomesticate women.[22]

Sexology was disseminated in popular magazines and books, where it focused on questions of marriage and child-rearing. The primary object of analysis in these works was female sexual development, made precarious, according to the general account, by a long period of sexual latency. The "sexually unawakened" woman was prey to various evils en route to monogamous heterosexuality. (Even Edna Millay herself was subject to this stereotype—at the hands of Floyd Dell, no less, who, at an early point in Millay's career, cast himself as her sexual savior.[23]) Feminist activism, a career, or even college could divert the unwitting woman from marriage, beguiling her into missing her ultimate sexual fulfillment in the timely production of children. On grounds of their own scientifically established biological needs, women were to be kept to the traditional path by their parents and the intervention of husbands. Sexology thus took up the consumerist rhetoric of personal fulfillment and the feminist concern with women's sexual expression by invoking medical authority to declare what was finally for women's own good.[24]

The principles of sexology had their culmination in the notion of companionate marriage. As the telos of individual development, it was implicit in the era's various handbooks on women, girls, adolescence, and marriage. Judge Ben Lindsey, its foremost popularizer, described "the companionate" as simply a nonreproductive period preceding traditional marriage for the purpose of establishing the permanence of the marital union.[25] His *Companionate Marriage,* first serialized in the popular *Redbook* before it was published as a single volume in 1929, illustrates, in clearer fashion than its more strictly "scientific" sexological counterparts, certain mechanisms by which heterosexual monogamy came to be compulsory in the contemporary culture.[26] Having declared his scientific neutrality in his introduction to the book, Lindsey uses the remaining four hundred or so pages to relate various of his out-of-court experiences as a family court judge, most of which come in the form of fictionalized dialogues with individuals in crisis over marital and sexual issues. The typical anecdote begins with the "subject" expressing gratitude for what he or she knows will be Judge Lindsey's confidence and open-mindedness. What follows is, in most cases, a confession of extramarital sex, framed by a rationale instantly recognizable to the reader as "modern" in its privileging of freedom and variety. Judge Lindsey (trusting to his by-now reiterated if not exactly proven disinterest) responds with arguments intended to reveal the naiveté, if not the hypocrisy, underwriting digressions from fidelity—never through recourse to religious or moral standards but purely on the basis of scientifically established terms of psychological well-being. For the most part, however, this line of argument does not produce the persona of the detached scientist; as the anecdotal form of his book suggests, Lindsey's rhetorical power depends on his constantly reminding the reader that his is a wisdom born of practical experience. He is finally a model of gruff but benevolent paternalism, dispensing expertise to society's wayward "children."

Companionate Marriage embodies two major strains of the ideological pressure that redomestication brought to bear on women: the impersonal authority of science and the patriarchal authority that under wrote it, here rendered explicit by the necessity of a persona for Lindsey's narrative. While sexology worried the question of female sexual adjustment, advertising zeroed in on the resultant free-floating anxiety. The cumulative effect of these discourses was to give a pointedly teleological cast to gender and sexuality, such that maturation *meant* heterosexual monogamy, particularly for women.

Despite its reputation for scandalous living, Village bohemia by the twenties was basically allied with the heterosexism of sexology.[27] Though unconventional sexuality was central to bohemian self-definition, though Edna Millay herself was known to have had lesbian relationships, Village writings kept silent on the subject of gay and lesbian Village subculture.[28] Perhaps most striking was the rhetorical apparatus common to both sexology and bohemian Free Love. The one tailored psychoanalysis to traditional bourgeois values; the other generated a literary counterpart that promoted romantic love.[29] Not just any love aesthetic, romantic love was a model of gender relations structurally and historically bound up with artistic sensibility itself.[30] Combined with sexology's psychologistic framework and its assertion of a rational basis for intimacy, romantic love allowed for a sexual "redefinition" which only served to exalt traditional gender arrangements. Certainly, power relations were never brought to light. The success of this conception of heterosexuality in the era of the New Woman depended on the obfuscation wrought by what we may describe as a rhetoric of aestheticization.

Popular sexology was peppered with calls for "frankness" and scientific candor yet so often proceeded from the contrary discursive register of metaphor and even euphemism. Moreover, it commonly made use of an explicit analogy between sex and art. Havelock Ellis, arguably the most influential of the sexologists, implicitly rejected Freud's model of social repression and sublimation of unconscious drives to focus, instead, on what he called "the art of love," which was generated only under the highest conditions of civilization. "The lover is an artist," said Ellis, and "the art of love" is possible only among the "more developed races" (an assertion consistent with what we have seen of the unspoken nativism of bohemia). This language is taken up by other sexological authorities. Ellen Key, whose *Love and Marriage* earned her the status of spokeswoman for women's sexual freedom and fulfillment, stated in a characteristic moment, "All developed women desire to be loved not *'en male'* but *'en artiste.'* "[31] The use of art as a structuring metaphor finds particularly fertile ground in the cultural context of the Village, where, happily for "developed" women, *male* and *artiste* come together. Villager Hutchins Hapgood tellingly called the memoir of his life *The Story of a Lover*, from which historian Robert E. Humphrey captures the essence of Hapgood's self-understanding: "Unlike most men, who could only create a 'sketch' in the 'difficult' art of love, Hapgood called himself the exceptional 'artist lover' who had the 'patience to build a work of art' even if it took 'an eternity to finish.' "[32]

Whatever its contradictions, Village bohemia perceived itself to be the vanguard of liberatory social practices, grounding its identity in broad opposition to mainstream culture: where middle-class America was sexually repressive and materialistic, bohemia was an arena in which personal freedom and art were supreme values. Within its winding and subterranean Village spaces, Free Love and artistic expression could take shelter from a world hostile to both. Such was the nature of bohemia's utopian promise.

Bohemian Love and/as Art

True to form, Floyd Dell provides a high-profile articulation of the logic of bohemian ideality. From his earliest days in the more modest and unpublicized bohemian subculture of Chicago, Dell promoted psychoanalysis and feminism as interpenetrating liberations. In 1912, he published *Women as World Builders*. A celebration of feminism and its influence, *Women as World Builders* nevertheless included in its introduction the only half-ironic assertion that feminism was the natural outgrowth of women's innate desire to serve men by becoming more interesting mates.[33] By the time of *Love in Greenwich Village*, Dell's feminism had been fully absorbed (or subsumed) into its larger heterosexual aim. As I suggested in my discussion of Millay, Dell's first chapter, "The Rise of Greenwich Village," charts the way in which all bohemian ideals culminate in the experience of heterosexual romantic love.

> Vagabond youth has always ignored the codes invented by those who have settled down and have a property-stake in the world. Security means little to young artists, and the opinion of the world still less. Love, they know, is sweet while it lasts. In Greenwich Village this attitude quickly became the social norm. Secrecy and hypocrisy were unnecessary there. And there, if anywhere, youth could discover fearlessly for itself, and not out of the leaves of musty books, the truths of human nature. (35)

Then follows the love story of Paul and Rosika, and Dell's introduction to the Village is concluded. Clearly, the reader is to understand romantic love as the natural framework within which bohemian values must find expression. Romantic love, emblem of bohemian utopia, enacted Village oppositionality, simultaneously concretizing its identity as a subculture and inoculating heterosexuality against the more profound implications of feminism.

But there was unspoken antagonism between women and men, and its management, discursively speaking, led back to an ideologically more fundamental antagonism: that between artistic idealism and bourgeois materialism. The path between the two was somewhat circuitous but not unpredictable. On the one hand, feminism, as an acknowledged positive value, naturally belonged to art and the Village, while the repression of women was the business of the reactionary mainstream. On the other hand, bohemian individualism implicitly took the romantic artist as its center of consciousness, a paradigm of experience effectively and traditionally masculinist in its privileging of transcendence over materiality. In practice, this meant that the obligations associated with heterosexual domestic arrangements and the constraints they imposed on the pursuit of art could be relegated to the devalued bourgeois world, precisely because they were material concerns. But, of course, they were first and most obviously the concerns of women.

Insofar as love was seen to imply domestic practice, there arose a fundamental tension in its alliance with art. Depending on where they happened to fall on the continuum between "free" and traditional love, female-male relationships carried some degree of threat to the pursuit of art. As we have seen, certain of the stories in *Love in Greenwich Village* specifically thematize the tension between art and love, with complicated results. Despite the notoriety of Village sexual license, marriage and the begetting of children were not uncommon among the bohemians or necessarily incompatible with Free Love as it was ambiguously defined. (Indeed, Dell specifically praises sexologist Ellen Key, one of the feminist "world builders" he identifies in his early book, for raising monogamy to its properly exalted height.) The freedoms of the Village were part of a highly eclectic and unsystematic model of social revolution. Moreover, the structure of mature life—including advanced domesticity—merited little attention in a culture self-consciously identified with youth.

Consistent with the metaphoric identification of love with the Village itself, the final segment of *Love in Greenwich Village*—"The Fall of Greenwich Village"—begins with a scene of typical bohemian life nested ominously within a well-entrenched domestic scene. The story follows "a long night of talk and a few hours' sleep in some one's studio" (everyone together on the floor, "boho" fashion) with the invasion of the hosts' small children. The narrator listens wonderingly to them identify "two friends of mine . . . as Mr. and Mrs.—as though they were grown-up people, and not the most delightful and irresponsible artist-children in the world! So they went about, identifying us, calling us by the titles of our adulthood" (305). Though the narrator finds this recitation "funny" as well as "sad," and though the chapter goes on to the much more definitive tragedies of suicide for one aging (male) bohemian and prison for another, family domesticity is unquestionably central to the general demise. Our narrator ends up "[a] ghost, . . . walk[ing] about the midnight streets, meeting other ghosts—friends and comrades and sweethearts of those lost, happy years" (321), but not before a final encounter with the "doomed" Paul, who invites him " 'out to my place' " (in Connecticut? Westchester?). " 'Come,' " he says, " 'and bring your wife. Helen will be delighted to show off her two lovely babies' " (320). Paul's doom is presumably explained by Helen and her babies, while the narrator's doom is as yet only imminent (the babies still to come).

Domestic life exacerbated the contradictions of free love, with the result that the dichotomy of idealism and materialism, which constituted the very cornerstone of bohemian self-understanding, resumed its gendered aspect. Unmolested by domestic pressure, the role of artist was as apparently gender-blind as the ideology of antimaterialism itself. But in the grip of economic necessity, the mask slips to reveal a transcendent male artist fighting for his life and identity against the material demands of an essentially domestic woman—who, in turn, finds herself not only excluded from artistic identity but also the agent of bourgeois oppression. Ironically, to the extent that eschewal of economic power actually returned as a threat to male identity, the containment of economic need and desire had all the more scrupulously to be located in women (and those other Others, the bourgeoisie and the immigrants).

Problematic yet essential, bohemian love as an ideal depended for its coherence on bohemian art. Art provided the central, structuring metaphor for love, which took on an impenetrable surface of beauty and lyricism, such as to obscure utterly the heterosexual power relations beneath the surface. By force of the same convergence, love could repell any but the most uncritical gaze, hiding its flawed self behind the unassailable value of art. Therein lay the power of aestheticization.

Aestheticization itself had gender-specific meanings for those it implicated. For Taggard, it may well have been uncomfortably associated with the "lady poet" tradition from which she sought to disengage herself. In the introduction to her *Collected Poems, 1918–1938*, Taggard wrote, "I have refused to write out of a decorative impulse, because I conceive it to be the dead end of much feminine talent. A kind of literary needlework." Still, she maintained the category of women's writing, redefining it as universalizable rather than rejecting it for specifically gender-free writing. The same passage from *Collected Poems* reveals the difficulty of this position.

> Many poems in this collection are about the experiences of women. I hope these express all types of candid and sturdy women. . . . I think the later poems and some of the early ones hold a wider consciousness than that colored by the feminine half of the race. I hope they are not written by a poetess, but by a poet. I think, I hope, I have written poetry that relates to general experience and the realities of the time.[34]

If the fine line is to be drawn at the "decorative impulse," aestheticizing discourse raises artistic-professional anxieties for the woman writer at the same time that it poses sharp contradictions to the bohemian woman's experience of Free Love, which includes the pain of male domination as well as the exhilaration of equality, exclusion from art as well as identification with it.

Taggard's love poetry of the early twenties testifies abundantly to her investment in Greenwich Village ideals: the romantic artist is her implicit paradigm for human subjectivity, she casts love as the central human experience, she is openly critical of bourgeois materialism and implicitly treats love as a force of resistance against it, and, finally, art and love, artist and lover, are so closely identified in her work as to be almost interchangeable. Yet Taggard's poetry makes the unmistakably iconoclastic suggestion that *aestheticization* was both a force and a function of repression, submerging the sexual power relations which were, for Taggard, the very engine of art. Paradoxically, this critical perspective testifies further to Taggard's investment in bohemian ideality itself. Her deconstruction of the "aesthetic" character of sexual love comes in the interest of tightening the hetereosexual dyad, delving deeper to an even more profound sense of the artist-lover couple as inviolable.

Love and Revolution

A striking fact of Taggard's poetry in the twenties is the number of works that focus on a vision of apocalypse or its aftermath. "Ice Age," among her first published poems, is also the first of an apocalyptic series delving deeper into bohemian ideology over time.[35] Apart from the general preoccupation with end visions, particular images from "Ice Age" persist in subsequent works, but with the difference that they are specifically enlisted to the project of configuring the world with the romantic heterosexual couple at its center—a project suffused with all the difficulty of Taggard's real-life relationship to Robert Wolf. True to the high standard of intellectual clarity and integrity she consistently set for herself, the personal and the theoretical are here deliberately and inextricably intertwined, each tested against the other. Indeed, the aptness of pairing "love and apocalypse" seems at least partly to reside in a wry twist on "love and revolution"—and a conscious darkening of the classic bohemian formulation.

Edmund Wilson's rather trivializing declaration that "Ice Age" was "the first effect on [Taggard's] imagination of one of our Eastern winters"[36] had more truth to it than he probably intended, for in a sense Taggard's preoccupation with apocalypse comes directly out of her formative experience of "paradise." Having grown up in Hawaii, a white missionary onlooker to what she regarded as untouched native bliss, Taggard had so foundational a feeling for utopia that its dark inversion awaited only the right prompting in bohemia's unfulfilled promise.[37] As its title suggests, "Ice Age" stages a slow, silent end to the world, a gradual going to sleep at twilight in the snow. Its human victims offer almost no resistance at all. Utterly divided by gender, seen only as the vaguely tribal units of "the women" and "the men," their passivity and ineffectualness in the face of disaster stem from the very social arrangements that thwart the human charge generated by individual hetereosexual coupling. So runs the strong implication. Thus, in 1921, Taggard was clearly at work on a poetics consistent with bohemian ideality.

By 1926, she had moved beyond the promise to interrogate the reality of dyadic heterosexuality: ''Doomsday Morning'' weaves love into apocalypse in such a way as to suggest Taggard's fierce but skeptical commitment to the romantic couple as a force of utopian resistance in the world. For all of the familiarity of doomsday as an ''occasion,'' ''Doomsday Morning'' depicts what is nevertheless an alien scenario. This doomsday has none of the grandeur of an apocalypse; even more striking is the indeterminacy surrounding the actors, not only in their identities but also in the power relations among them. The authority of ''God'' is clearly open to question, though whatever may be his ultimate power, the lovers respond to him with indifference and even contempt.

Deaf to God who calls and walks
Until the earth aches with his tread,
Summoning the sulky dead,
We'll wedge and stiffen under rocks,
Or be mistaken for a stone,
And signal as children do, ''Lie low,''
Wait and wait for God to go.
The risen will think we slumber on
Like slug-a-beds. When they have gone
Trooped up before the Judgment Throne,—
We in the vacant earth alone—
Abandoned by ambitious souls,
And deaf to God who calls and walks
Like an engine overhead
Driving the disheveled dead,—
We will rise and crack the ground
Tear the roots and heave the rocks,
And billow the surface where God walks,
And God will listen to the sound
And know that lovers are below
Working havoc till they creep
Together from their sundered sleep.

Then end, world! Let your final darkness fall!
And God may call and call and call.[38]

The imagery associated with ''we'' proceeds in a kind of evolution from something prehuman (1.4–5), to children (1.6–7), to social identity (1.8–15), and finally to lovers (1.16–22). The effect of this progression is to suggest that lovers are in some way the culmination of human possibility, an idea borne out by the narrative, for it is as lovers that ''we'' finally rise to challenge God.

The figure they defy is named as God but, in the course of the poem, accumulates associations which additionally identify him with the more impersonal authority of capitalist-industrial society.[39] The first hint of this synthesis appears in the effect of his "tread" on the earth, which causes it to "ache" as if he were in an abusive instrumental relation to it. Having summoned the "sulky dead," God then appears as an "engine," "driving" his "disheveled" and reluctant laborers against their own inclination to sleep. As God becomes a figure of authoritarian culture, his "doomsday" offer of immortality comes to be equated with society's offer of simple material survival, each offer exacting the high price of submission. The lovers clearly reject this bargain, but, having reduced God to Boss, the poem suggests no alternative to industrial society apart from the nonsociety of an apocalypse. Where all this leaves the lovers is someplace outside the social contract, antagonists to society itself.

Taggard grants the lovers the status of revolutionary subjects in their "ris[ing to] crack the ground" but refuses to render them overtly heroic and even takes pains to undercut what might otherwise be their unambiguously positive character for the reader. "Doomsday Morning" responds to the mainstream effort to domesticate sexuality with an emphatic assertion of resistance to the authority and demands of production-oriented society. The poem's spatial imagery implies that sexuality is a dormant force of revolutionary potential: the lovers occupy the bottommost stratum in the poem's geograpical hierarchy, and they are literally "walked on" by the powers that be; they are "underground," and they derive the power to elude authority and disrupt society precisely from that vantage point. Such identification with the driven masses serves the same normative function as may be seen for art in other of Taggard's works from the twenties; that is, it implicitly puts the lovers in a position outside and "above" (because "below") bourgeois society.

But all of this is contained at the level of metaphor; the overt assessment of revolution in the poem, whether political or sexual, is ultimately ambiguous. It is already "doomsday" when the poem begins, hence the end of the world is a foregone conclusion, brought about by Christian-industrial society according to its own teleological design. The poem renders this end as an oppressively regimented inevitability, to which the organic upheaval generated by the lovers presents a welcome opposition. But the apocalyptic outcome is the same in either case. The lovers neither defend the status quo nor offer a new utopian order; they simply detach themselves from societal structure per se.

Taggard makes ironic use of her setting, downplaying "doomsday" to emphasize "morning" in its mundane aspects, so that wakefulness, rather than moral purity, turns out to be the salient criterion for Judgment. And yet, there is a deeply embedded moral value attached to "early rising" in bourgeois capitalist society, and naming the speaker and her lover as "slug-a-beds" would seem deliberately to undermine our reader's sympathy for them—surely these characters are at least marginally lazy and unsavory. In the second half of the poem, the lovers "rise and crack the ground": now indisputably active, they have seemingly turned to purposeless destruction. The poem is nearly over before we even learn that our protagonists are "lovers." Given that audiences—bohemian *and* mainstream—are highly disposed to favor lovers, almost unconditionally, the question arises of why Taggard withholds their identity, keeping them out of range of our willing sympathy. This choice seems deliberate: Taggard effectively defies her audience to sentimentalize and domesticate the heterosexual couple, which, as the poem reveals, is neither ornamental nor a force for social stability but, in fact, nonproductive, disruptive, and, in the strict sense of the term, antisocial.

"Doomsday Morning" assigns love a privileged critical vantage point in relation to society as a whole, but not without raising questions about the nature of love itself. Such violence as the lovers exhibit must surely have implications for their relationship. Focused as they are on their mutual antagonist, society, their mutual destructiveness is kept at bay. In the war that ensues absent such external opposition in others of Taggard's poems, the heterosexual couple seem strangely to grow only more symbiotic. Indeed, the argument generated by Taggard's love poems in this period seems to be that self-containment alone gives heterosexuality what we are to understand as its necessary and permanent character. Taggard's palpable ambivalence arises from the combination of her insight into the precarious ability of bohemian monogamy to sustain itself and the absence—or necessary refusal—of a gender critique that would offer the possibility of an alternative vision. But however conflicted her sense of its viability, her conviction that heterosexuality is a field of power relations gives her a clear position from which to address aestheticizing discourses (cultural or countercultural) which would deny the relation of love to power and domination.

"Quarrel" and "Truce" are presented in Taggard's 1926 collection, *Words for the Chisel* (68–69), as a pair and together, serve to schematize Taggard's conception of heterosexual dynamics: a closed, stable, but warring economy. Most immediately striking in this narrative of sexual conflict are the rhetorical dynamics generated by the speaker as she alternately coaxes, scolds, and threatens her addressee, in a manner sometimes playful and maternal, then seductive, then somber. The manifest effort of this persuasive movement is such that it implicitly constitutes its object—the conflict, the man, or both—as formidable in its resistance. So practiced a rhetorical facility suggests a long history to the relationship, while the substance of the poems' conclusions suggests the speaker's perseverance is quite unsupported by stability.

The two poems are placed on opposite pages, and the obvious parallel of their titles invokes the comforting inevitability of a truce throughout the quarrel; this quarrel, we are assured, will have a resolution. And yet the "truce" has the paradoxical effect of retrospectively escalating the quarrel into what, on reflection, it more properly is: a war.

Quarrel

Stop fighting! It's the armour that I hate
And not the boy beneath it. Will you run
Out from your anger, put the quarrel straight—
(I will not always be the vanquished one!)

Or shall we go on raging, while we wait
Each for the other to come crying out
Like demons in the bible, so too late,
With frantic tears, bewildered by a doubt:

If I must anger and possess you so
And make you turn on me so black an eye
Your anger may not let you out but grow
To be your only being, by and by;
And we will go down clattering at last,
Two empty people, murderously fast.

Truce

Fling down your weapons, weary enemy,
And I will bind the wounds I just now gave;
Ah, keep your strength and all your poise and save
Your passion for tomorrow, when with me
You meet in naked grapple. Who but we
Should heal each other, wounded, who but we,
My tall antagonist, terrible and brave?

Some day beside each other we shall lie
And bleed, and ebb, and separately die:
Beyond this shock of battle, there will be
No warrior for our valor, in the grave.
Forbear to wound me utterly, unless
The time has come for that long loneliness.

The pairing of these poems conveys a sense of emotional closure on the episode they describe, the sense that the economy of this relationship is self-rectifying, self-sufficient, and viable, explicitly underscored in the lines "Who but we / Should heal each other, wounded, who but we." Yet there is considerable violence in the poems, and we are not always certain that, in the dialogue of love and hate, love will win out. Taggard deliberately makes this balance precarious, and there is a palpable undercurrent of fear in the images the speaker articulates. Furthermore, both poems end with the deaths of the lovers by violent means. The empty clattering of "Quarrel" continues the armour metaphor employed in stanza one, but also carries the suggestion of a metaphysical emptiness, the lovers as hollow men. The deaths of "Truce" are without these inorganic overtones but are only slightly more comforting, nonetheless. The violence of love at all phases of its dynamics is so much a presence that the specter of death never leaves, and only changes shape.

Taggard puts the danger of love in the forefront of the poems yet signals its containment within the bounds of monogamy. Moreover, within the controlling metaphor of chivalry, the lovers are equals in an ordered antagonism. In spite of the real and present danger of mutual destruction, Taggard charges this framework with the mediation and even ennobling of violent heterosexual dynamics. The threat to survival would seem to be a necessary part of love, as integral to the whole as sex itself. In repeatedly projecting forward to their mutual deaths, the poems implicitly assert the lovers' fates as inextricable, their bond to take them through till death parts them.

This pairing of the terms of stability and violence carries a certain irony, however, and assurances that monogamy works are principally to be found at the level of form. By contrast, the poems' narrative content depicts an excess of turbulence, the self-consciousness of which is evident in the suggestion that the lovers are given to melodrama: the addressee is a "boy"; they "fight" like children and, like children, work themselves into "frantic tears," representing their conflicts in the awkward and self-aggrandizing terms of "demons in the bible." It would be remiss to ignore the playful undertones of these images, but I would argue that they emanate from something other than a sense of security. Rather, they seem to signify Taggard's skepticism about the project these poems propose: the deliberate imposition of a stable structure on what is patently a volatile relationship. Nevertheless, the episode of "Quarrel"-"Truce" moves in circular fashion, originating and running its course toward resolution (however qualified) from within the lovers' intersubjective world. Permanent because self-contained, heterosexuality depends on a tautology. More specifically, the lovers' (k)nightly combat gives them an aura so allegorical and mythic as to suggest that they are all there is of the world. However much Taggard's lovers may live out their affair on the brink of self-destruction, the world and their relationship are so much mutually identified as to make male and female indivisible. There is no outside context from which to seek resolution or separation.

"Quarrel" and "Truce" lay down certain founding principles of heterosexuality in Taggard's universe—namely, that it is volatile, dubious,—and the very framework of existence. Recognizing its precariousness, she yet determinedly asserts it as "the only profound experience." With her subcultural identity, her ideality, and her artistry at stake, Taggard embarks on a crusade to defend what she sees as the truth about love against those who would obscure its force with aestheticizing rhetoric.

"Just Introduced" (1922) goes right to the heart of the problem of aestheticized love. The lovers' dynamics in this early poem may be seen as perfectly consistent with those of "Quarrel"-"Truce," with the difference that they are suppressed beneath a pointedly aesthetic surface, which the poem foregrounds as such. "Just Introduced" depicts a whirlwind modern romance, of a type carrying immediate cultural recognition. The first line ("Only a few hours!") carries a strong sense of speaking for itself, of saying much, and the following stanza fulfills our expectations with suggestive details built from the tropes of conventional romance:

We danced like wind,
Our faces like noon flowers
On one slim stem were lifted, turned aside.
You flew, I followed, matched your stride,
And held your pause, and swung and parted wide. . . .[40]

The freedom of Free Love is represented here in the kinetic images of dancing, wind, flying, and swinging. But already, embedded within this first, ascending half of the drama, we see the traces of precariousness and imminent collapse. The flowers are "noon flowers," their very existence dependent on the delicate balance of an apex; their faces are "lifted"—and the lovers' relationship rests—"on one slim stem." But before we consign Taggard's flower trope to a purely conventional signification—that, say, love is ephemeral—we should consider the poem's second and final stanza.

Rather than illustrating a self-consuming passion, "Just Introduced" depicts an aesthetic moment which depends precisely on the suppression of sexuality. After beginning exactly like stanza one, stanza two takes an abrupt turn, which is all the more disruptive for our having been lulled by the initial repetition of lines.

Only a few hours!
We danced like wind,
Thirsty as blown flowers,
Heavy lidded, fearful eyed. [original italics]

Here we see the poem's opening images imploded: the choreographed physical control of dancing reduced to the sheer physical need of thirst, the carefree potential of wind fulfilled in the helplessness of being blown. The demure faces ("lifted, turned aside") now meet for the first time, and in the intimacy of eye contact, reveal (to each other as well as to us) the terror of their own mutual need. This fear arises from the conjunction of sexuality and power relations: through the progress of her narrative, Taggard implies that, while romantic love may be adequately depicted by aestheticized discourse, sexuality introduces an underlying field of power relations characterized by domination and even violence, dynamics over which the amorous subjects have little control. In light of these closing lines, what had earlier seemed delicately suggestive now emerges as euphemistic and false. As "Just Introduced" illustrates, Taggard's critique of aestheticization is effected through the deployment of what may be called a *poetics of repression*: through the use of suggestive details of form and imagery, Taggard creates the sense that just beneath the aesthetic surface of romance lies sexual violence and struggle. Images that, in the discourse of Free Love, are taken to encompass the full scope of heterosexual union are here revealed not as metaphoric of the whole but as precisely dependent on the repression of the "thirst," "heavy lids," and "fearful eyes" of sexuality.

"Just Introduced" typifies the suggestion in Taggard's work that lovers take up the forms of conventional romance in order to distance themselves from intimacy. "Elegy in Dialogue" (1926) renders this mechanism explicit in order to critically examine its motivations, with the paradoxical result that the tie between aesthetics and love—like Taggard's identification with bohemian ideality—is tighter than ever. Another of Taggard's postapocalytic poems, "Elegy" situates two lovers in a landscape of death and describes their "elegiac" activity in relation to it.

See . . . we find pathways
All overgrown,
Prod [a]n old spider,
Turn a damp stone,
Until in a loop a spider spun
We start at a silver skeleton.

This is death—this exquisite
Quiver of hollow coral. Try—
The delicate thing is all awry—
Put it in order, gently, knit
These dangling stems together tight;
Put on the flesh, put in the light,
Peer at the wee imagined face,
Pretend—you cannot—pretend you can
Start a little thud in the skeleton man.

So we shall struggle—you or I!

One of us will shortly die
And leave the other alone in the end
Stunned, too weary to pretend.
—Is this death? This delicate tangle,
Caprice of bones at an uneasy angle?

This is the trellis-frame beneath
The bruised and crumbling spray of death.

Death is a reckless lunge—a sprawl
Of naked limbs on a narrow wall.

So shall we struggle, you or I.
One of us will shortly die
And leave the other a callow mask
Or an idiot smile to remember by,
And a granite body to conjure and turn.

Against such massive unconcern
One will labor. The other lie
Tall and quiet. Tell me why. . . .[41]

What comes through on an initial reading of the poem is the lovers' struggle against death, a struggle rendered valiant for being isolated and, ultimately, doomed. The poem offers no other form of opposition to death than theirs. Death is paralleled with love in the progress of the poem, thus reinforcing and clarifying the duality of "elegy" and "dialogue." Twice in the poem, death is explicitly defined. The first time is delicate: "This is death—this exquisite / Quiver of hollow coral." Toward the end of the poem, it has become cruder, more violent: "Death is a reckless lunge—a sprawl / Of naked limbs on a narrow wall." Despite their contrast, both passages put sexual imagery at the center of their death imagery, with the implication that one is the obverse of the other. Hence, in addition to thematizing aestheticization as a conscious process (the construction of an elegy), the poem foregrounds the nature of the threat that prompts it: death, we are to understand, is a constant and oppressive specter for those "in dialogue." It is the dark underside of sexuality, and creativity defends against this awareness.

Yet the converse is also true: without the deathly landscape of intimacy, there would be no framework or reason for the production of art. Basic to this poem is the contrast between the ugly world the lovers find and the beautiful world they attempt to leave in its place. How does Taggard judge this surely more honorable attempt to turn reality into art?

One kind of judgment is implicit in the fact that she puts this instance of aesthetic activity in an implied context of revolutionary labor: after the extensive passage in stanza two, in which the lovers engage in the delicate reconstruction of the skeleton, we have a refrain which, in content and hortatory style, gives their activity decidedly ennobling overtones: "So we shall struggle—you or I!" By contrast, the diction that describes this work suggests that its practitioners are naively childlike and their product, toylike. Most obviously, the skeleton is tiny, though its reconstruction is serious business—but possibly only in the way that a child's exploration of an attic is serious. A sense of anticipation is palpable from the beginning of stanza one, as, with the pause following "See," the speaker guides our concentrated gaze through the promising debris until "We start" in delighted terror "at a silver skeleton." We may sense the reconstruction of the found object is a child's game from the stark semantic simplicity and imprecision of the verb "put," repeated to encompass qualitatively different tasks: "Put it in order," "Put on the flesh," "put in the light"—and in the latter case, the word seems an apt part of a childish demand for the impossible. The next active verb is also repeated: "Pretend—you cannot—pretend you can," and then again in the subsequent stanza, "too weary to pretend." In their mutual efforts to transform death, "pretending" is a central tool. The reason appears in the subsequent line, where what has remained at the level of undertone comes out as a fully realized ironic taunt: ''pretend you can / Start a little thud in the skeleton man.''

Ultimately, Taggard's view of aestheticization in this poem can be said to be cynically sympathetic. Here, ''aestheticization'' has its basis in physical interactions with a vividly particularized material world; by contrast, the absence of illusion leaves the world abstract and anonymous, one of ''massive unconcern.'' At the metaphoric level, ''massive unconcern'' offers no access to human hands; there is nothing to ''knit together'' or even to ''pretend'' over. Love, even as mutual delusion, offers the possibility of human work, providing the framework necessary for a perception of the world as concretely particular, accessible to human intervention, and hence ripe with possibility. When the delusion drops away, as when ''one of us . . . die[s],'' the world withdraws its luminous textured surface (gone the sense of a wonderful old attic) and becomes irredeemably separate. With the world an undifferentiated blank, all human choices amount to the same futility:

Against such massive unconcern
One will labor. The other lie
Tall and quiet. Tell me why. . . .

''Elegy in Dialogue'' typifies a central assertion of Taggard's bohemian poetry: that art—the art of lovers—is the generative human force which makes a ''silver skeleton'' of a ''granite body,'' however ''callow'' the belief that drives it.

Taggard holds fast to this conviction throughout her bohemian career. The next chapter, ''Aestheticized Love and Sexual Violence,'' explores what for Taggard are the most difficult internal pressures on the artist-lover couple as an ideal: the physical violence of men and the destructive sexuality of women.

THREE

Aestheticized Love and Sexual Violence

> The pioneer woman was a dynamo—and her man nearly always ran out on her. From the bitterness in such women many of us were born. Where was her mate? Did she destroy him? Did he hate her for her strength? Was he weaker because she was strong? Where is the equilibrium, anyway? I do not know, for sure, although I spend much time wondering.
>
> Taggard,
> "Poet out of Pioneer"

Female Sexuality

In her anonymous essay for the Nation, "Poet out of Pioneer," Taggard reflected at length on what she saw as the severe disparity in strength and power between her parents, quite explicitly treating their situation as paradigmatic of "the problem" of heterosexual relationships. Several of the other women invited to contribute to the *Nation's* 1926 series on "These Modern Women" gave similar attention to the dynamics between their parents and similarly seemed to assume that marriage was a site of conflict between a strong and thwarted woman and a man who fails to "*be* a man." Any number of contemporaneous influences might have fostered this common perception, for though they were all "modern" as professional and independent women, these essayists had widely varying backgrounds. But sexology certainly made its subtle, scientific contribution to the general climate. Havelock Ellis, for example, warned that a woman's "frequently repeated orgasms . . . render her vigorous and radiant [but] exert a depressing effect on her husband," whose pride and health she must learn to protect.[1]

For Taggard, such a pronouncement from popular science would only have echoed the cry from literary high (male) modernism, to whose culture she must, as a writer, have felt some special susceptibility. As Sandra M. Gilbert and Susan Gubar have shown (and as any moderately attentive reading of Lawrence or Eliot confirms), male modernist writings tended to depict female sexuality as dangerous and destructive to masculinity. Gilbert and Gubar suggest that anxiety over the feminization of culture in general and the artist in particular was constitutive of the dominant literary discourse of male modernism. Threatened by women's incursion into the literary profession (well established since the nineteenth century) and their more gen-

Photograph on preceding page: Scene from the farcical play *Hobohemia* (1919). (Museum of the City of New York)

eral assault on male social privilege and control (exemplified by suffrage), high culture came to be a kind of masculine preserve, and its conservation a defense of "virile" civilization itself. Gilbert and Gubar go beyond noting the thematization of this anxiety to suggest that female power may actually have been a "motive" for high male modernism, which created a "community of high culture" in which "only an initiated elite [could] participate."[2] The cultural dialogue over female and male power which Gilbert and Gubar identify as underwriting modernism was not, they argue, restricted to the aesthetic preoccupations of an international elite but had its roots in broad social trends in the Anglo-American world. The evidence of works produced by writers of the Village literary community suggests that practitioners of more traditional literary forms were also concerned with the "problem" of female power. Taggard's own response is consistent with the ambivalence Gilbert and Gubar attribute to many women writers of this generation, for whom male literary authority seemed suddenly "fragile," requiring "a reassuring female commitment to [its] reconstruction."[3] We might understand Taggard's peculiar editorial decision to devote an issue of Measure explicitly to "Men Poets" in this light, particularly given the editorial spin Taggard imposes with "If You Are a Man."

But as that essay demonstrates, the problem of emasculation registered less for Taggard as a failure of literary paternity than as a day-to-day struggle for artistic survival in the lives of her male contemporaries. Women had the responsibility for assisting this struggle, not only out of the obligation of what she took to be their greater strength but also because, at some level, they were the root of the problem. Their culpability lay partly in what Taggard assumed to be the truth of the modernist notion of a devouring female sexuality and partly in the threat posed by female power at the level of social relations between women and men. Within the matrix of such beliefs, Taggard's sense of psychosexual dynamics as inherently violent (explored in the previous chapter) comes to be conflated with the definition of specifically *female* sexuality. But by the same logic, disrupting the aestheticized surface of romantic love simultaneously allows Taggard to give voice to a sexualized female subject.

Needless to say, the literary expression of female subjectivity takes up the more local problem of speaking as a woman from within masculinist bohemian subculture. In this endeavor, as in her treatment of heterosexual relations, Taggard trains her critical energy on aestheticizing discourse and the distortions it produces. But the clear opposition she is able to posit between aestheticized romance and a sexuality based in power and violence does not translate in this instance, for aestheticization is not so neatly extricable from female subjectivity. Certainly, femininity suffers the repressive effects of aestheticizing discourse to a profound degree, but Taggard's desire to break through its lies competes with her ambivalent sense of the "truth" about women: that they are in some way monstrous. We have seen that Taggard's own editorial voice is emphatically strong, determinedly unencumbered by the dilemma described here. But her poetry, the writings which struggled to concretely render bohemia(n utopia), are haunted by the fears she expresses about her "dynamo" pioneer mother: "Where was her mate? Did she destroy him? Did he hate her for her strength? Was he weaker because she was strong?"

Whatever mix of reverence and condescension allowed Taggard to keep the dynamo woman at arm's length, she could hardly have dealt so neatly as a woman writer with a subcultural discourse of objectified femininity. In a milieu in which masculinity and artistry were so closely identified, the pervasive notion of woman as art object served to entrench women's exclusion from creativity. And yet, as the subsequent discussion shows, Taggard did succeed in reconciling the identities of woman and artist—again, and paradoxically, through her very identification with the bohemian ethos.

"The Enamel Girl" (1922) takes up directly the conjunction of femininity and aestheticization (beginning with its title) to find them inherently incompatible. At the first level of signification, the poem's speaker tells a narrative of sexual awakening and loss within a conventionally feminine and delicate language.

Fearful of beauty, I always went
Timidly indifferent:

Dainty, hesitant, taking in
Just what was tiniest and thin;

Careful not to care
For burning beauty in blue air;

Wanting what my hand could touch-
That not too much;

Looking not to left nor right
On a honey-silent night;

Fond of arts and trinkets, if
Imperishable and stiff

They never played me false, nor fell
Into fine dust. They lasted well.

They lasted till you came, and then
When you went, sufficed again.

But for you, they had been quite
All I needed for my sight.

You faded. I never knew
How to unfold as flowers do,

Or how to nourish anything
To make it grow. I wound a wing

With one caress, with one kiss
Break most fragile ecstasies. . . .

Now terror touches me when I
Dream I am touching a butterfly.[4]

As in "Just Introduced," the sheer homogeneity of the poem's aesthetic surface implies its sufficiency to the task of describing the speaker's experience: she is a conventional feminine type, and her story is fully contained by a conventional feminine discourse. But there are significant pressures at work here. To begin with, the poem prepares us for oppositions it fails to sustain. The title, "The Enamel Girl," in the context of a work about "maidenly" sexual awakening, implicitly anticipates the lover who will shatter the "enamel" and transform the girl by poem's end. The girl describes her presexual self as "timidly indifferent: // Dainty, hesitant," her movements constrained, her emotions safe. Indeed, the lover enters on cue, at the midpoint of the narrative—but then abruptly departs. Our readerly expectations dictate that his entrance be metaphorically powerful, that it usher in an imagery that directly contrasts with what preceded it or, better yet, specifically undoes the brittle preciosity of enamel. What we get, however, is a deliberate *repression*: the lover and the love affair are buried in the lines of a single couplet, subsumed by the girl's discussion of "trinkets," which goes on unbroken despite the crisis in her narrative—"They lasted till you came, and then / When you went, sufficed again."

The break in this poem, the dynamic reversal churned up by the speaker's sexual experience, never penetrates to the level of language; the metaphoric surface of the poem remains homogeneous and unruffled. The delicately feminine "enamel" is succeeded by the equally poetic and feminine (for the two qualities converge at this point) flowers, bird, and butterfly. The language of the poem is hence consistent in its self-consciously aesthetic quality, even though the poem explicitly posits a contrast between delicacy and power. This undeviating linguistic register is also present in Taggard's treatment of the speaking female subject. We may see "I never knew / How to unfold as flowers do" as an expression of alienation from cultural ideals of femininity; likewise, "Or how to nourish anything / To make it grow." The import of these lines is striking in light of the fact that the speaker has until this point described herself and her experience in pointedly feminine terms. Both types evoked in the lines quoted are associated with "natural" femininity, whereas the "enamel" imagery is associated with a passionless, "overcivilized" femininity; probably this is the logic of their contrast. But within the assembled stereotypes, the girl's consignment to identification with "enamel" turns, ironically, on the actual power of her sexuality: incapable of channeling it into nonthreatening maternal ("nourishing") or aesthetic ("flower") forms, she finds safety and containment in its repression. "Enamel" is, of course, a *coating*, and an appropriately hard and opaque one.

The advent of physical force in such a story is no surprise, but the form it takes certainly is. We would expect the girl to be its object in a sexual initiation that is at least part violation. Not only culturally overdetermined, such a scenario has been telegraphed by the metaphor of enamel, which suggests an invitation to shattering force. But the end of the poem reveals a role reversal in which the girl inflicts wounds on the man. She turns out to have been justified in her extreme repression, for it is neither the world nor men that are dangerous, but rather, her own, now awakened sexuality. At the level of everyday social interaction, the girl is "enamel," hence predictably "timid" and "dainty," but her sexuality is contrastingly powerful, overwhelming, and destructive. And whereas the man is implicitly the contrast to all of her little "arts and trinkets," in the sexual context he is figured as a "butterfly."

The words "break" and "fragile" in the penultimate couplet ("I wound a wing/ / With one caress, with one kiss / Break most fragile ecstasies") harken back to the metaphor of "enamel," underscoring the fact that a gradual shift of properties has occurred. No longer is enamel associated with the girl but with "ecstasy" itself. As conceived within romantic Free Love, ecstasy is aesthetic and consequently fragile, like a figurine. The final couplet comes after the formal break of an elipsis, and its imagery concretizes the reversal that has been only subliminally suggested thus far: "Now terror touches me when I / Dream I am touching a butterfly." The repetition of "touch" physicalizes the speaker, and both the "terror" and "dream" states suggest her dangerous position outside the realm of conscious control. The imagery of this couplet metaphorically counterposes Taggard's conception of human sexuality to the "butterfly." Their incompatibility suggests that reconciliation of sexual and aestheticized love is impossible; more important, it implies a fundamentally disproportionate relation between female sexuality and its fragile male counterpart.

The speaker of "The Enamel Girl" tells of a personal discovery of sexuality and power, but in a language that admits of neither and, hence, necessarily distorts both. The problem of female sexual power appears again in "The Desert Remembers Her Reasons" from the same year, this time in a configuration which, in forgoing the critique of aestheticization, more directly foregrounds Taggard's ambivalence about female sexuality per se. The jump from figurine to desert suggests the metaphoric range of which Taggard necessarily availed herself in working to express a truthful and subculturally relevant feminine subjectivity.

Another dramatic monologue, "The Desert Remembers Her Reasons" begins in a tone of deliberate pathos with the desert/woman's lament at being forsaken in love and concludes with her commitment to what must be seen as justifiable vengeance.

How many rivers swerved aside
Rather than take a stony bride!
Rather than take a stony bride

Rivers and rivers swerved aside
And I grew desolate and died.

At my hot breath they checked their rush
And reared a wave, a head, and hush. . . .

Then fell and fled and would not come
To kiss the color of my loam.

The young bright rivers backed and fought—
And I lay thirsty and unsought.

They married valleys. If I caught
Water in my hand, it seeped. . . .
Rivers around—rain over me—leaped;
I was unwatered and unreaped.
Rather than take me for their bride
Rivers and rivers swerved aside
And I grew desolate, and died.

—(They shook their silver manes and curved
Aside. Aside they swept and swerved
Past my dull grandeur. River droves
Dared do no more than pound their hooves
And skirt my sombre purple. . . . White
Galloping cataracts took to flight.)

Why have I the lustre of stone?
Color of scorn, and scorn's tone
Brood over me. I move beneath
Pale dust with an edged breath.

Sliding under cover of sand
I throttle young rivers with a bold hand.[5]

The point of the poem, as the title makes clear, is that, indeed, the desert *has* her reasons, and she narrates them by way of justifying herself to a cultural audience who would otherwise take her destructiveness as merely given. The desert is figured as a woman,[6] and the speaker does not argue against the literary/cultural paradigm she embodies, that of a destructive female principle; nor, at the psychological level, do her "reasons" counter the stereotype of the "man-hater" as sexually frustrated, a passed-over "old maid." In this sense, it must be said that Taggard appears to accept the popular, medicalized understanding of female anger and aggression.

But within this conventional construction there is significant protest. Taggard endows the female figure in this poem with the authority and dignity of a primordial, even mythic, history. Rather than render a personal story of twisted and stunted female sexual development, Taggard takes up the transhistorical metaphor of the desert and provides her with a creation myth appropriate to her size and "grandeur." The character of the desert/

woman is the product of her heterosexual experience, but the metaphoric content of the figure as desert gives her an irreducible core of something larger than and prior to heterosexual society.

The encounter between male and female in this poem must be seen in light of the historical overtones it carries. The "men" the desert speaks of are, like the speaker herself, represented by a natural vehicle, in their case, water. But while the desert's actions are consistent with her singular identity, those of the rivers only multiply their metaphoric identifications: they no sooner have appeared as rivers than they take on the character of horses, while, of course, all along they are "really" men (stanzas 1–3, and 5). This particular fusion of images produces the strong suggestion of chivalric knighthood, and it is on these terms that the male side of the poem's gender equation finally encounters the woman/desert. At the level of metaphor, then, the failure of this meeting lies in a simple incompatibility of terms: the desert, an elemental principle of primordial nature, and chivalry, a social structure of ritualized and arbitrary, merely human interactions. Not coincidentally, chivalry represents an extremely rigid social construction of gender relations within which female sexuality—the "hot breath" of the desert—is inadmissible. Indeed, chivalry and the civilization it stands for must actively beat back the desert or be reclaimed to its leveling power. The poem specifically distinguishes between "presocial" desire and socially sanctioned gender relations in the lines, "And I lay thirsty and unsought. // They married valleys"—the pure physical need of "thirst" contrasting with the merely ritual act of "marrying," presented here with no stated relation to desire.

And yet, quite apart from the desert's necessarily distorted and misunderstood identity within chivalry, she is undeniably and inherently destructive to the "young rivers." By the last stanzas, she has even taken on murderous and calculating intent, moving "with an edged breath" to "throttle young rivers with a bold hand." Though by this point we understand her "reasons," it must be admitted that, for the rivers, this hatred is indistinguishable in its effects from desert love: "If I caught / Water in my hand, it seeped. . . ." However variable the desert's self-understanding, her destructiveness to rivers/men is an irremediable fact from the first. Furthermore, the destruction she finally wreaks is clearly linked to the earlier "hot breath [which] checked [the horses'] rush"; it originates with her desire. At the level of concrete imagery, the poem conveys the sense that, out of proportion to the capacities of civilization and men to accommodate it, female sexuality must be banished from the social world.

Taggard constructs this subjectivity for female anger without directly undermining any conventional assumptions about femininity; to that extent, she works within conventional modernist wisdom. But in deploying the harsh primordial mother (an equally conventional female stereotype) Taggard refuses modernism's masculinist trivializations. Like the speaker of "Galatea Again" (1926), the poem I examine next, the desert is a transhistorical presence that ultimately overwhelms her antagonists, the small, multiple, historical men. Furthermore, her assertion of power occurs in direct response to men and through the forms they impose on her. The speaker of "Galatea Again" is particularly resourceful in this way: she turns the fact that she is made the site of multiple objectifications into a powerful indeterminacy. In the process of defining herself, she moves through a series of feminine roles, ending with Medusa, whose deadly gaze she deploys against her implied male audience.

The speaker of "Galatea Again" expresses her wish to be turned back into the statue she once was, that belonging to Pygmalion, the mythic king who created his own ideal of womanhood out of ivory. The original myth depicts Galatea as a perfect beauty and a paragon of virtue; by contrast, the temporarily human speaker of the poem is marked with the signs of her humanness: "wild frantic eyes," a "bruised mouth," and the experience of whatever emotionally charged episode (typically repressed by the text) produced them.

Let me be marble, marble once again:
Go from me slowly, like an ebbing pain,
Great mortal feuds of moving flesh and blood:
This mouth so bruised, serene again,—and set
In its old passive changelessness, the rude
Wild crying face, the frantic eyes—forget
The little human shuddering interlude.

And if you follow and confront me there,
O Sons of Men, though you cry out and groan
And plead with me to take you for my own
And clutch my dress as a child, I shall not care,
But only turn on you a marble stare
And stun you with the quiet gaze of stone.[7]

The rhythmic "ebbing" of stanza one creates a sense of human yearning which combines with the poem's tropes of idealized womanhood in such a way as to present us with—not a personalized view of a mythic figure, as the title might suggest, but rather—the mythic, objectifying context in which an individual human female must define herself. As the poem progresses and the speaker, judging from shifts in rhythm and tone, is gradually getting her wish to be "marble once again," the rhetorical situation of the poem moves from the intimacy of a woman addressing her lover to a transhistorical female principle addressing the generations of patriarchal society with the fully apostrophic "O Sons of Men." Through the allusory language of the last two stanzas, she effectively takes on the personae of mother and Medusa, in addition to Galatea. By the final couplet, she has so accepted the terms of her objectification that she has made the Medusa's power her own and threatens to turn this and the other feminine ideals invoked by the poem back on the male culture that imposes them.

The poem begins from a situation of victimization, which, through purely rhetorical means, becomes one of domination. In the course of her self-articulation, the woman of "Galatea" utilizes the instability of the relations between victim and oppressor which the situation offers in order to orchestrate her own objectification. The vehicle for this transformation is a configuration of highly invested stereotypes projected onto women by patriarchal culture but here actually turned back on the male audience by a female object who is ultimately powerful and, as the rejecting mother of stanza two, even cruel. As an instance of Taggard's closely tended female power, "Galatea" is a poem barely in control: the woman who wills herself into the status of object also apparently cannot resist the dark irony of indulging the power latent there—just enough to let the "Sons of Men" know from what, and to what extent, she routinely protects them.

In taking the self-willed transformation of a woman into a marble statue as her dominant metaphor, Taggard suggests the possibility of empowerment from within objectification. But what of Taggard's own claim to the status of a *producer* of art? Her notion of heterosexual relationship resolves itself into the dichotomous figuration of female object and male artist often enough to cast serious doubt on bohemian claims to both gender equality and female access to artistry. And yet, typically, the solution she forges draws her closer into bohemian identification: faced with gender-based exclusion, Taggard circles back to the unified heterosexual couple and the quintessentially bohemian fusion of love and art—but all on significantly transformed terms.

Male Violence

> my broken-edge love . . . beautiful and frail . . . the realest most exquisite thing that ever happened to me.
>
> Genevieve Taggard,
> letter to Josephine Herbst (1921)

Taggard's most immediate concern with male violence may have been directly personal. In their frequent—and frequently cryptic—references to the difficulty of her marriage, her letters carry the suggestion that Robert Wolf might have been physically abusive toward her during their years together.[8] Were this the case, it would have posed a serious challenge to the bohemian idyll. Then again, there is a sense in which male violence is perfectly assimilable to the terms of aestheticized romance and is even suggested by them. To the extent that the couple's artistic agon was weighted toward the male lover, it would have been underscored and even exalted by his eruption into violence. And though her victimization threatened her claim to gender equality, the female artist had both culpability and strength enough that male violence against her would have fulfilled a kind of perverse bohemian justice, allowing her to share equally in his privileged pain. However much Taggard's poetic treatment of male violence avails itself of this logic of containment, it comes perilously close at times to sacrificing the ideal loving dyad to sexual domination.

Like destructive female sexuality, male violence (or its threatened possibility) often gets expressed in Taggard's work through the articulation of a female subject in whose construction it has a constitutive role. "Man in the Wind" (1926) presents a smooth surface of ethereal romance, beneath which runs a current of violence manifesting itself in the female speaker's very cognition of her world. The poem is a portrait of a woman whose perceptions are largely hallucinatory—or so it is implied. Certainly, the title strongly suggests as much: a man in the wind would seem to be no man at all, but rather a psychological projection or a fantasy. Beneath the lightly musical meditation that comprises the substance of the poem is a glimpse of the woman's ongoing attempt to order the random signals of her world around the idea of this man:

When you come you come so lightly,
I can never know you rightly;
Vines it might be from the eaves;
You have fingers like the leaves;
You can veer upon my door
Batter there, be off, before
I can even turn the lock.
It is hard to tell your knock
From the elements I love
From the tap, the knuckle of
Autumn gale or winter storm;
Always when you come, your form
Speeds upon the spinning air
And I stand and stare.[9]

This passage establishes a spatial division between the woman's presumably calm domestic interior and an exterior world in constant flux, then focuses on the woman's tentative encounters at the boundary between them. In the midst of consistently kinetic imagery, one line stands out as incongruously still and reflective: "You have fingers like the leaves." It is furthermore remarkable as the poem's single suggestion of physical contact between the speaker and the man. Thus concentrated into a single phrase, the character of their imagined interactions appears analogous to that between the house and the elements: the woman a still, passive object subject to random advances from the man. Moreover, her reception of him is ambiguous; the sensation of leaves on skin, while not directly unpleasant, is more on the order of nervous irritation than sensuality—as much as anything, because it has no larger goal, erotic or otherwise. She thus appears to be a woman who is simultaneously desirous enough of a man to conjure him up persistently in her imagination and fearful enough of him to dread his touch.

We must wonder, then, whether she is "turning the lock" to open or secure the door.

The speaker emerges as a specifically female neurotic—afraid of the intrusion of the world on her domestic space and/or afraid of the intrusion of a man on her body. The sense of this portrait as drawn within a psychologistic framework is reinforced by the compulsive quality of the poem's opening and closing couplets: "In the end I'll open, find / Nothing knocking but the wind," and "So tonight I open, find / Nothing knocking but the wind." At the formal level, they serve to frame and contain the experience described within the long stanza, the dangerous commerce with the outside world. And in anticipating a safe outcome to the experience before it begins, the first couplet provides the speaker a sense of security against danger—or disappointment. All this is consistent with the contemporaneous preoccupation with female neurosis and sexual repression. But close examination of the woman's "hallucinations" reveals an important difference from the sexologist's paradigm.

The woman's fears are not produced from her own innate proclivities but arise in response to an objectively based threat. The man in the wind, as it turns out, may not be an imaginary romantic ideal, neurotically feared by the speaker for the sexual potential he represents. In fact, there are strong suggestions that he is not only real but also dangerous and violent. The central stanza contains key evidence of such violence, most strikingly the words "batter," "hard," "knock," and "knuckle." Furthermore, the sense of instability and vertigo, which at first appears to emanate from the speaker, may, in fact, originate with the man, for he not only comes "lightly" but also "veers," and his "form / Speeds upon the spinning air." Taggard undermines the association of the man with the lightness of wind by transforming the vine-rustling breeze to a full-blown "gale":

It is hard to tell your knock
From the elements I love
From the tap, the knuckle of
Autumn gale or winter storm;

In thus semantically realizing the violent potential of the wind, Taggard suggests the same possibility for the man. We witness this development and the seamless ease with which it may occur in the slide from "tap" to "knuckle": "From the tap, the knuckle of."

"Man in the Wind" implicitly asserts the fact of male violence through the vehicle of a culturally familiar female stereotype, whose basic form, to all appearances, it maintains. Yet, despite her disdainful invocation of the psychologically "delicate" woman in certain of her writings, Taggard here challenges the assumptions that underlie the stereotype. The ontogenesis of her sexually repressed woman departs from the purely intrapsychic model and moves into conditions of intersubjective domination. Furthermore, this fairly complex depiction of a female subjectivity shaped by male violence is contained within a language and thematics that are consistently "light" and lyrical. As such, "Man in the Wind" illustrates the way in which the ideology of romance confounds women's perceptions and self-understanding by its aestheticized construction of heterosexual love.

While the aesthetic quality of the poem serves a strategic function in veiling the inadmissible truth of overt male violence, it would be wrong to overestimate Taggard's critical distance from the assumptions of her own cultural context. Of all her works, treatments of female subjectivity are by far the most openly ambivalent and unresolvable in terms of "modern" equality and stability in heterosexual relationship. Several points bear repeating here: first, alongside the implicit critique of a culture which denies female sexuality and power, there is in Taggard an equal, if not stronger, tendency to fall back into the widely prevalent notion of female sexuality as inherently pathological. Second, simply at the level of relative emphasis, male violence has not nearly the prominence of destructive female sexuality in the poems and furthermore tends to be subsumed to sexual violence per se. Just as often, the suggestion of male violence is deflected by an ostensibly larger object of critique, such as bourgeois materialism. So while violence in men reflects their societal victimization, destructiveness in women has the status of a biological essence. Third, the use of conventional paradigms of love and gender identity as the framework for their very critique suggests the belief—or hope—that these are not incompatible projects, that change can and should be contained within traditional gender relations.

"Beach Cabin" (1922) enacts this vision by placing an assertive female voice squarely within two dominant discourses of heterosexuality: romantic love and psychoanalysis. Brief and imagistic in structure, the poem holds out to its audience a "moment" self-consciously overcharged with meaning.

I dreamed you were the sea;
I dreamed you pounded
With foamy fists, the sad face of the shore.
Waking, I lay beneath you,
And the room resounded
With the hoarse fury of the mounting ocean's roar.[10]

The poem draws on the tradition of dream-truth, legitimated by psychoanalysis in the 1910s. Thus overdetermined, the speaker's statement that "I dreamed you were the sea" carries automatic authority: the dreamer has a privileged access to truth which commands our attention. Hence, we accept her intuition that, at some level, her lover *is* the sea. In this light, the subsequent lines take on the quality of an accusation: "I dreamed you pounded / With foamy fists, the sad face of the shore./Waking, I lay beneath you." Having so nearly spelled out the literal case, the speaker then reasserts the metaphor: "And the room resounded / With the hoarse fury of the mounting Ocean's roar." Ambiguous is whether she has thereby brought the dream out into waking reality—or only retreated into euphemism.

Whether toward reconciliation or repression, however, the romantic underpinnings of the poem demand the metaphoric outcome. The violent truth of the dream contrasts with the poem's imagery, which is aesthetic and romantic. The speaker communicates with her lover through this surface because it represents the terms of their self-understanding as a couple. They are at a beach cabin, a lovers' idyll. We know this is significant because the poem's title has no direct link with the poem itself except as a stark description of setting; it is somehow important that this utterance be framed by a scenario of ideal romance. Having started with the beach cabin, the speaker quite naturally conjures images of "dream[s]," "sea," "shore," "foam," and sleeping lovers. In the context of the poem, such romantic tropes are the fabric of reality, and when violence breaks in through the dreaming "unconscious" of the speaker, it is contained within this aestheticizing discourse. By channeling an ugly truth about power and domination through her dream, the speaker can express her intuitive sense of the underlying dynamics of her lover's otherwise presumably loverlike behavior without risking the dissolution of the world they have constructed. Indeed, the closing lines of the poem demonstrate the incorporative capacity of romantic discourse, the figure of the sea encompassing the feared—or possibly, manifest—escalation of violence.

In the picture of the relationship that emerges, the man's implied violence is repressed not by the woman's specific utterance but by the broader framework of the lovers' self-understanding as romantic couple. But in contrast to the female personae who find themselves bewildered and their self-constructions distorted by the processes of aestheticizing discourse, the woman of "Beach Cabin" (not unlike Taggard herself) moves with instrumental purpose within her discursive confines. As a communication to the lover, the poem represents a deliberate search for intersubjective truth, truth that points beyond itself to protest—yet never endangers the structure of romantic love itself. Finally at stake in this negotiation is the universe of values within which Taggard locates her coherence as an artist.

"Unacknowledged Dedication" (1922) turns the lens on artistry explicitly. Though superfically much more direct than "Beach Cabin," the basic situation of intersubjective domination which "Unacknowledged Dedication" describes has been radically distanced in a mode consistent with Village bohemia's tendency to refer questions of gender relations back to art and the artist. The speaker identifies herself with the artworks of a paradigmatic "he," taking a posture of apparently total self-sacrifice and submission to his violent renunciation of them both. With an explicitness not seen elsewhere in the poems, she attributes to this artist figure specific acts of destruction.

These were his songs. Now he has broken them.
All he has made, that has he also slain:
Seeing my beauty budding, broke the stem;
Finding his likeness here, where he has lain,
Finding the flame of his hurt spirit here
In this small pool that motioned with his shade,

> Seeing himself, he smote me with his fear—
> He only lives to break what he has made.[11]

So begins the poem, and as is evident from this first stanza, male violence is its primary focus. Given the careful way Taggard treats and contains this subject elsewhere, such seeming explicitness comes as a surprise. But, in fact, explicitness is limited to the naming of destructive acts; the identities of perpetrator and victim shift and remain vague throughout. Attention to the shape of this evasiveness suggests that, in this instance, Taggard has constructed male violence as a function of artistic temperament, specifically, an enigmatic hostility of the artist toward his own created beauty. Taggard thus removes conflict from the realm of sexual politics, taking it up as a problem of artistic process.

In the recoding of male and female to creator and beautiful object, Taggard's female speaker revisits the persona of Galatea, forthrightly identifying herself as a male creation.

> Now it is time to go, softly away;
> We will grow fragile songs, soon we will fade.
> He has no place for us, we cannot stay—
> He cannot bear the beauty he has made.

Such dramatic self-denial, including relinquishing artistic agency, occurs in the interest of a more immediate priority within this work: the sublimation of concrete gender oppression into an abstract aesthetic struggle.

Yet there are discernible breaks in this construction; neither the self-effacement of the speaker nor the power of the male artist is seamless. In the second half of the poem, the speaker claims the "songs" as her own works: "Where will we go, my songs, under the sun?" and again "Where will we go, my songs?" So determined and quiet an assertion of her own authorial credit is a characteristic instance of "safe" protest, as are the moments of slippage in the gender dichotomy established in the first lines. The male figure as male is introduced simultaneously with his violence ("Now he has broken them"); the female speaker first appears as an aesthetic object ("Seeing my beauty, broke the stem"). Thus dichotomized, their respective roles are implied to be a function of gender. Yet, in stanza four, the male artist loses his status as the sole force of violence: "The sea is like him, careless of all things, / Beating her own, and mourning that they die." Figuring the sea as female is conventional enough, but within the context established by the first three stanzas of the poem, any female appropriation of violence is significant. In fact, in this world of forces hostile to beauty, the sea threatens to dwarf the mere man. The strength of the sea as a figure comes largely from its associations as the primal mother, and these have a concrete basis for resonance in the poem. Stanza two begins, "All, all he fathered," referring to the relationship between the male artist and his works. In subsequently introducing the sea, Taggard suggests a patently unequal competitive tension between paternal and maternal forces (we have seen this pitting of male/human against female/primordial in "The Desert Remembers Her Reasons"). Yet the contest is contained at the level of metaphor, hence the defeat of the male is permitted to go unacknowledged and his ostensible reign of terror, technically undisturbed.

The poem's final subversion occurs in the concluding lines. The speaker leaves off bewailing her fate and that of the songs and grants to "him" the consequences of his destruction, depicting the scenario that lies beyond the "breaking" and denial of his works.

Let them follow him.
When all the sky is darkened at the rim
And he and we have stumbled in its shade,
No one will know the beauty he has made.

In speaking of "he and we," in throwing his lot together with her own in the mutual stumbling, the speaker definitively equates their two positions as artist and artwork. By the same mechanism, she reveals the limits of his power. As happens so often in Taggard's work, the appearance of a formidable third element levels the relative positions within a given sexual dyad. This typical deflection of an internal conflict outward to the repressiveness of an authoritarian society, is here also deployed as a weapon by one of the pair against the other. Having portrayed herself as devastated by the man's power, the speaker brings him down to her level in the final lines simply by turning his own actions against him: the male artist and the female creation become equals in the face of historical obscurity, which finally is what the "shade" of the "darkened" sky represents.

Taggard's strategic use of a third party in mitigating gender conflict finds its fullest development in her depictions of heterosexual conflict as the product of bourgeois society's utilitarianist hostility to love (like its hostility to art). The basic narrative framework for these poems is a pair of lovers figured as inhabiting alien and hostile environs. This relation is starkly and succinctly put forth in "Two Captives" (1926), beginning, of course, with the title.

I cannot keep the pompous years
From their poor task of taking you
Down the next alley-way of spears—
A gauntlet to be hurried through;

But now I watch them with a frown
Impassive as I try to be
And break a twig and throw it down
And look for them to come for me.[12]

Within Taggard's bohemian vision, coming of age for men means compulsory conformity to societal norms (specifically, bourgeois materialism), represented here in concentrated form by the imagery of medieval chivalric ceremony. Whatever the resistance of an individual man, the struggle would seem to be a losing one, hence the sense of inevitability about the male addressee's submission to the "gauntlet." The female speaker, by contrast, though herself without any great hope of escape, has at least kept her freedom thus far and shows signs of agency: in the knightly challenge of "break[ing] a twig and throw[ing] it down," she confronts her would-be oppressors on their own terms, as a dignified, if not equal, contender. Again, this is consistent with Taggard's notion of women as relatively free of cultural constraints and (partly as a result) as stronger individuals. As it appears in the poem, this gender differential implies that the antagonism of society toward lovers determines roles and relations within heterosexuality itself. The "two" of the poem are distinguished only by their different relations to the authority that persecutes them. Moreover, they are physically separated by the same means, with the implication that, again, it is only external pressure that prevents their otherwise unproblematic solidarity, and even sameness.

"Epithalamium" (1922) specifically takes up the "entry" of the heterosexual couple into society in order to reveal the consequences that follow. The traditional epithalamium is a lyric ode to a bride and bridegroom, hence we may be justified in reading Taggard's poem as addressing the meaning of institutionalized male-female union. In this work, Taggard develops more fully the paradigm of heterosexual relationship suggested by "Two Captives": the ostensibly autonomous unit of two lovers actually shaped by its relation to a powerful and antagonistic third party.

Within the triangulated sexual drama of "Epithalamium," the female lover is marginalized to a striking degree. She is a "little doe," an uncharacteristic figure of female as prey. Complex power relations structure the poem's narrative content, but "Epithalamium" reads first as a celebration of male sexuality.

Out of the forest, panther, come,
Silken, supple, silent, lone—
Out of the forest, drooped with night—
To your delight.
Under bloom and over stone,
Out of the forest, panther, come.

Something sees and slips with you,
Something huge and gaunt and blue,
Lashes its tail and follows you:
You, pursued, still pursue. . . .

Sky with thunder on its rim
Closes and closes after you:
Trigger loin, swinging limb,
Go and go and go from him!
Brushing haunches, taut with dew,
Follow, follow, follow you.

Now the doe with lifted ears
Rears in the bramble, looks and hears.
Sway a little, creeper, creeper;
After you comes, more gaunt than you
And lean for prey, and quick, the leaper,
—And the little doe will sleep with the sleeper.

Out of the forest, panther, come,
Silken, supple, silent, lone,
Out of the forest, drooped with night,
To your delight:
Under bloom, and over stone,
Out of the forest, panther, come.[13]

Beyond directing and encouraging the "bridegroom" in his pursuit of "delight," the speaker is clearly caught up in the struggle between panther and storm. In fact, the immediate occasion of the poem—its specific character as an utterance appropriate to a wedding—is in its warning to the panther-bridegroom of the danger he faces from the "[s]omething huge and gaunt and blue" which pursues him and whose movements the speaker monitors from her position of omniscience. The panther is beckoned repeatedly to come forward, yet his leaving the protective covering of the forest for the "clearing" of sexuality is what has brought on the attentions of the stalking "something" and begun the chain of pursuit in the first place. It would seem that sexuality is inevitably attended—even structured—by phallic rivalry, a rivalry in which, moreover, the mere man (or panther) is fated to lose. The possibility that sex may consequently not be worth the struggle is definitively precluded by the celebratory quality of the poem. But "Epithalamium" holds the valorization of male sexuality in close tension with an underlying critique of its societal determinants and its consequences for women.

Judging from this poem, we may say that Taggard defines male subjectivity as the point where individual desire intersects with societal imperatives—where panther meets storm. The imagery of the poem focuses on masculine beauty: the panther enters as a highly charged and arresting figure, its power augmented by details of positive male sexuality. The use of chanting rhythms and repetitions focuses the poem as a whole around the panther's movements, and in the moment of its encounter with the storm, these rhythms are intensified. We come inexorably to see the male subject's conflict with patriarchal authority as perfectly compatible with his given nature; however uncertain its outcome, the panther is ideally suited to this necessary battle.

Such a masculine rite of passage contrasts sharply with what we have seen of Taggard's "enamel girl," whose sexuality threatens to shatter completely the fragile reality she inhabits. The only possible resolution of the girl's encounter with society (as aestheticization) is the repression of her basic nature. In its determining force as a metaphor of sexuality, the panther may also be compared to the female desert of "The Desert Remembers Her Reasons." Both are defined by their power, but each has a qualitatively different role within its respective metaphorical context: although the desert can only destroy her surroundings, the panther is completely integrated with his. The deliberateness of this depiction is underscored in the fact that the slaughter of the doe—the explicit telos of the hunt—is suppressed or, at best, only suggested. At the climactic moment of attack, the narrative breaks off:

After you comes, more gaunt than you
And lean for prey, and quick, the leaper,
—And the little doe will sleep with the sleeper.

The particular euphemism of this last line suggests both death and sex. Phallic rivalry may be ultimately fatal to the doe/woman, but it is not wholly divorced from pleasure; most important, however, the doe—in her desire or in her demise—is marginalized in the interest of a positive depiction of the panther.

Where Taggard's women are typically prominent and actively desiring beings—and in some cases not even directly distinguished by gender from their lovers—the "little doe" is mere passive "prey," unworthy of descriptive detail. But, the female presence in "Epithalamium" is not encompassed by the doe; womanly agency and power find their way into the poem in the voice of the speaker. From her position of omniscience, she is simultaneously celebratory of the "natural" man and solicitous of his welfare, a posture we recognize as Taggard's own stated position on male struggle and female responsibility.

Taken as a whole, "Epithalamium" is finally a tribute to the masculine agon anchoring Taggard's bohemian vision. Yet the imperative to secure women's place in that vision dictates that emphasis fall more commonly on the heterosexual couple as a unified force against a greater outside evil, not only for the sake of its own survival but also for the cause of good—that is, the production of art. "Black Laughter," written at the height of Taggard's bohemian commitment, goes furthest of any of her works in particularizing the oppositional world bearing down on the artist-lover couple. Like "Elegy in Dialogue," "Black Laughter" is one of the cluster of apocalytic poems, and it participates in the basic scenario of two lovers defending themselves against an evil world through art.

Harsh, unuttered thunder
Stood like a stone wall
Above the marsh's silver line.
Crooked cranes, white as lightning—
Flattened for an instant, flashing from the cloud—
Came driving toward us; toward us fell
The long lines of the shade-laden trees,
Soundless slanting thunder:

And the snail-like hills
Dragged nearer
The marsh's slime.

Borne down so
By sullen immensities,
Two caught children we stood,
Waiting the flash, the oblique arm of the parent,
Waiting for speech from the jowl
Of the irritated horizon. . . .

Our love began
Between flash and crash,—
Terror seen and terror heard.
See what a cripple our love is!
It is sullen; sometimes it makes walls of black laughter;

It is fond of words, fond of thick vowels,
It mimics thunder.
Between us it limps:
We wait for it, when we must, faces averted.[14]

The poem builds itself up out of spatially defined relationships: stanza one depicts the external environment of the lovers; stanza two places them within it; stanzas three and four describe what arises, literally, between them. This larger framework is underscored in the metaphors of stanza one, for the landscape of "Black Laughter" appears in consistently geometrical images: thunder is "like a stone wall"; the marsh is a "silver line"; the cranes are "crooked" and "[f]lattened"; the parent's arm is "oblique"; there are "long lines of . . . trees" and "slanting thunder." The picture that emerges is one of randomly intersecting lines, with the lovers literally caught in the cross-fire.

The combined violence and linearity of these images suggests a war zone, the "thunder" and "lightning," the noise and flashes of artillery. In this work, Taggard gestures toward a distinctly historical context for the drama of lovers in a hostile world. Herein lies a crucial difference between "Black Laughter" and "Elegy in Dialogue": while the apparition of death plaguing the protagonists of "Elegy" is a function of their own sexuality, the violent landscape of "Laughter" has a definitively prior existence to the love relationship. In the progress of the poem's spatial hierarchy, the causal relation is unmistakable: the ills plaguing heterosexual lovers—here figured as literal deformity—originate in the world around them.

Taggard puts a definite face on the lovers' antagonist by casting the tensions between them and the natural landscape in terms of patriarchal relations and, specifically, patriarchal retribution. The storm advancing on the couple in stanza one evolves in stanza two into a threatening parent, while the lovers come into focus as his children. The subsequent "love" that "beg[ins] / Between flash and crash" is precisely a reaction to this angry father. In imitative identification with its parent, it is "sullen," it "makes walls of black laughter," it "mimics thunder." Like the landscape, this love has been assigned its own objective existence from its first appearance in the poem. Indeed, the final lines suggest that its identity outside the metaphorical context of the poem is art itself, specifically, literature: "It is fond of words, fond of thick vowels, / It mimics thunder." Art, for Taggard, is the concrete embodiment of love, is what lovers produce. The specifically "aestheticizing" art generated by the lovers of "Elegy" was seen to be ultimately inadequate to staving off death; in "Black Laughter," the creation of a space insulated from the war-torn world never even arises as a possibility. If the tradition of art since the Renaissance is to fix beautiful moments against the force of death, the modernist art that "makes walls of black laughter" is too ironically conscious of its own impotence to have any such illusions.

"Black Laughter" is perhaps the most concerted of Taggard's efforts to theorize the problems of heterosexuality in terms of external causes. The poem puts the categories of love, art, and oppositional context in their sharpest terms: the third party, elsewhere rendered abstractly as death or society, becomes the historical context of World War I; the lovers are members of the postwar generation, caught in a world not of their making; and their art, a bitter and ironic retreat into form.

Having articulated this vision, we must recognize it as one of classic Lost Generation futility. But Taggard had little use for what she saw as the lugubrious and aestheticist branch of modernism and, beginning in 1928, even expressed this contempt in a series of often scathing poetic portraits.[15] How can we explain the unholy convergence of her supreme center of value with the object of her deepest scorn? The answer comes back to what we have seen of Taggard's self-defined role in bohemian subculture: guardian of its ideals and necessary critic of its reality. "Black Laughter" is a moment of unsparing criticism that turns the klieg light on bohemian heterosexual failure (her own included) to force a damning admission of self-indulgence from its lover-artists. These moderns, Taggard implies, have been flirting with the pose of tragic children in a world for which they take no responsibility—and on which they blame their own failure to meet the demands of the great struggles of heterosexuality and artistic production. It is illuminating at this point to return to Taggard's autobiographical "Poet out of Pioneer," which concludes with an implicit reprimand to her generation, quoted from *Spoon River Anthology*.

What is this I hear of sorrow and weariness,
Anger, discontent, and drooping hopes?
Degenerate sons and daughters,
Life is too strong for you—
It takes life to love Life.[16]

Taggard's preoccupation with love and sexual struggle was grounded in her own attainment of subcultural and artistic identity as a woman. As we noted throughout this discussion, the lovers who form the subject of Taggard's works of the twenties are implicitly artist-lovers, and what the poems examine is not heterosexuality per se but specifically bohemian romance. This distinction is crucial for Taggard because it keeps love within the general framework of oppositionality, the core of artist identity in Village culture. Rebellion against bourgeois society had its roots in the romantic and American literary traditions and was, consequently, integral to a long-standing paradigm of artist identity. The rebellion—and artistic identity itself—proceeds from the notion that industrial society is the betrayer of cultural values and dehumanizing of the individual in its single-minded emphasis on "productivity," as against, in particular, "nonproductive" artistic pursuit. But artist-rebels must initially perceive themselves as the implied subject of the culture they reject, beginning from a sense of cultural *identification* to incur a sense of *betrayal* and of themselves as the object of social expectations in order to experience them as a burden, to be accepted or overcome. Given these parameters, the full experience of artistry as a vocational identity that carried a recognizable social status and content was one reserved for men. As interlopers in the public sphere of cultural value, women were neither as invested in the status quo nor as directly pressured to perpetuate it as were men, hence, their oppositionality could not have the same defined cast. The woman's experience of artist identity on this model must always have been, to a certain extent, vicarious. It may be that it was only to the degree that they were allied with the men of Village bohemia that the many women of the subculture could see themselves as artists, with the full social valence that term carried. Under these circumstances, Taggard's commitment to an intersubjective relation whose problems she perceived as stemming from society's persecution of the male artist is inextricable from her own claims to artistry. Whatever the cost, she must embrace the heterosexual dyad so as to identify her interests—and her very victimization—with those of the male artist-lover.

But even by 1926, the ideological and personal strain of bohemian married life had forced Taggard to uncouple her artistic and heterosexual commitments. Quoting again from "Poet out of Pioneer," more fully this time,

> Marriage is the only profound human experience; all other human angles are its mere rehearsal. Like every one else I have wanted it. And yet having it, it is not all I want. It is more often, I think, a final experience than a way of life. But I am a poet—love and mutual living are not nearly enough. It is better to work hard than to be married hard. If, at the beginning of middle age, we have not learned some of the perils of the soul, in this double-selved life, we are pure fools. Self-sufficiency is a myth, of course, but after thirty, if one is a serious-minded egoist (i.e., artist) it becomes more and more necessary. And I think it can be approximated. (67)

The subcultural ethos which exerted so profound a force in Taggard's early professional life was not to be so simply and rationally dismissed, however. Let me close the discussion with a rather chilling excerpt from a 1934 poem testifying to the difficulty of that very separation. "Two in a Dark Tower: No Child Roland (In which two silent people think and know they think the same thoughts)" constitutes a painful parting shot at the Bohemian ideal.

> Leave this house at last, that was
> Just a fortress barred and fenced
> For our fear to fling against.
> . . . .
>
> There is no antagonist.
> No one comes. No ones cares
> If we wall ourselves with airs
> Built of terror. No one takes
> Notice how the tower shakes.
> Guilty we, divided by
> Each the other, see the four
> People pushing at the door.
>
> Keep the secrets separate.
> Either,—both of us will wait,
> While both take the other role,
> Bring assault on the mutual soul;
> Each assigned the part outside,
> And the role Antagonist.
> Taking turns, each, leaving one
> Always walled to tread and moan . . . [17]

FOUR

The Algonquin Round Table and the Politics of Sophistication

> The group had become more than a clique or coterie. It had begun to take shape as a public institution, one defined by the careers of its members and the cravings of a new public taste of which all of them, in various ways, were becoming premier retailers.
>
> James R. Gaines, *Wit's End: Days and Nights of the Algonquin Round Table*

In recent years, traditional notions of modernism and its meanings have given way under the challenges posed by once-unrecognized, nondominant literatures—those of women, African Americans, and immigrants. And yet the cultural register known as "middle-brow"—or, as I will call it, popular modernism—still goes missing from our accounts of early-twentieth-century literary history. The periodical forms of popular modernism—cartoons, newspaper columns, farcical sketches, short fiction, and the glossy magazines of urban life—comprised the most prominent arena in the 1920s for the negotiation of modern selfhood, a selfhood that came to be (and in many ways, still is) defined by irony, urbanity, and humor. More visibly than any other discursive project of the time, middle-brow culture made modern selfhood its explicit and relentless business. Meeting modernity head-on, it answered the crisis of value and dislocation with the heartbreakingly (and deceptively) simple panacea of style.[1]

As the epigraph from historian James R. Gaines suggests, the Algonquin Round Table occupied a central place in the production of popular modernism in the 1920s. Structured around personalities and the phenomenon of personality as such, the Round Table provides a relatively stark depiction of writing as a construction of self in a public context of desire. In its founding use of seemingly central and enduring categories like gender warfare and democratizing style, the Round Table also offers insights to identity formation in mass-mediated culture. The drama of modern selfhood that preoccupied the popular modernists positioned a woman writer like Dorothy Parker to play both protagonist and world: not just the modern subject she imagined herself to be, she must also stand in for modernity itself as the mass-cultural New Woman. Like Taggard and Millay, Parker faced her own subculturally specific contradictions in assembling a writerly praxis. But the particular significance of what we shall see of her literary-cultural struggles resides in the power and normativity attaching to middle-brow culture.

Photograph on preceding page: 5th Avenue and 42nd Street in the 1920s. (Archive Photos)

FROM THE START of her career, Dorothy Parker's celebrated criticism, fiction, and verse were shaped by the demands of New York's self-consciously sophisticated magazine journalism. Parker, a native New Yorker, had returned to Manhattan after getting what education she would from an exclusive New Jersey girls' school.[2] Sometime in 1914, she had settled into a boarding house to begin at the bottom as a serious writer, but the pressures of making a living quickly and permanently deflected her from her goal of becoming "the next Edith Sitwell." To supplement her income as a dancing school pianist, Parker wrote captions for the fashion pages of *Vogue*, moving on in 1915 to *Vanity Fair* as occasional drama critic, the first of a series of magazine jobs she was to hold more or less continuously throughout her career.[3] That career was still in its early stages when Parker found herself at the very epicenter of New York literary sophistication, a founding member of the Algonquin Round Table.

The world of popular literature and journalism in the teens and twenties was based in midtown Manhattan, a long thirty-five blocks from the Village. Unlike their bohemian counterparts, the midtown crowd were regularly paid to write; many of them were even paid well, a circumstance key to magazine writers' relation to themselves, their work, and their audiences. Within this larger professional class was the Round Table, a highly visible subset of assorted journalists, critics, columnists, playwrights, and press agents, as well as the occasional musician and actor.[4] The group's reputation stemmed from their daily sessions at the Algonquin Hotel on East Forty-fourth Street, where they ate lunch and generated witty banter for most of the 1920s. The Round Table lunch was a cultural institution with a regular audience: the crowd of eavesdropping tourists obligingly seated by the management at adjacent tables and the even larger crowd of newspaper readers who got the highlights of Algonquin goings-on in the daily gossip columns (often written by Round Tablers themselves).

The Round Table was unquestionably a masculine preserve. Its composition shifted and expanded over the twelve years of its existence, but throughout there was a central and basically unchanging core of members who did most of the talking, trading quips while the others sat in attendance: newspaper columnist Franklin Pierce Adams (known as F. P. A.); playwrights George Kaufman and Marc Connelly; drama critic Alexander Woollcott; columnist, critic, and sports writer Heywood Broun; film critic Robert Sherwood; parodist and playwright Donald Ogden Stuart; humorist, drama critic, and sometime comedian Robert Benchley; and Harold Ross, editor and founder of the *New Yorker*.[5] Within this elite, Parker was the only woman.[6] The Round Table had numerous women associates, most of them professional actors or journalists and some of them luminaries like novelist Edna Ferber and playwright and columnist Alice Duer Miller. But all of them were more or less peripheral to the action, often recognized only as wives or girlfriends of the male members. Indeed, when women first began appearing at the Round Table in numbers, some of the men objected to having them there at all.[7] The fact of a large contingent of (second-class) women in the outer circle may well have heightened Parker's felt imperative to conform to the inside: not only must she prove herself a real (male) Algonquinite but she must also demonstrate her palpable distance from the (female) hangers-on.[8]

The case of Ruth Hale, feminist, journalist, and wife to Heywood Broun, suggests something of Parker's isolation as a woman within the elite. At a certain moment in 1921, Hale lit up a cigarette in the lobby of the Algonquin—a modest enough claim to equality in the very temple of sophistication—only to be informed by manager Frank Case that no woman was permitted to smoke in his lobby. "Then this one leaves," she replied, but according to Gaines, "her years-long boycott of the hotel was seconded by no one."[9] Hale also founded the Lucy Stone League, an organization whose purpose was to defend women's right to keep their own names after marriage. In this venture, only two other Round Table women—actress Jane Grant and commercial painter Neysa McMein—joined her actively.[10] Parker in particular was conspicuously uninterested in claiming such a liberation for herself, asserting that she "got married to *change* her name," which had been Rothschild.[11] The deflection of the feminist-political issue into a joke—in this case, anti-Semitic and at her own expense—is characteristic for Parker. Such rhetorical evasiveness is just as fully on display in the following theater review from 1919:

> The moral [of the play] is, of course, that woman's place is in the home; would it had been taken to heart by the woman sitting in front of me, who was seized with a severe cough just as the curtain rose and who paused for neither rest nor refreshment all through the play.[12]

The deliberateness of the response suggests the extent of Parker's refusal of feminist or even gender identification. Called upon to make a public judgment on a blatantly masculinist ideal (one which she might at least have found personally insulting), she stubbornly refuses to render anything but a diversion, throwing up the Round Table wit as a bulwark against the uncomfortable demands of womanly protest.

And yet the evidence of Parker's poetry suggests that sophisticated wit gave her more than tactics of evasion. In a crowd of sardonic Algonquin wits, Parker was superlatively sardonic and witty. But Parker used the Round Table ethos and aesthetic to evolve a model of heterosexual love lyric that—whatever its constraints—liberated her into public self-definition at the same time that it ensured her national status as a supremely modern icon of New Womanhood. This chapter delineates the complicated Round Table ethos that surrounded and informed the space of Parker's poetry.

Geographically and metaphorically situated at the center of New York and the national magazine industry, on continuous public display, the Round Table was a product, a source, and an embodiment of popular American modernity. The first best evidence was their distinctively frenetic rhetorical pace: they were all humorists. Highly marketable in a culture of self-conscious sophistication, humor also had distinct rhetorical advantages for the imperatives of this subculture. Principally, it afforded them license for detachment: they could be clever without the implication of intellectualism, critical without affiliation with any positive ideological model, and ironic in relation to themselves, rendering their own social identifications indeterminate.

Humor of the Algonquin sort also carried potent social meaning in the context of a certain sea change underway in popular American culture, a change with profound implications for the relationship between ethnicity and national identity. *Vanity Fair*, the vanguard journal of the new sophistication, had begun its active promotion of wit and urbanity for New York and the nation as early as 1914, with its first issue. By this time, F. P. A. had for ten years been presiding over a daily newspaper column of wit, a genre he was credited with having "invented" for the New York newspapers when he arrived from Chicago in 1904. With readers submitting much of the column's material, we might note that he also "invented" an interactive form of address that challenged the public to be witty.[13] Within a few years, F. P. A. had instituted an annual awards dinner for contributors to the column (the best of whom got a gold watch). In some ways the unsung precursor to the Algonquin Round Table itself, this group had its own sense of collective exceptionalism, calling their dinner the "Contribunion."[14] The undercurrent of mission nascent in these early formations grew to be a driving force of Round Table existence: in a nation which for decades had laughed itself silly at such vaudeville gems as "The Sport and the Jew," "Irish by Name, but Coons by Birth," and "Two Funny Sauerkrauts," wit constituted a forceful move to shift the terms of American humor. The equation of ethnicity with humor was long-standing and pervasive in vaudeville, and had carried over with some success to the Broadway play, as evidenced by the five-year run of *Abie's Irish Rose* and the fact of its many imitators—*The Cohens and the Kellys*, *Kosher Kitty Kelly*, and *Frisco Sally Levy*, to name a few.[15] Yet under assault from the considerable cultural clout of the New York sophisticates, the ethnic was losing ground to the socially transcendent, the "Hebrew impersonation" and "Coon song" replaced by the bon mot as comedy's stock-in-trade.[16] Not just the mark of the New York elite, then, Round Table wit did double duty as the banner (or promise) of a new democracy of middle-brow national culture.

For the Jews of the Round Table—F. P. A., George Kaufman and Parker herself, as well as Edna Ferber, Harpo Marx, Howard Dietz, Jascha Heifetz, and others—the new witty aesthetic they inhabited and helped to create was not only elite and democratic but, to some degree, necessarily assimilationist.[17] Indeed, the broad effect of mass-mediated American modernity was a flattening out of difference and a submersion of the past, a project most visible in its home base of New York, where modernity's slick utopian sameness was challenged on all sides by immigrant life. And yet, arguably, modern style carried this immigrant presence within itself as a nostalgic underside, a pull toward ethnicity that, given modernity's self-confinement to the crystalline irony of wit, came to be equated with genres of idealism and romance. Indeed, for many modernist writers, the poignancy of urban existence is captured in the figure of the Jewish immigrant. In her 1918 epic poem *The Ghetto*, Australian emigrant and Greenwich Villager Lola Ridge locates passionate romantic radicalism among the young Jews of the Lower East Side garment industry. *Manhattan Transfer*, John Dos Passos's 1922 novel of the brutalizing New York experience, begins with an orthodox Jew shaving off his whiskers and ends with the hardened and successful modern girl, Ellen, groping to remember something she forgot after a chance encounter with Anna Cohen, the disfigured victim of a sweatshop fire.[18]

That a Jewish immigrant writer like Anzia Yezierska would center her stories of assimilationist struggle on Jewish immigrant characters comes as no surprise, but worth noting is the widespread popularity of those stories and the fact that two of them even became Hollywood movies in the early twenties. Equally important is Yezierska's own self-conscious projection of "Jewish passion" through her female characters—*and* in her autobiographical publicity sketches.[19] After winning the O. Henry Award for 1919 and a three-year contract from the Goldwyn studio in 1920 for the film adaptations of her books, Yezierska was herself a celebrity of midtown—all the while standing for the *other* New York and the generic/idealistic potentials outside modern wit. Luminously Jewish in the Algonquin dining room, she must have given complex symbolic definition to Parker's home turf.[20] Seen in the light of that presence, Parker's exemplary modernism may be recognized for an embedded, even structuring pull toward the ethnic past. As the next chapter's examination of her poetics suggests, the "jaded" sexual independence of Parker's personae and the rhetorical structure of her humor channeled her erotic investments away from the amnesiac modern lovers' dyad, reaching instead toward a specifically premodern sense of communal values and belonging.

By the same token, the madcap and befuddled masculinity which motivated some of the most significant Round Table work—that of F. P. A., Kaufman (in collaboration with the Marx Brothers, themselves occasional Algonquinites), and Benchley—may be seen as a parodic response to the male Jewish encounter with 100 percent American, normative manliness (to say nothing of anti-Semitism). That a non-Jewish writer like Benchley actually epitomized the nervous, inept, intellectual, feminized, and (of course) funny marginality that defines this modern masculinity suggests the extent to which the Jewish encounter with modernity was inscribed on modernity itself.[21] Put differently, modern style was coming into being as the expression of "assimilation," not as ethnicity's prior and presumptive opposite.[22]

But if a shared sense of "Jewishness" was behind much of the Round Table style, the sheer heterogeneity of the group's regional, educational, and class backgrounds probably reinforced their characteristic posture of general detachment.[23] The Round Tablers divorced themselves from identification with serious intellectual pursuit, particularly from the politically committed intellectualism of the neighboring Village radicals (whom they considered exhibitionistic and phony).[24] Indeed, parodies of bohemia were a staple for *Vanity Fair* readers. Though much Round Table work was social satire, it rarely implied a positioned social critique. The oft-reiterated notion that the Round Table comprised an "aristocracy of intellect" gave the group license to place themselves above the cultural and political fray without incurring the situatedness implied by a specific class identity. But as significant producers and emblems of democratizing style, they were fully immersed in a national culture which itself worked to blur class difference into a utopian sameness.

Within Round Table culture, the complexities of this self-understanding found significant expression in what was perceived—in classically modernist terms—as a crisis of authentic masculine culture under siege by a degraded feminine mass.

The Culture of Publicity

The late 1910s and 1920s marked a new national orientation to personal fulfillment through leisure and consumption. Accompanying and promoting this shift was a cultural fascination with private life as it was lived by public figures, people who had the means to live ideally and who could guide their audiences in creating and refining private happiness for themselves. The cult of celebrity generated by Hollywood was a powerful force in this context. Tabloids like *Photoplay* provided celebrity advice on beauty and health, as well as tours of celebrities' homes and a steady supply of gossip about their private lives. For major Hollywood actors, such a media apparatus meant private life as display: in their personalities, residential palaces and "playgrounds," they provided the "reality" of the personae and consumer utopias projected on-screen.[25] But if ideal consumption had its symbolic center in Hollywood, sophistication, the dominant intellectual aesthetic of the twenties, was generated out of New York. There was no New York writers' equivalent to the powerful promotional machine of Hollywood, yet for those Round Table writers who embodied the new sophistication, there was an analogous imperative for "personality" and a blurring of public persona and private life.

Members of the Round Table attracted public attention outside their lunchtime forum as well as within it; their extravagance and prankishness earned them their place as a living embodiment of the Roaring Twenties, the quintessence of the age. But even within the larger class of popular journalists—many of whom also spent a fair amount of time at the Algonquin Hotel—the Round Table was distinguished by a distinct intellectual style and its very cohesiveness as a group. Edmund Wilson once complained of how persistently the Round Tablers clung together, rarely venturing beyond their own turf.[26] His critique finds a sardonic echo in the commentary of gold digger Lorelei, Anita Loos's heroine of *But Gentlemen Marry Bru-*

nettes (1928) (sequel to *Gentlemen Prefer Blondes* [1925]). Having gone to the Algonquin to view the resident "geniuses," Lorelei makes the following entry in her "Diary of an Illuminated Lady" (and please note the pun on publicity in Loos's subtitle):

> So then they all started to tell about a famous trip they took to Europe. And they had a marvelous time, because everywhere they went, they would sit in the hotel, and play cute games and tell reminisences about the Algonquin. And I think it is wonderful to have so many internal resources that you never have to bother to go outside of yourself to see anything. . . .
>
> So then they told Mr. [Ernest] Boyd, that every time they met somebody new, they had to stop and explain all of their personal illusions before their jokes could be laughed at, and it only wasted everybody's time. And I really do not know why the geniuses at the Algonquin should bother to learn about Europe any more than Europe bothers to learn about them. So they came back, because they like the Algonquin best after all. And I think it is remarkable, because the old Proberb tells about the Profit who was without honor in his own home. But with them it is just the reverse.[27]

However irritating some of their contemporaries clearly found it, Round Table cliquishness was apparently a necessary function of their identity as a group.[28] While many writers (including Loos and Wilson) chronicled and analyzed the twenties, the Round Table sought deliberately and publicly to embody its popular spirit. Ideal "sophistication" meant continuous fun, conspicuous flouting of authority and responsibility, and a discourse structured as a series of self-contained (and quotable) bon mots. Such behaviors derived their meaning from a paradoxical sense of audience: speaking from within the heady sophistication of the elite circle, seeming only to address one another, the notoriously exclusive Round Tablers were yet acutely aware of the mass of outsiders they seemingly ignored. Though Gaines and others assume the unmitigated snobbery of the Round Table, the evidence of their individual writings (explored later in this chapter) suggests a palpable wish that "the masses" were, or could be, equals in sophistication.[29] Round Table dynamics were premised on the artificiality and ironic inversions of the comedy of manners. (Sympathetic chroniclers describe them as "Wildean.") Intellectualism, seen as ponderous and self-important, was antithetical to sophistication, and several observers noted the apparent inability of the Round Tablers to sustain a topic of conversation long enough to develop it in any kind of depth or complexity.[30] As Parker apologetically explained it years later, "It *was* the Twenties and we had to be smartie."[31]

Round Table conversation fed the daily newspaper columns, while the columns, in turn, profiled the group for public consumption. The Round Table included several reigning members of the journalistic establishment who used the Algonquin conversation as a source of material and an opportunity to promote each others' work.[32] F. P. A., in particular, had a longstanding career of mixing culture criticism and poetry with gossip and the quips of emergent writers in his "Conning Tower" column. By the 1920s the presiding genius of several syndicated columns, F. P. A. was a formidable power in the culture of publicity. But while a plug from F. P. A. was generally a boon for men, its effect was more complicated for women. Indeed, publicity itself—the matrix of Round Table existence—presented an intensely gendered terrain, one with distinctive (and appreciably heightened) risks and rewards for the women who inhabited it.

In F. P. A's ''Diary of Our Own Samuel Pepys,'' a column he alternated with ''The Conning Tower,'' remarks and anecdotes like the following were extremely common.

> . . . home by omnibuss, and a very windy night it was, and near 110th Street a young woman made as to alight, saying, My hat hath blown off, so I got off and ran back four blocks but could not find it, owing to the great wind, and I went back, and found her, and she said, I fear I have taken cold, and thanked me prettily, with as fine a smile as I have seen in a week.[33]

Rather than true supplication, this parodic chivalry seems pretty clearly to express masculine resentment of feminine privilege; it also provides a volatile context for the treatment of real-life female ''personalities.'' Indeed, we need not look far for the visible traces of F. P. A.'s assertion of power over the images of the women he names. The following entries concern Elinor Wylie, appearing for the first time in F. P. A.'s column in 1922.

> Saturday, June 24
> To luncheon, and saw a lovely girl at another table, and asked who it was, and they said it was Elinor Wylie the poet.
>
> Sunday, June 25
> . . . so to Mrs. Elinor Wylie's and drove her to Travers Island.
>
> Monday, June 26
> To call for Mistress Elinor Wylie, and to dinner with her, and as pleasant a talk as ever I had.[34]

After this point, Wylie abruptly (and typically) disappears from the diary. These entries are openly challenging on several fronts, all with the effect of enhancing F. P. A.'s masculine-literary prerogative. Most immediately, F. P. A. challenges his status as a married man, or, more accurately, he challenges his wife with his extramarital interests (the couple finally divorced two years later). He also challenges Wylie's status as a well-established poet—as, in fact, a higher caste writer than Adams himself—by treating her as his own nonliterary ''discovery.'' Finally, the sheer triviality of the events he describes suggests the display of power for its own sake. F. P. A. enters the woman writer into public discourse and banishes her at will; most important, he enters her not as a writer but as the lover of his courtly narrative.

The sexualization of the woman writer could also be more oblique. The entry for January 31 of the same year describes a dinner with Dorothy Parker herself.

> . . . in the evening E. Parker [Edwin, Dorothy's husband from 1917 to 1924] come with his wife, whom I like no less with the passing of days, but she saith ere long I will chuck her aside like a withered nosegay. Which is hard to promise, one way or another.[35]

What appears as the public subordination of his close colleague to her wifely status is most likely a backhanded put-down of her husband. Eddie Pond Parker was a Yankee investment banker and dullard by Round Table standards. This point was so well thematized in the group that the gesture of identifying him as the primary dinner companion over Dorothy is probably ironic. Whether this comment was intended to insult Parker or to draw her into a smirking complicity at her husband's expense (which she does not seem to have been unwilling to do in general[36]), it addresses her at the level of her status as a fellow wit.

Given this beginning, the impact of the concluding remarks is quite devastating, however playful their tone. Having ironized Parker's status as a mere wife, F. P. A. immediately resexualizes her in terms of their own relation. Whereas "E. Parker" may be less than a fit husband for Dorothy— and if there were any question of this, his rhetorical cuckolding sees to it— F. P. A. commands the real masculine dominance to put her in her place. The romance metaphors have no referent in their real-life relation, and the context invoked by the entry itself makes that more or less clear to the public audience. But the pose of capricious and desirable lover serves to naturalize F. P. A.'s professional power over the emergent female writer as a function of his masculinity, while her public status, in turn, comes to depend on her feminine allure. The exact measure of F. P. A.'s professional power over a writer like Parker is hard to gauge (and, indeed, we can wonder if rhetorical assertions like the one under discussion might not have been motivated by anxiety on this very point). Nevertheless, for Parker, the effect of writing in a popular context which demanded of her a "personality" was that she entered the public eye as a sexualized woman or not at all.

In the world projected by Round Table publicity, this gender determinacy was ultimately bound up with relations and identifications of class. In the "Pepys" selection, the capriciousness on which Parker waits and the nosegays F. P. A. figuratively tosses aside are consistent with the dandy posture F. P. A. fostered in his writing. As prototypical moderns, the Round Tablers propagated a notion of themselves as aesthetes, simultaneously elevating themselves above the commercialism with which they were implicated and justifying that commercialism through the valorization of a sophisticated cynicism. Alexander Woollcott, arguably the dominant personality of the group, was appropriately an extreme case: hyperbolically snobbish, addicted to genteel games of all sorts, and known for his signature opera hat and silk scarf.

In modeling themselves on upper-class dandies, the writers of the Round Table adopted a preoccupation with manners that pervaded both their literary and nonliterary social expressions.[37] The Round Tablers saw themselves as the defenders of taste in an era overrun by mass entertainment and fatuous "jazz babies." This conservative impulse manifested itself in an aesthetic preoccupation with the English language, revealed in their famous banter as well as the punning that structured most of their obsessive parlor games. Parker in her book reviews and F. P. A. in his columns directed substantial sarcasm at the malapropisms and flawed grammar of contemporary writers, librettists, and other columnists.[38] In clear opposition to the new raciness of contemporary mass culture (and in stark contrast to their own promiscuous habits), most of the group were publicly fastidious about sex.[39] Many were consciously mannered in their behavior, though always with tongue in cheek; for example, the trio of Parker, Robert Benchley, and Robert Sherwood (fellow editors at *Vanity Fair*) habitually referred to one another as "Mrs. Parker," "Mr. Benchley," and "Mr. Sherwood."[40]

Upholding tradition became evidence of a cultured transcendence—a self-understanding that served to shore up a somewhat shakier sense of economic transcendence. Several members of the Round Table, including Parker, spent a good deal of time with Long Island millionaires such as the Fleischmanns and the Swopes.[41] The relations between artists and the rich in this circle were those of classic patronage: witty writers were expected to provide amusement to an otherwise dull society in tacit exchange for material support of various kinds, the most common of which was the standing, open-ended invitation to be houseguest—in effect, to partake of upper-class life. Parker, in particular, was disgusted with what she declared the ignorance of her benefactors and "hated their money but wished it was hers."[42] Such seemingly blatant hypocrisy might well have looked like simple justice from a Round Table perspective, a redistribution of wealth from the merely rich to the transcendently witty. Parker's sense of cultural insulation worked in both directions on the class continuum: secure in the essential aristocracy of wit, she could go schmoozing in the Hamptons without losing her soul and, as we shall see, write for the mass reader without "commonness" by association. Interestingly, she did not consider wealthy Hollywood actors (or herself as a highly paid Hollywood writer in the thirties) to be among "the rich."[43] Film historian Lary May argues that the singular popularity of the early movie stars stemmed in large part from their ability to inhabit the American dream without apparently wielding and abusing power over others, as industrialists and politicians were seen to do.[44] We can imagine that this rationale had substantial force in Parker's case, for she had surprisingly strong populist sympathies, which only grew more defined and articulate in the post-Algonquin decades.[45] Clearly, Parker and the Round Table shared the pervasive fantasy that a national culture had replaced class difference with democratizing style—of which sophistication was the premier expression.[46]

In the paradoxical way of the era's urban cultural hegemony, sophistication and wit were promoted as mainstream cultural values even as they served to mark the elite. *Vanity Fair* made a special mission of disseminating sophistication on a mass-circulation basis, not because its editors believed that readers were sophisticated but because it believed that they *should* be.[47] Anita Loos credited *Vanity Fair* and Mencken's *Smart Set* in particular with having had "an enormously civilizing influence on the United States."[48] In an essay of 1922, Round Tabler Robert Benchley argued that F. P. A.'s humor worked to counter American anti-intellectualism: "In F. P. A. we find a combination which makes it possible to admit our learning and still be held honorable men. It is a good sign that his following is increasing." Benchley himself was named to the 1924 *Vanity Fair* Hall of Fame for "mercifully inject[ing] into our national humor the quality of sophisticated and cultivated good taste."[49] As New York took its place on the cutting edge of urbanity, the new national youth culture emerging on college campuses everywhere looked to the acerbic essays of H. L. Mencken and the cynical love poems of Dorothy Parker as models of personal style.[50] What the writings of the Round Tablers in particular offered to a mass audience was, according to Gaines, "nothing less than an inside line to the new sophistication" (48). What sophistication might well have offered to the Round Tablers was a means to deny the mass character of their mass audience.

Certainly Round Table expressions of sophistication seem to have occasionally bordered on unintelligibility to the outsider.[51] The strength of this group idiom notwithstanding, several key members of the Round Table built their individual literary careers around an emphatically *inclusive* rhetorical mode—not only Dorothy Parker but also Robert Benchley and F. P. A. And such seeming contradiction vividly testifies to the class ambiguities of the modern culture they represented. Historian Roland Marchand's study of advertising copywriters from this period provides a highly suggestive analogue to the complex sociology of the Round Tablers as subjects and producers of modernity. Not poets or personalities, advertisers were nevertheless self-identified intellectuals in the unusual position of working the machinery of mainstream culture (rather than languishing in its margins). College-educated, urban, and paid to be consciously manipulative of consumers in the interests of corporations, advertisers might easily have been the most hardened of cynics. Yet in *Advertising the American Dream: Making Way for Modernity, 1920–1940*, Marchand argues that the worthiness of their profession and the dignity of their audience were matters of constant negotiation and anxiety for them. Advertisers, according to Marchand, were "the 'most modern of men,' " with the consequence that "they experienced with particular intensity many of those qualities of modern life that had gradually been coming to unsettle the wider society."[52]

"Men" may be the operative word here, not just for the advertisers but for the Round Table as well: the most visible experience of the situation we are calling modern was one of male crisis, and the most quintessentially modern response was a clearly marked style of masculinity. Their conspicuous sophistication notwithstanding, F. P. A. and Benchley expressed their modernness more as a sense of anxious bewilderment than glib mastery. In their perpetual mock-heroic struggle with incomprehensible machinery and social relations, F. P. A. and Benchley lived out the ambivalence of modernity in their public personae. Speaking from within his most characteristic rhetorical posture, Benchley declared in an essay entitled "The Real Public Enemies,"

> The hundred and one little bits of wood and metal that go to make up the impedimenta of our daily life . . . are bent on my humiliation and working together, as on one great team, to bedevil and confuse me and to get me into a neurasthenics' home before I am sixty. I can't fight these boys. They've got me licked.[53]

For his part, F. P. A. derived many of his humorous effects from positioning himself as a naive reader, taking on the modern world armed with the (often fatal) advice of popular experts and, occasionally, poets. Inspired by Sara Teasdale's "Summer Night, Riverside," "F. P. A." goes in search of the romance he sees reflected on the page. Full of inspiration and trust, he ventures forth.

In the wild, hot summer subway
What time I journeyed home from work,
O Sara,
I read your verses.
Free and fetterless as any barefoot girl in Arcady,
And I detrained at One Hundred and
Sixteenth Street
And walked
One block west, to Riverside Drive.
I sat upon a bench, avid for Adventure,
Athirst and overyearnful for Romance;
And a girl came along
And I thought of the blossoms clinging
in the coils of her hair;
And I said, "Good evening."

She said: "You fresh guys ought to be arrested for mashing."

And so I sat there, senseful that Romance
and such
Were not for me.
All that paid attention to me were mos-quitoes;
And I went home,
And, dreamily before my mirror,
I anointed myself
With Oil of Citronella.[54]

Typically, what stands between F. P. A. and fulfillment of the modern promise of glamor or social mastery is a hardheaded "modern woman." In his "Samuel Pepys" column, this role is most often taken up by his "wife." F. P. A. presents himself as a self-deluded figure whose fantasies are repeatedly crushed in the encounter with his wife's brutal (and castrating) realism. Take, for example, this entry from March 1922.

> [Crossword] puzzles are so popular, as the ability to solve them is mistaken by the solvers for intelligence. Lord, for a few minutes after I solve a puzzle I am as vain as any peacock, and strut about the house till my wife takes my vanity away by calling me silly or some such thing. But she away this day, in Orange, so my inflation endured for an hour.[55]

Clearly, Round Table inclusivity—no less than Round Table exclusivity—gets staged across a highly gendered public terrain of address and self-presentation. Defying the conventional wisdom that women are the subjects of consumer culture, the male F. P. A. derives his identity from advertisements and "advice," while his wife remains solidly anchored in "reality." Indeed, as the preceding examples testify, there is a distinctly feminized component to the F. P. A. persona, which most often serves to situate him precisely in the role of consumer. For all his high culture references, and in spite of his Pepysian diction, F. P. A. presents a highly accessible figure of identification for his "average" reader, the male subject of—and to—modernity. (Indeed, his blatant and humorous feminization may even provide this reader with the opportunity to consciously *dis*identify, to shore up his own masculinity in laughing at F. P. A.'s loss thereof.)

The dual sense that, while the man is a fool, the problem may lie with the modern world suggests links to what certain critics identify as the shtetl humor of the schlemiel. Charlie Chaplin, surely among "the most modern of men" and relevant to any mapping of popular modernism, is typically spoken of in precisely these terms. Hannah Arendt called his Tramp "a little Yid," arguing that he had "epitomized in an artistic form a character born of the Jewish pariah mentality."[56] Even closer to home, given their connections to Broadway (where they played successfully before turning to films), the Round Table (where Harpo especially was a regular), and George Kaufman (author of their hit plays *The Cocoanuts* and *Animal Crackers*), the Marx Brothers have also been seen as "acting out Jewish identities" and, in particular, as staging a specifically Jewish experience of social marginality.[57] In thinking of Benchley and F. P. A. in the vocabulary of this critical paradigm, the figure that stands out is less the schlemiel than the *schlimazl*, who, with his

> keen, rational mind . . . tries to integrate more information than he should. . . . [N]ew information bombards him. He cannot revise quickly enough to keep up with events. . . . [H]e is constantly modifying his system of beliefs, trying fruitlessly to find a place for everything, then trying to put everything in its place. . . . He learns all the rules, obeys all the laws, lives by all the orders . . . and yet, somehow, for some reason, he never quite prospers.[58]

Capturing as uncannily as it does the essence of what Benchley and F. P. A. implicitly assure us is the modern experience of manhood, the *schlimazl* again suggests a latent Jewish dimension to the popular modernism of the Round Table.

Yet we know that the sense of freedom from ethnic limitations is critical to modernity's appeal. In reviewing Eddie Cantor's vaudeville act for *Life* magazine, Benchley is perfectly willing to cite the ethnic matrix, which, in truth, vaudeville foregrounded. Offended by Cantor's blackface routine (which "for years . . . [has] meant considerably less than nothing to us as entertainment"), he nevertheless approvingly (and seemingly unprompted) finds Jewishness in Cantor's unmasked performance.

> Last year at the Winter Garden, he washed up, and in place of the neurotic Negro appeared a Jewish boy with large, bewildered eyes and mild manner, an apologetic calm superseding the offensive assurance, and, oddly enough, a considerably more sanitary batch of songs and jokes.
>
> Both Eddie Cantors are in the Follies this summer and you can take your choice. Ours is the Jewish boy, especially in his scene with the traffic policeman, where his eagerness to conciliate and his humility in the face of a terrific injustice borders on high tragedy.[59]

Benchley's willingness to embrace a Jewish-cultural line of interpretation is, however, limited to this atavistic form of humor (even as he values the modern within it, the "humility" over the "offensive assurance"). When the stakes are not the already moribund genre of vaudeville but the very definition of madcap modernity, he is suddenly vehement in beating back the ethnic tide.[60] Under the pretext of reviewing the Marx Brothers, Benchley takes aim at a British reviewer who had gone on record with the judgment that Groucho was "the sublimation of the Jews' attitude toward life, 'the exteriorization of this faithful power of laughing at themselves.' " Benchley dismisses this interpretation with an aggressive appeal to common sense, underscoring his point by appropriating the Marx Brothers' joke to his own, non-Jewish voice.

> The Marx Brothers ought to be very easy to enjoy. We find it absurdly simple. . . . When Groucho says to Chico: "You look like Emanuel Ravelli," and Chico says: "I *am* Emanuel Ravelli," and Groucho retorts: "No wonder you look like him. But I will insist there is a resemblance," we detect no symbolism of an oppressed Jewry, but rather a magnificently disordered mind which has come into its own.[61]

Indeed, it is the pure abstractness of the "magnificently disordered mind" which is at stake here, Benchley's (and the wider democratic-elite's) equal access to modern sensibility. In effect, Benchley reserves the right of any disordered modern man to "come into his own" and be transcendently, stylishly funny.

Whatever its importance to the motivation and definition of Round Table modernity, ethnicity and the complications to identity upon which it insisted were forcefully subsumed to the one overriding difference of gender. The broad paths of self-parody laid down by so many Round Table men were diverted in any number of cases away from self to "Woman" and "the eternal struggle of the sexes." Such persistent displacement leads finally back to an anxiety about the status of the commercial writer; indeed, many individual Round Tablers struggled with the sense that they were putting their talents to unworthy use. As a whole, they assumed a fashionably cynical stance toward their work, claiming they were in it for the money. In a remark much quoted at the time, George Kaufman tacitly summed up the basically commercial nature of the enterprise: "If you have a *message*, call for Western Union."[62]

F. P. A.'s "Pepys" column, in particular, was largely premised on the very triviality of his own life and commentary, and the underlying absurdity of its public display.

> Bespoke Mistress Julia over the telephone, and asked her how she was, and she said she was well; and she asked me how I was, and I gave a not dissimilar reply. So to my scrivening, and at it all day.
>
> Mr. Harding is become President this day. Did on my new blue cravat this day, making a brave show.
>
> Noting in The Globe I have been nominated for Mayor of this city, I gave a statement saying I bow to the will of the people.
>
> Up by times, and to the office, and there all day at my stint, and was hard put to it to think of aught to write, and filled with alternate merriment and dismay to think how little it mattered what I wrote, or whether I wrote anything soever. Now if everybody who ever wrote thought that way, I mused, what sort of place would the world be? which was a question I could not answer.[63]

But F. P. A.'s take on the gender-specific motivations of commercial writing comes through forcefully in his cultural criticism. His collection *Column Book* is full of such gibes at popular fiction as "The Passionate Magazine Writer to His Love."

CORYDON

Ah, sweet, the songs I sing to thee
  Nor wondrous are nor many,

PHYLLIS

And mind thou gets a weighty fee,
  And copst a pretty penny.

CORYDON

Dear love, thou hast my brimming heart
  Till that I near must die for it.

PHYLLIS

Ay, sell the magazines thine art,
  And soak'em in the eye for it.[64]

In earlier collection called *Overset*, F. P. A. offers this mock book dedication to the writer with candor enough to use it:

TO
MY DAUGHTERS
SPENDA AND BLOWA
but for whose extravagant
idleness I should not have
had to write this unworthy novel[65]

Most striking of all is the real-life dedication of *Half a Loaf* to his wife:

TO
ESTHER
who continually urges me to
write more—and more[66]

As these examples suggest, the self-denigration of the (male) Round Table writer has certain limits, as does his inclusivity. However much he may be willing—even anxious—to confess his prostitution, he would have us understand that it is the vulgar world of commodity culture that drives him to abandon artistic purpose. More specifically, it is the parasitical female whose boundless consumer appetites are the instrument of his degradation—and the engine of mass culture itself.

Even Benchley, whose work in this period was far less preoccupied with dichotomous gender values and roles, occasionally grew hysterical at the specter of the feminine mass:

> One of the most embarrassing experiences that a man can have is to find himself alone at a matinee where Sex is rampant on the stage in either double, or simple *entendre*. Scenes of seduction, like those in "Fata Morgana" for example, which in the evening are taken with at least a modicum of the seriousness intended by the author, become, at matinees, occasions for giggling and obscene hilarity, making the lone male feel that perhaps, in spite of its traditional temporary advantages, the whole institution of Sex has been a mistake. Woman, however lovely she may be in stooping to folly in individual cases, is never so unlovely as when giggling at it in a group over boxes of chocolates.[67]

Again, the Round Tablers' self-understanding and relation to the culture they helped create may be usefully compared with those of contemporaneous admen.

> As a last resort, in the protection of their self-esteem, and as a psychological weapon against cultural engulfment [*sic*] by the tastes of the consumer masses, advertisers could always emphasize the stereotyped gender distinction between advertisers as men and consumers as women.[68]

The parallel continues: in addition to this gendered opposition between themselves and their audience, Marchand finds "admen" of the twenties personally invested in an identification with the upper class and high culture. And yet, according to Marchand, "the class distinctions that advertising writers drew between themselves and their broad audience were not nearly so sharp as the disparities they perceived in intelligence and in cultural tastes.''[69]

These parallels with Round Table identifications suggest that the latent but palpable Algonquin masculinism served an important insulating function for its members, bolstering their ''aristocratic'' status through distancing the ''mass'' associations of femininity—even in the midst of a sincerely democratic appeal to the ''average'' reader. Such a structure of identifications may account for one of Parker's most famous and disturbing puns: challenged to find a sentence in *horticulture*, she threw out ''You may lead a horticulture but you can't make her think.'' Though perhaps more multiply nasty than the typical Parker utterance, the line suggests the intensity and precision with which a woman of the Round Table might have had to draw the boundaries of inside and out.

At the more immediate emotional level, Parker's anchor in the Algonquin subculture seems to have been Robert Benchley. The two were close friends and, at the time of the Round Table's inception, coeditors of *Vanity Fair*. Their mutual devotion was such that when Parker was fired for writing a drama review unfavorable to Billie Burke, the actor wife of the powerful Florenz Ziegfeld, Benchley resigned in protest, despite his status as sole provider for a family of four. Parker called it ''the greatest act of friendship I have ever known.''[70] Unemployed, they moved their playful rebelliousness into a tiny rented office, where they behaved ''like impoverished pseudo-newlyweds'' while waiting for freelance business. When business was not forthcoming, they let the rest of the Round Table (and, of course, the world) know that they were going to lure prospective customers in with a sign on the door bearing the single word *Men* (which seems ironically appropriate).[71] The ''newlyweds'' reference notwithstanding, the available evidence suggests a relationship of siblings united in defiance of a stuffy and unfair world. This sentiment is captured in Parker's poem ''For R.C.B.'':

Life comes a-hurrying,
    Or life lags slow;
But you've stopped worrying—
    Let it go!
Some call it gloomy,
    Some call it jake;
They're very little to me—
    Let them eat cake!
Some find it fair,
    Some think it hooey,
Many people care;
    But we don't, do we?[72]

As foundational as this relationship was for Parker, Benchley seems to have found it important to keep his hooks in staid conventional masculinity. He commuted to sophisticated New York from suburban Croton, where he lived with his wife and two sons, and from which he drew much of his comedic material. As the twenties wore on, he established a steady pattern of patronizing prostitutes (at the famous Polly Adler's, where he had his own monogrammed robe, and where Parker would go along for the champagne) and "keeping" young mistresses—through it all preserving his marriage to his childhood sweetheart intact.[73] Moreover, he was not above sacrificing Parker to male solidarity with her hated ex-lovers, a couple of whom he went so far as to share city apartments with.[74] Although Benchley was unquestionably a Round Table sophisticate, he was also clearly invested in his existence as a "family man," even to all its attendant hypocrisies.

While Benchley evidently exercised a substantial measure of control over his life, including "his" women, Parker invested a lot of angry emotion in the conviction that her friend and colleague was trapped and victimized—by suburbia but, most of all, by his wife. There are several available accounts of Parker's unprovoked attacks on Gertrude, but perhaps the best register of her notion of Benchley's "other life" is her short story "Such a Pretty Little Picture." The protagonist is Mr. Wheelock (and the name suggests something of Parker's diagnosis), a man in every respect alienated from his suburban roles: he is a mediocre provider, inept with tools, intimidated in his marriage and only faintly attached to or aware of his child—a male misfit, but, crucially, without the modernizing humor. He nurses a fantasy of escape, which never progresses beyond the details of leaving for the train, so daunted is he by the unthinkable task of standing up to Adelaide, his wife.

Adelaide is the embodiment of oppressive domesticity and the antithesis of sophistication. We meet her as she sits

> on the spotless porch of the neat stucco house. Beside her was a pile of her husband's shirts and drawers, the price-tags still on them. She was going over all the buttons before he wore the garments, sewing them on more firmly. Mrs. Wheelock never waited for a button to come off, before sewing it on. . . .
>
> Passionately clean, she was always redolent of the germicidal soap she used so vigorously. She was wont to tell people, somewhat redundantly, that she never employed any sort of cosmetics. . . . Adelaide Wheelock's friends—and she had many of them—said of her that there was no nonsense about her. They and she regarded it as a compliment.[75]

To the extent that she can be said to have an opinion of him at all, Mrs. Wheelock seems to regard her husband as childish and inept. For the duration of the story, she continues to sew buttons while Mr. Wheelock—"Daddy" to his wife as well as his child—clips hedges. He remains absorbed in his fantasy and virtually silent while Mrs. Wheelock speaks peremptorily to him on various domestic matters. At the conclusion of the story, a passing neighbor woman, "barren, and addicted to sentiment," comments on the scene: " 'Look, Fred; just turn around and look at that,' she said to her husband. She looked again, sighing luxuriously. 'Such a pretty little picture!' "

Mr. Wheelock is classically misunderstood; no one but the narrator knows his true feelings. In fact, she knows them far better than Mr. Wheelock himself. If Adelaide would stifle him with ridicule and drudgery, the authorial voice has denied him not only the strength to change his situation but even the imaginative capacity to understand his own victimization and to generate humor from within it—this lies within her power alone.

At the first level of signification, "Such a Pretty Little Picture" depicts Wheelock/Benchley's fight with suburban domesticity, but, more fundamentally, it stages Parker's own struggle with Adelaide/Gertrude, first for control over Robert and, ultimately, for definition of herself. To the extent that the authorial voice/Parker is the sole guardian of Wheelock/Benchley's oppression, her identification with him is secure; equally secure is her distance from Gertrude. Emphatically not a wife (just as she had no part in the mass female identities of matinee audiences or feminism), going along to brothels to drink champagne in the parlor, Parker could be a boon companion to Benchley, provided she defined herself in terms of her distance from the kind of overt, traditional femininity against which he, in a different way, defined himself. Seen through the lens of his city life alone, Benchley was the Round Tabler whose madcap modern masculinity most converged with his "personality," the one who epitomized modernity if only because—well—he was the funniest.[76] For these reasons, Benchley was the genuine article in a way that Parker, as a woman, could not be. In this light, her pitying and protective identification (misread, I would argue, by biographers and a certain filmmaker as unrequited love)[77] are an emotionally forceful way of anchoring what was necessarily a vicarious experience of modernity.

But turning to the larger body of her work, we find that Parker had made for herself another, more stable, if rather abstract, emotional home at the heart of her poetics. Writing as a woman from within the Algonquin Round Table and the culture of publicity, Parker forged a modern public place for herself through an intimate bond with her audience. An early poem published in *Life* generates this dynamic even while cynically denouncing the business of writing. "The Far-Sighted Muse" displays the "backstage" view of poetry alongside the poetry itself, blasting any pretense to artistic purity.

Everything's great in this good old world;
(This is the stuff they can always use,)
God's in his heaven, the hill's dew-pearled;
(This will provide for the baby's shoes.)
Hunger and War do not mean a thing;
Everything's rosy where e'er we roam;
Hark, how the little birds gaily sing!
(This is what fetches the bacon home.)[78]

Any discussion of "Muse" must begin from the fact that Parker never wrote the kind of poetry to which the work refers; from the beginning of her career, she built her reputation on cynicism and bitterness—and in specific response to the tastes of popular editors and audiences. Hence, we need to look beyond the substance of the "complaint" to explain the poem and, instead, explore its rhetorical mode as a pretext for inviting just the sort of intimacy "Muse" ultimately affords.

The use of a double voice, common for Parker, thematizes a hopeless rift between the speaker and her rhetorically implied audience at the same time that it asserts their actual and seemingly unmediated contact. The speaker makes her audience the ironic confidante for her dilemma as a lonely public persona at the mercy of a degraded commercial imperative (from which she invites her magazine-buying audience to imaginatively dissociate themselves). She has not only made her readers privy to the problem but also constructed them as allies against a common oppressor. The force that reduces her to turning out saccharine verse, she implies, is one they will recognize immediately, for it is equally operative in their own lives. They, too, must "bring the bacon home," but more to the point, under the prevailing self-consciousness generated by aggressive advertising, they will feel equally burdened with the necessity for a public persona. The newly mass-mediated urban life of the modern period projected a public sphere of anonymous personal scrutiny dictated by the normative standards of advertising and the social sciences. Even the ordinary citizen met those standards or faced personal and professional failure (or so the ads implied).[79] By invoking her own enslavement to the public sphere, Parker offers her audience a point of identification with one who is presumably a controlling agent in an arena where the average reader feels merely subject. The characteristic Parker bitterness, which would seem to repel rather than invite identification and intimacy, actually functions as evidence of the speaker's sincerity. It is writers (and sellers), she implies, who aestheticize the world; she and her readers—"real people"—know better.

The rhetorical structure of "Muse" parallels that of many contemporaneous advertisements as described by Marchand: both begin by invoking a merciless public world, then shift the ground to a private communication between the "persons" of speaker and reader. In the case of the ad, there is first an insinuation of the "reality" of the reader's shortcomings from the "disinterested, judgmental" voice of public standards, after which "the advertiser quickly befriended the consumer. Assuming the role of coach and confidante, he offered the consumer advice and encouragement as together they faced the external challenge."[80] For her part, Parker is not selling a solution but, rather, offering up her own victimization as a point of communion with her readers. The effect of the writer (or advertiser) coming down on the side of the reader (or consumer) is one of an underscored refusal of power—a denial of the authority to render "solutions" to modern living. In ways less obvious but even more emphatic than what we have seen of other Round Tablers, Parker presents herself as the *subject* rather than the *manipulator* of modern culture.

But, again, the struggles of the modern subject are irrevocably gendered struggles. The gender polarity deployed by F. P. A. and, to a lesser extent, Benchley defines the modern experience as a crisis of masculinity—and implicitly defines the modern challenge as a feminine threat. "The Far-Sighted Muse" comes at this dichotomy slantwise, heightening rather than undermining its terms but in the interest of a telos that accommodates a differently gendered modern subject. The confidential voice, identified with reality and the burden of "bringing the bacon home," is that of the "bread-winning" man; the poetic voice, identified with sentimentality and denial, is that of the tyrannical feminine mass—an emphatically *unsophisticated* mass, at that. Though "he" is producer and "she" consumer, the cultural power resides with her. The double voice reflects a more fundamental division for Parker, though, for if F. P. A. and Benchley could make themselves at home in modern masculinity, however mitigated its thrust, Parker was truly caught between the impossible alternatives of male subject and female world. And yet her stark ideological arrangement of those alternatives in this poem points outward to a different terrain: forced out of the modern gender polarity, the speaker slips between the terms of male and female to seek a relation with her audience on new, nonheterosexual ground.

The full exploration of that ground requires bringing into visibility a final piece of Parker's discursive context. Parker's literary survival as a woman within a masculinist subculture was importantly enabled by Round Table participation in a national discourse that could function to flatten out gender difference even as it foregrounded gender roles. The last section of this chapter describes the contemporaneous preoccupation with urbane heterosexuality and gender antagonism—what I am calling "modern love" and its "war of the sexes."

Modern Love and the War of the Sexes

By the mid-1920s, most of the Round Tablers had come to make extensive use of "modern love" and its primary narrative premise, the "war of the sexes." After some early and passing use of Modern Love in his *Vanity Fair* pieces from the teens, Benchley had fully incorporated the war into his domestic sketches. Whereas husband-wife relations had been subsumed to the drama of the lone man in (and out of) suburbia, now readers got a black comedy of sex strife, complete with flashes of sadism.[81] The war of the sexes appears in F. P. A.'s column starting in 1922, sometimes accompanied by embittered reflections on the courtly standard it replaces.[82] In the same year, F. P. A. and Parker collaborated on a "war" piece for the *Saturday Evening Post* called "Women I'm Not Married To [F. P. A.'s contribution]; Men I'm Not Married To [Parker's contribution]." The fact that this generic shift coincides with the beginning of the Round Table itself as a significant theme in F. P. A.'s writings suggests the intrinsically "modern" aura surrounding this treatment of heterosexual relations. But while her male colleagues worked up to it slowly, Parker had made the war and its encompassing discursive medium, Modern Love, foundational to her work from the time of her first *Vanity Fair* success.

Parker had had only marginal success getting published in *Vanity Fair* when, in 1916, she finally succeeded in impressing editor Frank Crowninshield. What apparently won him over was the malicious theme of her poem "Women: A Hate Song," which gleefully dissected a long string of affectedly "feminine" types.[83] Having established this "hate" as her first credential of sophistication, she took on the men in "Why I Haven't Married." Crowninshield subsequently commissioned a series of "Hate Songs,"[84] now fully capitalizing on the quintessentially "sophisticated" lashings of a "sharp" female tongue. If sophistication meant cynicism and a barbed wit, women, with their "innate" bitchiness, were prime to be dominant in this discourse. Indeed, by the time of her first best-selling collection in 1926, Parker had made a national career for herself as the most sardonic (and luckless) lover on literary record. Modern Love and Round Table sophistication were key to her success, providing the terms by which she could forge an alternative—and highly enabling—model of self-other relations.

Though more diffuse and culturally pervasive than "free love" or "companionate marriage,"[85] Modern Love was similarly concerned with negotiating the new social terrain defined by the modern woman and the focus on heterosexual couples, as opposed to the actively reproductive family. But whereas both Free Love and Companionate Marriage referred implicitly and even explicitly to utopian social visions, Modern Love took its driving force from the assumption that gender relations were permanently and intrinsically flawed.

Free Love and Companionate Marriage presupposed that gender equality was an accomplished fact or, more accurately, that it was the "natural" state of male-female relations. Their focus was ideal, almost mythic, and, apart from a certain reliance on a eugenicist telos to underwrite their authority, largely privatized. By contrast, Modern Love described a mundane world of daily life and social pretensions. The players of Free Love and Companionate Marriage were highly agential beings with a strong, not to say, lofty, teleological focus; those of Modern Love were identifiable social types to whom the modern world had happened. The readers of Free Love fiction and Companionate Marriage manuals presumably came away inspired to work toward heterosexual bliss with little reference to the social world outside the insular dyad. By contrast, readers of Modern Love could only conclude that heterosexuality was flawed at best and take comfort in the fact that the whole project was too comical and inevitable to bear much analysis, or even emotional investment.

Modern Love rendered a heterosexual world whose chief appeal was perhaps the opportunity it offered for cynical detachment from a common obsession; in the process, it flatteringly inscribed its readers as sophisticates. Indeed, one of the principal compensations of Modern Love discourse was its very modernness: the combination of a self-consciously risqué preoccupation with sex, a certain glib cynicism, and a humorous aesthetic suggesting the fast pace of modern life generated a palpable aura of sophistication around the work and, by association, its reader. Modern Love was to be found as early as the late teens in newspapers and fashionable magazines as the basis of short fiction, humorous "dialogues," satirical sketches and cartoons, and the occasional novel.[86] Crossing many genres, widely diffused throughout public speech about sex and gender, and without a defined or activist agenda, Modern Love was somewhat amorphous as a discourse but nevertheless had certain identifiable features. Principal among them was a focus on the social identities of its lovers to the virtual exclusion of any notion of private self or of attributes such as individuality, introspection, and intimacy. Rather, Modern Lovers took their definition and "character" from a set of common sociological types: the debutante, the college man, the gold digger, the Don Juan, the Newlyweds, and so forth.

In taking its subject as a social rather than a private phenomenon, Modern Love posited what was in effect an ambiguously valenced heterosexual couple. The couple was, of course, paramount in Companionate Marriage and Free Love; while one valued gender difference as the means to happiness, the other emphasized variety and the "experience" of love. Both discourses were structured around a utopian center: the heterosexual couple as the site of pleasure and primary emotional investment. Modern Love, by contrast, saw the heterosexual couple not as a private refuge but as continuous with heterosocial society, the new mingling of the sexes brought on by women's encroachment on formerly all-male turf, the public spaces of campus, office and street.[87]

The central structural mechanism of Modern Love narrative was the war of the sexes, within which there were no serious threats to the institution of heterosexuality (though particular alliances might fail), and no ultimate victories or defeats for either its male or female participants. Instead, fictive couples carped and bickered in response to assaults on their easily shattered illusions about the opposite sex and married life (a favorite theme was the break precipitated by an annoying habit like not recapping the toothpaste). Modern Lovers were emotionally shallow and two-dimensional, consistent with a wider generic relation between Modern Love and the humor of farce. When they were not governed by outright greed or desperation, the desires of Modern Lovers often followed facile illusions; men and women seeking commodified ideal images in one another were destined to pursue them across a series of individuals.[88]

Since Modern Love understood itself as, above all, a sophisticated response to a newly problematized heterosexuality, its impetus was conventionally foregrounded as reactive, its tone as ambivalent. Cultural observers—male and female—seemed to take up Modern Love whenever they engaged that other highly charged subject, the New Woman (or her trivial sister, the flapper). At first making a show of their perplexity and surprise at her values and behavior, they inevitably discovered, by article's end, the eternal feminine just below the modern surface or the innocuously beneficial nature of the changes she represented. The typical title was redolent with sophisticated irony: "Prue Enlightening the World: A Disadvantage of the New Freedom for Women" or "The Doom of the Home: And What about Children? and Rubber Plants?"[89] The humorous enactment of the "upset" caused by the New Woman, the ultimate tone of unruffled calm and sometimes even celebration with regard to her, and the rhetorical dismissal of the threat she posed were all equally important expressions of her effects on sophisticated observers. It may even be argued (as Gilbert and Gubar have done with respect to literary high modernism) that sophistication itself arose in part as a response to the New Woman.[90]

F. Scott Fitzgerald's rendition of the modern New Woman highlights the contradictory ideal that lurks within Modern Love: successful heterosociality through the "masculinization" of its women. Fitzgerald was a significant force in defining the new heterosociality, and his work appeared in many of the standard vehicles for Modern Love.[91] The most central trope of Fitzgerald's jazz-age narratives was the world-weary, beautiful, and intensely male-identified flapper. In "Bernice Bobs Her Hair," a short story from 1920, Fitzgerald compares this highly desirable woman to a tedious "old-fashioned girl":

> As a matter of fact Marjorie had no female intimates—she considered girls stupid. Bernice on the contrary . . . longed to exchange those confidences flavored with giggles and tears that she considered an indispensable factor in all feminine intercourse. But in this respect she found Marjorie rather cold; felt somehow the same difficulty in talking to her that she had in talking to men. Marjorie never giggled, was never frightened, seldom embarrassed, and in fact had very few of the qualities which Bernice considered appropriately and blessedly feminine.[92]

Blessed femininity is not an incorrigible condition, however, and under Marjorie's reluctant tutelage Bernice achieves the modern variety. Significantly, her accomplishment is marked not by manly sobriety and courage but by the capacity to draw male desire to herself through sophisticated banter. The final measure of her break with "femininity" (or blessedness) is her willingness to turn classically "catty" aggression on the woman with whom she had once "longed to exchange confidences." (Bernice snips off the sleeping Marjorie's braid in a fit of vengeance for her own coerced "bob.") The crux of modern femininity as exemplified by "Bernice Bobs Her Hair" lies more in a woman's choice of alliances than the specificity of her character; Bernice has arrived when she recognizes the rightness of forgoing homosocial for heterosocial investments.

One of the central engines for Modern Love was, of course, *Vanity Fair*, which (along with its chief competitor, *The Smart Set*) was not coincidentally also the central vehicle of the larger discourse of sophistication. *Vanity Fair*'s implicit editorial promise was to bring its readership into a state of desirable sophistication in and through successful heterosocial relations.[93] Structurally, this glossy magazine embodied modern heterosociality through its designated readership, which was expressly identified as both male and female—a distinct break from past and concurrent patterns of gender-specific markets for journals.[94] Even more pointed was the editorial policy expressed in each issue through a page-long feature that drew the reader in through the absorbing quality of its narrative before finally revealing itself to be a combination advertisement and mission statement for *Vanity Fair* itself.[95] Presumably for the sake of variety and disarming the reader, this editorial feature took various forms—essay, play, or diary entry—but each negotiated a terrain defined by sophistication and gender relations, with the strong implication that the two were inextricably intertwined.

"A Word about Debutantes," from the January 1915 issue, was in the form of a letter from "George" to "Harry." "My Dear Harry," it began, "You ask me for the hottest news from New York—for items sizzling on the griddle of Fifth Avenue life." Harry is apparently laid up at a remote sanitarium and wants to be kept abreast of events in Society. George's response is to tell him about the New Women, specifically the new debutantes. True to the form of such discussions, George begins by sounding alarmed at their transgressions. Then, as the mark of his own sophistication (over the secluded Harry), he declares them exciting—though he makes his ambivalence sardonically evident.

> The chief change in the world of fashion during this winter and last—has been directly due to the debutantes. They now run everything. Their energy, ability and knowledge of the world are simply appalling. . . . You left here in 1912, and already the social fabric has taken on—solely because of these youngsters—a new pattern, a pattern which you, in your ignorance, might think a devilish loud plaid. . . . But once you become used to them—to their intelligence, ability and energy, and to their remarkable knowledge of life—one finds it hard to leave them and go back to the old 1912 models. . . . No, my boy, this year's lot are as quick as hawks, as strong as lions, and as keen as game-cocks.

But these fabulous monsters inspire real terror when it comes time for George to make his entrance at a dance in an all-women's club:

> Entrance to the Colony is made, for modest men like ourselves, a little less conspicuous and galling by the presence of a gentleman's entrance. This corresponds to what, in our more select liquor saloons, is usually designated the "family" entrance. . . . As I entered that little door my heart stood still. (The clash of sex is a terrible thing!) To be, perhaps, the only man in a feminine club, behind closed doors, with two hundred or more ladies and debutantes—all of them strong and active, and most of them protected by mysterious club minutes and club by-laws—was a thing almost too perturbing to contemplate.

He goes on to compare himself to Dante entering hell and Achilles going among the women, but as it turns out, his fears are all for naught.

> Any one expecting to find fluted frills in the Colony Club, and French musk, and *punto a rilievo* lace, and ice cream soda, and Pomeranians, and a colored

> maid, and a booth for the sale of bon-bons, and all such pleasing secondary sexual characteristics, will be greatly disappointed, for I found it to be nothing more than a very sensible and well-regulated club. It was, indeed, quite like a man's club, save that the dinner was cooked with more art, and served with hanged sight more alacrity. I also found the manicuring of the waiters to be more unexceptionable, and the decorations more vivid and cheering.

Having entertained the range of horrors female power suggests to him—from ravishment to captivity in a garish boudoir—George discovers that the New Women are, in fact, very much like men with certain improving touches, for which he very gallantly gives them due credit. How have they achieved their transformation?

> I asked them what they read and they all assured me that they never read anything but Vanity Fair. . . . It appears that it is solely due to Vanity Fair—and the rage for it here—that the debutantes have ceased being simpering little idiots and have developed into able and intelligent human beings.[96]

The scene of George's adventures among the women is important, for both his anxiety and its resolution are centered on society (in both senses of the word) and society's ability to sustain its structure and the identities of its members in the face of disruption. Here we are assured that the style of presentation and interaction known as sophistication—acquired through studious attention to *Vanity Fair*—makes the requisite new "equality" and proximity between the sexes not only possible but also relatively painless.

It was painless, in the first instance, for the men involved. As the story of George and the debutantes reminds us, the struggle for sophistication was most prominently a male drama enacted over the female terrain of society. Typically, "In Vanity Fair" featured a man trying to make a favorable impression on a New Woman, whose desires were elusive.[97] In this context, the answer to the threat of women's advancement became a continual posing of the question of "what a woman wants"—to which the reassuring response was a style that offered modernness and heterosocial survival, qualities that could be said to call each other into being. When F. P. A. was asked to contribute to "In Vanity Fair," however, he provided an unusual and revealing lapse from the formula, first of all, by addressing the woman reader:

> Listen my dear, to the words of the oracle
> If you would be a much sought after
> fluff,
> Drop all your Latin and volumes historical—
> Read clever stuff!
> Girlie, attend me while now I elucidate
> What I have said in the stanza above.
> (Such pearls of wisdom should quickly
> produce a date
> With him you love.)

Banish your novels, prolix, episodical,
Turn to the pages with sparkle and
flair,
(Meaning America's First Periodical:
Vanity Fair.)[98]

Here the self-directed irony embedded in *Vanity Fair*'s editorials is foregrounded. Of course, a single glossy magazine cannot produce comprehensive knowledge—as George puts it—of "books, drama, music, golf, art, fashion, humor, dogs, sports, opera, motors, dances, sculpture, essays, restaurants, shops—and Heaven only knows what!" But what F. P. A. baldly states here (seemingly in flagrant disregard of tacit editorial policy) is that sophistication has actually an antithetical relation to knowledge. When F. P. A. constructs the consumer of sophistication as a *female* reader, sophistication takes on an unmistakably degraded cast. Yet, what the poem describes is nothing more or less than a conventional opposition between a woman's knowledge and her sexual desirability. No great feminist himself, F. P. A.'s suggestion that sophistication is a discourse of containment is only a by-product of a more urgent—if submerged—revelation: that the aura that attaches to sophistication (and modernity itself) depends on a woman embodying these qualities *naturally,* as intrinsic properties of her New Womanly femininity. The specter of a woman who actually had to read her way to sophistication would be deflationary indeed. By contrast, thinking back to F. P. A.'s foiled Riverside romance, we recall that the male protagonist's ignorance of the modern rules did nothing to tarnish the glamor of modernity itself; as the poem concluded, we left him the "dream[y]" consumer "before his mirror, anointing [himself] with Oil of Citronella."

Put more emphatically, the burden of cultural coherence and heterosexual desire in the new modern society fell to the modern woman—even as she was cause for its disruption. This doubleness is beamed provocatively from the cover illustration for the *Vanity Fair* of May 1915 (Figure 4.1): in the foreground is a young woman, physically boyish but for a coquettish sway to her back, who, powdering her nose, stands dressed in a full tuxedo tapering down to high heels. In the background stand two young men, more traditionally tuxedoed, and looking off in random directions. The relations among the three are ambiguous but nevertheless to be understood as capturing the ambivalent thrill of having a woman be one of the boys. On the one hand, the scene is fully suffused with desirable, blasé sophistication. On the other hand, the incongruity of the woman's dress with her posture, even (on second glance) the inevitability of the feminizing touches to her costume, serve to undercut her claim to masculine privilege. Meanwhile, the abstractedness of the men, their apparent lack of interest in the foregrounded woman—despite her prominence for the reader—suggests boredom or perhaps uneasiness with her similarity to them (which may amount to the same thing).[99] But as finally open-ended as this image is, certain things come through clearly enough. Not only occupying the foreground but also

Figure 4.1 Cover of *Vanity Fair*, May 1915. (Condé Nast Publications)

preparing to face a public of some sort, the woman is the implicit star of the scene. By contrast, the men stand around idly; while they ignore her, we ignore them. Perhaps this picture expresses the fear that, in the dynamic between the desirable feminine image and her desiring audience—anchoring the intersection of publicity, modernity, and sophistication—men may be altogether redundant. And yet, the hope that men may be pulled into the circuit of sophistication (or the foreground of this picture) lies with same new woman who usurps the male tuxedo.

The sophisticated female "personality" held out the promise that, indeed, the New Woman's self-assertion would be titillatingly invested in the new heterosociality. The phenomenon of "Dorothy Parker" participated prominently in this larger tension between disruption and recuperation. The discursive space Parker was able to create for herself depended partly on the gendered character of sophistication and partly on the distinction between mass femininity, as represented by the *Vanity Fair* debutantes, and individual women. While the one embodied female threat, the other concentrated the characteristics of New Womanhood in iconic self-presentation without any suggestion of alliance with the feminine horde—and, indeed, with the strong suggestion of abhorrence of such alliance. For the sophisticates, discursive domination by a sweet-smelling, soft-eyed gamine with an amusingly sharp tongue was a way to embrace the modern world through a relatively painless enactment of female supremacy.

Given this cultural niche, Round Table femininity (by contrast with the masculinity of Benchley, F. P. A., and the others) worked to repress the ethnic overdetermination beneath the modern achievement. In discussing the representation of Jewish femininity, Sander L. Gilman has argued that Sarah Bernhardt "more than anyone else," embodied the destructive stereotype of the *belle juive*, the Jewish femme fatale, in turn-of-the-century Europe.[100] Paradoxically, Bernhardt's association with the Jewish seductress, predatory to non-Jewish men, linked her to her seeming polar opposite, the unsexed feminist. Referring to Bernhardt's performance in Oscar Wilde's scandalous *Salome*, Gilman says:

> Bernhardt as the exemplary Jewish woman is represented as the diseased Salome, the destructive seducer, but also has all of the overtones associated with the "bluestocking." Her image in this text is "mannish" in her demand for control over the world—but this is also Jewish. . . . She represents precisely the anxiety about "modern woman" that is associated, as early as 1849, with the emancipation of women. . . . After the turn of the century, the discourse about the destructive Jewish female as the epitome of the modern woman becomes a commonplace. (205)

Though Gilman is concerned with the European context and Germany in particular, his analysis suggests a further constraint on Parker's embodiment of New Womanhood in anti-Semitic postwar America.

Certain biographers assert that Parker deliberately distanced herself from her Jewish family roots, Leslie Frewin even going so far as to say that "she loathed her Father for being Jewish" (her mother and stepmother were both Gentiles). In this light, her emphatically ladylike persona seems a deliberate contrast to the "noisy, boisterous" Rothschilds.[101] Gilman's Bernhardt also brings Parker into negative alignment with her contemporary and fellow Jewish, New York, woman celebrity, Anzia Yezierska. As captured in the words of syndicated columnist Frank Crane, Yezierska's public image was the polar opposite of Parker's.

> I got a new slant on America from Anzia Yezierska. She walked into my office one day and brought the Old World with her. She had not said three words before I saw farther into the heart of Russia and Poland than I had ever been able to do by reading many heavy books. She was Poland. She was the whole turgid stream of European immigration pouring into our home country. . . . Here was an East Side Jewess that had struggled and suffered in the desperate battle for life amid the swarms of New York. . . . From a sweatshop worker to a famous writer! All because she dipped her pen into her heart.[102]

Yezierska encouraged the public perception of herself as "the sweatshop Cinderella" but also as a radically unassimilable Jew. The protagonists she identified herself with were too passionate and impulsive—too "Jewish"—to ever be happy with the polite and sanitized New World, and especially the hyperrational and unfeeling New World man. But however undone he was by Jewish passion, this man always recognized what we as readers were also to see: that the "Jewess" brings vitality to a dried-up white America and, through the raw force of her desire, authenticity to the American ideal of success. (We will see another version of this racial/national discourse associated with the "New Negro" and the Harlem Renaissance.)

But that Yezierska could call her most straightforwardly autobiographical work *Salome of the Tenements* underscores the degree to which, even for her, Jewish femininity retained associations of perversion, destructiveness, and ambition. For the detached and sardonic Parker, the greater sin of *Salome* may well have been its insistent melodrama, a genre anathema to the Round Table moderns. But if style put them worlds apart, Parker and Yezierska could hardly have avoided rubbing actual elbows. Yezierska's national visibility through her fiction and films coincided with the local visibility of a midtown address and a social circle that included the Algonquin Hotel and even certain members of the Round Table. Wit itself did much of the necessary work of insulating Parker from association with Yezierska; she, after all, was the New Womanly sophisticate, figure of reconciliation between the sexes, of reassurance for the modern world. Perhaps silence did the rest. Remarkably, in her writing Parker seems never to have mentioned Yezierska or her work. While early-twentieth-century anti-Semitism focused on men to an overwhelming degree,[103] cultural anxiety about female power made the ethnic association far more problematic for Parker than for her male colleagues, who might even be said to have capitalized on it.[104] As we shall see in chapter 5, however, Parker's relationship to ethnicity did inscribe itself upon her literary modernism in significant, if attenuated ways.

A different sort of illumination comes of comparing Parker's career with that of another popular modernist New Woman, Anita Loos of Hollywood. Both were writers and humorists (Loos worked primarily on movie scripts but also wrote satirical novels), yet contemporaneous accounts of them always stress their appearance. Given their intellectual powers, they had (and, of course, cultivated) very reassuring—and remarkably similar—bodies: "tiny," "dark," "fragile," "feminine," and especially in Loos's case, "childlike." Because of her Hollywood context, Loos was even photographically featured in film tabloids on occasion, "getting," as she put it, "the soap job usually reserved for actresses." This heightened objectification may also have been linked to her more pronounced intellectualism; in fact, she considered the Round Tablers (with the notable exception of Parker) intellectually inferior to her true midtown idol, H. L. Mencken. When D. W. Griffith sent Loos to New York on a crucial publicity tour for *Intolerance*, he told her, "those 'learned' remarks of yours, coming from the mouth of a flapper, ought to amaze the gentlemen of the New York press."[105] Far from worrying over the potentially threatening nature of her intellect, Griffith clearly put his faith in the pleasure "the gentlemen" would derive from the juxtaposition of learned remarks and precocious/promiscuous femininity. Integral to this pleasure was the context in which it would have occurred: a lone woman, redolent with heady modernness, transgressing traditional femininity for the benefit of an all-male audience who had ultimate control over her public image even as they were enthralled to her charm.

The point is not to reduce Parker or Loos to the innocuous and thoroughly appropriated figures that patriarchal power brokers like Crowninshield and Griffith would have had them be, but rather to try to account for their enormous success and popularity. The aura of modernness was at a cultural premium, and those who would inhabit it had to come to terms with its New Woman. The Parker persona was desirable to the extent that it was modern and reassuring to the extent that it left certain basic femininities intact. Parker's rhetorical modernness lay in her daring sexuality (for which she paid by having her heart routinely broken) and in her sophisticated tone (which was feminine bitchiness revealed). And yet she successfully projected beauty and style, a near-total preoccupation with love and men, and a ladylike suppression of hostility (expressed only "in confidence" to her audience). The success with which Parker maintained this tension made her an extremely appealing figure to a public ambivalent about women's sexual freedom and the modernity it stood for. For Parker herself, the public context in which she was to maintain the tension of old and New supplied its own ambivalences. Providing an alternative to conventional heterosexuality, it yet left her inescapably embodied as a woman. But Parker's writing engaged the totality of her situation, and the literary strategies explored in the following chapter derive as much from her constraints as from her freedoms. Her literary response to modern publicity was to exploit it for its utopian possibilities, to treat it as the enabling matrix that it arguably was.

FIVE

"Oh, do sit down, I've got so much to tell you!"

Dorothy Parker and Her Intimate Public

If you and I were one, my dear,
A model life we'd lead.
We'd travel on, from year to year,
At no increase of speed.
Ah, clear to me the vision of
The things that we should do!
And so I think it best, my love,
To string along as two.

Dorothy Parker, "Day-Dreams," in *Enough Rope*

Oh, lead me to a quiet cell
  Where never footfall rankles,
And bar the window passing well,
  And gyve my wrists and ankles.

Oh, wrap my eyes with linen fair,
  With hempen cord go bind me,
And, of your mercy, leave me there,
  Nor tell them where to find me.

Oh, lock the portal as you go,
  And see its bolts be double . . .
Come back in half an hour or so,
  And I will be in trouble.

Dorothy Parker "Portrait of the Artist,"
in *Enough Rope*

Through what conjunction of subcultural identity, publicity, love discourse, and poetic conventions did Dorothy Parker generate the singularly popular and critically acclaimed Parker verse? What cultural and imaginative negotiations allowed her to make love modern and herself a modern lover? Parker's career in the twenties, continuous with that of the Algonquin Round Table, was significantly structured and even constituted by publicity. The genre of poetry, meanwhile, had a complex relation to modernist culture. To begin with, it was ubiquitous in the new newspaper "columns," the "little magazines" of the Village and Harlem, and mass circulation journals of all kinds, from the *Ladies' Home Journal* to *Vanity Fair*. Thus ephemeral and public, "verse" carried the meaning of cultural currency and circulation, at the same time that, as "literature," it suggested the stability of cultural tradition. In its structure, the essence of lyric (at least since the Romantics) arguably lay in its atemporality, its ability to clear and fix dis-

Photograph on preceding page: New York Bathers, 1919. (Bettman Archive)

crete spaces apart from the historical and discursive flow. "All lyrics," argues Sharon Cameron in her fine work on *Lyric Time*, "oppose speech to the action from which it exempts itself, [and] oppose voice as it rise[s] momentarily from the enthusiasms of temporal advance to the flow of time that ultimately rushes over and drowns it."[1] Lyric poems, Cameron says, "slow temporal advance to the difficult still point of meaning" (25).

This lyric potential could be channeled to various ends, as the present work attempts to demonstrate (compare this chapter especially with chapter 8). Among Parker's multiple uses for lyric was the disruption of the narrative about herself that would otherwise have sprung up in the wake of her celebrity (her lyrics' triumph over the "enslavement to temporal narrative"[2]). While her public image was obviously critical to her career, its status as specifically modern depended on staving off the entanglements of socially situated identity. Again, the comparison to Yezierska is instructive: the image we know Yezierska to have cultivated through her fictional and autobiographical writings—that of the "sweatshop Cinderella"—would have been meaningless outside the context of narrative's teleological trajectory. Likewise, her highly prominent ethnicity—as Frank Crane put it, Yezierska "*was* Poland" by virtue of the fact that "she had hungered and strived and endured" to make the journey "from a sweatshop worker to a famous writer." This interdependence of ethnic identity and narrative holds equally for the nonliterary example of Fanny Brice; the other funny woman of New York in the twenties,[3] this vaudeville star generated her (ambivalently) Jewish identity through frequent tellings and revisions of her life story. While making a career of "Yiddish numbers" (featuring enactments of other ethnic stereotypes done up in a Yiddish accent, such as "Oi, oi, oi, oi, I'm a terrible squaw!"), she constructed a public identity around the prototypical "success story" she shared with a host of other Jewish vaudeville performers. This narrative took her from the Lower East Side to the Great White Way, and though she waffled on the degree to which her Jewishness was "natural" (sometimes claiming perfect racial identification, other times hyping her need for periodic ghetto research to get the accent right), Jewish she was in the public imagination.[4]

Thus identified with a premodern ethnicity, Yezierska and Brice found their "progress in America"—as *women*—tied to what inevitably became their "love careers." Whatever expressions of love they fed or let slip to the public immediately became fuel for the narrative machinery producing them as "Jewish women."[5] Yezierska's female protagonists quite explicitly sought the promise of America through alliance with "American" (i.e., WASP) men who epitomized the project of enlightenment through education.[6] This dynamic in her fictional writings is matched so closely by that of her autobiographical statements that they are almost indistinguishable. But whether through fiction or nonfiction, the story Yezierska tells never reaches resolution. The heroine/Yezierska is always searching for American happiness—and, therefore, always irreducibly Jewish. To find happiness—to end the story—would be to give up the identity.[7]

Fannie Brice's long-standing relationship with gangster Nick Arnstein was highly publicized and woven tightly into the mesh of Brice's American life story, beginning with their first meeting: "I was introduced to a man who stood then and forever after for everything that had been left out of my life—manners, good breeding, education and an extraordinary gift for dreaming."[8] The many troubles of the Brice-Arnstein marriage were widely publicized (*Vanity Fair* even honored Fanny Brice in its 1925 Hall of Fame for making Arnstein's criminal trial "the most diverting one on record"). When in 1921 Brice added "My Man," an uncharacteristic ballad of feminine masochism, to her repertoire, audiences ate it up as public sentimental revelation—and Brice made it her signature number thereafter.[9] When the couple finally divorced in 1927, Brice claimed publicly that the nose job she had gotten four years earlier (with full photographic coverage in the dailies) had generated "an inferiority complex" in her husband, causing him to be unfaithful.[10] Palpable evidence for the interdependence of romantic destiny and ethnicity, certainly—but, equally, testimony to the contradiction at the heart of the immigrant success story itself, in which, in the words of Waldo Frank, "Hebrew" is "the seed" and "American the fruit."[11]

At the time, Brice presented her surgery quite explicitly as an intervention in the generic possibilities of her stage performance. She wanted to move from comedy (where a "Jewish" nose forecast the laughs to come) to serious drama (where the ethnic body could only confuse the high seriousness of feminine beauty).[12] As it turned out, Brice's bid for a "straight" career was short-lived, her promotional campaign notwithstanding, and Benchley himself announced her return "home" to comedy in his *Life* column.[13] Meanwhile, Parker, having kept her own career innocent of even a whiff of the Old World, could safely pronounce judgment from the sidelines: Fanny Brice, she declared, had "cut off her nose to spite her race."[14] But even so snugly wrapped in sardonic cool, Parker was not without her own relation to the racial dimension of romance.[15] The urbane intellectual playwright Elmer Rice (né Reizenstein) was apparently "too Jewish" for the romantic involvement he sought with her,[16] while the investment banker Edwin Pond Parker III, "a handsome Gentile"[17] with "a nice clean name," was good enough to marry.[18] Round Table modernity—and the lyric in particular—kept the implications of such contradictions at bay (or seemed to). Within the frictionless space of lyric poetry, Parker could explore love for its modern, self-fashioning potentials. Safe from the autobiographical constraints of narrative, she could fulfill her personal charge as an icon of manifest modernity and New Womanhood.

Of course, the atemporal freedom of lyric was at least partly a fiction. Parker was a great admirer of Edna Millay (newly famous at the start of Parker's career), of whom she once remarked, "Millay did a great deal of harm with her double-burning candles" (a reference to "First Fig"), making "poetry seem so easy that we could all do it but, of course, we couldn't."[19] We might as well take this as a judgment on the larger project of public New Womanhood, for Parker was, indeed, to become a poet of equal stature, with equal cultural responsibility for the serious business of feminine transgression and heterosexual reconciliation—though in a sardonic mode which turned Millay's lyricism on its ear. Parker herself put it more humbly: "I was following in the exquisite footsteps of Miss Edna St. Vincent Millay, unhappily in my own horrible sneakers."[20] Embedded within Round Table discourse, such an identification might also have resonated with the midtown mockery of Village idealism, suggesting the possibility of a more pointed edge to Parker's emulation. But however variegated this identification, Parker's choice of a professional path occurred with full benefit of Millay's warning about public life, that "a person who publishes a book willfully appears before the populace with his pants down [*sic*]"; she had, moreover, the lesson of Millay's literary imitativeness to signal the degree of determining force exerted by the poetic tradition.[21] For Parker, a woman writer attempting to project and sustain a highly public and appropriately sophisticated identity, lyric love poetry—and, more generally, the traditional literary role of woman lover—had its own inherent problems, founded as it was on feminine self-effacement. While Millay drew her New Womanly strategies out of the literary tradition, Parker mined the possibilities of her public context. Through figurations and rhetorical modes that incorporated the public into her poetics, Parker provided her speakers the possibility of self-definition outside the heterosexual dyad. As we shall see, to the extent that this was a deliberate gesture toward public identity and speech, it was an identity defined not as sexual, but civic.[22]

WITHIN THE LEGACY OF ROMANTICISM, love has conventionally been premised on the uniqueness of the lover for the Other, and the context for mutual recognition of this uniqueness has been the dyadic intersubjective relationship.[23] Roland Barthes's *A Lover's Discourse* captures the critical interdependence of love and individual identity for the amorous modern subject, expressed here in the text's characteristically cumulative, collage style.

> "Ah, whatever I know, anyone may know—[but] I alone have my *heart*."
>
> I divine that the true site of originality and strength is neither the other nor myself, but our relation itself.
>
> Once, speaking to me of ourselves, the other said: "a relation of quality"; this phrase was repugnant to me: it came suddenly from outside, flattening the specialty of the rapport by a conformist formula.
>
> The other whom I love and who fascinates me is *atopos*. I cannot classify the other, for the other is, precisely, Unique, the singular Image which has miraculously come to correspond to the specialty of my desire. The other is the figure of my truth and cannot be imprisoned in any stereotype (which is the truth of others).[24]

Within the ideology Barthes describes, lovers are not answerable to common moral or aesthetic standards—"the world and I are not interested in the same thing'' (52)—but perceive themselves as inhabiting an intersubjective space with its own private ethos.[25] The romantic relationship, then, is seen as irreducible to objective cultural criteria of worth and compatibility. Most important, it is inaccessible to outsiders.

But within such a hermetic universe, differential positions become crucially important. Critic Jan Montefiore has called the traditional literary expression of heterosexual romance the ''I-Thou dyad.'' Focusing on the love sonnet in particular, Montefiore argues for the historically entrenched and psychoanalytically overdetermined nature of the gender polarity these poems employ.

> The love poem as it appears in the Western tradition of poetry represented by Petrarch and Sidney is characteristically spoken by a male poet celebrating the beauty and virtue of an unattainable woman who is at once the object of his desire, the cause of his poetry and the mirror which defines his identity. . . . Problems arise [for the woman poet] from the complex processes of self-definition at work in the classic love poems. In the great tradition of Petrarch and Shakespeare, the lover-poet is principally concerned with defining his own self through his desire either for the image of his beloved or for his own image mediated through her response to him.[26]

The male speaker, then, is the subjective ''I'' to the female addressee's objectified ''Thou,'' a dyad in which the woman is reduced to a function of her lover's narcissism. John Brenkman identifies this one-sided dynamic as a form of ''cultural domination,'' an aesthetic of love that ''refus[es] the play of the desire of the other in all its negativity and conflict''[27]—refuses, that is, the productive exchange that occurs when both lovers are accorded full status as subjects. Montefiore notes, moreover, ''the obvious difficulty of speaking in a form which defines one as muse, not maker.''

Feminist criticism has identified a wealth of women's strategic responses to the gendered character of the traditional canon, from literary cross-dressing to subversion of the genres themselves. At the broadest level, Parker undercut her own ascension to muse or loved object through her irony, a stance built into her subcultural imperative to perform as a humorist. More important, in sacrificing the sober intensity of romantic love to humor, she broke up the loving dyad with the implied intervention of her audience, for whom the jokes were staged. Thus triangulated, the lovers lose the psychodynamic logic supporting their lopsided interrelation.[28] Humor about love—not the dramatic irony attending the spectacle of bunglers but the acerbic wit of a sophisticated lover-narrator—has the power to rupture the charmed circle of intersubjectivity by constructing its audience as a complicitous third party to the ridicule of one lover (the man) by the other (the woman).

Parker also refused the passivity and objectification that the love tradition would assign her at the thematic level of her work, where her historical-discursive manipulations were most evident and particularized. Her explicit response to the romantic love tradition often went beyond protest of her designated position as female within the dyad to rejection of the very form of hermetic intersubjectivity itself. The profoundly jaundiced notion of love structuring Modern Love discourse gave Parker license to displace the heterosexual relationship as the necessary center of her poems and, instead, make the poems' public the site of her primary psychological investment.[29]

Parker's self-declared lesser-little-sister relation to Millay translated quite directly into a poetry of the antilyric, which evoked key lyric conventions only to invert them. Intended for public consumption, lyric poetry nevertheless issues from an intensely private voice traditionally understood as "not heard but overheard."[30] Parker's most significant manipulation of the lyric was to foreground the listening audience that was usually suppressed. Her very fame carried with it the spectral presence of the public which constituted her as a "personality," while her writing actively transformed the solitary musings of a speaker addressing only herself or the figure of her lover into essentially public space and speech.

In "Plea," humor constitutes the female speaker's first level of resistance to her lover's attempt to impose upon her a tyranny of privacy.

> Secrets, you said, would hold us two apart;
> You'd have me know of you your least transgression
> And so the intimate places of your heart,
> Kneeling, you bared to me, as in confession.
> Softly, you told of loves that went before,—
> Of clinging arms, of kisses gladly given;
> Luxuriously clean of heart once more,
> You rose up, then, and stood before me, shriven.

In this first stanza, the speaker mockingly renders her lover's self-indulgence in the terms of his own self-justification, terms the contemporaneous audience must recognize as a species of "enlightened" Free Love: the couple are to have no "secrets" to keep them "apart," anything that would sustain their separateness being self-evidently a bad thing. But as the poem so clearly demonstrates, this relation is not one of equality, and modern mutual honesty appears to be neither actively mutual nor, strictly speaking, honest. Rather, we see the male lover, under the guise of Free Love intimacy, attempt to reduce the woman to a function of his own psychic economy, an ego ideal to whom he can confess himself a sexual adventurer and thus emerge "luxuriously clean of heart."

Parker's speaker is conscious of her lover's instrumental use of her but goes beyond a mocking tone and the joke she has with her audience at his expense.

> When this, my day of happiness, is through,
> And love, that bloomed so fair, turns brown and brittle,
> There is a thing that I shall ask of you—
> I, who have given so much, and asked so little.

Some day, when there's another in my stead;
Again you'll feel the need of absolution,
And you will go to her, and bow your head,
And offer her your past, as contribution.

When with your list of loves you overcome her,
For Heaven's sake, keep this one from her![31]

The Round Table ethos mitigated against anything so humorless as direct protest of gender oppression, but note how this requisite aloofness dovetails with Parker's own desideratum for the love relationship. Underlying the ironic depiction of gross inequality in "Plea" is an almost palpable disgust with the sort of relationship this modern love affair implies, even in its ideal (that is, genuinely mutual) form. It is not merely the self-serving use to which it is put in this instance but the very idea of "the intimate places of [the lover's] heart" that is held at a critical distance; the speaker's distaste is clearly and extensively drawn around the idea of intimacy as such.

Read in terms of the relationship's gender inequality, the speaker's relative passivity may be seen as a function of her femininity and the exclusion of her own "contribution" as anything more than confessor. But her silence may also be deliberate reticence: beyond her marginalization within the relationship as defined and controlled by her lover, the language of the poem suggests that, in fact, she imposes her own alternative framework on their interactions. Stanza one is devoted exclusively to the male lover's construction of love. The first word, *Secrets*, deliberately set off by a comma, signals the lover's self-infatuated exhibition to come. Lines like "Kneeling, you bared to me, as in confession," and "Luxuriously clean of heart once more" join images of sensuality and religious asceticism in a way that renders both faintly obscene. Ironically, this sense carries over to the programmatically unashamed Free Love paganism underwriting the lover's revelations of "clinging arms" and "kisses gladly given." The speaker's repugnance is thus plainly evident from the poem's beginning; when in stanza two she goes on to speak from within her own, more dignified model of love, it stands as a reproof to the version that preceded it.

Leaving the lover to stand "before [her], shriven," she establishes a loving arena according to her own terms before making the request with which the poem culminates. In defiance of her lover's attempts to contain her within his narcissism, the female speaker chooses to view their relationship in the discreet and lyrical terms of flower imagery ("love, that bloomed so fair"), oppositional in its invocation of emphatically traditional rather than modern love paradigms. Here it becomes apparent that the struggle to set the terms of love in this poem goes beyond the opposition of romantic intersubjectivity and its absence in Modern Love. The model the speaker offers combines the cool cynicism of Modern Love with the traditional lyricism of love poetry. The essence of this hybrid mode is *decorum*, continuous with the drawing room dimension of Round Table identity. As we have seen, a mannered and proprietary aesthetic functioned for the group as a whole to establish their modernist "aristocratic" detachment. But for Parker in particular, decorum provided the foundation for an intrinsically social alternative to private love.

Stanza two of "Plea" highlights the stark difference of the speaker's assumptions about the status of this affair in her life. The lover uses the ostensible telos of unbounded and unending mutuality to justify his lurid self-revelations, a pretext mocked by the very nature of the confessions themselves. The female speaker, by contrast, augments the dignified distance she puts between herself and him by assuming, with lyrical calm, the unlamented finitude of their affair. She makes no pretense of being absorbed with him in particular but explicitly derives her pleasure from the experience of love itself. Their affair at its height is *her* "day of happiness," and the love that blooms, then wilts, as the metaphor suggests, has its own objective existence and its own immanent course to run independently of either of them. The assertion that she has "given so much, and asked so little" apparently expresses (ironic) feminine self-effacement but more pointedly functions to emphasize—even to flaunt—her restraint and self-sufficiency. Her protest to him to, "For Heaven's sake," keep their affair secret from his next lover, is ostensibly a plea for her own future privacy, but the force behind the expletive, the force that has been building steadily throughout the previous stanzas, derives from her disgust with the absence of privacy in their present interactions. One hears in this woman's voice the distinctly preromantic echo of Congreve's Millamant, who demanded of her husband-to-be that they "be very strange [reserved] and well bred: let us be as strange as if we had been married a great while," she says, "and as well bred as if we were not married at all."[32]

Intersubjective love, what one Parker poem refers to as the "mist of a mutual dream," places its practitioners in an unbounded relation to each other while sequestering them away from the emotional reach of the ordinary world. But Parker's writing works actively toward a more viable sexual-literary praxis through her characteristic bitterness and the theme of an endless series of doomed relationships. Thus surrounded by the apparatus of love and men, the Parker persona remains legitimately within the sphere of "women's concerns," and she addresses her audience unquestionably as a woman. But by virtue of her amorous "failures," she is free from the all-consuming rapture that would bar her access to the world (though granting her the "success" of submersion in a single adored man). With love established as more or less a dead end, Parker's poems channel their energy toward the more interesting task of elaborating a life in public.

The opposition of isolation in romance versus community in the world structures the poem titled, significantly, "Now at Liberty."

Little white love, your way you've taken;
    Now I am left alone, alone.
Little white love, my heart's forsaken.
    (Whom shall I get by telephone?)

Well do I know there's no returning;
  Once you go out, it's done, it's done.
All of my days are gray with yearning.
  (Nevertheless, a girl needs fun.)

Little white love, perplexed and weary,
  Sadly your banner fluttered down.
Sullen the days, and dreary, dreary.
  (Which of the boys is still in town?)
Radiant and sure, you came a-flying;
  Puzzled, you left on lagging feet.
Slow in my breast, my heart is dying.
  (Nevertheless, a girl must eat.)

Little white love, I hailed you gladly;
  Now I must wave you out of sight.
Ah, but you used me badly, badly.
  (Who'd like to take me out to-night?)
All of the blundering words I've spoken,
  Little white love, forgive, forgive.
Once you went out, my heart fell, broken.
  (Nevertheless, a girl must live.)[33]

In her characteristic use of a double voice, one ostensibly straightforward, the other an aside to the audience, Parker opposes affected lyricism to urbane sophistication. The first is the realm of love, and its most striking features are its relative atemporality and the absence of an actual lover. Love, it seems, is not an event or even a relation with another human being, but a solitary state of being. It is, moreover, the realm of poetry, specifically, women's love poetry.

Of course, the asides are no less in the poem and even take their rhymes from the lyric lines, underscoring their status as an alternate register of the same voice. But if the love lines attend to the state of the speaker's womanly soul, the urbane lines are focused on "tonight" 's very material "fun." The love poem (and, by implication, the love) is oppressive and the speaker is palpably relieved to be out of it, but there is a sense in which it is the necessary precursor to "liberty." For the Parker persona generally, license to flout the normative structure of female sentiment comes from the well-demonstrated way in which the world of romance has failed her. Justification for her rebelliousness comes first of all from the fact that she is a wronged woman. But she seeks more from her audience than tolerance; she wants them to claim her as their own, just as she, implicitly, claims them. The public figuration that begins as the enabling condition for Parker's lyric heterosexuality quickly becomes a charged and overdetermined affective site in its own right.

Beyond the abstractly democratic sense of (consumer) identification with her middle-brow reader that we saw evident in "The Far-Sighted Muse" (chapter 4), Parker shares in what Casey Nelson Blake has identified as a pervasive modernist attraction toward communitarian values. In his study of the influential cultural critics known as the "Young Americans"—Randolph Bourne, Van Wyck Brooks, Waldo Frank, and Lewis Mumford—Blake finds the formative influence of Deweyan pragmatism and republicanism more generally in their "insist[ence] that the search for self-fulfillment was a search for communities that engaged the self in the language and civic association of a democratic culture."[34] This communitarian ethos, disseminated through New York City journals like *Seven Arts*, contributed powerfully to the broader intellectual milieu in which popular modernism was nested. And indeed, pragmatist communitarianism had much to offer a public woman love poet seeking a praxis on her own terms: a shift from metaphysical to "consensual reasoning" and "collective inquiry" for the basis of moral truth (about love, for example) (88), as well as the achievement of self through cultural engagement, including equal access to intellectual and artistic resources (despite the femininity that rendered one otherwise "uncivil") (87). Especially significant were the specific advances to Pragmatism promulgated by these contemporaries of Parker: critical of Dewey's Anglo-Saxon elitism, they saw "ethnic communities [as] anticipat[ing] a new center to American culture, one in which traditional bonds of shared experience reinforced modern ones of rational inquiry" (117). As Blake summarizes it, "here was a community that Americans could *rationally shape and also love,* a form of experience that engaged their capacities as moderns while fulfilling the functions of tradition" (118; my italics). Significantly, this combination is bound up with *cosmopolitanism* (117), a sensibility encompassing the aesthetic of sophistication. The crucial sense of the modern ideal as underwritten by ethnic social dynamics maps suggestively onto the public imagined by Parker's poems, which invoke middle-brow modernity even as they gesture toward the more concrete yet spectral public of ethnic/Jewish New York, somewhere beneath Fourteenth Street but out of sight of midtown.[35] As an imagined Other projected from her writing, this palimpsestic public, a modern-ethnic convergence, gives Parker back a self that is easily larger than "woman lover."

The dynamics of "Rainy Night" may stand as an example. Ostensibly about love, "Rainy Night" conveys the sense of a young adventurer soliciting the indulgence of her protectors. "Rainy Night" seems at first to reverse the valuations of "Now at Liberty": of the two opposing realms the poem evokes, it is the mythic, "poetic" one that is favored. The speaker of "Rainy Night" is poised between the dead and the living.

Ghosts of all my lovely sins,
    Who attend too well my pillow,
Gay the wanton rain begins;
    Hide the limp and tearful willow,

Turn aside your eyes and ears,
    Trail away your robes of sorrow.

You shall have my further years,—
 You shall walk with me to-morrow.

I am sister to the rain;
 Fey and sudden and unholy,
Petulant at the windowpane,
 Quickly lost, remembered slowly.

I have lived with shades, a shade;
 I am hung with graveyard flowers.
Let me be to-night arrayed
 In the silver of the showers.

Every fragile thing shall rust;
 When another April passes
I may be a furry dust,
 Sifting through the brittle grasses.

All sweet sins shall be forgot
 Who will live to tell their siring?
Hear me now, nor let me rot
 Wistful still, and still aspiring.

Ghosts of dear temptations, heed;
 I am frail, be you forgiving.
See you not that I have need
 To be living with the living?

Sail, to-night, the Styx's breast;
 Glide among the dim processions
Of the exquisite unblest
 Spirits of my shared transgressions.

Roam with young Persephone,
 Plucking poppies for your slumber . . .
With the morrow, there shall be
 One more wraith among your number.[36]

In a general way, the same opposition that held for "Now at Liberty" applies here: the realm of myth and classical allusion (presumably the proper realm for the woman poet) and the world of "fun," specifically, the sexual freedom of the New Woman. But here in "Rainy Night," the speaker's consistent use of lyrical poetic diction greatly blurs the opposition, burying the New Woman so starkly present in "Now at Liberty" behind a properly romantic (even gothic) poetess until the final lines, when her true worldly intentions and character are revealed to humorous effect. Against the force of her New Womanly exploits, the speaker's lyrical expression demonstrates to her well-intentioned "ghosts" her solidarity with them, as well as her worthiness of their protective concern.

Yet however instrumental her lyricism appears to be, the world of the ghosts and poetry actually constitute the site of the speaker's greatest rhetorical investment. Though we infer, reading backward from the last lines, that the speaker's immediate plan is to meet a lover, the only image she counterposes to the ghostly world she must first escape is that of the rain; like the realm of love in "Liberty," this one is described as effectively solitary. And again, typically, what remains from past exploits is her experience of her "lovely sins" rather than the memory of any significant Other.

In fact, the loveliness of her sins, once they have been immortalized as such, presents a significant contrast to the crude materiality of the actual life of the body insofar as it even appears in the poem. Given the speaker's telos, one might expect her to oppose sensuality to etherealized love, yet she figures death rather than sex and employs jarringly unaesthetic language to do so. Much of the effect derives from her positioning of soothingly poetic words just before the shockingly ugly ones: as a "fragile thing," her body shall "rust" (1.17); "When another April passes / [she] may be a furry dust, / Sifting through the brittle grasses" (1.18–20); and finally, the starkest contrast, "nor let me rot," embedded in a sibilant stanza of "sweet sins," "siring," "Wistful still, and still aspiring" (1.21–24). This explicitly gruesome treatment of death is typical for Parker. One of its functions is to permit her to exclude sex from her treatment of love and thereby maintain the essential effect of decorum and measured distance, at the same time that the details of rot and decay allow her to be more shockingly physical than she would be permitted, were she, in fact, describing sex. For the point is not to be daring and titillating; it is to deflate the romance of heterosexuality.

Bodily experience—sex or its degraded form, death—is compared in "Rainy Night" to the community of ghosts and poetry and found to be horrifying. As the speaker suggests, the "ghosts of all [her] lovely sins" are the narrativizations of her experience. As a collective figure, they embody both the telling and the audience who realize the telling, making it a heard and remembered thing. Parker's literary praxis thus participates in the "native (New York) modernist" ideal of the "beloved community," which "could only be realized . . . in a society that returned aesthetic experience to the center of everyday life" (3). Parker's community is—almost by definition—quintessentially modern, but a sense of perceived public vulnerability is evident in the way her poems supplement the elective membership in modern "America" with the security of heredity rights to what is, in fact, an *accomplished* "small-scale communit[y,] knit together by shared cultural traditions, mutual aid, and a sense of the common good" (3). In "Rainy Night," then, the process of aesthetic work embedded within the text brings the woman lover out of solitude and effacement and into community and power, *as a loved charge of the culture.* Poetry *is* community and power, whereas a love affair is, in the best of circumstances, only a love affair.

The principal difference between "Now at Liberty" and "Rainy Night" is that the poems appear to value opposite worlds. In fact, both speakers actively seek community, wherever it may be. In "Liberty," the community is split between the modern life of the New Woman thematized within the poem and the poem's audience, whom the speaker cajoles with apologies ("Nevertheless, a girl must eat") and with appeals to their common modernness in rejecting the stifling world of the "poetic" woman. The audience of "Rainy Night" is figured within the poem itself as the ghosts who tend to the speaker and her immortality, realizing her personal experience into social space. But the plea she levels at them is of the same order as that of her sister in "Liberty": she wants consent and approval for her sexual freedom as a New Woman.

This sense of imperative raises the suggestion of ambivalence on the part of the speaker in relation to her audience, however much she may value them. In "Rainy Night," the ghosts are "dear" and "sweet" but they also "attend too well [her] pillow." They must be persuaded to "turn aside [their] ears and eyes" in order that the speaker may fulfill her "need" to spend time with her own kind, whatever the risks. They are, in short, like cultural elders, and the speaker, like the modern American child over whom they keep a solicitous watch. In fact, Parker's claim to the dignity of a heroine striking out before a communal audience of supporters often collapses into the more confining family drama of a child reined in by her parents. Relational models, it would seem, present a slippery mix of possibilities. Modern Love, for instance, may not worship the male or marriage, but neither does it offer much in the way of positive alternatives to the romantic love it critiques. Its vision of heterosexual relations is static and circular; a writer who would make interventions in this vision—even (or especially) the intervention of speaking through a female persona that is fluid and independent—must do so with reference to alternative genres of love as well as literature. In this light, romantic love, whatever its problems, supplies the dignity of an elevated context for reception of the poetic work and an ideal of love; ironically, it also establishes an interiority for the woman speaker. That Parker works assiduously to undercut these characteristics does not detract from their importance as a framework to her poems. Out of the matrix of these models, Parker finally turns outward to her audience, constituting herself in relation to an Other with whom she may be a fellow subject of a common culture. While this dynamic turns out to have a distinctly infantilizing potential, it holds out the hope of a new ground for female identity—and a place in the interesting world.

At another level, the sense of confidence and familiarity with which Parker approaches her audience may be explained by her experience of public life in the Round Table. New York writers in general may have had a justifiable (if tautological) sense of identification with the New York culture of which they were the primary producers and promoters. The cultural power of New York (particularly in the eyes of New Yorkers) and the concomitant presumption of an identifiable New York mind-set may well have contributed to Parker's sense that when she spoke publicly she was largely received with comprehension and sympathy.[37] Some popular modernist writers invoked an opposition between New York and provincial culture, either explicitly or through a self-consciously madcap or erudite style (with the sense that they were eluding their audience). Parker was among those who consistently assumed the worthiness of even those readers beyond the borders of Manhattan. This assumption was not simply generosity on her part but an index of the centrality of her imagined audience to her work, the adequacy of whom was essential for the investment she made in them. The Parker public could present an alternative to the heterosexual dynamic of domination and submission only if it was comprised of her equals.[38]

In imagining this public for herself, Parker drew on various imaginary relations, as we have seen, but whatever its shifting dimensions, it proceeded from an ideal of cultural consensus: a higher court of cultural authority to which a woman love poet could appeal the injustice of her lot as lover. The poem "Folk Tune" explicitly asserts the worth of consensual culture over a privatized ethos, and in those terms. Typically for Parker's work, it is structured as a single extended setup for a final punchline. For two stanzas, the speaker lays out objective criteria by which her addressee must be judged unworthy as a lover. We are to recognize this as a rational argument with no ultimate force in what we know to be a matter of the heart; consequently, we are fully prepared for a conclusion based on what is ostensibly the radically different ground of feelings.

Other lads, their ways are daring:
    Other lads, they're not afraid;
Other lads, they show they're caring;
    Other lads—they know a maid.
Wiser Jock than ever you were,
    Will's with gayer spirit blest,
Robin's kindlier and truer,—
    Why should I love you the best?

Other lads, their eyes are bolder.
    Young they are, and strong and slim,
Ned is straight and broad of shoulder,
    Donald has a way with him.
David stands a head above you,
    Dick's as brave as Lancelot,—
Why, ah why, then, should I love you?
    Naturally, I do not.[39]

The movement of this poem—the force that leads us to expect a conclusion that flies in the face of all reason—depends on the conventional assumption that object choice in love is inexplicable or, at least, highly idiosyncratic. This expectation is, of course, humorously subverted, and it is easy enough to see the reversal in "Naturally, I do not" as a surprise about the character of the speaker. She turns out to be not a "genuine" lover at all but a cold-hearted cynic.

The alternative reading I would propose takes the concluding line and—rather than deflecting its import onto a revelation about the speaker—turns it back on her utterance to overturn the model of love it invokes. Love choice, the poem suggests, *does* in fact proceed out of a kind of rational deliberation; more accurately, it follows from culturally agreed-upon standards. Here is where the title, "Folk Tune," reveals its aptness to the poem beyond a certain quaintness of diction. If we take the final line to be continuous with what precedes it (rather than an ironic reversal), the poem presents a logic for love based on common consensual wisdom. Love alliance is forged according to the standards and blessings of the "folk," not as a private expression of individual taste. In addressing herself to the potential lover—seemingly appealing to what would be their shared arena of private values—the speaker's ultimate rejection of him on grounds of his objectively verifiable shortcomings must be seen as the rejection of the intersubjective ethos itself. The distinction between a consensual culture of "folk" and an impersonal society within which couples take private refuge suggests the speaker's positive motivation for rejecting her would-be lover. More than just the expression of hardened modern femininity, the poem's eschewal of the privatized world of this love relationship gains the speaker access to a broader community of cultural common ground as well as affective investment.

Still a lover, yet allied with this broader community, the Parker persona could deploy its terms within the romantic context to her own advantage, even circumventing her own gendered fate. A stark example is "Finis."

Now it's over, and now it's done;
    Why does everything look the same?
Just as bright, the unheeding sun,—
    Can't it see that the parting came?
People hurry and work and swear,
    Laugh and grumble and die and wed,
Ponder what they will eat and wear,—
    Don't they know that our love is dead?

Just as busy, the crowded street;
    Cars and wagons go rolling on,
Children chuckle, and lovers meet,—
    Don't they know that our love is gone?
No one pauses to pay a tear;
    None walks slow, for the love that's through,—
I might mention, my recent dear,
    I've reverted to normal, too.[40]

The speaker lures her lover into contemplation of the opposition between the everyday social world and their private universe—more specifically, into a vision of her own lonely vigil in the closed space that they no longer share. But having spent two stanzas reestablishing their mutuality, she effectively abandons him to uphold it himself—the fate that was to have been "rightfully" hers, as the woman in the dyad. Simultaneously, she reveals that she has all along been speaking from the other side of the dichotomy invoked by her words; she is among the free social beings who profane their lost love. Conventionally, the love poem is the "unconscious" display of private values for a public audience with worldly values. The ultimate betrayal is the breach of this divide; by figuring her audience within the poem (as the "people"), Parker provides her speaker the structure within which to commit this treason. Her betrayal is worse than the lover's betrayal of infidelity; it is the nonlover's betrayal of being "normal."

Rejecting privatized intimacy and its dangers for her as a woman, Parker adopts an antiromantic model of love governed by decorum and propriety. As I have argued, the psychodynamic effect of such love is to infuse a certain construction of the social field with the erotic investment that would otherwise be fixed in a single defined locus, the heterosexual male Other. Not coincidentally, this model of love turns out to be consistent with the drawing room aesthetic dominant in the culture of sophistication generally and the Round Table in particular. "They Part" uses an arch and mannered voice to directly counterpose decorum with the emotional excesses of romantic love.

> And if, my friend, you'd have it end,
> There's naught to hear or tell.
> But need you try to black my eye
> In wishing me farewell?
>
> Though I admit an edged wit
> In woe is warranted,
> May I be frank? . . . Such words as "———"
> Are better left unsaid.
>
> There's rosemary for you and me;
> But is it usual, dear,
> To hire a man, and fill a van
> By way of souvenir?[41]

Whereas "Plea" depicts the lover's lack of taste as a programmatic modernness, the lover's behavior in "They Part" appears at first as a mere lapse in decorum without the justification of any social code, however misguided. In the world of this poem, the only protocol for love seems to be that set forth by the speaker. The poem is structured so that each of the three stanzas begins with a detail of amorous etiquette whose subtlety (the second half of the stanza reveals) is completely lost on the lover-addressee. The values that structure normative love in "They Part" are restraint, both thematized and enacted by the speaker, and tradition, as evidenced by the folkloric symbol of rosemary for remembrance.

The behavior of the lover, however, though seemingly shown merely for its vulgarity, does in fact emanate from an opposing model—that of romantic love—in which passion drives the lover to the behavioral excesses that are the testament to its authenticity. The quality of the lover's feeling is conventionally gauged precisely by the degree to which it impedes his ability to adhere to social codes of behavior; in the long shadow cast by *Young Werther*, social propriety and love are seen to be mutually contradictory. From the speaker's perspective, clearly the reverse is true. Love is to be enacted within the matrix of the social; protocol and the tropes of consensual culture are of paramount importance. "They Part" reverses the notion of "falling in love" as an escape into hermetic intersubjectivity. Building a notion of love around decorum and propriety means turning it into a publicly known and shared field of behaviors and roles into which lovers can then—freely and independently—interpolate themselves.

Parker's "Threnody" foregrounds the social character of love in order to overturn the tragedy of the bereft woman. A lament, the poem is constructed of tropes of romantic suffering but deployed in such a way as to dispel the profound isolation in which these tropes conventionally fix the mourning female lover.

Lilacs blossom just as sweet
Now my heart is shattered.
If I bowled it down the street,
Who's to say it mattered?
If there's one that rode away
What would I be missing?
Lips that taste of tears, they say,
Are the best for kissing.

Eyes that watch the morning star
Seem a little brighter;
Arms held out to darkness are
Usually whiter.
Shall I bar the strolling guest,
Bind my brow with willow,
When, they say, the empty breast
Is the softer pillow?

That a heart falls tinkling down,
Never think it ceases.
Every likely lad in town
Gathers up the pieces.
If there's one gone whistling by
Would I let it grieve me?
Let him wonder if I lie;
Let him half believe me.[42]

After invoking the full weight of the pitiable romantic tragedy in a succinctly conventional opening, the speaker takes up her own sacred lover's "heart" and commits a double outrage upon it, literalizing the metaphor to mere object, then "bowl[ing]" it in vulgar denial of its preciousness. The deflation complete, she is ready to assess her more readily visible attributes.

What is traditionally repressed in the lyric, the specularization of the grieving woman as an erotic object, is here foregrounded and put to practical good use. The intrinsic value of romantic suffering, the poem suggests, is nil, but there is significant sexual capital in inhabiting the image. Adherence to the role of tragic woman in all its proper particulars—white arms, bright eyes, and so on—assures her the ultimate benefits of the social contract it supports. In the same way, the metaphor of the tragic heart provides its own solution: as the bereft and brittle unitary heart shatters into a liberatory multiplicity, the speaker's erotic investment is freed from the doomed dyad of self and (absent) Other and goes out to multiple sites of desire, to "every likely lad in town."[43] In this instance, Parker's redefined heterosexuality and her emotionally enlisted public converge to heightened effect. To an extraordinary degree, the publicness of "Threnody" provides Parker with the utopian relation of self to a cathected social body and a field of conventional tropes in which to construct and manipulate this relation.

Yet many of Parker's poems express significant anxiety over the management of such complex publicity. "Braggart" contrasts two models of inhabiting a public persona and public space in order to suggest both the supreme value of community and its attendant dangers.

The days will rally, wreathing
Their crazy tarantelle;
And you must go on breathing,
But I'll be safe in hell.

Like January weather,
The years will bite and smart,
And pull your bones together
To wrap your chattering heart.

The pretty stuff you're made of
Will crack and crease and dry.
The thing you are afraid of
Will look from every eye.

You will go faltering after
The bright, imperious line,
And split your throat on laughter,
And burn your eyes with brine.

You will be frail and musty
With peering, furtive head,
Whilst I am young and lusty
Among the roaring dead.[44]

The speaker taunts her (ambiguously gendered) addressee with the dismal details of her or his future life, gloating over her own escape into a quite different fate. The contrast of their respective worlds carries with it certain expectations. We are prepared for "hell" to be the atemporal antithesis of the relentlessly time-driven "life"; more specifically, we are prepared for hell to parallel that truly abstracted alterworld, heaven. Knowing that the salient point of her association with hell is that she is "bad" rather than "good," we are likely to overlook its other implications.

But while this braggart's reversal of values is shocking and iconoclastic in typical Parker fashion, it introduces complications beyond those suggested by a mere inversion. The addressee will suffer the physical ravages of old age, and yet the speaker, presumably dead, has not herself been released from her body. She is in hell, a place whose whole purpose depends on the continued embodiment (as capacity for suffering) of its subjects. Yet from the three lines of description the poem offers, we learn that hell provides the speaker with safety, youth, "lust[iness]," and—most important—company. Having surprised us first with an embodied alternative to life, the poem goes on to surprise us with the physical comforts of hell.

But the underplayed embodiment of the dead speaker is purposefully overshadowed by that of the live addressee, whose body is a source of pure agony. In the first two stanzas of this extended prediction (or curse), the addressee undergoes the disorientation and pain of aging, substantial enough in itself. But stanza three marks a crucial shift away from the subjective to an even more horrifying dimension of the process: as the surface of the body "crack[s] and crease[s] and dr[ies]," it becomes an increasingly opaque boundary dividing the person within the once "pretty stuff" from the "every eye" without. By the final stanza, the addressee has been reduced to a "peering, furtive" relation to the world, embodiment having finally—and paradoxically—given way to invisibility. The still-young speaker, meanwhile, belongs unproblematically to a powerful community.

In "Braggart," both alienation and community are founded on embodiment; if the body has the power to tragically isolate, it is also the only means to connectedness. Which it will be is a matter of control, specifically, management of one's public persona. The woman who holds to a conventional image of femininity finds herself at the mercy of publicity's "crazy tarantelle." Acceptable while she is able to conform, she must be put out of sight as soon she shows signs of losing the hypostatized youth which is the essence of her appeal.

The alternative represented by the poem's speaker is to refuse the embodiment of feminine perfection and, instead, go to hell—and by her own volition. This takes two forms for the speaker: she positions herself as a "bad girl," and she constructs a community and a relation to that community which is not in any way subject to living time. Typical for Parker's use of the bad girl persona, the "lusty" speaker of "Braggart" functions to elicit from her audience the protectiveness and "safe[ty]" that the "roaring dead" provide within the poem. The community that grants her the kind of seemingly unmediated connectedness suggested here is precisely the one this chapter has attempted to describe: an imaginary relation of self and other staged across the public space of a poem. Yet, though this relationship often seems to transcend embodiment, the presenting problem of the "braggart" is the effect of aging on her public identity, and her solution is to "die" into permanent youth. While she may be able to negotiate a femininity that circumvents the imperative for youth and beauty, her identification with her audience as she has imagined it depends on her own personification of the New York culture of sophistication, a culture defined by youth and modernity. The loss of either quality casts her irrevocably adrift. From this perspective, the relationship Parker has fashioned as an alternative to the heterosexual dyad presents her, ironically, with the same criterion for acceptance.

For Parker as a writerly persona, embodiment proves to be an inescapable and peculiarly feminine component of public identity, just as love itself proves to be her only means of entry into public speech. "A Well-Worn Story" stands as a kind of allegory of ambivalence for both these moments in Parker's literary practice—an ambivalence unrelieved by humor.

In April, in April,
My one love came along,
And I ran the slope of my high hill
To follow a thread of song.

His eyes were hard as p[or]phyry
With looking on cruel lands;
His voice went slipping over me
Like terrible silver hands.

Together we trod the secret lane
And walked the muttering town.
I wore my heart like a wet, red stain
On the breast of a velvet gown.

In April, in April,
My love went whistling by,
And I stumbled here to my high hill
Along the way of a lie.

Now what should I do in this place
But sit and count the chimes,

And splash cold water on my face
And spoil a page with rhymes?[45]

The intersection of love and publicity structuring this narrative has an implicitly feudal cast in the proprietary stance the lover takes toward the speaker—his silver-handed possession of her like his visual possession of "cruel lands." This context accounts for the nature of their peculiarly joyless love affair. The single stanza describing it is concerned exclusively with the relationship between the lovers and their public, the town. The lane which they "trod" was secret, apparently the more oppressive for that; the town they walked was "muttering."

But if the public and even the male lover have the luxury of maintaining privacy within their ritual communication, the female speaker is bound by her position to total self-revelation. Where she had had freedom and privacy on her "high hill," in the town she must provide visible proof of her worthiness: a "wet, red stain" of hymenal blood testifying to her virginity, to her possession by this man, or even to her repentance, à la Hester Prynne. Typically for Parker, this image bypasses sex itself for a shockingly antiromantic physicality. Wearing one's heart on one's sleeve, thus violently literalized, even suggests the equation of falling in love with being slain. But beyond these narratively motivated stains, the singular obligation to bear a "wet, red" brand suggests the extranarrative expression of femaleness per se, menstrual blood. Where the town and the male lover mutter, sing, and chime, the woman's expressions are all graphic. In the same way that, as a lover, she wears a stain on her gown, she later "spoils a page with rhymes" after being spurned. The equation renders her love poetry as involuntary feminine revelation before a public; at the same time, the poem's feudal resonances suggest that such revelation is an obligation if a royal—or celebrity—woman is to find acceptance among her followers.

Of Parker's various responses to public embodiment, the most spectacular are undoubtedly her many death poems—poems of wry suicide, rotting corpses, and grotesque visitations.[46] Most of her books are titled with an eye toward cultivating this association with the macabre: *Enough Rope* (1926), *Sunset Gun* (1928), *Death and Taxes* (1931), and *Here Lies* (1939). Biographers have attributed this element in Parker's writing to a morbid personal obsession related directly to Parker's several real-life suicide attempts.[47] Yet at least as salient for our purposes is the way in which the trope of the dead or doomed body becomes a carnivalesque flouting of the *sexualized* body that public visibility (in the press or in the street) would impose on a woman. Parker did not just write the occasional morbid lyric; she let it be known that she subscribed to mortuary science trade journals and wore tuberose perfume, the scent favored by morticians in what Parker delightedly thought of as their grisly ministerings.[48] As in her unrelenting focus on love, Parker took the womanly constraint of embodiment for granted—and used it directly to forge a literary identity. To varying degrees of success, Parker's work managed a central contradiction: that of *speaking* to a public and *appearing* as a woman. More than simply releasing her from heterosexual claustrophobia, Parker's "public love" offered her *female citizenship* as a horizon of possibility—rather than as a contradiction in terms.

S I X

"The New (and Newer) Negro (es)"

Generational Conflict in the Harlem Renaissance

The *Dictionary of Literary Biography* names Gwendolyn Bennett "one of the more active and promising authors of the New Negro movement" and Helene Johnson, "one of the youngest and brightest of the Harlem Renaissance poets." Gloria T. Hull has likewise identified Bennett and Johnson as "the stellar poets of the [Harlem Renaissance] younger generation."[1] Yet for scholars and readers generally, it is Zora Neale Hurston who has come to define Harlem Renaissance women's writing, despite the fact that her work (though invaluable) is more idiosyncratic than representative of the renaissance literary matrix. Ann duCille has argued recently that African American literary criticism itself has come under the spell of what she calls "Hurstonism," "the utopian trend in contemporary cultural criticism that readily reads resistance in such privileged, so-called authentically black discourses as . . . the folkloric fiction of Zora Neale Hurston, while denigrating other cultural forms for their perceived adherence to and promotion of traditional (white) values."[2] While duCille is concerned with the larger question of African American literary value, I would like to propose that an understanding of women's writing in the context of the Harlem Renaissance in particular might also fruitfully put Hurston aside in favor of Bennett and Johnson.

Like many of their female contemporaries, Bennett and Johnson forged their artistic identities in close engagement with Harlem Renaissance concerns. Uniquely among women writers, however, they also laid claim to active membership in the renaissance subcultural core, joining the avant-garde elite of young renegades like Langston Hughes and Wallace Thurman in developing a subculturally specific *aesthetic*.[3] Such an affiliation went distinctly against the grain of renaissance gender arrangements. In a mode widely identified as typical of modernist avant-gardes, the vanguard of Harlem took much of its drive and identity from defiance of the bourgeois establishment (embodied in long-standing race leaders like W. E. B. DuBois) and expressed that defiance through a "revolutionary" aesthetic. To the extent that key icons of black femininity served to organize the symbolic universe of Harlem's subcultural life, the terms of this aesthetic implicated (even targeted) African American womanhood. Through a rhetorical assault on the genteel African American woman as the emblem of bourgeois propriety, the younger generation put critical distance between itself and its elders; likewise, the celebration of working-class street life established for them their own radically oppositional space. Both projects made avant-garde identity highly problematic for women writers, particularly in the context of an ongoing struggle to secure mainstream legitimization for black femininity. Johnson and Bennett took up the challenge, however, each of them forging a distinct path to arrive at a feminization of renaissance avant-garde speech.

Photograph on preceding page: Scene from the Broadway musical *Lulu Belle* (1926). (The Billy Rose Theatre Collection, New York Public Library at Lincoln Center)

Neither Bennett nor Johnson had the opportunity to produce more than a scant body of work, and in this they are typical of Harlem Renaissance women writers. Johnson wrote a total of twenty-eight poems, and Bennett a mere twenty-one. In reading renaissance journals, one is struck by the sheer number of women writers publishing fiction, essays, and especially poetry. But equally impressive is the virtual absence of poets whose literary output persisted beyond that charmed decade "when the Negro was in vogue" or was voluminous enough to suggest the shape and concerns of a definable artistic career. With the exception Alice Dunbar-Nelson and the stellar Georgia Douglas Johnson, who were already well established at the start of the renaissance, individual voices remain partial. While we may lament the thwarting of so many lost talents, we should note that renaissance artistry was generally viewed as collective culture building, the individual work as explicitly part of a greater effort to elaborate a racially specific artistry. Attending first to a broad sampling of the collective, then, we find in the case of women's poetry a lyric voice that only emerges from the totality, a voice running counterpoint to the primitivist modernism of the (largely male) avant-garde and to one side of the genteel modernity of the largely male establishment.

The chapters that follow explore this collective tendency of women's poetry, as well as certain literary strategies of women's prose against the background of renaissance generational tensions, with the ultimate goal of illuminating the specificity of Bennett and Johnson's literary achievements. As we shall see in chapter 8, " 'Our Younger Negro (Women) Artists,' " Bennett and Johnson were strongly allied with the women's tradition, on friendly terms with the establishment, and yet uniquely determined to embrace the masculinist avant-garde—the quintessence of the renaissance—as their own. Chapter 7, " 'Exalting Negro Womanhood,' " takes up in detail a range of representative works in various genres by women in order to render more fully the kind and degree of cultural pressures and literary negotiations indicated by the rubric "women writers of the Harlem Renaissance." But first, to lay the groundwork for apprehending the nature of renaissance women writers' individual and collective achievements, the present chapter explores the discursive matrix within which they wrote, reading Harlem's journals to delineate the renaissance public sphere of self-understanding.

> There have been times when we writers of the older set have been afraid that the procession of those who seek to express the life of the American Negro was thinning and that none were coming forward to fill the footsteps of the fathers. . . . But even as we ask "Where are the young Negro artists to mold and weld this mighty material about us?"—even as we ask, they come. (W. E. B. Du Bois)[4]

> Youth the world over is undergoing a spiritual and an intellectual awakening, is looking with new eyes at old customs and institutions, and is finding for

> them interpretations which its parents passed over. . . . And so it is not to be wondered at that the young American Negro is having his Youth Movement also. (Countee Cullen)[5]

> In Harlem, Negro life is seizing upon its first chances for group expression and self-determination. It is—or promises at least to be—a race capital. . . . Harlem has the same role to play for the New Negro as Dublin had for the New Ireland or Prague for the New Czechoslovakia. (Alain Locke)[6]

> There had been throughout the nation an announcement of a Negro renaissance. The American Negro, it seemed, was entering a new phase in his development. He was about to become an important factor in the artistic life of the United States. . . . Novels, plays, and poems by and about Negroes were being deliriously acclaimed and patronized. . . . And yet the more discerning were becoming more and more aware that nothing, or at least very little, was being done to substantiate the current fad, to make it the foundation for something truly epochal. (Wallace Thurman)[7]

> Negro intellectuals who have the itch to write . . . should by all means move immediately to New York City. . . . Having arrived at the mecca of suckers, sharpers, cabaret proprietors and other such bandits, they should immediately get in touch with that group of about twenty New Negroes who represent the intellect of the Negro race so admirably. If they aspire to write it is suggested that they join one of the Young Writers' Guilds. It is not necessary to be either a writer or a youth to qualify, since many of the members do not write at all and some of them are rather elderly. . . . Very shortly some of the white writers or editors who dote on having an "intelligent" Negro protégé under their wing, will invite them to offer a manuscript for scrutiny with a view to publication. (George S. Schuyler)[8]

Critics have long debated the meaning and significance of the Harlem Renaissance, some arguing that the very designation of the decade between *Cane*'s first appearance and the early Depression as a discrete artistic period artificially distorts the internal logic of African American cultural development.[9] Indeed, questions about the meaning and existence of the Harlem Renaissance date from the period itself, when, for every use of the term (or its more common alternate, "The New Negro Renaissance"), one finds a second use with "so-called" appended to it.[10] For a race leader of long standing like W. E. B. Du Bois, the renaissance is less a revelation than the assurance (albeit shaky) that the next generation will have the will and ability to carry forward the work of their elders. Indeed, given his careful attention to the global context of race relations, Du Bois conspicuously failed to elevate the renaissance in Harlem to an event of world historical status.[11] Alain Locke, by contrast, saw the renaissance as nothing less than the African racial nation coming to consciousness as part of worldwide nationalist resistance. For conservative satirist George Schuyler, the renaissance epitomized the way a delusional notion of African essence could serve the pretensions of a few, while dangerously obscuring the transracial common ground of American experience. To Wallace Thurman, one of the ''Younger Negro Artists'' expected to produce the artistic outpouring that would justify the fanfare, the renaissance belonged to the schemes of his controlling elders. And for women writers generally—who, as these epigraphs intentionally suggest, were squeezed out of the frontline deliberations altogether—the emergence of a cultural phenomenon garnering national attention seems to have necessitated an apotheosis of abstract femininity: women found themselves ''elevated'' to mute iconic status by the same mechanism that drew forth and canonized a battery of male cultural commentators to ''speak'' the renaissance.[12]

Successful or failed, putative or real as a discrete artistic period, the 1920s were certainly a time in which African American writers and cultural commentators worked with an inescapable consciousness that something definitive was supposed to be happening for the race (whether or not they thought it *was* happening). And the strong sense among the bourgeois Harlem intelligentsia was that it fell to them to bring this something about.[13] In the course of an ongoing discourse of definition, Harlem writers pursued questions which the fact—or specter—of a modern renaissance raised: the meaning and value of publicity and the relationships between national and racial identity, aesthetic expression and political progress, and African heritage and modernity.

Perhaps the strongest distinction between the self-understanding of the Harlem Renaissance and that of the Algonquin Round Table or of Greenwich Village bohemia was the profound aura of responsibility that enveloped the Harlem intelligentsia. The Village bohemians took their marginal status as central to their self-definition—indeed, as the foundation of their moral authority. In their more conflicted self-understanding, the Round Tablers saw themselves as articulators of modernity for the modern mass, but a middle-brow ''mass'' that was as socially abstract as they themselves—''personalities'' all—were exceptional. By contrast, writers of the Harlem Renaissance had a ready-made and inescapable constituency in the African American population, a constituency which they understood to have a great deal at stake in their success. Indeed, the Harlem Renaissance began less as a group or (in Raymond Williams's term) ''fraction'' collectively evolving their sense of difference from the world than as a cultural wish—of race leaders *and* white moderns—which artists then found themselves inhabiting (to varying degrees of comfort) as their own. Whatever their ideological and social differences, the Harlemites nevertheless cohered around the ongoing discursive project of defining (or denying) the ''Renaissance'' which had sprung up among them.

The bohemians and Algonquinites encountered publicity as a new and quintessentially modern phenomenon, but for the African American leadership, public relations was a long-standing fact of racial life whose prominence was only heightened in the age of mass media. Unchanged was the need to use public attention to chip away at mainstream racism, to seize the spotlight for the purpose of persuasion and education. Whereas publicity was in other cases an experience of the self writ large, that self was here also automatically in service to the overriding racial imperative. And implicit in that imperative was the centrality of the national audience and culture, not as a point of resistance (as for the bohemians) or as the matrix of narcissistic identification (as for the Round Tablers) but as the object of clear social goals. Their instrumental relation to publicity notwithstanding, the Harlemites were subjects as well as manipulators of the mainstream culture. Their public expressions bear witness not only to strategy but also to ambivalence and resistance, desire and identification.

Harlem's high-stakes relation to the national culture profoundly affected its internal gender arrangements, both symbolically and materially. To begin with, the close tie between the artistic project and its possible social consequences disabled the usual fixation on the embattled male artist in America, which we have seen serve as the functional default for our other modern subcultures. Unlike the bohemian and Algonquin men who lived in anxious relation to the world of "real" masculine endeavor, Harlem men who would divorce their art from the serious project of racial advancement had to actively seek and defend alternative, non-utilitarian definitions of artistic production (which, as we shall see, was a key struggle for the renaissance avant-garde). While the equation of artistic production with serious race work seems to have allowed masculinity to recede significantly as a source of anxiety, still, as Gloria T. Hull has observed, the material conditions of the renaissance as a patronage-driven movement greatly reinforced male privilege in the form of an old-boy lock on resources. Women writers suffered significantly reduced access to money and contacts among publishers and patrons simply because, as women, they lacked the currency of confidence through which these alliances were built. In myriad ways, their work bears the evidence of the consequent stress.[14]

But if the historical woman writer found herself squeezed out in the scramble for resources, the iconic woman had the same centrality to the Harlem Renaissance economy of meaning as she had to those of other modern subcultures. The era's national New Woman, refracted through the ideals and anxieties of the locale, split to become two diametrically opposed figures: the "exalted Negro woman," icon of bourgeois gentility, and the primitive "Brown Girl," icon of racial authenticity. Perfect opposites, their necessary interdependence emerges most clearly in the work of women writers, who speak from the faultlines of the subcultural ethos this complex femininity supports. As we shall see, the dichotomy of genteel and primitive femininities anchors a subcultural public sphere that variously defined and positioned (representational) women in its interarticulations of race, politics, and aesthetics.

Publicity, National Culture, and the Race

In the words of literary historian Chidi Ikonné, "the role of black journals in the birth and growth of the New Negro cannot be overemphasized."[15] The major magazines—*Crisis, Opportunity*, and the less prominent *Messenger*—served as essential vehicles for sustained culture building, both in keeping artists' work before the public and in continuously theorizing the relations among aesthetics, race, and racial progress. Ikonné has also suggested, however, that the mission of the journals was at odds with the spirit of the renaissance: while the renaissance sought a free modernist self-actualization, *Opportunity* and *Crisis* pursued traditional racial uplift (113). Certainly, this perspective echoes the express consensus of the younger Harlem Renaissance artists, as we shall see. *The Messenger*, for its part, began as an instrument of Marxist revolution and gradually took on the very different political-cultural agenda of bringing African Americans into mainstream modernity—the popular middle-brow culture associated with the midtown sophisticates. Obviously, this project had its own points of convergence with and divergence from the renaissance. My interest in the present analysis, however, is not so much to isolate the "true" renaissance from the local distractions of competing and appropriating impulses as to delineate the range of discussion going on within the boundaries of "renaissance discourse" in order to speculate about its effects on women writers.

The two central vehicles for public discourse within the Harlem Renaissance were principally geared to charting and promoting racial progress in an era of mass black migration and urbanization. *The Crisis*, edited by W. E. B. Du Bois, was founded in 1910 as the official organ of the NAACP, while *Opportunity*, under the editorship of Charles S. Johnson, came along in 1923 to disseminate the sociological analysis of the National Urban League. Both encounter the renaissance as appropriable but finally secondary to their sociopolitical agendas. This is not to say that Du Bois's and Johnson's absolutely essential efforts to support the cultural movement were compromised or made in bad faith. But within the terms of Harlem Renaissance self-understanding, the journalistic status quo can usefully be seen as representing one pole, and the modernist aestheticism of the avant-garde youth the other. The fullest expression of this avant-garde as a self-conscious force must be the "little magazines," but, as the single, bankrupting issue of the infamous *FIRE!!* in 1926 attests, little magazines were no match for their big counterparts, a discrepancy in power which itself helped fuel the sense of avant-garde difference so central to renaissance dynamics.

For the renaissance cultural establishment, the stakes in its conflict with rebellious youth were greatly raised by the presence of a third party: the national mainstream public, which served not only as a critical audience to the progress of the race but also, in the way of a mass-mediated representational matrix, as a site of identification and desire for black writers themselves. In this context, publicity—always of paramount importance to African American racial goals—took on a more diffuse character and a more pervasive significance. Both *Crisis* and *Opportunity* designated regular and explicit outlets for the purpose of monitoring the public life of the race. Each journal chronicled the key racial moments of the mainstream press: *Crisis* had its intriguingly titled "The Looking Glass," which treated an extensive range of discursive events from the larger public sphere in the characteristically strong editorial voice of W. E. B. Du Bois. *Opportunity's* "Pot Pourri" brought together items from a variety of newspapers, wherever "the race" found its way into the national spotlight; "Interracial Forum," also a regular feature, focused specifically on public discussions of "the race problem." *Opportunity* even provided an annual, feature-length assessment of the Negro press. For its part, *The Messenger* weighed into the discussion with "The Month's Best Editorial (Selected from the American Negro Press)."[16]

But the preoccupation with publicity far exceeded such focused outlets and served—especially in the case of *Opportunity*—as a general grid of interpretation for nearly everything that appeared in its pages. In a 1926 editorial on "The 'Charleston,' " for example, editor Johnson concludes his breezy, humorous overview of this dance craze with a serious assessment of its public racial import:

> More maligned and extolled than jazz it goes its merry pace. And here is the paradox: It is a purely Negro dance, and yet they would claim that Negroes are the greatest imitators; it is not a vulgar dance or a sensuous dance—one cannot swing arms and legs wildly and at the same time be guilty of the most common dance hall evils. And again, no one as indolent as some people think Negros are, can ever hope to learn this Negro dance. It contradicts a dozen popular and detractory notions about Negroes even tho this contradiction is accomplished in a light and flippant manner.[17]

In the August 1923 issue, we find Cleveland G. Allen reporting on the progress of "Our Young Artists" with the story of sculptor Augusta Savage being denied her art school scholarship on racial grounds, his final word on the subject being an assessment not of the art world but of the press: "The New York World was the first American newspaper to carry an account of this incident. The exposé of the actions of the [adjudicating] committee by the World is in line with its usual policy of fairness."[18] The editorial pages of the same issue take the opportunity to lament the effects of racialist humor: "Through most of what passes for humor runs a constant tone of caricature, directed at those type-figures we select as the stools on which to elevate ourselves. A little of this may not do us much harm; but dwelt on time after time, as in fact it is, it breeds a biased social outlook."[19] Still in the August 1923 number, we find a remarkable racial meta-statement buried in the book review section. Commenting on Georgia Douglas Johnson's *Bronze*, white novelist and regular contributor Zona Gale raises publicity to the level of a full-blown racial theory:

> The American Indians never had one of their number to speak out of their wo[e] and injustice in English verse. Withdrawn, incurious of an audience, and without hope, they lamented or prayed or sang, wrapt in absorption, intent on their own paths and their own gods. But the colored peoples have voices, crying with power over barriers.[20]

We should note that, like most such articulations of the classic racial axiom that publicity equals progress, this one bears evidence of a specifically modern conception of the national public sphere as a space of redemption for any race that can connect (as against those that cannot). The extreme of such logic resides in the raw marketplace thinking of the time that equated social success with personal commodification; if advertisements are any gauge, the Harlem press had a hand in this as well. The following text comes from an ad that ran in the December 1926 issue of *Messenger*.

> ARE YOU UNKNOWN? YOU—May have accomplished much; May own beautiful property; May fill a position of responsibility; May own a flourishing business; May be honored and respected in your community
> BUT—The outer world knows nothing of you; Nothing about your refinement; Nothing about your culture; Nothing about your achievements; Nothing about your influence; Nothing about your family
> WHY?—Because information about you has not been properly disseminated, if at all—Because you have not been ADVERTISED.(28)

As the ad continues, the attenuated instrumentality of its pitch comes through in the emphasis on private life (as opposed to, say, business connections).

> LET US Put you before the world in a dignified and artistic manner, with an excellent, human interest biography, beautiful portraits of the members of your family and photographs of your property.

Indeed, the ad is quite explicitly driven by the understanding that general and diffuse salutary effects flow from the application of market principles to all phases of social life. In particular, it assumes the desirability of a public presence and circulation.

> DEMAND INCREASES VALUE This is true of commodities and individuals. One must be recognized in order to have value and one's value and importance increases as one is more widely recognized and one's attainments are broadcast to the world.

In this ad (as in so much of *The Messenger*) the implicit racial imperative for (good) publicity dovetails with the quintessentially modern conception of publicity as constitutive of self—the visible, specular, Other-produced-and-endorsed self at the core of mass-mediated national culture. Indeed, the modern journalistic necessity to generate desire and interest around readers by sweeping them up into this public aura was not lost on the African American press.

> As long as the Negro society woman can read about her clubs and social activities only in the Negro paper, as long as the Negro paper is the only one

> in which she can see her picture, her neighbor's picture, read about her pastor's sermon, then so long will the Negro press have reader interest.[21]

Equally obvious to the publications identified with the renaissance was the imperative to hook this local circle of reflective glamor into the larger, national network of desire, generated and expressed by mainstream mass culture. A key instrument was photography, which serves magically to fuse the local and the national. W. E. B. Du Bois explicitly linked photographic image making to racial politics in a *Crisis* editorial from 1923.

> Why do not more young colored men and women take up photography as a career? The average white photographer does not know how to deal with colored skins and having neither sense of their delicate beauty of tone nor will to learn, he makes a horrible botch of portraying them. From the South especially the pictures that come to us, with few exceptions, make the heart ache.[22]

Du Bois's sense of the need for good photography is apparently such that it warrants a virtual call to arms. It is worth rehearsing the dynamic context in which the failure of photography could generate such urgency.

The national, mass media–driven culture that had evolved in America by the 1920s ushered in a palpable national erotics: a charged and luminous representational field out of which individuals and groups derived new identities and identifications, drawn in by their desire for commerce with the collective, national desire generated out of commodity capitalism. As we have seen, the image of woman became an increasingly standardized commodity in this context, deployed as a point of general access to the national circuit of desire (or a fantasy thereof).[23] This backdrop of a national culture is particularly important to the subcultural dynamics of the Harlem Renaissance. The idea of the Americanness of "Negro" identity, of a revitalizing Negro contribution to American culture, and, in particular, of an intrinsically dramatic Negro life bringing the American theater out of its abortive stagnation had great currency in this period.[24] Such phenomena as *The Messenger*'s long-running photo series, "Exalting Negro Womanhood," as well as their and *The Crisis*'s policy of using women's faces for cover illustrations might reasonably be interpreted as overt expressions of national identification achieved through the commodified beautiful woman.[25] Here we come to a key reason for the resiliently iconic status of contemporaneous bourgeois African American womanhood, a category that included the women of the renaissance intelligentsia: it was through the image of beautiful, genteel femininity that the race could most fully participate in a libidinally charged national culture and identity.

Indeed, something needs to explain how the image of the bourgeois woman comes to be seen as doing all the racial work with which it is credited. The original announcement of "Exalting Negro Womanhood" begins, as one might expect, with reference to the situation of African American women:

> It is quite commonplace to see every Sunday morning in the photogravure section of the daily papers, page after page of pictures of white women. If a colored woman commits some crime or does something very indecent and censurable, her picture may be presented.

At this point, however, the discussion shifts suddenly to the publicity of men and, in doing so, heats up considerably.

> Or space will be given to something comical like a parade of the U.N.I.A. [Garvey's Universal Negro Improvement Association] or to some clown-like Marcus Garvey regaled in robes, ribbon and gold braid. The buffoon, the clown, the criminal Negro will be seen, but seldom the Negro of achievement, culture, refinement, beauty, genius and talent. As we frequently say, "Let a Negro make a scholarly address on some public occasion and you need a microscope to discern it in the paper—if, indeed, it be there at all. On the other hand, let a Negro snatch a white woman's pocketbook and he will be given headline on the front page of most of the daily papers."

Now the surprising solution to this race problem is ushered in.

> The Messenger is going to show, beginning with 1924, in pictures as well as writing, Negro women who are unique, accomplished, beautiful, intelligent, industrious, talented, successful. We are going to take them by states, displaying two or three pages of these women artistically arranged each month.[26]

Riding on what one assumes is a presumption of common sense, the image of the bourgeois African American woman is offered up as the logical advance guard in the publicity battle.

In the context of the "page after page" of white women, the exalted Negro woman constitutes a clear bid for racial inclusion in the definition of American life and a point of access through which to suffuse the race in the national-erotic-public charge. But importantly, she also epitomizes the invisibility suffered by her class as whole, and, as such, her prominence is a bid for acknowledgment of the African American bourgeoisie per se. She further epitomizes an intrinsic doubleness, built into the historical context of African American publicity: her image simultaneously raises and blots out the specter of the grotesque stereotypes by which mainstream (white) America "knows" the black woman—the animalistic breeder, the lascivious temptress, the unsexed mammy. Mainstream resistance to the idea of genteel black womanhood in particular resided in the perceived contradiction between a class identity premised on transcendence of the body and a racial body historically saturated with sexuality (or its cousin, bestiality).[27] Accordingly, the sense that acceptance of the bourgeois woman was somehow the final test of racial status was implicit even as early as 1892 in Julia Ward Cooper's famous declaration, "Only the BLACK WOMAN can say 'when and where I enter, in the quiet undisputed dignity of my womanhood, without violence and without suing or special patronage, then and there the whole Negro race enters with me.' "[28]

Quite apart from all the obstacles to its reception, the bourgeois publicity fostered by the exalted Negro woman seems to have carried an ambivalent charge for the bourgeoisie themselves. While Harlem discourse contains the frequent lament that "our better people" are invisible to the mainstream, it also bears evidence that this invisibility may well be cause for relief.[29] In her *Opportunity* review of Gertrude Sanborn's novel *Veiled Aristocrats*, Eunice Roberta Hunton concedes that the white Sanborn's grasp of black high society is "indeed, founded on the real contacts of one who has lifted the veil that a willfully blind nation has draped around our aristocrats." But Hunton also qualifies her endorsement.

> With the protective instinct of the outcast, one momentarily resents that one of the enemy alien should know so well the soul and the mind of us; but immediately one remembers that not until this knowledge is complete can there be peace on earth among men.[30]

Such anxiety about race, class, and publicity is even more often expressed in inverse terms, with representation of the black bourgeoisie as precisely working to veil the hidden "truth" of the race. Such is the case with this March 1928 cultural commentary from Countee Cullen, which coincided with the publication of Claude McKay's bestseller of street life, *Home to Harlem*. Cullen urges that discretion

> might improve race relations more than the wholesale betrayal of racial idiosyncrasies and shortcoming which seems so rampant. Every house worthy of the name has an attic or a bin or an out-of-the-way closet where one may hide the inevitable family skeleton. But who inviting a prominent guest to tea, or dinner, and hoping to make even the slightest of good impressions, feels called upon to guide that guest sedulously through every nook and corner of the house, not omitting attic, bin, and the dusty retreat of the skeleton? In most well-regulated households one's guest would not get further than the parlor.

In Cullen's metaphorical mapping, the private sphere stands ready for public scrutiny, serving as a protective front to the unfit, the repressed racial secrets. The ethos (and of course, the metaphor) are distinctly bourgeois, and they render the working or peasant class the family "dirt" of their responsible caretakers, who maintain the parlor (in the form of bourgeois writing) as a matter of moral duty: "Decency demands that some things be kept secret; diplomacy demands it; the world loses its respect for violators of this code."[31] Bourgeois publicity, then, functions simultaneously as an unveiling (of the black middle class itself) and a concealment (of the race generally, as represented by the lower classes). By the same logic, lower-class publicity also conceals the race by perpetuating the use of racial masks derived from minstrelsy.

Beyond this hall of mirrors is a paradox at the core of bourgeois publicity: public display by its nature threatened to erode the very class-bound dignity it was intended to project. And given their special place within race publicity, not to mention their gender-specific sexual vulnerability, bourgeois women were particularly sensitive to this threat. The writers among them also had a characteristic response: undergirding many literary "performances" is a symbiosis of femininity, a network of feminine "others" which provides a context of possibility for a relatively stable bourgeois heroine. In this textual economy, bourgeois women get help managing the dynamics of public "performance" from their (imaginary) working-class as well as their (imaginary) peasant-class sisters. Among the latter was the icon of the primitive African American woman, magnificently sensual, regal and mute, in whose rapturous "barbaric" dance was embodied the mystery of the racial past and the vitality of the racial future.[32] Perhaps as a defense against her power, she was most often referred to by the diminutive appellation of "brown girl." Ubiquitous in the pages of renaissance literary journals, the Brown Girl satisfied the call for a trope of racial essence, a call which issued equally from an exoticizing white public and renaissance artists seeking to define a truly "Negro" art.[33] Just as important for the present discussion, the "primitive" woman often absorbed the potentially degrading sexual implications which paradoxically emanated from the genteel woman's "exalting" performances.

Though the problems of class and publicity had particular force for renaissance women, the intelligentsia as a whole manifested class anxiety over definition of (and identification with) "the race." The renaissance demand for racial authenticity was never far from the rhetorical surface; yet, for all the time the intelligentsia devoted to ferreting out and celebrating the race, they kept it pretty consistently at arm's length. One becomes aware of a "primal scene" of class confrontation staged repeatedly in the poetry and short fiction of the time, in which the middle-class intellectual stumbles (narratively or rhetorically) upon the race in its essential embodiment. Eunice Roberta Hunton's sketch of 1923 is exemplary. "Digression (To Three Companions in Adventure on a Spring Night)" recounts the story of a group of young urban intellectuals who—presumably in response to the pagan summons of spring—venture out into the southern countryside (site of the same primal blackness that draws down the northern intellectual protagonist of *Cane*). The "digression" belies the inevitability underlying their adventure, for whatever bohemian impulse leads them out of town, there could be only one generic outcome to their journey. Sure enough, they come upon a peasant dance and, among all the ordinary rustics, discover in one particular girl the icon of primitive womanhood.

> [A]nd such a girl—barely out of her teens, scarcely more than an inch or two over five feet, slim and lithe, with short black curls framing an oval face of rare olive richness. Dressed in a short blue skirt and white sailor blouse, she looked more like some child playing with grown-ups—that is, she looked that way until one saw her vivid red mouth so alluringly full, and those dark eyes whose depths revealed a glimpse of things. . . .[34]

The ellipsis is Hunton's, inviting us to fill in the primitivism (as sexuality) which is "unspeakable" or, at least, bounded only by the degree of desirable threat we are willing to withstand. This initial glimpse prepares the way for a full-scale descent into primitive abandon, which comes with the dance itself:

> The music stirred the blood; it blinded reason; it stripped away the veneer of civilization; and leaving the senses bare and unprotected, it played upon them tauntingly, cruelly. The air was stiflingly heavy and there was quiet. . . . Everyone was completely submerged by the music. . . . On and on they danced, the air growing more fetid, the dancing growing more and more abandoned, men and women clinging passionately to each other in savage caresses. (381)

Concluding her story, the narrator moves back to the girl and finally outside into safety.

> As we left the crowded rooms with the eyes of little scarlet lips desirously intent upon a member of our party, it seemed as though we were entering another world; and yet as we sped once more through the sweet, clean night, there suddenly came to me on the air the fragment of a song . . . (381)

Reentering this "other world," the bourgeois friends are restored to their own "sweet, clean night," rescued from the "fetid" air, the "submergence," the "savagery" of the racial Other whose only lasting claim on them is the remembered fragment of a song.

Hunton's description of the dance is remarkably like that of Nella Larsen's narrator in *Quicksand*, when ex-"Naxos" (Tuskegee) teacher Helga Crane has her first serious encounter with racial "essence." Yet where Hunton portrays her "primitive" woman explicitly through the eyes of a middle-class observer—with the distance between them foregrounded—Larsen leaves Helga Crane to confront the "primitive" within herself. In the narrative's cabaret scene (a central and weighty trope of renaissance writing), we see Helga

> drugged, lifted, sustained, by the extraordinary music, blown out, ripped out, beaten out, by the joyous, wild, murky orchestra. The essence of life seemed bodily motion. And when suddenly the music died, she dragged herself back to the present with a conscious effort; and a shameful certainly that not only had she been in the jungle, but that she had enjoyed it, began to haunt her. She hardened her determination to get away. She wasn't, she told herself, a jungle creature. She cloaked herself in a faint disgust as she watched the entertainers throw themselves about to the bursts of syncopated jangle, and when the time came again for the patrons to dance, she declined.[35]

Larsen focuses sharp critical attention on the function of denial for the Harlem intellectual. Consistent with the narrative's strong critique of middle-class hypocrisy, Larsen seems deliberately to ironize the self-delusion of her fellow writers by refusing to grant her heroine the safety of the standard racial voyeurism.

But even at the extreme of painful denial, Harlem's intellectuals were motivated by more than flight from racial identity. We need also to note the evidence for a positive identification with a transracial intellectual class. Indeed, such conscious affiliation was often primary. Alain Locke's introduction to the landmark anthology *The New Negro* includes the remarkable lament that "what has been *the most unsatisfactory feature* of our present stage of race relationships in America . . . [is] that the more intelligent and representative elements of the two race groups have at so many points got quite out of vital touch with one another" [my italics].[36] The short-lived little magazines *FIRE!!* and *Harlem: A Journal of Negro Life* suggest that many avant-garde writers manifested this intellectual identification in fairly acerbic self-directed irony. But more on this later.

Meanwhile, *The Messenger*, in its determinedly middle-brow modernness, waged war on what it saw as the pretensions of intellectual Harlem. Indeed, its most significant contribution to renaissance discourse might be its attempt to displace intellectualism and the class structure it implied with the ostensibly democratic middle-brow sensibility—the "transcendence" of class which defined the Round Table and popular modernism. The "third" journal after *Crisis* and *Opportunity*, *The Messenger* drew vital energy from the Harlem discourses of race and aesthetics, art and political progress, even while generally taking the position that the renaissance in African American culture was "Hokum."[37] George Hutchinson has identified *The Messenger* as distinctively concerned with merging the definitions of Americanness and blackness, thereby establishing the equivalence of the two terms.[38] While *Crisis* and *Opportunity*—and cultural critics generally—showed some of the same impulse, what particularly distinguishes *The Messenger*, to my mind, is its definition of the national culture as a specifically modern culture.

The Messenger brought the national culture home—and pushed Harlem toward modernness—through regular feature-length attention to those hot buttons of modernity, love and psychoanalysis, as in the series "Who's Who: The Mirrors of Harlem—Studies in 'Colored' Psycho-Analysis."[39] Moreover, readers were specifically enjoined to embrace contemporary American culture as their own and to recognize the "machine-age" character of black urban life. Just as critical was the modern rhetorical style of key *Messenger* contributors, reminiscent of those truly "high moderns," the Algonquin Round Table. Unlike the oratorical W. E. B. Du Bois[40] or the self-effacing Charles Johnson, George S. Schuyler and Theophilus Lewis made "personality" and humorous irony (i.e., sophistication) the central framework of their cultural commentary. Between March 1924 and September 1925, Schuyler and Lewis cowrote the satirical "Shafts and Darts" column, playing up the duo dynamic to almost vaudevillian effect while skimming lightly across myriad points of modern male self-deprecation.

> *In Imitation of Yahveh*—In the matter of politics the compilers of this page of bushwah have never been able to agree; one of us inclining far to the left while the other is as reactionary as it is possible for a man owing his landlady back rent to be. Nor have we ever been able to compromise on the most

> efficacious method of making a gal. One is hot for the modern realistic method, while the other is just as strongly attached to the mid-Victorian romantic school.

Once they have assured us that the ideological rift described here disappears on the subject of religious tolerance—that is, they both agree to tolerate the religious—they resume their public self-denigration.

> We do not claim there is anything exceptionally chivalrous or virtuous in our conduct. It is simply the attitude we like for people to assume toward our threadbare clothes and the bald spot one of us has. Then, too, we always have an eye out for the safety of our persons. Sometimes, if you make fun of a man's religion he will knock your brains out or tell your wife he saw you with a cutie one day last week.

The affiliation with the parodic midtown masculinity of the Round Table is unmistakable in such passages, just as the stamp of "Pepys" is all over newspaper-style bits like the following:

> *Minor Tragedy*—I had a clean collar on one day last week and not one of my so-called friends saw me.
>
> *Fashion Note*—Mr. Schuyler has a new overcoat. London papers please copy.[41]

Aside from buttressing the important identification of African Americans with national culture and identity, the discourse of sophistication makes available certain possibilities for social transcendence, with specific local utility. To begin with, there is the self-invention of "Schuyler" and "Lewis," who use public speech to generate an aura of publicity within which to create peculiarly modern "private" selves. As for the midtown sophisticates, the elaboration of a public "private" sphere of personality calls into being a class of readers that is precisely *outside* class identity. Schuyler, in particular, directed a great deal of satire at the peculiarities and pretensions of class as masking a truly American commonality. Indeed, the root of his critique seems to have been that class identity of any sort is a pretense for African Americans.[42] As in the case of Modern Love, Schuyler's insistent attention to class finally has the paradoxical effect of clearing a rhetorical space for an identity free of class and disengaging blackness from any kind of class specificity. However reactionary Schuyler's motives,[43] his was a significant intervention in a public discourse so strongly defined by the polarization of bourgeois and working class, with the meaning of African Americanness alternately fixed in one location or the other. Schuyler's popular modernism or, rather, his Americanism-as-modernism, presents at least the possibility of racial/subcultural self-definition on terms other than those of the reigning, class-ambivalent intelligentsia.

Consistent with *The Messenger*'s cultivation of modernness is its abiding interest in heterosexual love, from the featured philosophical speculations of Chandler Owen[44] to "The Adventures of Davy Carr," a serial (and clearly fictional) "study" of romantic intrigue and manners among the black upper class of Washington, D.C.,[45] to Schuyler's own increasing reliance on the war of the sexes for the material of his columns.[46] Love emerges as the matrix of society, with women as the locus of society's mysteries—and vice versa. "Davy Carr" must get his worldly education by deciphering the gestures and language of a certain well-to-do flapper who, like Emma's Mr. Knightly, is in our hero's life long before he realizes she is in his heart. Eulalia Osby Proctor's regular feature, "La Femme Silhouette," does *Vanity Fair*–like spadework in establishing the links among love, women, and societal truth. Her March 1925 column, for example, tells the brief story of a vacuous flapper, whom our disinterested narrator, Pygmalion-like, endows with an educational subscription to *The Messenger*. Three issues into the regimen, "her laughter [had the] new and deeper vibration" of sophistication, and our intellectual male has become her ardent suitor (134). In February of the same year, Proctor declared the advent of "The Bronze Age," in which, thanks to the discovery of King Tut and the vogue in African American musicals, brown skin had come to be equated with the cutting edge of desirable modern femininity for "Mr. Man."

Love in *The Messenger*, then, appears to work in ways consistent with conventional popular modernism. Yet Modern Love's generic focus on women as matrix and barometer of society is fundamentally in conflict with the local practice of making women the face of the race. As we saw in chapter 4, the equation of woman and society assumes a sympathetic male protagonist whose education or fate will depend on a woman who is the object of his journey in the world, its antagonist, or both. By contrast, when woman is the face of the race, our identification is with her; however much she may be objectified, our best hope rides on her hopes, and we can take no pleasure in her demise or even the suggestion of her denigration—assuming we are on board the project of racial uplift. In the larger context of Harlem Renaissance discourse, the protective impulse toward the iconic bourgeois woman does, indeed, correlate with an investment in racial uplift, while antagonism toward her is pretty consistently associated with an aestheticist avant-garde. The latter dynamic is explored more fully later in this chapter.

Meanwhile, we begin to see the difficulty of feminine self-positioning in the matrix of renaissance representation. One of the love formulae dominating the journals is particularly direct in representing the dilemma. In a wide range of works, both poetry and prose, a young woman negotiates between the security of domesticity (concretely rendered as the apartment) and the excitement of urban working-class pleasure (viewed or heard through the apartment window); in a larger sense, she must choose between the bourgeois feminine imperative to be "exalted" and full participation in the cultural phenomenon of the Harlem Renaissance, whose topos is "the street" in all its seamy romance. Helene Johnson's 1926 "Futility" succinctly renders the opposition.

It is silly—
This waiting for love
In a parlor
When love is singing up and down the alley
Without a collar.[47]

The speaker's bravado in fact testifies to the difficulty of the choice she faces, for Johnson was peculiarly determined to fight for her place "on the street," to wrest the terms of the renaissance to grant her feminine inclusion. But this trope of parlor versus alley occurs with the greatest frequency among the more faint-hearted majority of women writers in the renaissance, suggesting a pervasive need to stage the difficulty of access to "Harlem" for the woman who is obliged to be "exalted."[48]

Dorothy West's "Hannah Byde" captures succinctly the critical scene of a woman caught between domesticity (in the form of a petit bourgeois husband) and the life she has missed outside.

> One comes upon Hannah in her usual attitude of bitter resignation, gazing listlessly out of the window of her small, conventionally, cheaply furnished parlor . . .
>
> Holiday crowds hurrying in the street . . . bits of gay banter floating up to her . . . George noisily rustling his paper . . . Wreaths in the shop window across the street. . . . a proud black family in a new red car. . . . George uttering intermittent, expressive little grunts. . . . A blind beggar finding a lost dollar bill. . . . a bullying policeman running in a drunk. . . . George, in a reflective mood, beating a pencil against his teeth—
>
> With a sharp intake of breath she turned on him fiercely, her voice trembling with stifling rage, angry tears filming her eyes.
>
> "For God's sake, stop! You'll drive me mad!"[49]

West's example is clearly antidomestic (typical for her work in this period), though it is Hannah Byde's very gentility that is the source of her conflict with her "crude" husband. Other writers enlist the same dichotomy to the opposite valuation. Anita Scott Coleman's Nancy, in the short story "Silk Stockings," lives in mutual devotion with her husband but strays with an unscrupulous man who can give her the silk stockings she loves. At first, the street is the site of their illicit trysts.

> Nancy started slipping out to meet him. They would drop into a "movie" while it was dark and steal out again through the throbbing, people-jammed blackness. They would wander about and find a snug seat in the park where the night scent from flowers and shrubbery pressed upon them while they exchanged confidences.[50]

Nancy finds her rightful way home to her "plain, humdrum duties," but, interestingly, the journey back comes via a redefinition of the street itself as the space of domestic values.

> Gerald [the lover] was an adept at oogling and talking baby-talk. . . . But his oogles never included the beggar down on the corner or caused him to drop

> a coin in to the old beggar's hat . . . [original ellipsis] as did John [the husband]. . . . [original ellipsis] Nor did it ever include a wistful child with his face pressed to the window of a candy-shop. . . .
>
> Gerald would not join her in the pastime [of picking out objects in the moonlight] though she went on tripping along beside him, with her hand still lying on his arm. (231)

Having thus revealed Gerald's unworthiness, the signifying street finally presents the wayward wife with the vision that sends her home for good: a clothesline with

> a man's sox, cheap and coarse, even in the moonlight, and beside them dancing—the cream of silk and wool, pink at the heel and toe; the finest they could buy—
>
> An infant's tiny stockings. . . . [original ellipsis] (231)

In planting laundry in the once-"throbbing" street and underscoring the gesture with the ironic flourish of handing the emblematic silk stockings over to an equally emblematic infant, Coleman insists on the greater authority of domestic values in a woman's life. And perhaps she also gestures at the utopian possibility that a "good" woman need not forgo the street altogether. The forgoing examples suggest that, in the tension between urban and domestic spaces within which women's relation to the core avant-garde trope of "the street" is staged, heterosexual love functions as both bridge and moat between the street and the walled apartment.

The Avant-Garde Core

By definition, the poetics of the street—the assertion of this topos as the essential Harlem—finds its fullest expression in works by avant-garde insiders like Claude McKay's best-seller of 1928, *Home to Harlem*, and Langston Hughes's 1926 collection, *The Weary Blues*. At this point, we need to explore more fully the self-understanding of these caretakers of the "true" Harlem aesthetic, the group I am calling the renaissance avant-garde. As I hope to demonstrate, the term both acknowledges the explicit gestures of affiliation to be found in their work and usefully describes their structural position within the universe of African American cultural politics in the 1920s.

The sense of collective identity among these writers as a maligned and threatening fringe emerges first with the publishing venture called *FIRE!!* which definitively entered the avant-garde voice into the public sphere of renaissance discourse. As Langston Hughes narrates its origins, avant-garde self-understanding comes through clearly in the assault on bourgeois values, the revolutionary aesthetic, and the youthful collective behind the enterprise.[51]

> Wallace Thurman, Zora Neale Hurston, Aaron Douglas, John P. Davis, Bruce Nugent, Gwendolyn Bennett, and I decided to publish "a Negro quarterly of

> the arts" to be called *Fire*—the idea being that it would burn up a lot of the old, dead conventional Negro-white ideas of the past, *epater le bourgeois* into a realization of the existence of the younger Negro writers and artists, and provide us with an outlet for publication not available in the limited pages of the small Negro magazines then existing, the *Crisis, Opportunity*, and the *Messenger*—the first two being house organs of inter-racial organizations, and the latter being God knows what.[52]

Hughes goes on to describe the critical reception of this Young Negro venture, his gleeful exaggerations (not *everyone* over twenty-five hated *FIRE!!*) the best testimony to his sense that status quo disgust was a direct measure of avant-garde success.

> None of the older Negro intellectuals would have anything to do with Fire. Dr. DuBois in the Crisis roasted it.[53] The Negro press called it all sorts of bad names, largely because of a green and purple story by Bruce Nugent, in the Oscar Wilde tradition, which we had included. Rean Graves, the critic for the Baltimore Afro-American, began his review by saying: "I have just tossed the first issue of Fire into the fire." Commenting upon various of our contributors, he said: "Aaron Douglas who, in spite of himself and the meaningless grotesqueness of his creations, has gained a reputation as an artist, is permitted to spoil three perfectly good pages and a cover with his pen and ink hudge pudge. Countee Cullen has written a beautiful poem in his 'From a Dark Tower,' but tries his best to obscure the thought in superfluous sentences. Langston Hughes displays his usual ability to say nothing in many words. (237)

The actual content of *FIRE!!* has immediately recognizable avant-garde meaning in the local context of Harlem Renaissance cultural politics. The first thing the reader of *FIRE!!* encountered after the table of contents was a full page drawing of an African woman under a coconut tree—but this was not the woman of noble heritage (Figure 6.1). Toes pigeoning in, knees knocking, face burrowing down into her shoulder in a coy gesture rendered grotesque by her nudity and jungle setting—her body is an inversion of every feature of "primitive womanhood" generally admired in contemporaneous Africanist discourse—large flat breasts pointing straight down, fat belly, bunchy thighs, nappy hair. On the opposite page, just under the *FIRE!!* logo, was the large-lettered title, "Cordelia the Crude." Though the short story it named had no literal connection to Richard Bruce's illustration, together they set an unmistakable tone—one might even say they declared a mission for the publication: the antiexaltation of Negro womanhood.

In fact, Wallace Thurman's "Cordelia"—a Southern country girl recently arrived in New York—does turn out to be sister to Bruce's African. The key to their affinity is the Harlem Renaissance discourse (well established by 1926), which, as we have seen, finds in the African American peasant girl the embodiment of a noble (or threatening) racial past. Yet Cordelia herself gets not an iota of romanticization or even much respect. Our introduction to her establishes this from the first.

Figure 6.1 Richard Bruce [Nugent], Untitled, published in *FIRE!!* (1926). (Schomburg Center for Research in Black Culture, New York Public Library)

> Physically, if not mentally, Cordelia was a potential prostitute, meaning that although she had not yet realized the moral import of her wanton promiscuity nor become mercenary, she had, nevertheless, become quite blasé and bountiful in the matter of bestowing sexual favors upon persuasive and likely young men.

And later: "Cordelia, sixteen years old, matronly mature, was an undisciplined, half literate product of rustic South Carolina" (5). And when the speaker-protagonist finally encounters her,

> She clumped down the aisle [of the movie theater] before me, her open galoshes swishing noisily, her two arms busy wriggling themselves free from the torn sleeve lining of a shoddy imitation fur coat that one of her mother's wash clients had sent to her. She was of medium height and build, with overly

> developed legs and bust, and had a clear, keen light brown complexion. Her too slick, too naturally bobbed hair, mussed by the removing of a tight, black turban was of an undecided nature, i.e., it was undecided whether to be kinky or to be kind, and her body, as she sauntered along in the partial light had such a conscious sway of invitation that unthinkingly I followed, slid into the same row of seats and sat down beside her. (6)

In a pointed inversion of the standard renaissance meaning that renders the lowly "colored girl" transcendent by virtue of her continuity with Africa, Cordelia's tawdriness has somehow spilled over to the "woman of Africa" on the opposite page, bringing them both down to the level of the contemptible.

From what perspective could such deliberate denigration be desirable? What cultural positioning makes such devastating iconoclasm satisfying? Here we might go back to the pages in *Fire!!* before the table of contents. *FIRE!!*, we learn, is "A Quarterly Devoted to the Younger Negro Artists," a group whose credo is presumably expressed in Langston Hughes's unsigned Foreword.

> *FIRE . . . flaming, burning, searing, and penetrating far beneath superficial items of the flesh to boil the sluggish blood.*
>
> *FIRE . . . a cry of conquest in the night, warning those who sleep and revitalizing those who linger in the quiet places dozing.*
>
> *FIRE . . . melting steel and iron bars, poking livid tongues between stone apertures and burning wooden opposition with a cackling chuckle of contempt.*
>
> *FIRE . . . weaving vivid, hot designs upon an ebon bordered loom and satisfying pagan thirst for beauty unadorned . . . the flesh is sweet and real . . . the soul an inward flush of fire. . . . Beauty? . . . flesh on fire—on fire in the furnace of life blazing. . . .*
>
> "Fy-ah,
> Fy-ah, Lawd,
> Fy-ah gonna burn ma soul!" (1)

Yet another bit of self-definition lies in the note that concludes the editors' solicitation for patronage of upcoming issues: "We make no eloquent or rhetorical plea. FIRE speaks for itself" (2). Taken together, these texts suggest an ethos which the journal material bears out: a self-conscious claim to youth and its privileges (including defiance of the world's opinion) and commitment to a revolutionary aesthetic threatening to bourgeois complacency (whether personal or institutional).

By itself, such an ethos allies the editors of *FIRE!!* with the subcultural revolutionaries of the international avant-garde. Indeed, the very name "Fire!!" seems deliberately to echo "Blast!" the journal of Wyndham Lewis's 1914–1915 Vorticists, while the "cackling chuckle of contempt" comes directly out of the manifestos of the Italian Futurists.[54] Like other manifestations of the historical avant-garde, *FIRE!!* explicitly promises a violent assault on the sensibilities of the status quo in a rhetoric highly conscious of itself as delivering a wake-up call to an (aesthetically) revolutionized future. The militant rhetoric with which the journal begins serves to signal Negro Youth's emphatic rejection of the bourgeois propriety urged upon them by their elders at *Crisis* and *Opportunity*, as does, arguably, the refusal to "plead"—to see language only and always for its instrumental value to the racial cause. The convergence in Harlem of establishment politics and a social progress agenda accounts for the generally apolitical character of this avant-garde. Unlike their European counterparts, who took social transformation as the telos of their aesthetic innovations, the Younger Negro Artists saw avant-garde meaning in freeing art (and the artist) from social (i.e., racial) necessity. (And "art for art's sake" may well be what draws certain conspicuous renaissance avant-gardists to an aesthetic alliance with the Decadents of the 1890s.)

Aside from the avant-garde rhetoric of destruction-as-creation, *FIRE!!*'s Foreword also lays claim to the "pagan" redemption of the body identified with the bohemians of Greenwich Village ("beauty unadorned," the "sweet and real flesh"). Historical sources point to significant social commerce between the Younger Negro Artists and the Village;[55] perhaps more important, representations like Wallace Thurman's 1932 roman à clef, *Infants of the Spring*, stress the Harlem literati's independent embrace of bohemian values in a manner that points as clearly back in time to the Decadents as to contemporaneous lower Manhattan. As we shall see more fully in the example of Richard Bruce Nugent, bohemianism with a Wildean spin has avant-garde force in the local context.

One final significance to the foreword is its identification with African American—rather than African—heritage. In citing a spiritual as opposed to tom-toms (the conventional trope of primal African power, which the avant-garde purpose might well seem to call for), the Fireites put space between themselves and the "primitivism" that serves as the authenticating flip side to bourgeois exaltation. At the same time, they challenge the dichotomy of civilized and uncivilized, whether laid across the grid of race (white and black) or class (bourgeois and peasant).[56]

We must note one important point of convergence between the rhetoric of Harlem's avant-garde and its establishment: the trope of "youth." "Our Younger Negro Artists" was a powerfully resonant phrase used by all sides to refer to the acknowledged creative center and, by implication, the future potential of the race. In the era of the New Ireland, the New Czechoslovakia, and the New Jew, the "Younger Negro Artist" served as a redaction of the New Negro, sweeping Harlem's cultural renaissance into the tide of global nationalism (to quote Locke again: "Harlem has the same role to play for the New Negro as Dublin had the New Ireland or Prague for the New Czechoslovakia"). Conversely, the emphasis on youth implied the freeing of a world's generation from its specific national (and racial) moorings into a modernist sense of *inter*nationalism. It is this vision which inspires the younger Negro artists to align themselves with the larger world of avant-garde and even high modernist aesthetics. But the most widespread (and shared, even by many white writers) point of reference for "Negro youth" was the spiritual awakening the New Negro would or could provide to an exhausted and moribund civilization. In his role as *Opportunity* columnist, Countee Cullen used this framework to defend Negro lyricism against the "soulless" formalism of the high modernists (Amy Lowell in particular). Interestingly, when the prominent drama critic Theophilus Lewis articulated the same general vision, his language actually converged with that of the revolutionary avant-garde.

> Now the Negro Problem is this: It is the question whether a youthful people living in the midst of an old and moribund civilization shall die with it or find themselves able to shake loose from its complexities and build their own culture on its ruins. This is a condition of extreme uncertainty and cannot be faithfully interpreted by the definite art forms which adequately enough express the life-spirit during its periods of stability and order. Rather, this condition of doubt will find its esthetic expression in dissonances of sound and color, and such explosive comedy and tragedy as results from the struggles of a passionate people to escape the restraints of the calvinist version of the Ten Commandments.
>
> The task for the Negro artist, then, is to observe the confusion of rusting flivvers, migratory populations and expiring faiths which confronts him and reveal its meaning in a felicitous manner. *He will show us, perhaps, the convulsions of a world breaking down in chaos. Perhaps the nuclei of a new world forming in incandescence.* [my italics][57]

With due acknowledgment, then, to the ways in which renaissance discourse was harmonious, if not completely unified, we return to its internal divisions, which are critical to the situation of the renaissance woman writer. In its campaign of resistance to the cultural-political establishment, the avant-garde element of the younger Negro artists seemed to set its sights on bringing down the exalted Negro woman, emblem of the establishment. Just as the Italian Futurists had targeted the female nude in its war on the artistic establishment that kept European sensibilities complicit in bourgeois values,[58] the Harlem avant-garde took the iconic Negro woman as a central locus of resistance to the racial elders and all that the elders would presumably impose on them—instrumental art and a life in public in the name of racial duty.

The pages of *FIRE!!*, though certainly expressive of the artistic individualism the journal was determined to liberate, have a strong unifying current of pointed iconoclasm. "Smoke, Lilies and Jade," six prose pages by Richard Bruce [Nugent] listed as "A Novel, Part I," is perhaps most determinedly calculated to shock. Going beyond libertinism to bisexuality, beyond aestheticism to decadence, "Smoke, Lilies and Jade" pointedly explodes the image of the Harlem renaissance artist as a noble New Negro. This new artist is a bohemian in the Decadent tradition and asserts himself unapologetically as such from the very first lines of the story (and note that the ellipses are in the original, modernist-phenomenological form):

> He wanted to do something . . . to write or draw . . . or something . . . but it was so comfortable just to lay there on the bed . . . his shoes off . . . and think . . . think of everything . . . short disconnected thoughts—to wonder . . . to remember . . . to think and smoke . . . why wasn't he worried that he had no money . . . he *had* had five cents . . . (33)

While it was the manifest bisexuality that reportedly led Bruce Nugent to sign the story "Richard Bruce" in deference to his family, it was arguably the denobling of the renaissance that led to the virulent critical responses Hughes cites.

Another selection, Zora Neale Hurston's "Color Struck (A Play in Four Scenes)," portrays a dark-skinned African American woman so obsessed with the real and imagined privileges accruing to women of light skin that she ruins her chances at a happy life and even allows her light-skinned daughter to die out of jealous neglect. The play's setting is vintage Hurston: an all-black, Eatonville-like society, within which white racism counts for very little, but the foibles of black folk are on prominent display. Hurston's other contribution, the short story "Sweat," is similarly set and focused, telling the story of an abusive husband who attempts to drive away and, failing that, to kill his long-suffering (but "too skinny") wife in order to move his plump mistress into the house his wife has bought with her years of "sweat" as a laundress. Poetry selections included such works by Langston Hughes as "Elevator Boy," which depicted the consciousness of an ordinary working-class man doing (and thinking) what he must to get along. Through his eyes, we glimpse the meaning of success ("Two new suits an' / A woman to sleep with") and aspiration ("I been runnin' this / Elevator too long. / Guess I'll quit now"). Lewis Alexander's "Little Cinderella" is a sexually aggressive woman (whether prostitute or sheba[59]) who offers herself as an erotic object in stanza one ("Look me over, kid! / I knows I'm neat,—/ Little Cinderella from head to feet") then turns her own eroticizing and actively seductive gaze back on the man in stanza two.

> Daddy, daddy,
> You sho' looks keen!
> I likes men that are long and lean.
> Broad Street ain't got no brighter lights
> Than your eyes at pitch midnight. (23)

Edward Silvera's "Jungle Taste" performs some subtler cultural work, drawing fine lines within the race/class/gender complex of "exoticization." The first of his two stanzas denies the "Otherness" of the implicitly working- or peasant-class black man and thus sets his speaker apart from the bourgeoisie of both races who secure their own identities in opposition to the "primitive."

> There is a coarseness
> In the songs of black men

Coarse as the songs
Of the sea.
There is a weird strangeness
In the songs of black men
Which sounds not strange
To me.

Moving on to women in the second and final stanza, however, the speaker is quite insistent on their exotic character.

There is beauty
In the faces of black women,
Jungle beauty
And mystery.
Dark, hidden beauty
In the faces of black women
Which only black men
See.

The difference between standard exoticization and what Silvera would carve out here is, first and most obviously, that this mystery is unavailable to voyeuristic whites. It is furthermore not a function of class but of gender alone, something women have and men see. The paradoxical effect of this declaration of difference is to emphasize the speaker's commonality—along lines of race—with the people he observes. If finally ''jungle taste'' and ''jungle beauty'' evoke primitivism as usual, the poem itself emerges as a concerted effort to get outside the class dichotomy which leaves the (black) intelligentsia unimplicated in the race they celebrate. Silvera finally defines Negro womanhood in terms of heterosexuality instead of publicity (which may or may not be an unqualified victory for Negro womanhood).

A key issue for the writers of *FIRE!!* is the function and status of the Harlem intelligentsia. Having declared themselves free from the traditional responsibility of racial uplift, the Younger Negro Artists seem simultaneously to be grappling with their collective social definition, if only in negative terms. Wallace Thurman's ''Fire Burns: A Department of Commentary'' launches a straightforward attack on the Harlem critical establishment for its condemnation of white patron and writer Carl Van Vechten's sensational novel of Harlem life, *Nigger Heaven*. The critical scandal attendant on *Nigger Heaven*'s publication provides an easy vehicle for a ''younger Negro'' self-positioning, requiring little more than a reversal of values—a staunch defense of the lurid exotic representation of cabaret life that Du Bois and company excoriate, of Van Vechten's independence as an artist from any claims on his loyalty from the race who hospitably showed him around Harlem, and of his even more fundamental artistic independence (as a white man writing of black life) from racial identity per se.

More complicated is the essay preceding Thurman's editorial, ''Intelligentsia,'' written by Arthur Huff Fauset, folklorist and younger brother to

Jessie Redmon Fauset. In general stylistic terms, we might see this piece as a typical example of the Menckenesque debunking made popular in the twenties through *The Smart Set*—and hence as another gesture of external affiliation, this time with the national mainstream culture. The opening paragraph of the essay signals immediately the acerbic dismissiveness of H.L.M. (as Fauset offhandedly refers to him later in the essay)

> Of all the doughty societies that have sprung up in this age of Kluxers and Beavers the one known by that unpronounceable word, "Intelligentsia," is among the most benighted. The war seems to have given it birth, the press nurtured it, which should have been warning enough, then the public accepted it, and now we all suffer. (45)

Fauset continues in this vein for the rest of a page and a half, skewering the "intelligentsia" on grounds of their pretentiousness, uselessness, and parasitic relation to "truly intellectual types like Sinclair Lewis, Dreiser, H.L.M., and Shaw, men who are in every respect creative critics and thinkers." One is struck in general by the whiteness of this list, and in particular by the omission of W. E. B. Du Bois, a giant of contemporaneous intellectual life, who surely meets Fauset's criterion of making a positive and original contribution to solving social problems. Perhaps, then, Fauset's point is to put the African American critical establishment in its place by invoking a canon of "Nordic" untouchability. We might explain such a seemingly self-defeating strategy as an excessive manifestation of, again, the avant-garde refusal to "promote" the race. But while Fauset's conspicuous omissions seem to identify the Harlem Renaissance status quo as the target of his backhanded criticism, the details of the essay's caricature lead much more readily to the bohemian avant-garde: this intelligentsia "measure [literature] by its mystic qualities or its pornographical settings," and best of all, "they are actually proud of their nonaccomplishment: it shows their artistic temperament, they boast" (46).

Before we dismiss such self-ridicule as implausible, we should look back to "Cordelia the Crude," the short story by *FIRE!!*'s chief editor, which begins the journal. Appended to the concerted deflation of Negro womanhood we saw in Cordelia is an equally devastating commentary on the intelligentsia, as embodied in the story's speaker. We have already witnessed his reflexive response to Cordelia's charms: "her body . . . had such a conscious sway of invitation that unthinkingly I followed, slid into the same row of seats and sat down beside her." As the story continues, our hero backs out of the sexual encounter at the last moment.

> I abruptly drew away from her, opened my overcoat, plunged my hand into my pants pocket, and drew out two crumpled one dollar bills which I handed to her, and then, while she stared at me foolishly, I muttered good-night, confusedly pecked her on her cold brown cheek, and darted down into the creaking darkness.

In the final lines (set six months later), our hero discovers that Cordelia has gone from "potential" to actual prostitute—and that his own attempt at chivalry has been the means of that transition. Spotting her at a rent party "in a well known whore house," he greets her; more specifically, he watches her dance with various men, then "seeing that she was about to leave the room[,] . . . rushed forward calling Cordelia?" She, "finally recognizing me[,] said simply, without the least trace of emotion,—'Lo kid . . ." (6). His romantic sensibility thus fully contrasted to her vulgar one—that is, his identity as an artist secured against her whorishness—the story finishes with a dramatically ironic flourish.

> And without another word [she] turned her back and walked into the hall to where she joined four girls standing there. Still eager to speak, I followed and heard one of the girls ask: Who's the dicty [high-toned] kid? . . .
>
> And Cordelia answered: The guy who gimme ma' firs' two bucks. . . .

After so unrelenting a deflation of Negro womanhood, Thurman aims his final, most devastating blow at the pretensions of modernist artists—people like himself—who are so busy aestheticizing their own encounters with "the people" that they fail to see themselves as implicated in the human society to which they play voyeur.

Thurman's 1932 postmortem on the renaissance, *Infants of the Spring*, devotes several hundred pages to anatomizing the untenable social position of the artist, and the evidence is that self-denigration and self-pity may have been Thurman's peculiar lens for cultural observation.[60] But beyond Thurman as an individual writer, there is a more general contradiction at work in the subcultural refusal to locate meaning elsewhere than with the individual artist. Renaissance avant-garde identity rests on a rejection of the notion that art and artists can or should produce social progress; instead, individual aesthetic vision should be the only guide to artistic production. But while meaning must come from the individual self, the individual artist must also be deflated as a racial example, as a (non)member of the Talented Tenth. "The folk" are a source of meaning and value for some, but with the proviso that they must not be romanticized or "promoted." The resulting ambivalence for avant-garde artistic self-positioning vis-à-vis the world manifests itself in self-directed irony (of the sort seen in "Cordelia") and in the impulse to elide the distinction between artist and world. *FIRE!!*'s best example of the latter is Aaron Douglas's "Three Drawings," in which the typical Harlem "types" of the preacher and the cabaret waitress sandwich between them the "type" of the artist (30–32).

In the midst of what we have identified as avant-garde speech and preoccupations, three contributions to *FIRE!!* stand out as anomalous: those by Countee Cullen, the favorite son of the critical establishment (and, just briefly, the actual son-in-law of W. E. B. Du Bois himself),[61] and our representative Renaissance women, Helene Johnson and Gwendolyn Bennett. Though unquestionably a "younger Negro Artist," Cullen took a conservative position on the critical question of "appropriate" Negro art (as we have seen), used traditional romantic ("white") forms for his poetry, and, perhaps not coincidentally, served as literary editor and columnist for *Opportunity*, giving him a voice in the renaissance public sphere unrivaled by any other "youth." His poem, "From the Dark Tower," stands out in the midst of so much avant-garde rebellion as an unrelentingly earnest protest poem couched in a far-off nineteenth-century diction, as the opening lines convey: "We shall not always plant while others reap / The golden increment of bursting fruit" (16). Neither Bennett nor Johnson takes anything like the style of Cullen, and yet they share with him, uniquely in this collection, the focus on white oppression which was the centerpiece of art as propaganda. Johnson's poem, "A Southern Road," though modernist in its elliptical and compressed imagery, settles in its final lines on the figure of a lynched man. Bennett's short story, "Wedding Day," tells of a black American expatriate, embittered by racism, who is beguiled into marrying a white woman only to be jilted by her at the last minute—on grounds of race.

At this point, we should note that Johnson and Bennett are two of only three women contributors to *FIRE!!*, along with Zora Neale Hurston; moreover, only Bennett and Hurston have a place on the editorial board. Hurston is the more powerful presence of the two, both in the renaissance generally and within the pages of *FIRE!!*, of which she gets nearly fourteen to herself. But Hurston is also thirty-five years old in 1926, well-established as a writer and even more so as a personality.[62] By contrast, Bennett is only twenty-six, and Johnson is a mere twenty-one. The five years separating Bennett and Johnson are perhaps the most critical with respect to subcultural participation: at the moment in 1922 when Charles Johnson launched the Renaissance with his dinner honoring Jessie Fauset, Johnson was a high school sophomore in Boston, while Bennett, at twenty, was enough of a New York artist to write the commemorative poem for the occasion ("To Usward"). Just three months before the publication of *FIRE!!* Bennett had begun reporting "informal literary intelligence" and "the lighter side of Negro letters" in her "Ebony Flute" column for *Opportunity*, a post which ensconced her officially at the hub of Renaissance goings-on.[63] Bennett was at her peak of involvement with the renaissance in 1926—and at the apex of her poetic productivity—but Johnson would really hit her stride as a writer only in the subsequent year.

Bennett's "Wedding Day" actually does locate itself in the street, though that street is not Lenox Avenue but Rue Pigalle in Montmartre; nor does it come in for much "celebration" or "local color." The protagonist, Paul Watson, is a boxer, a club musician, and a violent criminal—a quintessential urban character of the sort the establishment loathed to see given literary life. And yet, all his exploits are motivated by an unimpeachable anti-racist motive. For reasons we explore in chapter 8, some degree of deflection from the avant-garde path is built into Bennett's self-positioning as a feminine speaker. It will be for Johnson to fully appropriate and inhabit the poetics of the avant-garde; *FIRE!!*'s only intimation of this eventuality is the high modernist aesthetic (and, by implication, identification) of "Southern Road." Note in particular the nihilistic vision with which the poem closes, a lynching-as-anti-Cruxifixion:

> A hidden nest for beauty
> Idly flung by God
> In one lonely lingering hour
> Before the Sabbath.
> A blue-fruited black gum,
> Like a tall predella,
> Bears a dangling figure,—
> Sacrificial dower to the raff,
> Swinging alone,
> A solemn, tortured shadow in the air. (17)

FIRE!! collapsed in debt after its first issue (its hundreds of unsold copies lost in a warehouse conflagration). It was not until 1928 that the editorially driven Wallace Thurman once again attempted to give avant-garde speech an institutional home in the renaissance public sphere. *Harlem: A Forum of Negro Life* had a distinctly more pragmatic and conciliatory air than its predecessor. The new journal carried plenty of paid advertising and gave generous space to conservatives like George Schuyler and establishment powers like Alain Locke. Thurman's inaugural editorial cast *Harlem* as the synthesis of the old dichotomy.

> The old propagandistic journals had served their day and their generation well, but they were emotionally unprepared to serve a new day and a new generation. The art magazines, unsoundly financed as they were, could not last. It was time for someone with vision to found a wholly new type of magazine, one which would give expression to all groups, one which would take into consideration the fact that this was a new day in the history of the world and that new points of view and new approaches to old problems were necessary and inescapable.

But even as mediator among "all voices," Thurman retained his claim to youth and the "new"—that is, to modernist relevance over establishment obsolescence.

In fact, the *Harlem* materials devoted to avant-garde expression were largely unmitigated from the heady days of *FIRE!!*, in some cases even intensifying the radical assault on bourgeois sensibility. Roy de Coverly's "Holes" concerned an artist driven by the power of a prostitute's eyes to paint and then strangle her; Langston Hughes's "Luani" tells of an African woman's inexplicable sexual power over a doomed European man—both stories clearly authorized by a certain misogynist bravado within high modernism. William Hill's poem "Conjure Man" generates two stanzas of exotic mystique, only to bring the man and his magic rudely down to (mercenary) earth in the final line: "Conjure doctor's fee is due" (45). More obscure at the present historical remove is Leon Noyes's cartoon, "Deep Harlem, a

Study in Sepia" (42). Two near-minstrel figures—very black and shiny-faced, with prominent white lips—stand off, one a policeman, the other a cab driver apparently in violation of the law. The humor presumably resides in the rundown quality of the cab, the muscularity of the cop, the sheer blackness of the men, and especially in their antagonism and the relish with which the officer wields power—all deflationary of racial solidarity and the New Negro. The most direct and perhaps playful gibe at the New Negro Renaissance comes from Thurman himself in his "Harlem Directory: Where to Go and What to Do When in Harlem" (43). Beginning with "There are four main attractions in Harlem," Thurman baldly develops the notion of Harlem as a tourist center, even leading off his list of nightclubs with the notoriously jim crow Cotton Club. He furthermore makes the first of his "four attractions" churches—followed by gin mills, restaurants, and nightclubs. In all likelihood, Thurman intends his "Directory" to say out loud and in the worst possible taste what all the renaissance worries might be the case, that Harlem is not an autonomous African American cultural mecca but a sideshow dependent upon white interest for its existence.

Clearer in 1928 than might have been possible in the time of *FIRE!!*'s publication was the degree to which theater held a utopian status in establishment renaissance values; more than ever, it had become invested with the promise of acceptance into and transformation of American culture. The avant-garde of Harlem accordingly targeted theater, along with the still-exalted woman, often merging the two, just as they tended to be merged in mainstream renaissance representation (a phenomenon explored in chapter 7). As he had two years earlier, Richard Bruce [Nugent] provided this latest avant-garde document with shocking feminine iconography. His single illustration, titled "Salome: Negrotesque I" (Figure 6.2) interrupts—or augments—the George Little short story "Two Dollars." As was the case in *FIRE!!* the story has no explicit narrative link to the drawing, yet their juxtaposition generates significant avant-garde meaning.

To begin with, "Salome" evokes the Oscar Wilde play of the same name, which had been enjoying a craze in the United States for ten years or so.[64] The many theatrical productions, movies, and at least one derivative novel included a production by the Ethiopian Art Players, an African American company who chose this play to inaugurate their first season in 1923. The choice may seem a strange one or, at least, as cultural commentator Esther Fulks Scott put it, "an ambitious and hazardous undertaking" for a black company of social and philanthropic purpose, given the fact that Wilde's play was a virtual emblem of sexual decadence.[65] Yet Scott was typical of the Harlem critics in her defense of this particular production as the reverse of decadent. The difference, according to Scott, resided in Salome herself at the scandalous climax of the play: actress Evelyn Preer's "Dance [of the Seven Veils], while done with intense emotional expression, was yet chaste." Understandably defensive about such a claim, Scott enlisted Preer's own testimony on this point, as well as corroboration from the white press. Cited alongside a large publicity shot of herself in an unmistakably demure pose,

Figure 6.2 Richard Bruce [Nugent], 'Salome: Negrotesque I,' published in *Harlem: A Forum of Negro Life* (1928). (Schomburg Center for Research in Black Culture, New York Public Library)

Preer said, "I believe Salome was a religious fanatic and a virtuous girl who had given her heart to Jokanaan. . . . Her dance then would necessarily be a chaste and restrained one" (20). And among many the many reviewers Scott cited, Sam Putnam of the *Chicago Evening Post* declared, "Salome was a saint, rather than a devil. Her dance was one of the most chaste exhibitions I have ever seen. It was almost austere" (23).

Whatever its popularity, the subject matter of *Salome* had not been entirely domesticated, as evidenced by the occasional banning of performances. An operatic *Salome* was canceled at the Metropolitan, and even the Ethiopian Art Players themselves were prevented from playing in Boston by that city's mayor. The question arises, then, as to why an organization centrally concerned with racial reputation, and especially the reputation of its women, would launch its career in so precarious a craft as fin de siècle debauchery (however restrained). The discussion within renaissance establishment journals like *Crisis* and *Opportunity*, exemplified by Scott's article, suggests strongly that *Salome* was a challenge, a paradoxically perfect vehicle for dramatizing the race's successful conquest of bestial emotions in the context of "civilized" psychological depth—in effect, for staging the bourgeois redemption of a world-historical female pervert.[66]

When, five years and at least one black production of *Salome* later, Richard Bruce [Nugent] published his drawing, he might well have been thinking more of the original Aubrey Beardsley illustrations of Wilde's play and the international context of Salome's scandalous production history than of any local attempts to make the play the site of race work. Beyond his presumably strong avant-garde identifications with modernist aesthetics and Decadent bohemianism, Nugent might well have been drawn to the sexual nonconformity that made *Salome* an intensely personal endeavor for both Wilde and Beardsley. Indeed, Nugent's drawing echoes those of Beardsley in certain key ways, in particular, the hair with a life of its own and the broken-lined adumbrations woven into the figure's costume. Moreover, the face, though marked as racially African, has more the look of an African mask than an African American person, suggesting that even on the point of racial identification, Nugent weighs in as more a international modernist than a citizen of Harlem. It seems likely that this expression of allegiance to the broader context was an attempt to reclaim *Salome* as a powerfully charged symbol of radical perversion in defiance of local attempts to sanitize her.

Returning to "Negrotesque," certain details now come into legibility: Salome's impotent hands, fingerless and downturned[67]; the twisted splay of her legs, suggesting the contortion of minstrelsy; her hairy underarms and hairless genitals, sexual power become mere unkemptness; and, most striking of all, the tawdriness of Salome's scarves, with their polka dots and obvious string attachments—the artistic dance of the seven veils become mere striptease. Nugent's drawing targets both the theatrical and the feminine ideal in renaissance discourse, but his "Negrotesque" is more than doubly devastating, for she exploits mercilessly the contradiction at the ambivalent core of racial uplift: that between bourgeois dignity and public display.

At this point we begin to see the way the seemingly unrelated short story within whose pages "Negrotesque" appears actually contributes to its meaning. "Two Dollars," by George Little, tells a self-consciously tawdry tale of gambling, two-timing, and jealous murder—just the sort of story to raise the hackles of the publicity-conscious establishment. The descriptions of the opening cabaret scene are pitched toward broad, derisive humor in portraits like the following:

> a plump brown skin girl with protruding front teeth, thick lips and straightened hair sticking out ludicrously was playing the piano.

> a dowdy little brown skin woman approaching stout middle age. Her hair was streaked with gray, her hat perched precariously on top of her head as if

> undecided which way to fall, the pince nez with long gold chain which [she] always affected [standing] out in austere and dignified contrast to her abandoned gestures.

> a baldheaded old man with the face of a mischievous pickaninny, all the more ludicrous because of an artificial eye which stared steadily and unwinkingly when he gazed at anyone. (27)

> [the carddealer who] looked like a brown slug. (29)

Embedded within this local-color pageant is the distinctly out of place figure of genteel femininity.

> She was almost black, her head was small and well shaped. She wore her hair long and caught back in a roll at her neck. She was slightly above medium height and had a figure in which suppleness and voluptuousness were combined to a pleasing degree. Her calves and ankles were exquisitely proportioned—a delight to the eye. She had a voice of strength and clarity. She sang without effort. She moved her body in rhythm with her song. After she had finished singing she lifted the curtain on an exquisite scene of chiffon lingerie and blond hose and danced the Charleston.

While we are invited to be amused by all we see (as, indeed, the cabaret's patrons are), only this woman is ensconced on the stage and officially designated "the entertainer." Every detail of her person and her performance contributes to the portrait of bourgeois feminine perfection—the decorous hairdo, the perfect symmetry of physical proportion, and, most especially, the reserve, underscored by the narrator's shift to matter-of-factly short, declarative sentences, and in sharp contrast to the usual abandonment of the jazz singer. But when ultimately she "lift[s] the curtain on an exquisite scene of chiffon lingerie and blond hose"—concentrating into a single symbolic gesture what has all along been her situation as the woman on stage—the pretense that she can control the terms of her performance (that she can be on stage *and* bourgeois) is exploded by her "cruder" brethren. She begins to dance the Charleston, and we learn that

> Her efforts were abetted by exclamations from the patrons such as,
> 'Ah, play wid it!'
> 'Stan' up in there!'
> 'Do that thing!'
> 'Now do it!' (27)

Not only does her audience respond overtly—and exclusively—to the carefully suppressed sexual dimension of her performance, they get the last defining word on her status, since at this point the narrative moves away from this bourgeois interloper and on to the working-class story. If the story needed any help making its point, Nugent's "Negrotesque" is there to underscore its purposes. One effect of this intertextuality is clear: Salome is the sleazy underside to the bourgeois woman who performs her genteel femininity for the good of the race. At still another level, "Salome" is a commentary on that other lower-class feminine icon, the primitive Brown

Girl. The woman of Africa is here degraded and by the same means as her genteel sister, both of them reduced to their common sexual vulnerability as performing women.

Perhaps more than any cultural statement we have seen till now, *Harlem: A Forum of Negro Life* forces the question of how a would-be avant-gardist might find a place for herself as a woman writer. Gwendolyn Bennett has ceased to try by 1928, having recently found herself unhappily married and exiled in Florida from the ferment of renaissance culture. Helene Johnson, too, is past the peak of her subcultural involvement and will retire to her hometown of Boston within the year—and from writing altogether within three years. It might be hasty to draw conclusions from the coincidence of the two primary female avant-gardists withdrawing their energies just as the avant-garde seems to consolidate its misogyny. It would be just as remiss, however, not to take note of a certain correlation between gender emphasis and ideological zeal. Just as the increasing national importance of the renaissance as a whole seemed to call forth a definitively masculine artistic leadership, so perhaps the heightened self-consciousness of its rebellious front line necessitated a renewed assault on propriety and on the woman in whom it was embodied.

Johnson is actually relatively well represented in the avant-garde roster of *Harlem*, the only woman with two poems in its pages (this pattern of diminished representation of women's work is widespread in the later years). Interestingly, these works suggest the best and worst results of her engagement with avant-garde masculinism. "Cui Bono?," in a standard, even cliché, avant-garde attack on convention, ridicules a sexually repressed middle-class woman for her hypocrisy and prudery. The first and final stanzas tell us all we need to know.

> She sat all day and thought of love.
> She lay all night and dreamed it.
> Our romance stricken little dove
> Grew truly quite anaemic.
> . . . .
>
> "I wish I'd let him kiss me tho.
> Oh, just the merest peck.
> I wish—I wish—I wish, but no,
> I'd lose my self-respect."
>
> And so she sits and thinks of love.
> And all night long she dreams it.
> And with regret our little dove
> Continues quite anaemic. (11)

Painfully arch and uncharacteristic, "Cui Bono?" easily represents the self-alienated nadir of Johnson's avant-garde career.

And yet the dismissive modernist psychologizing she deploys here becomes a serious psychological study in her other *Harlem* poem, "A Missionary Brings a Young Native to America." Out of the unlikely combination of the disdained bourgeois feminine psyche and the objectified exotic primitive comes a complex portrait.

All day she heard the mad stampede of feet
Push by her in a thick unbroken haste.
A thousand unknown terrors of the street
Caught at her timid heart, and she could taste
The city grit upon her tongue. She felt
A steel-spiked wave of brick and light submerge
Her mind in cold immensity. A belt
Of alien tenets choked the songs that surged
Within her when alone each night she knelt
At prayer. And as the moon grew large and white
Above the roof, afraid that she would scream
Aloud her young abandon to the night,
She mumbled Latin litanies and dreamed
Unholy dreams while waiting for the light. (40)

"Missionary" explicitly manipulates contemporary discourses of modernism. Even before we notice their effects on the woman of the poem, we are struck by the challenges Johnson's cityscape poses to the standard colonialist dichotomy. Rather than a jungle assault on the fragile sensibilities of the civilized explorer, it is the "timid-hearted" "native" who finds herself under siege by the city's "mad stampede of feet," its "thousand unknown terrors," her very body overtaken not by heat or fever but by urban "grit upon her tongue." And yet this is not the simple irony of reversal but a complex interpenetration of values in which to stage the commensurably complex psyche of the "Young Native."

In a dramatic flouting of modernist cultural codes, Johnson makes this "native" the subject of psychological repression rather than the object of fantasies about "the primitive" in the psychic drama of some bourgeois observer. In attributing psychology to the Brown Girl, Johnson violates the separation (upheld even by the Harlem avant-garde) of complex civilized consciousness and unmediated primitive abandon. Moreover, once the language of psychoanalysis is applied to the Brown Girl, the distance between her and the genteel Negro woman closes, pulling each of them into the matrix of historical struggle and out of their respective cultural/iconic exiles—off their pedestals, as it were: the pedestal of racial authenticity and the pedestal of aracial gentility. The Brown Girl thus becomes an articulator of the renaissance she so often merely symbolizes, and the genteel, implicitly "white-faced" Negro woman becomes an authentic African American with a claim to racial heritage. At the moment that she gains this heritage, she gains, too, a respectable origin for her infamous repression. In the face of colonialist cultural power—its "steel-spiked wave of . . . cold immensity"—

she prays for her life, ''mumbling Latin litanies'' to save herself from the direct confrontation with colonialist cultural might that her ''young abandon[ed] scream'' would surely bring on. The imperative of survival and not the fastidiousness of ''Cui Bono?'' chases her eroticism into the unconscious space of ''Unholy dreams.'' The centrality of the ''Missionary'' in the poem's title serves to insist on the historical origins of black womanhood in all its dimensions, at the same time that the missionary's rather remarkable absence in the poem itself allows the native some space of psychological autonomy—even giving her credit for a degree of complicity in her own subjugation.

''Missionary'' works to subvert the key ideological divides between artist and object, victim and oppressor, and good girl and bad. As we shall see, in her best poetic moments, Helene Johnson used the persona of a slangy urban modern to inhabit fully—and as a woman—the street, which is here the object of so much terror. In embracing the topos of Harlem itself, developing a poetics of place that renders Harlem luminous and unique, the rebels of the renaissance also laid claim to its essence. Anyone truly identified with the Harlem Renaissance had to find herself in this space and speak through this poetics. Bennett and Johnson felt the strong lure of the ''real'' renaissance, but they were also subject, as bourgeois women, to the imperative to carry the burden of racial publicity. Before we come to focus on them, chapter 7 explores the specific phenomenon of ''performing'' bourgeois Negro womanhood through the works of those who felt its effects most keenly: women writers squarely in the ''genteel school.''

SEVEN

"Exalting Negro Womanhood"

Performance and Cultural Responsibility for the Middle-Class Heroine

TWELFTH ANNUAL EDUCATION NUMBER

The CRISIS

JULY, 1923

FIFTEEN CENTS A COPY

> To no modern race does its women mean so much as to the Negro, nor come so near to the fulfillment of its meaning.
>
> W. E. B. DuBois, *Darkwater: Voices from within the Veil*

> We think there will be no denial of the fact that until a far-seeing race woman called attention to the fact that the colored woman owed it to herself and her loved ones to do all in her power to improve her personal appearance, in other words until this appeal was made to the pride of our womanhood, the great masses were not large users of hair and toilet preparations.
>
> F. B. Ransom, "Manufacturing Toilet Articles: A Big Negro Business"

Having set out the larger terms of Harlem Renaissance discourse, we now turn our attention to *women's writing*, with an eye to discerning strategic responses to complex subcultural imperatives. It bears repeating that women produced the renaissance as well as reacted to it, derived identity and value from its ethos as well as risked objectification through proximity to its icons. As the ensuing discussion shows, the enabling and constraining sides of this equation balanced out (or failed to) according to the ways generic and historical imperatives converged for individual writers. Chapter 8 explores the significant utopian potential of the *lyric poem* for renaissance women. By contrast, the space of *narrative*, pursued in the present chapter, emerges as almost claustrophobic in the ideological burdens it imposes. My point, however, is not to argue for a given ideological content to either genre but to discover the particular uses to which these forms were put by women writers of modernist Harlem.

As I argued in the previous chapter, Harlem Renaissance artists of all generations worked under a powerful sense of class-specific responsibility for the fortunes and status of the African American people, a situation with particular implications for women writers. In the configuration of cultural imperatives and possibilities that characterized the renaissance, the bourgeois African American woman found herself with the onerous task of endlessly "performing"—and proving—her identity to a mainstream public unwilling to believe in her existence.

Photograph on preceding page: Cover of the *Crisis*, July 1923 (photograph of Clarissa Mae Scott). (Beinecke Library, Yale University)

Performance itself has a prominent place, both literally and metaphorically, in renaissance women's writing, and the goal of this chapter is to derive a sense of its relevant historical meanings through readings of three representative texts.[1] At stake is how these authors dealt imaginatively with their cultural situation and how, in turn, that situation might illuminate the literary-aesthetic logic of their texts. The structural specificity of each work—the telos of doom in Ottie B. Graham's play *Holiday* (1923), the centrality of the narrator to Mamie Elaine Francis's short story "Souls for Gasoline" (1925), and the symmetry of the double plot in Jessie Redmon Fauset's novel *There Is Confusion* (1924)—arises to a significant extent out of the problem of performance, just as the conventions of each respective genre contribute to that problem's resolution. The formal differences among these texts signal even greater differences of substantive emphasis, as each text takes up a distinct aspect of bourgeois womanhood's predicament and evolves a distinct authorial negotiation of its terms. Running through the variety these texts present, however, is at least one common response to compulsory performance, deployed to different degrees: each bourgeois heroine depends in some crucial way on a feminine other for the meaning and stability of her identity. The nature and intensity of the relationship and the imperilment of the heroine herself reflect the author's assessment of the risks attached to performance and the possibilities she is able to imagine for surviving its disciplinary regime.

Ottie B. Graham and Mamie Elaine Francis

Though *The Messenger* had for some time been "specializ[ing] in the theatrical field,"[2] in May 1925 drama critic Theophilus Lewis took a strong, even polemical stand in expanding the title of his "Theatre" column to read, "The Theatre: The Souls of Black Folk." Sentiments regarding theater were mixed among the cultural commentators of the renaissance; critics alternately dismissed it as trivial, hailed it as the culmination of "Negro" artistic expression and American art, and treated it as a necessary if faintly distasteful facet of the project for racial uplift. For the Harlem intelligentsia, theater embodied the ambivalent history and contemporaneous state of the race in its relation to the white mainstream: perpetually on public display yet visible only through the performance of racialized conventions. At the same time, the theater presented a most immediate access to public opinion, and the pages of *The Messenger* as well as *The Crisis* and *Opportunity* were peppered with calls for a true "Negro drama" that would bring the race into its own and into American high culture simultaneously.[3]

Complexly interwoven with discussion of the African American theater was the larger, more diffuse effort to "exalt Negro womanhood," which we have seen exemplified by *The Messenger*'s photographic campaign. The woman worthy of exaltation was one of social standing and, more often than not, of personal accomplishment as well.[4] "Exalting Negro Womanhood" and its equivalents in *The Crisis* and *Opportunity* often read quite like "society" pages, publishing the credentials and connections of the elect. But whatever its compensations, the bourgeois woman soon discovered the glare and responsibility of publicity to be a compulsory condition of her own womanhood, a womanhood she could not take for granted but had always to assert against the tide of a cultural history that condemned her to grotesque stereotypes or invisibility.[5] The impact of this imperative would be difficult to overestimate, and much contemporaneous women's writing—often the very writing traditionally dismissed by critics as irrelevant to the true racial tradition—struggles with (or against) its constraints in fairly direct fashion.[6]

Ottie B. Graham's *Holiday* spotlights the tyranny of public performance and its costs to the private woman. The play describes a brutal cultural economy in which the bourgeois woman finds herself relegated exclusively to performance and martyrdom in the name of racial advancement. Margot Cotell is an African American woman who has attained theatrical stardom while passing for white. The opening scene finds her suffering extreme agitation under the combined burden of a dark, chilly summer day, a melancholy ocean surf, pounding away outside her summer cottage, and her enslavement to the constant demands of "the people" that she perform. Not in years, she laments to her maid, Bertie, has she taken a "holiday."[7] When the schoolgirl Claire, "tall, slender [and] wrapped in a cape," bursts mysteriously on the scene and collapses in hysterical weeping, she, too, attributes her distress to the weather and to the fact that "this [place] is a summer resort—a place for a good time, and everybody has it but me. They're all white—I don't want to go with them—but I am absolutely alone!" (13–14). The conventions of melodrama may largely explain the heroines' temperamental susceptibility to the elements, but it will also transpire that, for Margot, the ocean and "the people" are one and the same: her audience is for her an abstract and irrevocable force of nature before which she is helpless to cease acting (16). For her part, Claire registers the sense that the white world she feels closing in around her is as bleak and unwelcoming to a "colored girl" as the chill winds of the day. If Claire is thus a shivering waif, shut out of the general merriment, Margot, her long-lost mother, is just as tragically shut in.

Margot's story may be read as sociological reflection. Left to support an infant daughter upon the death of her husband, she chooses the stage as one of the few employment options available to her as an African American woman. Once she finds herself passing for white (having joined a white acting company), she is able to greatly enlarge her prospects, leaving vaudeville for stock, and eventually ascending to the pinnacle of success at which the play finds her. Except for Margot's Duse-like stature, this trajectory generally squares with institutional realities of race, economics, and the theater in the early twentieth century.[8] Within the play itself, however, we are made to feel that such real-life conditions are only a pretext for Margot, whose destiny as an actress emanates from her own improper, even pathological, ambition. Yet both the sociological and the psychological readings lend themselves to an understanding of Margot as a figure for the existential reality of contemporaneous African American bourgeois women in general.

Indeed, Margot's performances sit squarely at the intersection of the world stage and the stage proper. The ostensible conflict of the play is that Margot has chosen acting over mothering, supporting but not acknowledging her daughter, whom she has long ago given over to the care of fancy boarding schools and a succession of guardians. Of a piece with the refusal to mother is a racial refusal: Margot claims a "false" whiteness at the expense of her "true" blackness, and since the daughter is visibly "colored," Margot cannot claim her. This plot suggests a system of governing values: the interdependence of rightful maternal and racial identities, the authenticity of the individual at home in the private sphere, and the public sphere as a theatrical world characterized by black deception, racial disloyalty, and white dominance. But these meanings blur as the text unfolds and the private sphere reveals itself as having little of privacy (and private goodness) about it. Leaving the staged identities of the public theater, we will find only the same staged identities in the private theater of mother-daughter relations. For Margot, then, there will be no returning to a "true" self.

Alone with her maid, Bertie, at the start of scene I, Margot muses fretfully about—and within a language of—acting and performance. Even race itself is introduced as a theatrical by-product. In an early line clearly meant to telegraph to us the imminent crisis of her racial passing, Margot says to the disconcerted Bertie, whose wrist she has just fitfully grabbed, "look[ing] hard into [her] face," "Don't be alarmed, young idiot. I just wanted to look at your skin. It's *beautiful* Bertie—I—I just wondered whether I might brown well.—My next role will require it" (13). The discourse of performance still reigns when Claire turns up as a lonely schoolgirl, weeping and desperate for "colored" and maternal companionship. After comforting her, Margot asks "What under heaven's sun made you come to me?" For at this point in the play, Margot stands before Claire doubly masked: not only secretly colored, she is, of course, Claire's real mother. Claire's halting reply teasingly hovers between the racial and the familial revelation (in fact, she *does not* know Margot's true relation to her) before launching into what might best be described as the remembrance of a cherished past performance.

> Because I knew you were—I—I used to know you when you lived across from my uncle and me in Mersville ["motherville/seaville"]. . . . I used to watch you come and go from my play-room window, and when you had gone down the street I would try so hard to walk like you. You were the wife of every fine prince in my fairy-tale books; when you came over to see uncle I tried to talk like you. Oh, I remember so well—when you took me for walks and held me on your knee—I—I thought I was in paradise. (13)

She goes on to speculate that "It—it must be that I remember you so well all the time because you were the only lovely woman I ever knew in my home" (14).

For Claire, Margot has been a model of womanhood since early childhood, one who embodies explicitly remote cultural ideals, and one whose value she names expressly as the private performance of those ideals—"you were the only lovely woman I ever knew *in my home*." Moreover, the most immediate impetus for Claire to seek Margot out has been her stage performance in *Crinoline*, whose title strongly suggests Margot played a Southern belle.[9] Claire says, "I'm lonely.—I want Uncle. He's the only mother I ever knew. . . . I knew you were here. I saw you play in 'Crinoline' the other night—and—I—I—." Finally, the knowledge that Claire has been struggling with comes out, ironically anticlimactic, given what she might have known:

MARGOT: You came here because you knew—that—I—was—

CLAIRE: Colored. (14).

At this moment, Margot's secrets—her racial and maternal truths—function as interchangeable in the structure of the play. But truly, they seem to *be* interchangeable—or at least inextricable—for Claire: she explicitly seeks a "colored" companionship whose content is maternal nurturance. (This equation is most striking when Claire describes her lost uncle as a "mother".) Just as consistent is her attraction to Margot's performances, both private and public, raising the possibility that the form of performance actually satisfies rather than impedes what Claire seeks. She has, in effect, been following Margot's "career" all of her life; the official performance of *Crinoline* only highlights the nature of their relationship generally. Claire has watched worshipfully from a distance—even apparently when no distance was required—as Margot enacted an ideal womanhood. Though Margot's performances have been of abstractly white women, Claire's witness has always included the knowledge that Margot was indeed "colored." Hence, for Claire, Margot has always been performing—and modeling—"Negro womanhood."

When Claire comes to Margot for motherly comfort even without knowing the biological truth, she has *not* chosen Margot for this role on the basis of any nurturant or domestic characteristics she might seem to possess. She does not, for instance, identify Margot's apartment as a cosy refuge from the elements, which loom so large in the play and which she has just rather dramatically escaped. The strong suggestion is that Margot has been elected to maternal status on the strength of her stage performance. When Margot finally confesses the truth and offers herself to Claire as a "real" mother—in the same moment, necessarily revealing her race and giving up her stage career—Claire begins by simply rejecting but ends by actually disbelieving her: "How—how do I know you are my mother?" she says (15–16). Claire's rather baffling skepticism may be seen as a desperate gesture of self-protection from a far more profound orphaning than that she has known throughout her lonely life. As an African American bourgeois daughter in a white world, Claire's greatest need from a mother (biological or adoptive) is a legacy of legitimacy for her own bourgeois womanhood. When Claire sits in a theater and watches someone whom she alone knows to be a ''colored'' woman perform the Southern belle to an audience of anonymous white admirers, she experiences ''Negro womanhood'' as limitless and her own: limitless because it can incorporate even its own theoretical antithesis, the Southern belle historically held forth as illustration and legitimation for the subwomanly status of the enslaved African American; her own because the experience of being the lone sentient witness to the meaning of Margot's performance in an ignorant and undifferentiated crowd renders her claim to Margot uniquely valid—as well as rendering herself uniquely worthy, and Margot, uniquely worth having.

The play asks us to see a tragic flaw in Margot's stage lust but simultaneously enmires us in the conflict at the heart of bourgeois African American motherhood. In the white world that would deny African American women a claim to genteel womanhood, private mothering is insufficient to bring along the next generation of daughters, who need to witness their mothers' womanly legitimacy in the abstract gaze of a national public desire. It is not surprising, then, that Claire's ultimate response to Margot's confession is to throw herself into the sea—a gesture not of confusion or ambivalence so much as of loss. In the terms within which the play defines motherhood, Claire *has* lost her mother in the same moment that her mother has given up her public status. Likewise, with Claire's suicide, Margot imagines she has lost the only audience capable of providing the racial frame of reference to grant her performance the meaning ''exalting Negro womanhood.'' Cut off from even the hope of racial duty and authenticity, Margot follows Claire into the sea, where they finally have ''their holiday together.''

At the close of the play, an unanticipated advocate steps forward to proclaim Margot's true worth as a martyr to racial advancement. Bertie, the maid, expresses a unique perspective in this bourgeois drama, a perspective which, moreover, grasps the larger stakes of Margot's life and death. In her capacity as working-class realist and survivor (over the dead and demented heroines), she is ''the race'' for whom Margot must be sacrificed. In the more specific terms of the present discussion, she is the class Other who provides for Margot's viability, such as it is.

Merely sympathetic and unobtrusive in scene I, Bertie steps forth in scene II as the rightful adjudicator of Margot's life. As Margot lies prostrate with grief and sedatives on her chaise longue, Bertie learns from a member of the rescue team working to save Claire that news of Margot's true ''color'' has spread and upset the guests of the resort. Her impassioned defense lifts Margot out of the sentimental/Gothic framework of hereditary secrets and dementia, which is all the play has offered us for understanding her thus far. Instead, Bertie describes Margot in the surprising language of rugged individualism.

> Well, what'n the devil's [her color] got to do with it! She didn't bother a darned soul unless *they* came after *her*. She never told nobody what she was because nobody asked her. I'd like to tell these white guys something around here. I may not be so doggoned high-up, but I certainly know the real stuff

> when I see it. Margot Cotell's got in her what a lot o' folks around here need, and need bad! She took the chance that came to her, and she's let'em know what she is. (17)

Earlier in the scene, Bertie has stood in for Claire in Margot's grief-inspired hallucinations, and there is an important sense in which she *is* the true daughter, sympathetic and appreciative of Margot's accomplishments. At the same time, she breaks us out of the insular vocabulary of family by placing Margot's life in the wider context of gritty American independence. Not only venturesome and determined, Margot is more American than the whites with whom she is surrounded. *This* is the "truth" about Margot, not some contingency of race and image; she is "the real stuff" and Bertie, as a working-class pragmatist, knows it when she sees it.

Bertie's authoritative judgments are consistent with a Harlem cultural discourse that privileged national identity, focusing on the Americanness of the Negro as underwriting the future of the race and the country itself. All the more reason, it seems to me, that we should wonder at the tragedy of Margot's life and death. If she had what it takes, why did she not have recourse to a redemptive national identity transcending the racial and gender identities that so troubled her? The fight to publicly legitimate bourgeois Negro womanhood, Graham seems to say, essential though it may be, is fatal to the Negro woman herself. Though the crisis of *Holiday* is precipitated by the coincidence of Claire's appearance, Margot's life has all along been uneasy and, on the day in question, is quite pointedly doomed from the first. "Somehow," Margot tells Bertie, "I believe I won't act tonight." The relentless necessity for a public demonstration of genuinely genteel womanhood traps the bourgeois woman in an "identity" of ethereal abstraction, from which she can only fade into the feminine perfection of self-annihilation. However American her pioneer spirit and her pursuit of success, Margot's task of "exalting Negro womanhood" relegates her to playing the "princess," the "belle," and, finally, the romantic suicide.

It is left to Margot's "daughters" to work out her inheritance. Had she lived, Claire, with finally only a private mother, would only have gotten feminine fragility without the (white) public endorsement to sustain it. By contrast, Bertie, always free of the bourgeois burden of public relations, is in theory positioned to go forward with the legacy of racial advancement through national identification. And yet, in the very last moment of the play, as Margot's "final, wild, victorious scream" is heard in the distance, this stalwart maid "falls, fainting where she stands," in so doing, mirroring for us the demise offstage (17). What are we to make of this final twist of the drama? Though the sturdy working-class woman of the race may be possessed of the vision to see her American future, as long as "Negro womanhood" is in "dispute," the play seems to say, "the whole race" depends on keeping the bourgeois woman in the front lines. Margot and her kind must sustain the contradictions of their lives indefinitely.

Mamie Elaine Francis's "Souls for Gasoline" moves us out of the war zone of direct claims to genteel femininity and into a shadowy space of indirection. The story tells of one bourgeois Negro woman's highly strategic response to the performative imperative—a response so strategic as to verge on minstrelsy. Importantly, ''Souls for Gasoline'' carries the suggestion of fantasy: the fantasy of self-creation and control of one's own identity and perhaps the even more powerful fantasy of refusing to take up the duties of bourgeois Negro womanhood. At the most general level, this brief narrative concerns a woman who moves from one social situation to another, driven by the trouble her identity as a highly educated, beautiful, black, and bourgeois woman causes her. At the center of the text is her relationship to the narrator, a certain discerning white personnel worker from one of her many jobs. The heroine, Liane Leclerc, pointedly evades the limelight that ''exalting Negro womanhood'' would thrust upon her. And yet, her claim to bourgeois status is unmistakably asserted through her identification with the story's unmistakably bourgeois narrator. Both are educated, acutely aware of the ideological mechanisms of racism, and quite above confronting them directly—this, in fact, is their strongest commonality. But whereas the white narrator finds such transcendence alone sufficient to her social situation, the African American Liane requires the narrator's recognition to secure her identity for the time when she is ready to claim it directly.

Apart from its value as one Harlem Renaissance woman writer's assertion of mastery over her social predicament, ''Souls for Gasoline'' offers a virtual catalogue of performative venues and the performances they engender. Ostensibly focused on religious conflict, the narrator tells of her experience with Liane, a mysterious woman whose secret turns out (rather unsatisfyingly) to be the loss of religious faith she confesses at their final encounter. Liane's principled refusal to participate in the formalities of Christian worship has cost her more than one job (including the one at the factory where the narrator is personnel officer) and, in that sense, functions just like the racism she has encountered in many prospective employers. Forced to wrest a conventionally clear narrative line from the text, then, we could say that Liane is a heroic woman forging a difficult path through a world of racial and religious bigotry to a cherished personal goal (she wants to earn a Columbia master's degree). But to take the text so much at its word would be to ignore much of its strange substance, which more accurately adds up to a woman's education in the politics of performance.

Liane's story begins with her childhood in the Episcopal church, where ''the majesty of the processional, the glorious music, the soft, persuasive tones of the rector, were all woven into a shining fabric that was my spiritual life.''[10] The next lines underscore the innocent unity which precedes the split of her world into performers and audiences, with all its attendant power dynamics: ''I had not been out of New Orleans, had not met many of my people, and I was certain that this splendid fabric of faith was universally shared.'' But at sixteen, Liane is sent to Washington, D.C., to live with relatives, ''intensely religious, staunch Baptists.''[11] Liane names her resultant discontent as the change from religion as ''a happy thing'' to religion as a ''stern, ascetic fear, a terrible preparation for death.'' But the focus of her explanation is not the tone but the dynamics of the new service:

> "In our pew was an old woman, a former slave. It was her weekly delight to get happy. That's what they call it. And I would watch her in fascinated fear. She would doze fitfully through the service, and then awake to rhythmic punctuations of 'Amen, glory to de Lawd, Amen.' And as the minister heard these first reassuring cries, he would proceed with inspired fire. I can't ever drown out the sound. Gradually increasing in tempo and fervor, he would persuade and then exhort and command his followers to give up sin and prepare for heavenly joys. Most conservative ministers do that. But you must understand the psychology of my people to picture the effect of it upon them.
>
> "They have the true faith. It is pathetic and beautiful, such a faith. If they could only see my childish vision of true faith. [But] No! . . .
>
> "Soon the entire congregation would be sobbing a passionate prayer, seeking light, and truth. . . . That amazing acceptance of Divine guidance was brutally whipped into an orgy of emotional hysteria."

The young Liane finds the "shining [and] splendid fabric" of the serene and opulent Episcopal service rent and, in its place, a dangerous and flagrantly manipulative human interaction between minister and congregation, performer and audience. Liane's identification with the audience in the vulnerability to which performance subjects them is evident in her remark, " 'I hated to go to church. It was too much like tearing out the soul of my race, and saying, "There!" It responds so to the word of God.' "

Liane steels herself against religion but still goes to church with her aunt, who, one fateful Sunday, tricks her into presenting herself to a visiting evangelist as a sinner in search of salvation. Again, the church context is defined by manipulation and exposure, this time her own: " 'Neither passionate wishing nor relativity would enable me to vanish, so I stood there. I tried to shrink, but seemed to loom up until I filled the church. I dared not look around. Three hundred pairs of eyes were staring at me in shocked pity' " (177). Liane then experiences a brief resurgence of faith just before her final descent into lifelong cynicism. Again, the salient factor is not spiritual content but religious dynamics. The minister suddenly delivers what is to her an appropriate performance, one that is self-contained and consequently grants her the invisibility and serenity of an analogous audience role.

> "The evangelist was praying earnestly. It might have been the voice of John the Baptist ringing from the altar. For a moment I felt a happy return of the golden fabric of faith. It seemed to fold about me, and shield me from those terrible eyes burning through me from behind."

Yet the orderliness of this moment and relation quickly deteriorates into a demand for her to "give up her soul"—to become the performer. It is then that "a new light dawn[s] upon [her]" and she realizes the minister's true motive: " ' "I must buy food to eat [she imagines him thinking], and gasoline for my car, and if I do not save all, I cannot stay the week. Give it up, your damned rebellious young soul! They must say I saved all the sinners!" ' " The public arena of the black Baptist church now stands doubly indicted in the story: the site of emotional manipulation as well as corruption. But if the latter charge seems redundant, coming as it does well after Liane has lost her faith, it serves to free her of any illusion of authenticity and release her into a perfectly instrumental relation to interactions of all kinds. Liane will now embark on a career of "performance," using her knowledge to conquer myriad white audiences.

What distinguishes Liane's career in the white world at the point when we catch up to her is that, far from asserting her claim to bourgeois womanhood, she actively enters into the racial fantasies of her audience. The result is the power accruing to one willing to manipulate the established cultural machinery. She first enters the narrator's purview to present herself as an uneducated "colored girl" looking for a factory job. As she explains later, she had long since learned that "one cannot secure any sort of employment as a colored college graduate. Employers become annoyed. They cherish an illusion that we were born in ignorance and should in all decency die in ignorance" (176). Having threatened no one's illusions, Liane gets the factory job and is quickly promoted, with only the narrator privy to the intelligence quotient the staff psychologist has calculated for her ("higher than that of the foreman. Higher than that of the production manager, had it been known" [175]). After Liane quits the job (having been asked to lead an employee Bible class), she turns up in "the snappiest Hawaiian revue on Broadway" as that ultimate racial fantasy, the tropical dancer.[12] Here posing as a "genuwine [*sic*] Hawaiian princess" (175), she bears all the classic markers of exotic authenticity, and accordingly, " 'all the men are crazy about her,' " according to Anderson, the narrator's male coworker. In his enthusiasm, Anderson brings the narrator along to the revue. Unaware of whom she sees before her, the narrator describes Liane's performance.

> She was brown, and wore only a grass skirt, a jeweled breast bandeau, and a wreath of flowers about her neck. She was singing now. A sad, wailing melody, but what a throbbing, vibrant voice! . . . The song was ended, and bills seemed to snow about her. She was truly a riot. Someone was yelling for her to dance. She began the slow swaying movement of some strange tropical dance, and gradually worked into a thing [*sic*] of passionate abandon. (175–176).

This racial display is the more chillingly ironic since only at the conclusion of the performance do we and the narrator learn the "true" identity behind the "false" exotic rapture.

> Then she turned toward us. It was Liane Leclerc. She smiled at me and her eyes asked me to excuse her presence there. In a minute she was gone, and we left. I was glad Anderson [who had had his eyes closed!] hadn't found out who she was. Dreams shouldn't be destroyed. (176)

At this point, the narrative shifts from linear time to Liane's retrospective narration of her religious history, delivered "the next day during lunch," and thus ends "Souls for Gasoline." But the coherence of Liane's story and strategy as a bourgeois Negro woman actually depend on the details of the dance club performance we have just witnessed.

Though she has cast herself in the role which we noted earlier was the very antithesis of bourgeois womanhood, Liane as a "Hawaiian princess" is far from conceding her claim to her rightful identity. Insulating her from even the role of tropical dancer are two things: the sentient witness of the narrator (sharply highlighted in this scene by contrast with the dreaming Anderson) and Liane's own relentless deployment of performative power, a power that originates with the hard-won knowledge that surviving performance is a matter of ensuring that the roles are clear and the line of influence unidirectional. Liane recognizes the world as populated by people whose perceptions are a mesh of race-based fantasies, a world of sleepwalkers—like the racist prospective employers, the factory production manager, and, most prominently, Anderson, who, incredibly, "watches" Liane's entire Hawaiian performance with his eyes closed so as to have her "in his own setting" (175). In all her interactions, Liane exercises the power to create an enraptured audience—an audience who, acting on her influence, confirms the identity she performatively projects. Ironically, among the working-class "ethnic hodge-podge" of the factory women, Liane is able to assert a genteel class identity by "exert[ing] a refining influence." "One soft voice," the "welfare expert" reports to the unsurprised narrator, "had toned down forty harsh ones" (175).

Her first and most important conquest, however, is the narrator herself, a world-weary white personnel worker. The special dynamic between them begins with their first meeting.

> The office had only been open for a half hour and a steady stream of young girls had been pouring in, in response to our advertisement for unskilled factory workers. Girls of all types—black, white, Italian, Jewish—only one American. I went wearily through the routine. . . .
>
> I became conscious of someone standing before the desk. Another hopeless one to face. Without looking up I asked, "Name, please?"
>
> A low, crooning voice murmured, "Liane Leclerc."
>
> I was too lazy to guess, and she carefully spelled it for me. A soft, singing name, I thought. "French?" I was so sure of it I had already written it down.
>
> "No." There was a slight pause. "I am from New Orleans."
>
> It annoys me to be mistaken so early in the day. I stared at her and my mouth dropped open in rude astonishment. Liane Leclerc was certainly not French. The girl before me was of a clear copper brown, with superbly chiseled features. Her great black eyes almost caressed me in their smouldering warmth. It is the way a cat must feel before a low hearth fire. (175)

The narrator is both peculiarly attuned to Liane's personal power and uniquely conscious of her fantasy potential for others. In her capacity as gatekeeper to "girls of all types," the narrator has the transcendent perspective on the racial panoply to register the dynamics of racial reality as against the fantasies of whites and the white public imaginary.

> I could see that she had heavy black hair, bobbed and uncurled. I thought of [popular romantic racialist writer] Octavus Roy Cohen. If she ever got into the *Saturday Evening Post* she'd be a "High brown, about half-past eight." The fire of her eyes and the bronze gleam of that brown skin would certainly evade print.

As she prepares to send Liane to the foreman, she rounds out her assertion of cognitive racial mastery with a more local (if slightly confusing) speculation.

> I was almost gleeful. In there with that ethnic hodge-podge she ought to create a riot. We employed quite a few colored girls, and they worked together by choice. We never had any trouble or hint of prejudice, and we were proud of the fact. Then there was Anderson, the foreman's neurotic assistant, whose sole ambition was to abide forever beneath a permanent moonlit sky on some remote South Sea island. She would stimulate his imagination.

The identification of Anderson as the exemplar of white fantasy will be confirmed in the nightclub scene, as we saw.[13] In fact, the nightclub is where the extremes of Liane's exotic performance, Anderson's slavering fantasy, and the narrator's singular sentient witness converge to bring into high relief the text's structural economy of bourgeois feminine survival within racist publicity. As far from her true social identity as she may stray, Liane's bourgeois selfhood is secured through the comprehending gaze of the narrator and even enhanced by the distance between what the world sees and what the narrator knows (here harking back to Claire's witness of Margot in *Holiday*'s play within a play, *Crinoline*). Indeed, the narrator's authority to recognize the real Liane gets reinforcement in the nightclub, where she suffers her own bout with public exposure: "I felt somewhat uncomfortable. Anderson and I seemed to be the only ones present not listed in the social register. My evening dress laughed sadly at itself, and Anderson fidgeted in his cousin's extra dress suit. I wanted to leave" (175). The public scrutiny the narrator experiences is nothing to Liane's, but it does secure her ability to comprehend the truth of Liane's situation—even if, at the same moment, it quietly asserts her inadequacy to master publicity as Liane does. This is the difference of race between them: though equally bourgeois, Liane's way of being in the world is founded on a set of skills the white narrator has little need of. Moreover, the narrator gets access to her special knowledge only at the moment that Liane grants it: "*Then* she turned toward us. It was Liane Leclerc. She smiled at me and her eyes asked me to excuse her presence there." Though Liane may need this woman's recognition, she never gives her control of the situation.

Ironically, the specifically erotic power Liane exercises over the narrator is a function of the biggest race fantasy of them all: that of the overpoweringly seductive black woman. Even as Liane confesses her past to this woman whom she has asked to "excuse her presence" in a nightclub act, she "almost stroke[s] [her] with the melody of her voice" (176). The very fact that such remarks appear without any trace of homophobic anxiety suggests strongly their cultural intelligibility as expressing not so much a relation between two women as the "nature" of African American womanhood itself. In this final venue—the intimate proximity to a racially, economically, and sexually disinterested other, whose gaze is the guarantor of one's identity—it is Liane's deployment of erotic performance that secures the power relation. The text's critical distance on mainstream cultural stereotypes and its simultaneous insistence on the erotic power of the black woman thwart our expectation of a bourgeois feminine "truth" (articulated by the narrator) behind the minstrel facade (generated by Liane). In fact, truth is quite beside the point in this world, where performance is a given and the degree and locus of power the only questions.

But there is a limit to the radical pragmatism of this textual ethos. Liane is headed for graduate school and, one imagines, the fantasy of disembodiment intellectual life supplies. As the horizon of Liane's narrative, the abstract world of the academy holds the promise of a loss of bodily difference—one's own marks of difference and the distinction between bodies that implies power and necessitates performance. In the context of renaissance cultural politics, however, Liane's ascension to what finally will be a most overt claim to bourgeois womanhood can only initiate a new regime of performance, one in which she will trade the power of exoticism for the exposure of gentility.

Liane's knowing narrator allows her, in effect, to be both the exalted bourgeoise *and* the exotic primitive. The character of Margot, too, depends on sentient witness, not only that of her daughter but also that of the maid, who proclaims Margot's meaning to the world—who, in fact, commands the social vision that Margot herself lacks. A different sort of feminine economy structures the project of exalting Negro womanhood in Jessie Redmon Fauset's *There Is Confusion*. Rather than offering witness, the working-class Maggie acts as a lightning rod for the destabilizing publicity set off in the text by the bourgeois Joanna's theatrical performances.

Jessie Redmon Fauset, *There Is Confusion*

There Is Confusion is a romantic novel, and though the text decidedly exceeds this generic classification, it is through romance that Fauset finally resolves the problem of performance for genteel African American womanhood. Ambitious in scope, the novel spins out a saga of generations driven by urgent questions of racial responsibility, feminine destiny, and the challenge of life in public. Fauset works her story of three black Philadelphia families to elaborate the meta-narrative of a race—and, finally, a nation—in pursuit of its own progress. Though there is an overt determinism attached to the lineage of the characters, there is equally a sense of contemporary historical crisis about the generation whose story is the narrative focus: Joanna, Sylvia, and Philip Marshall, Peter Bye, Maggie Ellersley, and their community within the city's black middle class. The implication is that this group of young people stand at the threshold of a new era for the race, an era whose racial triumphs and failures will be triumphs and failures of *publicity*. The characters are clearly divided (with some crossover, in the course of events) into those who hearken to the racial call and those who fail to see the larger racial meaning of their own lives. But the presence or absence of a sense of mission and strategy is finally irrelevant to any given character's implication in publicity. The narrative economy of the two central women protagonists bears this out: the working-class Maggie Ellersley thinks only of her private concerns, while the bourgeois Joanna Marshall is possessed of visionary racial consciousness. Yet, in her capacity as (in essence) a "girl of the streets," Maggie is a magnet for the distress and volatility of life in public, hence the structurally enabling condition for Joanna's pursuit of a stage career that is sanctified and safely bourgeois.

Even apart from Maggie's role in their feminine economy, Joanna's theatrical ambition is carefully contextualized as one of a cluster of approaches to racial advancement. The line between a career in public and the professions and entrepreneurship is carefully blurred: old Joel Marshall, the family patriarch, forced by economic necessity to abandon his dream of being a minister "with a great name and a healing tongue,"[14] is at this point in his life a highly successful caterer whose reputation had at one point gotten him a banquet engagement with President Grant. Within the group we see growing up together, Peter Bye, Joanna's fiancé, is to be a "famous" doctor and her brother Philip, a national orator and race organizer, clearly on the model of Du Bois and the NAACP. In such a context, Joanna's own ambition to be a great singer and dancer seems blameless and even safe.

But Fauset goes beyond the ennobling effects of this framework in securing the meaning of Joanna's presence on the stage. Joanna's determination to "be someone great" comes not from some modern day fascination with celebrity but as a sanctified legacy from her father and her race, evident in Joanna from the moment in very early childhood when she declares that she wants to be a "great woman"—like the great slave women who "had won their way to *fame* and freedom through their own efforts" (14; my emphasis).[15] Joanna is a starkly and emphatically untheatrical personality: methodical, sober, even insensitive, and, most important, unadorned. We are told that "she had the variety of honesty which made her hesitate and even dislike to do or adopt anything artificial, no matter how much it might improve her general appearance. No hair straighteners, nor even curling kids for her"—as if even ordinary feminine self-fashioning would leave her open to the giddy lure of specularity (20). When, as a successful singer, she appears in beautiful costumes, it is the result of her sister's design efforts and, moreover, functions as another element of the racial mission: "Through me [Sylvia] certainly is teaching these colored people how to dress. We will not wear these conventional colors—grays, taupe, beige. . . . colored people need color, life, vividness" (132).

The details and particularly the dynamics of Joanna's actual performances get little attention for a text that takes Joanna's career as its narrative axis, and those few instances in which a performance is described are carefully managed. Joanna's effect upon her audience is palpable while their effect on her is virtually negligible. In an early scene, Joanna sings in the family church.

> Joanna was the soloist of the choir these days, sole *raison d'être* of her church-going. Her mezzo voice full and pulsing and gold brought throngs to the church every Sunday.
>
> "There is a green hill far away," she sang, and the puzzled, groping congregation turned its sea of black and brown, yellow and white faces toward her and knew a sudden peace.[16] Even Philip stopped his restless inner queries.
>
> At times like these Peter Bye felt his very heart leap toward her.
>
> Joanna with her cool eyes and steady head cared almost nothing about this. She never saw herself in this scene. Always in her mind's eye she was far, far away from the church, in a great hall, in a crowded theater. There would be tier on tier of faces rising, rising above her. And to-morrow there would be the critics. . . . (73–74; ellipsis in original)

Even within the imaginary scenario that rescues Joanna from the one at hand, there is a further deferral of performative context into the moment when all dangerous human dynamics are laid to rest in cool, impersonal print ("to-morrow would be the critics"). Obviously, in this scene Joanna's imperviousness appears through the perspective of an ironic distance (in fact, her single-mindedness is the subject of general friendly banter among the other characters). But even late into the narrative, after she has achieved the fame and the national audience she craves, other things intervene perpetually to defer the dangerous possibility of an open emotional circuit between her and her audience: her distraction at losing Peter, her sudden (and seemingly inexplicable) sense that fame is "an empty thing," and, finally, her use of the stage as merely an opportunity for winning Peter back.

Among the myriad fine lines that score the terrain of Joanna's performing is that drawn between singing and dancing. Singing is her first career and the one most defined by the dynamics we have so far been describing; dancing emerges as important only in the second half of the book, eventually taking to itself the dangerous qualities attendant on the crisis in Joanna's life and career—and the seeming reversal of values in Fauset's narrative, which I discuss later. But even here the boundaries are carefully laid out. Dancing, to be sure, is the site of a more conventional creativity and artistic *jouissance*. This dichotomy of values undergirds Joanna's first childhood discussion with Peter of her future. Singing is the province of methodical perseverance and racial integrity:

> "I never go to bed without getting my lessons. In fact, all I do is to get lessons of some kind—school lessons or music. You know I'm to be a great singer."
>
> "No, I didn't know that. Perhaps you'll sing in your choir?"

> Then Joanna astonished him. "In my choir—I sing there already! No! Everywhere, anywhere, Carnegie Hall and in Boston and London. You see, I'm to be famous."
>
> "But," Peter objected, "colored people don't get any chance at that kind of thing."
>
> "Colored people," Joanna quoted from her extensive reading, "can do everything that anybody else can do. They've already done it. Some one colored person somewhere in the world does as good a job as anyone else,—perhaps a better one. They've been kings and queens and poets and teachers and doctors and everything. I'm going to be the one colored person who sings best in these days, and I never, never, never mean to let color interfere with anything I *really* want to do."

Thus grounded in personal and racial integrity, she goes on to describe a more fanciful ambition: " 'I dance, too,' she interrupted herself, 'and I'll probably do that besides. Not ordinary dancing, you know, but queer beautiful things that are different from what we see around here; perhaps I'll make them up myself.' " Then the contrast with staid singing comes through sharply, as Joanna is classically transported by visions of her name in lights: " 'You'll see! They'll have on the bill-board, "Joanna Marshall, the famous artist,"—.' She was almost dancing along the sidewalk now, her eyes and cheeks glowing" (45).

Dancing will be consistently charged with meaning throughout the story, acting not only as the site of Joanna's greatest vulnerability as an African American woman in public (to racial slurs and exclusion) but also finally as the arena of her greatest public success. At virtually the same moment that Joanna finally succumbs to the racial prejudice she encounters in the profession, putting to rest her dream of dancing, she gets an offer to play "America" in a prominent Greenwich Village theater's production of *The Dance of the Nations*. With no interference from a choreographer, an artistic director, or even any generic or production requirements,[17] Joanna brings herself and the dance piece she has been perfecting since adolescence onto the stage in their unadulterated purity, and to instant acclaim. Fauset devotes such meticulous and uncharacteristic attention to this dance as to suggest that it embodies an exemplary aesthetic—and the means to an exemplary performance.

To begin with, Joanna's dance originates not in the professional dance world or in her own personal artistic vision; rather, it comes straight from the play of urban black children. Joanna first encounters this dance as a very young woman on the city street.

> Sylvia and Joanna . . . came upon groups of children playing games. Italians, Jews, colored Americans, white Americans were there disporting themselves with more or less abandon, according to their peculiar temperament.
>
> "Look," said Joanna, suddenly catching at Sylvia's hand. "See those children dancing! Wait, I've got to see that!"
>
> Out in the middle of the street a band of colored children were dancing and acting a game. With no thought of spectators they joined hands, took a

> few steps, separated, spun around, smote hands sharply, and then flung them above their heads.

Not just the innocent expression of children, this dance bears the democratic aura of the national ideal, arising as it does in the midst of the quintessentially "diverse" American street. Moreover, without a "thought of spectators," the children have none of the artificiality or self-consciousness of performers. Accordingly, they, and even Joanna herself, are permitted the passionate involvement that audience would render dangerous: "The little players were absorbed, enraptured with the spirit of the dance and the abandon of the music. Joanna, too, was in a transport." In the course of the next page, we get a detailed description of "Barn!" which turns out to be (prophetically) an elaborate wedding game. Having thoroughly conned its intricacies, Joanna is ready to join in.

> Joanna rushed forward: "I can play it! Girls let me play it, too!"
>
> The children stared at her a moment, then, with the instinct of childhood for a kindred spirit, two of them unclasped hands and took Joanna in. She outdid them all in the fervor and grace of her acting. Two white settlement workers stopped and looked at her.
>
> "Come on, Joanna," Sylvia called impatiently.
>
> Joanna came running, a string of the children after her. She bade them goodbye. "I must go now, but I'm coming back sometime soon, to learn some more." She blew them a kiss, "good-bye, oh, good-bye!" (48).

The noncommittal spectatorship of the whites—already, by virtue of their profession, an "audience" to the life of the street—affirms the "objective" worth of Joanna's dancing, while the simple affectionate attachment of the children (literally enclosing her in the circle and in a string) rescues her back into the unself-conscious unity of the cultural group.[18] Later, Joanna teaches "Barn!" to the Marshall family and friends as one of their parlor entertainments. Again, the description is detailed and conveys the message that "Barn!" is infused simultaneously with the meaning of African American community itself and Joanna's special entitlement to perform (49–50). In this rendition, even more emphasis is given the eros of the performance, perhaps because of the absolute privacy and safety of the Marshall family parlor as a venue: "Peter [on the piano], strumming a haunting, atavistic measure; Joanna, dancing like a faun" (49).

In her audition for the artistic directors of the prestigious District Line Theater, the biggest break of her career, Joanna performs this same children's street dance. She even goes so far as to request a supporting (and legitimating) cast of "colored children" for the occasion, which the directors promptly secure from the street below,

> of every type and shade, black and brown and yellow, some with stiff pigtails and others with bobbed curling locks. Most of them knew the game already, all of them took to Joanna and threw themselves with radiant, eager good nature into the spirit of what she was trying to display.

This performance is finally everything at once: the pinnacle of stage success couched in perfect personal and cultural integrity, and rightfully asserting the long-overdue equation of Negro and American identity. For, indeed, it is this "she was trying to display"—"America," defined as "us," the African American race and culture, in fulfillment of her youthful vow "to show us to the world." "I am colored, of course," she had said at that early point, "but American first. Why shouldn't I speak to all America?" (76). Bringing the race before the national gaze as Joanna does in this culminating performance could only be bested by the opportunity to give back to the race her acquired aura of national desire. When the African American regiments return from World War I (where the battles within their own racist army rivaled those they fought with the enemy) Joanna performs her dance for them.

> She surprised even her most intimate friends by her graciousness. Night after night, when the [District Line] performance was over, she appeared, splendid, glowing, symbolic before those huge dark masses in some uptown hall. The "boys," starved for a sight of their own women with their dark pervading beauty, went mad over her. She was indeed for them "Miss America," making them forget to-night the ingratitude with which their country would greet them to-morrow. (269)

But at this point, the reader cannot help but be struck by Joanna's failure to register emotionally what the narrative has prepared us to see as an overwhelming triumph: "She had gone . . . out of sheer graciousness—a willingness to do something for these brave men." It would seem that even here, in this most sanctified of all performative contexts, Joanna must be rescued from the possibility of losing herself in a collective transport—even to the point of insulating her with "sheer graciousness" from an ordinary sense of racial solidarity. Such a contradiction of our expectations occurs on the strength of what may be called the increasing heterosexualization of the text, the sense that love and marriage have displaced all other values. By the time Joanna performs her consummate art to perfect and complete recognition, she is in thrall to an overwhelming personal desire: "At none of these assemblies did Joanna find what she was looking for—a sight of [the estranged] Peter." But, as I argue later, this narrative "rescue" of the bourgeois heroine from the perils of performance needs to be seen not (or not merely) as a contrived evasion of the issues but as a seriously proffered solution to the racial and personal problems the text has raised.

Up to this point, Maggie Ellersley, in her capacity as Joanna's working-class analogue, has herself served as a "solution" or, at least, as a stay against chaos. Crucially, Maggie shares Joanna's most prominent characteristic, her single-mindedness. Peter's statement that "Joanna has the faith that moves mountains [and] . . . if anybody can make it she can" (50) echoes intentionally Mrs. Ellersley's comment of a few pages later: "If there's a way to be found out, Maggie'll find it" (58). Maggie often appears as Joanna's structural surrogate in the story. As Sylvia Marshall's constant high school companion and in her conventionally feminine interests, she is certainly more "sister" to Sylvia than the austere Joanna ever could be. She has the paternal admiration and interest of old Joel Marshall, who recognizes her entrepreneurial potential and gives her responsible employment in the family business. In this way, Maggie becomes the inheritor of Joel's real-life contribution to the world and the race, while Joanna, as we know, has taken on his dreams. Maggie's romantic destiny—to marry Philip Marshall—suffers the same agony and deferment as Joanna's and even includes an extended episode in which Maggie nearly marries Peter himself.

Yet, the differences that divide Maggie and Joanna are far more striking than their similarities, so much so that the two might be seen as inhabiting two distinct textual worlds. In fact, very late in the novel, Fauset makes explicit what has all along been suggested about Maggie, that, unlike the rational-realist Joanna, she is a sentimental-naturalist heroine with her own generic imperatives to serve. Maggie goes overseas as a war nurse, to the French town of Chambery, on which occasion the narrator delivers an uncharacteristically literary commentary.

> [Chambery is] the scene of a novel by Henri Bordeaux, "La Peur de Vivre," the story of a young girl who, afraid to face the perils of life, forfeited therefore its pleasures.
>
> Certainly Alice Du Laurens, the young woman of Bordeaux' novel, would have been no more astonished to find herself in New York than Maggie Ellersley, whom she so closely resembled in character, was to find herself in Chambery. (254)

But long before this virtual declaration on Fauset's part, we have been aware of Maggie's dramatic propensities, inscribed as they are on her very person from her first full introduction to the text (again, reminding us of Crane's precursor).

> Out of it all [her abject poverty] Maggie bloomed—a strange word but somehow true. She was like a yellow calla lily in the deep cream of her skin, the slim straightness of her body. She had a mass of fine, wiry hair which hung like a cloud, a mist over two gray eyes. Her lips, in spite of her constant malnutrition, persisted unbelievably red. When she met excitement those gray eyes darkened and shone, her cheeks flushed a little, her small hands fluttered. And she was nearly always excited. Something within her frail bosom pulsed in a constant revolt against the spirit of things that kept her in these conditions. (57–58)

Over the course of the novel, moreover, Maggie suffers many of the conventional fates of her generic ilk: marriage to a shadowy man, secretly violent and criminal; entanglement with murder and suicide, as well as the suggestion of prostitution; marital scheming; and consumer enthrallment.

Most important for the present discussion are the many opportunities Maggie's sort of life affords for scenes of public vulnerability, scenes in which she is caught on the street with her interior life exposed to (if sometimes misread by) the casual observer. Examples begin early in the text:

riding the subway and thinking of how she has come to love Philip, she smiles, and "a white man sitting opposite mistook the smile and leaned forward, leering a little" (81). In Atlantic City on her honeymoon with the nefarious Henderson Neal, she is ostracized by the public of respectable African Americans to whom, despite her anonymity, she is perfectly legible as an unwitting gambler's beneficiary—though she herself cannot "read" her own marital situation as such (115–117). Indeed, it is the failure of her class to secure the private space of the parlor that causes her ill-fated marriage in the first place: when an emotionally tormented Maggie ventures out of her bedroom in search of relief for her thirst, she is apprehended by Neal (one of many male boarders in her mother's house who might as easily have done the same), and her sentimentally apparent vulnerability prompts him to pressure her to elope with him (88–91). Finally, Maggie figures as a public spectacle even within the inner circle of characters: after a significant absence following her breakup with Henderson, she reenters the narrative publicly and incidentally as Peter, riding a street car, "idly . . . glance[s] out of the window. On the corner stood a woman. . . . the street light fell full on an old-gold, oval face, haggard and disillusioned. Peter saw it was Maggie Ellersley" (113). Thus, while Joanna gets public acclaim and stardom in the theater, Maggie fends off public degradation as the embodiment of theatricality.

Joanna has her own significant engagement with life on the street but as an avid observer rather than as the object of a specularizing public gaze. Instead of the sexual obstacle course facing Maggie, Joanna's street is a democratic vista, which feeds the authenticity of her art. Crucially, Joanna often has Peter as a protective escort.

> Joanna liked the foreign quarters, but she had never cared to stand around too long in those teeming, exotic streets. She was too conspicuous, attracted too many inquiring glances. With Peter she felt safe to stand for long moments watching the children play, to enter queer dark shops, to taste strange messes. Sometimes she spoke to women about their dresses, their headgear. One Spanish woman, grown used to the sight of this dark American girl and the good-looking boy at her side, took them into her quarters one day and showed Joanna how she dressed her hair. Another time she taught her an intricate Spanish dance. (99–100)

But even during the time of her estrangement from Peter, when she must face the street alone, Joanna is figured as a racial strategist, plotting how she will get restaurant service in white-dominated midtown, rather than as a feminine victim, buffeted by the unwanted attention of strangers (195).

Joanna's public invulnerability does have certain dramatic lapses, however, and I would argue that they are tied to the crisis that turns Joanna away from the stage and inward to marriage. This shift restructures the economy and meaning of Joanna's publicity, with the result that Maggie is displaced and eugenic marriage ushered in as the real (not to say, final) solution to the problem of Joanna's bourgeois identity. In one concentrated passage in the narrative, Joanna falls precipitously out of her bourgeois insularity and into what we recognize as Maggie's dangerous world of public vulnerability. Having received from Peter an apparently final letter,

> [s]he finished her engagement in the quiet Southern city before an audience which wondered vaguely what had happened to make Joanna Marshall different. Somehow she packed her trunk, thanked the persistent youth who had constituted himself her cavalier, and boarded the Jim Crow car. . . . After Washington she fell to wondering. . . . How could she endure it? . . . No wonder people "crossed in love"—she dwelt on the phrase distastefully—killed themselves. She toyed with the idea. Of course she couldn't; that sort of relief was not for her. . . . With her usual mental clarity she visualized the colored papers of Harlem. There would be notices telling how the "gifted singer, Joanna Marshall, daughter of Joel Marshall, died by her own hand—."
>
> . . . . As the train slid into the long shed at West Philadelphia she pressed her face against the window-pane and strained out into the dusk. . . . Her tears crept down the glass, the man behind her watching curiously. (174–175)

Joanna is suddenly exposed and vulnerable in every arena and in every way—professionally, racially, emotionally, even sexually. And when she arrives home, one paragraph later, she takes on fully the sentimental temperament that is Maggie's trademark.

> "Help me to get to sleep, Sylvia," Joanna said suddenly after a rambling account of her trip. Her roving eyes and twitching hands had already betrayed her need. "Help me to get to sleep or I think I shall go mad." (174)

Through moments like these, Joanna's character comes gradually to incorporate the public danger along with the public life, necessitating the imminent retreat into privacy.

The collapse of the opposition between Maggie's publicness and Joanna's performance ushers in the new (or, rather, latent) ideological regime of the novel, the shift from racial publicity crusades to heterosexuality as the final value in itself. And yet, this is heterosexuality in close negotiation with publicity. Peter has taken up with Maggie, providing us with a clear comparative perspective to bring into focus how much each woman's gender identity and heterosexual practice turn on the management of public and private. Their difference is figured neatly as the ambition they each inspire in Peter: "Five hours ago he had expected some day to be a physician and to marry Joanna Marshall. Now it seemed that he was going to be a musician and marry Maggie Neal" (171)—musicianship in Peter's case being equated with voluntary racial servitude (playing for white parties) and moral degradation (playing in black cabarets).[19] The next lines suggest the link between ambition and public-private management: " 'It isn't true,' he told himself fiercely. But it was true. There on the dresser were some cookies wrapped up in a red and white fringed napkin, Maggie's gift when he left her" (171). In a curious scrambling of conventional class wisdom (not to say history), the working-class Maggie turns out to be cloyingly servile (cookie-pushing), passive, and dependent, producing a lazy surrender to masculine privilege in the malleable Peter, while the middle-class Joanna briskly asserts her independence *and* her right to chivalrous attention from a man whose professional ambitions rightfully exceed her own. Put differently, the working class woman has no regard for the public values of professional accomplishment and eugenicist heterosexuality—that is, a marriage of social equals that moves the race forward, as much through the private exercise of rational living as through the public contribution of well-bred children and a high-profile *example*. Maggie is eager to retreat into the completely privatized heterosexuality of gendered indulgence and insularity; she effaces her own autonomous life and desires in order to fuss endlessly over Peter while encouraging his slothful resistance to professional achievement.[20] Joanna, by contrast, keeps a lively sense of public values in play in her private habits and in her relationship with Peter, striving constantly to live an exemplary life just as if she were always in the public eye—which of course, she is.[21]

One moment in particular reveals this consciousness as the very foundation of middle-class, eugenic heterosexuality. Peter and Joanna are on their way to the opera by way of the street, their old stomping ground and the site of their happiest times together. Their recent interactions having consisted of nothing but quarreling,

> they were a little stiff next day on the way to the matinee, talking politely and impersonally about the weather in Philadelphia and New York, Joanna's concert, and Sylvia's children. Walking up Broadway, however, they thawed a little. Joanna as usual was looking trim. She wore that winter an extremely trig [*sic*] tobacco-brown suit, with a fur turban and a narrow neckpiece of raccoon, the light part setting off the bronze distinction of her face. But Peter was superlative. His financial success with [musician] Tom Mason had made it possible for him to indulge in a new outfit which emphasized the distinction of his carriage, set off his handsome face. Several people looked at him on the crowded street. Joanna herself stole several glances sidewise.

Entering the street as tense private strangers, Joanna and Peter gradually discover each other as possessed of all the dignity and desirability of beautiful commodities, thus reawakening their private relation through a public gaze. Having arrived at this sense of themselves as luminous public figures, however, they move quickly to a mutual consciousness of how precarious is their control over their own public meaning.

> He caught her at it. "Joanna Marshall, if you look at me again like that, just once more, mind you, I'll snatch you up in my arms this minute and kiss you."
>
> "You wouldn't dare."
>
> "I dare you to try it. I'd do it no matter how much you kicked and struggled. Wouldn't the people stare?"
>
> Joanna giggled. "Can't you see the headlines in the papers to-morrow? 'Burly Negro Attacks Strapping Negress on Broadway!' "

> "Yes, and the small type underneath, 'An interested crowd gathered about a pair of dusky combatants yesterday. A Negro and Negress—' "
>
> Joanna interrupted: "Both of them spelt with a small 'n,' remember! Here we are at the Opera."
>
> He caught her hand. "Just because you jockeyed me out of that kiss that time, clever Joanna, doesn't mean that I'm going to do without it forever."
>
> In her heart she loved him. "Oh, Peter, be like this always," she prayed. (153–154).

The chapter ends here, and we might take a moment to acknowledge the remarkable turn this scene has taken. I would argue that it is of significance to Fauset's larger meaning.

As a rightful middle-class African American couple, Joanna and Peter find their happiness, their peril, and finally their life's work, together and in public. Draped in chic clothes and the approval of passers-by, Joanna and Peter attain the status of advertisements; relays of desire for a wide, abstract public, they lay claim to a public—even national—identity in spite of their racial difference from the cultural norm.[22] This process fuses race work with their own heterosexual desire, though, as the scene illustrates, collective and individual desires and the racial politics of publicity are finally so interdependent as to be inextricable. It is precisely at the moment when their own desires become visible, however—when Peter figuratively kisses Joanna on the street—that they fall out of the state of national/commodified grace and into racial stereotypes of animalistic sexuality. More precisely, they fall out of bourgeois visibility per se, for there is no mistaking the grotesque disparity between the scene we witness and the imagined newspaper description. We are reminded that the status quo cultural machinery goes on, despite its distance from the lives of actual African Americans like Joanna and Peter, bringing us and them into stark confrontation with what is at stake in the success and quality of their relationship. Their bourgeois life—the afternoon at the opera, the deferred kiss, the interior emotion ("In her heart she loved him")—must stand as a bulwark against the racist public sphere.

Importantly, though this moment comes as close as any other to registering Joanna's potential vulnerability, she is shielded from the full implications of life in public by Peter's more pronounced specularization. What this episode foreshadows is the narrative conclusion that critics find to be either a gross concession to formula romance or an ironic critique of its assumptions. But I think we can see Joanna's receding behind her husband's identity in terms consistent with the larger racial scope of the novel. Joanna departs from her own professional life to devote herself to Peter's professional and personal development, as well as the development of the future generation, their children (284–285). But by this point, Fauset has gone to some trouble to prepare the moment by refunctioning the meanings of "private" and "public." One remarkable scene in particular lays to rest any trace of the original meaning of public prominence as a noble cause. Joanna is at the height of her fame (and the nadir of her disillusionment) when she finds herself

> walking presently along teeming Lenox Avenue. Some young girls passing turned and stared. "That's Joanna Marshall. You know, the dancer." A dark colored girl wearing Russian boots and a hat with three feathers sticking up straight, Indian fashion, came along. Lenox Avenue stared, pointed, laughed and enjoyed itself, Joanna's admirer with the rest.
>
> This, this was fame—to be shared with any girl who chose to stick feathers, Indian fashion, in her hat. An empty thing—different, so different from what she had expected it to be. (274)

We should note that, rather than the more obvious and threatening comparison with, say, a cabaret singer or even a "streetwalker," Joanna confronts the image of her own degradation in the merely silly. So far has Fauset divested the public world of meaningfulness that she will grant it only as much power (even negative power) as can be wielded by a bad and motley dresser. At the same time, the eugenic family has become the site of personal happiness and racial progress; when the reunited Peter and Joanna discuss their future, they make no distinction between the two (283–285).

But if the one overriding fact of thus cutting through the racial "confusion" of the title is that the bourgeois Joanna must be safely sequestered in the family circle, then Maggie has by default become sole mistress of the public arena. She has acquired her own "chain of Beauty Shops. First class ones" (261). It is perhaps only at this point that Maggie's narrative career finally falls into place. In the novel's original schema of a generation moving forward into the promising future of publicity, Maggie has had an important though repressed role. The two Marshalls, Joanna and Philip, were clearly the core of this vanguard, in the text and by their own estimation: " 'There'll be a twin star constellation,' " says Philip, " ' "The well known Marshalls, Joanna and Philip." We'll make the whole world realize what colored people can do' " (79). Joanna's mate was not quite stellar, but still importantly public: Peter was to be a "famous doctor." Given his heritage as a son of old Philadelphia, we expect no less. But Maggie was an outsider to the privilege of bourgeois responsibility, and so her future as a beauty culturist easily eludes us as a piece of her generation's racial project. But in fact, for much of the book, Maggie was a leading beautician for "Madame Harkness"—a clear reference to the women-centered enterprise of the historical Madame C. J. Walker, whose hair-straightening formula made her a millionaire in the first decades of the century and raised up a thousands-strong contingent of saleswomen nationwide. Not a dignified middle-class pursuit, as Joanna is quick to point out, but the novel clearly recognizes its status as a venture in modern publicity, one peculiarly suited to the working-class urban woman.[23] Chapter 14 concludes with Maggie, at the end of her disastrous first marriage, plotting a new life over Madame Harkness's business card, the text of which we get in full.

> MADAME HARKNESS
> Hair Culturist
> 270 West 137th Street
> New York City
>
> [Maggie's] glance dropped to the left-hand corner. Yes, she was right, there it was: Branch offices—Washington, D.C. 1307 U Street, N.W.; Baltimore, 1816 Druid Hill Avenue; Philadelphia, 2021 South Street. (127)

One page into the next chapter, her lover, Philip, "evolved his new scheme. He proposed that an organization be started among the colored people which should reach all over the country" (129). Where Peter's and even Joanna's careers fall short of being identical with race work, Maggie's scorned hair-straightening venture echoes the unimpeachable "NAACP"—in its national reach, in its focus on service, and simply by virtue of the heterosexual symmetry that structures the text. Moreover, Philip finally abandons his work for health reasons (but not before "admitting" that he only pursued his public cause to assuage his private anguish at losing Maggie). Maggie, by contrast, has arrived at a sense of mission about her work as the noble alternative to her selfish pursuit of private (i.e., heterosexual) happiness.

Though finally reunited with Philip, Maggie's marriage is childless and lasts only as long as it takes Philip to succumb to the gassing he received in the war. Within the new regime of eugenic family values, the working-class/entrepreneurial Maggie must be finally peripheral to the racial future. But is she? Complex rationales aside, it is hard to get around the sense of strain about Joanna's fate. When we are told that "although she sang sometimes . . . she almost never danced except in the ordinary way" (291), the tang of masochism raises the specter of Fauset's own discomfort with the marital "happiness" she has bestowed upon her heroine. Perhaps the wish that bourgeois womanhood could find its racial duty not only clear-cut and safe but also fulfilling requires a companion fantasy that working-class womanhood be *unencumbered* and safe, in an empowering publicity of the free market.

AS JOANNA TAKES UP HER new roles of wife and mother within the now racially significant family, we might note that she fulfills a fantasy implicit in Margot's story, that of publicly sanctified private performance. Likewise, Liane's performative power and freedom emerge as the privilege of one who has somehow escaped the necessity to stake a claim in the social world—again, the fantasmatic contrast to Margot, who has everything riding on a fixed identity. These texts, in other words, different as they are, might fruitfully be seen as the interpenetrating fantasies of three women writers bearing the same cultural burden. They should also be recognized as illuminating distinct facets of a common task, that of exalting Negro womanhood. To illustrate, I want to take up a question that has gone begging in my analysis of *Holiday* to answer it (tentatively) with the message of "Souls for Gasoline."

"Souls" explores performative power in its relation to venue and dynamics. Within her own racial community of the black church—with its dialectical performance-audience relations, its emphasis on the collective totality as the site of identity—Liane faces the loss of her bourgeois self and flees as an act of survival. Herein lies a solution to the puzzle of *Holiday*: where is the African American public sphere in Margot's story? If performing Negro womanhood is a racial cause, why is there so little of the race in Graham's formulation? Like Liane, Margot has left behind her a predominantly African American audience, that of the cabaret and vaudeville. Though Graham's text goes on to develop a different set of issues, we might well speculate that, were they known, Margot's reasons would not be far from those of Liane. Such an audience demanded an interaction, even an intimacy that left the performer dispersed across the time and space of the performance, replacing her bourgeois illusion of a unified integral self with a collectively constituted and contingent presence, "degraded" in its implications of a woman "violated" at the intimate level of her ego boundaries. While a predominantly white audience of the so-called legitimate theater subjected a woman like Margot, who performed for it, to specularization, that woman—through the gaze that suppressed its own presence even as it fixed her in its penetrating beam—had recourse to the illusion of expressing a "private" interior self. Indeed, she had more self with the power and approval of the audience than without it, as Margot demonstrates in staging her "private" maternal confession to daughter Claire before a group of fascinated whites, who happen to have been invited to lunch on the fateful day. While Claire rejects the personal justification Margot offers her, the guests are "touched in spite of themselves" (15). Moreover, Margot seems genuinely dismayed that they are powerless to make Claire accept her as a mother: "Don't let her say that [I'm not her mother]—don't! Don't!," she screams, as Claire flees the scene (16). Here, of course, is where Liane and Margot necessarily part ways. For Margot's absolute faith in the white audience is the corollary to her desperately claustrophobic performance—and a key component of Graham's distinctive contribution: to render in full the bourgeois African American woman's potential for tragic isolation and fragility.

EIGHT

“Our Younger Negro (Women) Artists”

Gwendolyn Bennett and Helene Johnson

In introducing her valuable 1989 anthology, *Shadowed Dreams: Women's Poetry of the Harlem Renaissance*, Maureen Honey explores the reasons for Romantic poetry's evident aptness to the literary expression of African American women in the 1920s. After noting the largely forgotten fact that nearly as many poems by women as by men appeared in *Crisis* and *Opportunity* in the renaissance years—and to good critical response—Honey asserts that women's embrace of an apparently white-identified aesthetics, and of such apolitical subjects as love and nature, was, in fact, a conscious refutation of black inferiority. Taking inspiration from the English Romantics, renaissance women saw nature as a source of value in an acquisitive and industrialized white world, and the passion of love as elevating—in particular, as defying the slave-holding society's assault on black emotional bonds. Drawing simultaneously on their peculiarly modernist faith in the power of art, women poets (like their male counterparts) believed that art would bridge the divided races and force a recognition of black worth.[1] Gloria T. Hull's *Color, Sex, and Poetry*—the 1987 study that launched the current wave of interest in renaissance women writers—takes a more materialist approach to this question of genre. Hull points out that "lyric poetry has long been considered the proper genre for women," and, accordingly, the women of the renaissance "both kept themselves and were kept in their lyric sphere."[2]

Perhaps another reason for women of the renaissance to write poetry lay within the ethos of renaissance subculture itself—namely, that lyric poetry offered the possibility of an escape from the imperative to "exalt Negro womanhood." In its classic definition as the expression of a moment rescued from time and suffused with one individual's private feeling, lyric poetry radically opposed the performative drive intrinsic to narrative, with its relentless temporality and social dynamics.[3] In its very structure, then, lyric poetry suggested the possibility of a literary refuge to women whose social identity had to be perpetually asserted against the cultural denial of their existence. As Honey argues, renaissance women poets "found congenial poetic models in the Imagists and English Romantics because these forms allowed them access to a core self" (33). Ironically, then, the site of their greatest participation in renaissance discourse was also the one which most relieved them of their special renaissance pressures.[4]

In the emergent tradition of renaissance women's poetry, Helene Johnson and Gwendolyn Bennett took full advantage of the potentials of lyric, making their most significant contributions in bringing lyric to bear on the essential core of renaissance aesthetics. As discussed in chapter 6, this essential aesthetic was the acknowledged domain of a largely masculine avant-garde elite who staked out the street and the urban, working-class life they

Photograph on preceding page: On the roof (1924). (Schomburg Center for Research in Black Culture, New York Public Library)

found there as the site of their resistance to the racial establishment and the bourgeois values it promoted. The rebellious, agonistic element of avant-garde expression seems to have been of little interest to Bennett and Johnson; indeed, Bennett in particular was highly invested in her role as a unifier of rifts within Harlem culture. But for two writers whose artistic development was so closely tied to the rise of the New Negro renaissance, the street itself—the avant-garde topos—had undeniable appeal as the vital, luminous center of Harlem subcultural identity. Bennett and Johnson had a straightforward claim to the street as "younger Negro artists," and yet their access would necessarily be complicated and attenuated by their status as women. What we see in their poetry are two very different and sometimes oblique strategic responses to the conflict between gender and subcultural value, both of which develop the potentials of a specifically urban consciousness in ways that contribute to the democratization of renaissance aesthetics as a whole. In a subcultural context in which fringe is center, Bennett and Johnson's "feminization of the avant-garde" refers to the whole range of ways that they, as women, insist on the commensurability of the subcultural pulse and their feminine selves—including the feminine lyric tradition which fostered them.

Women's Lyric Poetry

The notion of the "lyric moment" has potentially profound implications for the speaking self the poem projects. Seeming to escape time and the social contract, suffused with the emotion of a single consciousness, the lyric poem echoes the perfect self-sufficiency of pre-Oedipal subjectivity, that state before the fall into "lack"—of maternal nurturance, of personal wholeness, of an unmediated relation to the universe—a state characterized by the utopian fullness of plenitude. I make this point not to characterize the practice of lyric poetry as infantile regression but rather to illuminate the way that a variety of lyric modes might tend toward the production of a speaker whose psyche was underwritten by a primordial experience of self-worth. If the context of Harlem subcultural imperatives made escape from a certain kind of performative femininity occasionally desirable, it also created the positive need for a feminine identity that was fundamentally noncontingent. In sharp contrast to the palpable presence of the Other in, for example, Parker's complex rhetorical dynamics, much of renaissance lyric principally concerned itself with the projection of an unassailable and free-standing feminine self.

Marion Grace Conover's "Comment" from 1928 is a straightforward use of lyric to establish an inviolable black femininity.

Perhaps you have forgotten
That a lotus flower
Pure, fragile, white,

May blossom in foul places
Far from the sun's pale light.[5]

We might be inclined to dismiss Conover's conventional association of whiteness with purity and fragility as false consciousness, yet, when the lotus expresses its inherent virtue despite adverse circumstances, it creates an imagistic space in which the same possibility exists for the speaker as a black woman. Two points from Houston A. Baker Jr.'s *Workings of the Spirit: The Poetics of Afro-American Women's Writing* are relevant here. The first is the importance of the larger historical context from which, according to Baker, any interpretation of African American women's writing must proceed. The foundational experience in this history is the massive and systematic rape that characterized the Middle Passage:

> A rejection of the assumptions, if not the conditions, of violation—an obstinate insistence on a deeper intimacy, as it were, provided conditions of possibility for the very existence of [an] Afro-American [cultural] system. The unmediated, above-deck world [where the rape takes place] reduces the scope of concern from a desire for possession of the Western machine to a psychic quest for an achieved and ordering intimacy of women's *self*-consciousness. The shift is something like that between world historic forces and embedded ancestral energies of survival and even poetic consciousness. (136; emphasis in original)

Baker's second point concerns the primacy of *space* as a set of luminous sites which gather meaning over the course of cultural generations—as against the white-Western pursuit of progress through *time* (which Baker associates with the writings of key male African American writers like Ralph Ellison and Richard Wright). Space "is a function of images," and though Baker has in mind a more or less constant "imagistic field" which constitutes the African American women's literary tradition, the general argument seems clarifying in the present case as well: images and the spaces they create provide black women writers with alternative values and meanings in a world whose given terms render black women's existence precarious.[6] When the speaker of "Comment" spins out a vision of a lotus fully and deliberately *being* a lotus regardless of the "foul[ness]" it confronts, she creates not merely an allegory of black womanhood for the benefit of the "you" she addresses but an imagistic space for her own habitation, a place in which the embedded logic of biological essence unfolds in space, escaping the temporal dimension in which any "foul" eventuality is possible.

An important source of the self-sufficiency we see in play in "Comment" may well derive from the black church. Explicitly Christian poems are fairly common among renaissance writers generally, nearly always figuring an analogy between the crucifixion and ostensibly nongendered Negro suffering, especially lynching.[7] But Christian experience may make itself felt at a more pervasive level and have particular significance for women. One dimension of this significance is more or less spelled out in Alice Dunbar-Nelson's "Of Old St. Augustine."

Of old, St. Augustine wrote wise
And curious lore, within his book.
I read and meditate, my eyes
See words of comforting, I look
Again, and thrill with radiant hope.
"They did not sin, those white-souled nuns of old,
Pent up in leaguered city, and despoiled
By knights, who battered at the peaceful fold,
And stole their bodies. Yet the fiends were foiled,
They could not harm their stainless, cloistered souls."[8]

What the speaker articulates here is the final preserve Christianity provides for noncontingent feminine selfhood: the soul, standing as bulwark against the bodily denigration of rape. Yet the radical split of soul and body expressed in this poem, while a commonplace of Anglo-European epistemology, is actually quite rare in renaissance women's poetry as a whole. Pervasive, by contrast, is the implicit notion that to believe in God is to be personally suffused with God's spirit. In her study *Conversions and Visions in the Writings of African-American Women*, Kimberly Rae Connor states that black women confront "a dominant culture that not only devalues but oftentimes erases their identity. . . . Conversion for these women yields to creation—creation of a self and of a story." More specifically, "for African Americans conversion is an experience . . . where women and men ask not for God's forgiveness but for God's *recognition*."[9] Connor offers a definition of conversion itself that bears a strong similarity to what I am arguing is the cultural function of lyric for renaissance women.

> Bearing qualities of both transcendence and immanence, the goal of conversion is to create: where there was absence to create presence; where there was no self a self emerges; where God was a transcendent listener on high, there is an immanent god participating in the lives of black women. (12)[10]

Lending significant force to the self called into being by lyric, this black Christian experiential framework also converges powerfully with the romantic sense of a world saturated with spiritual meaning.

Dora Lawrence Houston's "Preference," published in the June 1925 issue of *Opportunity*, projects the sense of overdetermined plenitude resulting from this convergence of generic and spiritual registers—and brings out another of its dimensions.

I love all quiet places—
Low prairies, placid seas,
The heart of woods in winter
When no wind shakes the trees.
People are much like places:
Oh I could travel far
With one who loves to ponder
The tip of a burning star. (164).[11]

Sexual love (along with religious feeling) is the classic approximation of plenitude, and as "Preference" finally suggests, the point of such love is not the lover or togetherness but the being loved, the enhancement of self that love provides. The speaker conjures places of perfect symmetry and stillness: the "low prairies" in balance with the "placid seas," the "heart of woods" where not even "wind shakes the trees." The completeness of the natural world she "loves" extends to the speaker herself, not just explicitly ("People are much like places") but in the unmistakable sense that the lover she invokes is nearly redundant to the psychical state she values. The exquisite rapture suggested by mutually "ponder[ing] / The tip of a burning star" is merely an intensification of the "quiet places" that precede it—an immanent, white-hot center to all that perfection and stillness. The shift from solitude to sexual love, then, is merely one of degree. In contrast to the compulsion we have seen for white women poets of the period to generate literary selfhood strictly within the confines of heterosexuality (or, at least, to appear to do so), black women poets had almost the reverse imperative: to present a womanly self luminous with "the desire of the other" yet extricated from the degrading implication that that self is sexually derived. The African American woman lover must be the product, not of her human lover, but of God, poetry, and, as we shall see, nature.

Honey argues that, for renaissance women poets, "Nature offered an Edenesque alternative to the corrupted, artificial environment created by 'progress' " (7). These writers "saw the cityscape as manmade," whereas "nature, like them, had been objectified, invaded and used by men seeking power and wealth" (8). Indeed, the evidence of African American women's strong identification with nature runs all through the period. Starting from this central observation, we soon see what a flexible tool the trope of nature provides in the literary construction of renaissance women's subjectivity. Jessie Redmon Fauset's "Rain Fugue" is exemplary in important respects: its feminine speaker's negotiations with desire are played out through nature, while nature functions not merely to reflect her emotions but, as an ontologically distinct entity, to actively engage them. The result is a dynamic process of self-construction.

The speaker traces four seasons of rain and eros—without the implicit denigration of either personal embodiment or the presence of a lover. The first season is summer:

> Slanting, driving, Summer rain
> How you wash my heart of pain!
> Ships and gulls and flashing seas!
> In your furious, tearing wind,
> Swells a chant that heals my mind;
> And your passion high and proud,
> Makes me shout and laugh aloud![12]

The sheer excess of the summer storm produces in the speaker an intense present-orientation. "Wash[ed]" of her "pain"—freed of her past—the speaker gives herself over to the "swell[ing] chant" of an insistent "passion[,] high and proud," which she matches with her own "shout[ing] and laugh[ter]." Only abstractly figured by her "heart" and "mind," she is yet concretely performative (though, indeed, her very willingness to shout and laugh in forgetfulness of her own pain serves ironically to underscore her physical elusiveness).

The rain of autumn is calmer, but more disturbing for all that:

Blotting, blurring out the Past,
In a dream you hold me fast;
Calling, coaxing to forget
Things that are, for things not yet.

Forcing her out of the full present of the summer, the autumn rain instigates desire in the speaker for that which she lacks (the "things not yet") but keeps her from pursuing them in the world by "hold[ing her] fast" in the "dream" of a still, pre-Oedipal suspension. The speaker resists such manipulation, however, with nature's own help, as intensity returns with the winter.

Winter tempest, winter rain,
Hurtling down with might and main,
You but make me hug my heart,
Laughing, sheltered from your wrath.
Now I woo my dancing fire,
Piling, piling drift-wood higher.
Books, and friends and pictures old,
Hearten while you pound and scold!

Though autumn gave her a coaxing whiff of "lack," winter is its very essence and here attempts to drive her forward into the cruel teleologically driven (narrative) world. She scornfully resists: "You but make me hug my heart, / Laughing." Ironically, in taking "shelter . . . from [its] wrath," she escapes winter's specific intentions without violating the larger natural order, which is, of course, to go indoors in a tempest. In typical fashion, this woman struggles with nature while staying always in harmony with it.

This is the specific meaning of her identification with nature: the two are autonomous and yet coextensive as a poetic space apart from worldly imperatives. In contrast to the unity of passion we saw in "summer," winter is the site of the speaker's differentiation from nature and development of her own desire. The domestic space we are conventionally given to see as bourgeois confinement here springs from the feminine speaker's own need as the very shape of her desire. Forced by winter to grapple with lack, she refuses the (futile) narrative pursuit of wholeness in the world and instead directs her grappling inward to the creation of her own domain. Ensconced in her hearth and thus defended against the world, the speaker's erotic self emerges with witchy abandon: "Now I woo my dancing fire, / Piling, piling drift-wood higher." The seemingly incongruous "Books, and friends and pictures old" of the subsequent line (assuming that she is not actually throwing these items in the fire) signal a crucial difference from the incipient erotics of the first two stanzas: having come into her own, the feminine speaker seeks not a particular, heterosexual locus of desire, but the multiple sites—and hence, the multiply grounded self—that domesticity affords.

Spring mirrors the muted power of autumn, but given a now-articulated feminine subject, its force all flows to her greater autonomy:

Pattering, wistful showers of Spring
Set me to remembering
Far-off times and lovers too,
Gentle joys and heart-break rue,—
Memories I'd as lief forget,
Were not oblivion sadder yet.
Ah! you twist my mind with pain,
Wistful, whispering April rain!

The poem now concludes by concretizing the difference of spring:

Summer, Autumn, Winter rain,
How you ease my heart of pain!
Whispering, wistful showers of Spring,
How I love the hurt you bring!

Having successfully resisted the "things not yet" held out to her by autumn, the speaker allows herself to be lured by spring into contemplation of the past. The past brings "hurt" that she "loves"—as against the pain of stanza one, which she was happy to lose. Whence the shift to pleasure in pain? The seasonal ordeal of autumn and winter has given the speaker a core self, whose boundaries are only enhanced by the look backward. Memory by definition pulls life into the orbit of a controlling consciousness. Pain under these circumstances is likewise an intensity lending itself to an even greater sense of the speaker's emotional world as subject only to her own control and as intrinsically, autonomously meaningful. (Indeed, numerous poems from the period suggest that literary masochism may have had this specific function for women writers.)[13]

In a subcultural context that renders the woman's love poem per se as an oblique genre—more explicitly about selfhood than body, less interested in the relationship than in the person it produces—the line between the love poem and the lyric tends to blur. "Love" finally becomes something about voice and eros—finding, directing and keeping them despite the cultural conspiracy to render one silent, asexual, or animalistic.

Bennett and Johnson in the Lyric Context

Though Gwendolyn Bennett and Helene Johnson both found their strongest literary identity in relation to avant-garde aesthetics, they came to write poetry within the matrix of this emergent women's lyric tradition. Moreover, they did so not by struggling against its "feminine constraints" but by exploiting to the fullest its significant potentials. The best testimony to that potential is the variety of lyric resources Bennett and Johnson drew on to forge their very distinct avant-garde voices. The subsequent discussion describes the central modes of each poet's participation in the women's lyric tradition while developing further dimensions of the tradition itself. Following the trajectory of Bennett's and Johnson's own uses of lyric, the analysis of their conventional lyricism slides inevitably into the unconventional appropriations that lead them to identifiably avant-garde expression.

Like many of their female contemporaries, both Bennett and Johnson were drawn to what might be called the "nightwoman" poem—simply, a poem in which night and woman are rendered in terms of each other. Bennett's "Street Lamps in Early Spring" suggests the genre's appeal for the Harlem Renaissance woman poet.

> Night wears a garment
> All velvet soft, all violet blue . . .
> And over her face she draws a veil
> As shimmering fine as floating dew . . .
> And here and there
> In the black of her hair
> The subtle hands of Night
> Move slowly with their gem-starred light.[14]

The first, most important characteristic of the nightwoman is her sheer scale. Larger than life, the center of her world, even the matrix of that world itself, her position bears certain key resemblances to that of the bourgeois Negro Woman—but without the strains of "exaltedness." Their differences are built into the particular cultural register that each inhabits: iconic status can provide the Negro Woman with only the protections and power attendant on the commodification she has undergone; by contrast, metaphoric status lends the Night Woman the magnificence and the imperturbable stillness of poetry—as well as the greater remove of metaphor itself.

Intrinsic to the figure of night is, of course, the elevation of darkness to a world on its own terms; indeed, the night has a persistent presence in renaissance poetry as a point of reference for black legitimacy, as in Langston Hughes's "Proem": "I am a Negro: / Black as the night is black, / Black like the depths of my Africa."[15] But the autonomous night has a special felicity for women writers, one which Bennett here exploits fully. The night is larger than life, metaphorically magnificent, but simultaneously *veiled*; prominent, powerful, yet unavailable to prying eyes; ubiquitously "public" yet private unto herself. Even beyond resolving what is a central contradiction of bourgeois Negro womanhood, the nightwoman eradicates a second, culturally imposed contradiction between black skin and genteel womanhood: in the metaphoric context of the nightwoman poem, *darkness* is intrinsic to (modest, demure—i.e., bourgeois) *femininity*. Johnson's "Night," from the same year, wraps the metaphoric woman in the additional mantel of Christian selfhood:

> The moon flung down the bower of her hair,
> A sacred cloister while she knelt at prayer.
> She crossed pale bosom, breathed a sad amen—
> Then bound her hair about her head again.[16]

Again, femininity is inextricable from the dark. The woman herself has become the "pale-bosomed" moon, but the darkness of night remains in her hair—emblem of femininity and the means of her "cloistered" modesty.

Johnson's "What Do I Care for Morning" explores the potential of the nightwoman metaphor within a more ambitious ideological framework. Contrary to convention, night is here explicitly contrasted with day, as the title suggests, while day itself is rejected as the disorderly realm of aggressive and disjointed activity.

> What do I care for morning,
> For a shivering aspen tree,
> For sun flowers and sumac
> Opening greedily?
> What do I care for morning,
> For the glare of the rising sun,
> For a sparrow's noisy prating,
> For another day begun?[17]

When the speaker chooses night, as she inevitably must, it is for the calm unity that emanates from that domain's central organizing presence, the moon.

> Give me the beauty of evening,
> The cool consummation of night,
> And the moon like a love-sick lady,
> Listless and wan and white.
> Give me a little valley
> Huddled beside a hill,
> Like a monk in a monastery,
> Safe and contented and still,
> Give me the white road glistening,
> A strand of the pale moon's hair,
> And the tall hemlocks towering
> Dark as the moon is fair.

In drawing day into the comparative shadow of night, Johnson invites certain oppositions: between industry and love, drive and contentment, desire and satiety. We can hear in this structure of values strong echoes of the (by 1926) long-standing argument among black and, increasingly, white intellectuals that African America had soulful qualities badly needed by the grasping, frenetic world of white capitalism.[18] The poem's final lines feed into this contrast of the ancient race with the hard, youthful one.

Oh what do I care for morning,
Naked and newly born—
Night is here, yielding and tender—
What do I care for dawn![19]

To the extent that the night is, indeed, identified with African America, the function of the metaphoric woman is significant. At the center of her world, she provides the magnetic charge from which comes order—and eros. Here the affective positioning of the speaker is significant, for whereas more or less straightforward identification is implied by the nightwoman lyric in its simpler forms, in this instance the speaker claims a place for herself as a woman distinct from the metaphor. She accomplishes this through a declaration of her desire. Having begun by asserting in broad terms the superior attractions of the night over the day, she finishes with a fairly precise articulation of the possibilities for intimacy each offers her. The "naked and newly born" morning asks her to be mother to the child who goes forth to strive with the rest of the striving world. This scenario leaves her behind and redundant, as, indeed, the dominant culture traditionally relegates the African American woman to its forgotten domestic and psychological spaces to do its drudgery. The "yielding and tender" night, by contrast, is the omnipotent mother of pre-Oedipal plenitude, the mother who *is* the world, and the invitation is to the "cool consummation" of "safe[ty]," "content[ment]," and "still[ness]." This language of adult sexuality signals the speaker's choice as a conscious return to a culturally sanctioned state: though premised on infant pleasure, this is the world of courtly love and monastic life, as well as the beauty and allusiveness of poetry itself. Indeed, morning has no trace of culture to its credit, only raw nature untouched by poetry. Johnson's poem thus extends the reach of the nightwoman metaphor to encompass culture itself, newly defined as feminine and African American.

Bennett's 1926 "Moon Tonight" situates the feminine speaker and her lover within the terms of a world emanating from the Nightwoman, granting this figure yet another province of meaning, that of the lover's psychology:

Moon tonight,
Beloved. . . .
When twilight
Has gathered together
The ends
Of her soft robe,
And the last bird-call
Has died.
Moon tonight—
Cool as a forgotten dream,

Dearer than lost twilights
Among trees where birds sing
No more.[20]

With the opening address, the speaker ushers her beloved into the night-world, asserting in the process her control over its meaning. First comes the twilight, and with the imagistic brevity to which she was so frequently drawn, Bennett evokes the privacy we have seen as typical for the night-woman, modestly "gather[ing] together / The ends / Of her soft robe." Having thus established the inviolable feminine space as the very matrix of their love, the speaker introduces the moon, traditional catalyst for romantic passion. Yet this moon brings only displacements of emotion—"cool," "forgotten," and a "dream"; "lost twilights" and birds who "sing / No more"—images signaling that this is an affair of the past (or the soon-to-be past). The felicity of the moon in this love scenario lies in the aesthetic residue it retains after the affair itself has burned away; left behind in the twilight and the nostalgia is a metaphorically and artistically enhanced self.

The imagist aesthetic of "Moon Tonight" suggests both Bennett's significant avant-garde affiliation with international modernism and her strong roots in graphic art. Though Bennett is remarkable for the variety of her renaissance pursuits (not only poetry and cultural commentary but also cover illustrations for *Crisis* and *Opportunity*), graphic art provided the principal educational and vocational structure to her career. First studying art at Pratt and Columbia and in Paris, Bennett then taught at Howard and Tennessee State College and, much later, directed the Harlem Community Art Center. Not surprisingly, then, graphic art also served her as a powerful resource in the poetic problems of love, self, and African American womanhood under conditions of compulsory publicity.

In "Purgation," Bennett uses the notion of aesthetic process and value as the basis for a love not in conflict with the complexities of her selfhood; like so many other Harlem Renaissance women writers, she strives for disembodiment as a context for love. This ascetic impulse is evident from the beginning of the poem.

You lived
      and your body
Clothed the flames of earth.

Now that the fires have burned away
And left your body cold,
I tremble as I stand
Before the chiseled marble
Of your dust-freed soul.[21]

The speaker of "Purgation" makes no appearance in the first stanza and thus avoids any proximity to the lover and his body while they "live." Once "the fires" have put an irrevocable distance between them, however, the speaker appears, passionately embodied in her "trembling"—but trembling in response to the work of art the lover has left in his place. Indeed, his worthiness to be loved at all seems to reside in the implication that his soul, or essence, is "chiseled marble." The purgation of the title, most obviously a reference to the lover's transition into death, more importantly describes the process by which the affair itself achieves the purity of art—and lends the woman speaker a comparably timeless and exalted self.

Bennett also rallied her visual artistry to tackle a more pervasive dilemma of artistic subjectivity in the renaissance and thereby extended her purview to critique of both establishment and avant-garde practice. Several of Bennett's poems implicitly target the tendency of bourgeois artists to render the racial subject they celebrate in the exoticizing terms of an alien Other. Drawing on a conception of nature implicit to the art deco aesthetic of her drawings, Bennett derives a poetics that is finally democratic in its implications. In the context of the renaissance, Bennett's "fairy sketches"—pagan fantasies of animistic nature—displace exotic Africa as the terrain in which to establish artistic positionality. Though its subject and tone are "light," the poem "Wind" suggests the contours of a world that neatly sidesteps the ruling, racially freighted dichotomies both of Christian good and evil and of awed artist and "aweful" primitive.

The wind was a care-free soul
That broke the chains of earth,
And strode for a moment across the land
With the wild halloo of his mirth.
He little cared that he ripped up trees,
That houses fell at his hand,
That his step broke calm on the breast of seas,
That his feet stirred clouds of sand.

But when he had had his little joke,
Had shouted and laughed and sung
When the trees were scarred, their branches broke,
And their foliage aching hung,
He crept to his cave with a stealthy tread,
With rain-filled eyes and low-bowed head.[22]

The casual destruction that follows from the exuberant expression of "a care-free soul" highlights the poem's refusal to impose a sense of evil or mystery on the natural world. The compunction that creeps over the wind at the close of the poem arises from a natural moral sense and demands neither redemption nor restitution. Or perhaps the "rain-filled eyes and low-bowed head" are only the tail end of a mood that has spent itself.

"Fantasy" is continuous with the amoral, animistic world of "Wind" and builds in an apparently direct translation of Bennett's art deco drawing into a verbal tapestry:

I sailed in my dreams to the Land of Night
Where you were the dusk-eyed queen,

And there in the pallor of moon-veiled light
The loveliest things were seen . . .

A slim-necked peacock sauntered there
In a garden of lavender hues,
And you were strange with your purple hair
As you sat in your amethyst chair
With your feet in your hyacinth shoes.

Oh, the moon gave a bluish light
Through the trees in the land of dreams and night.
I stood behind a bush of yellow-green
And whistled a song to the dark-haired queen . . .[23]

The scene Bennett puts before us is highly visual and echoes the drawing she made for the March 1924 cover of *Crisis*: fauns and nymphs dance and play pipes while a slight young black man reclines among them (Figure 8.1). In both representational worlds, subjectivity—including artistic subjectivity—is manifested and contained within its boundaries; no outside gaze exists to impose an exoticizing regime on the natural world. In the drawing, the young man—figure for the African American artist—is off-center and asleep. The nymphs, meanwhile, are distinctly separated from him in the background and are clearly pursuing their own ends, as indeed are the fauns, intent on playing their pipes. This visual decenteredness carries over to "Fantasy." The speaker of the poem begins explicitly as the controlling consciousness of the fantastic world depicted, which is, after all, her or his dream or "Fantasy." But, though "dusk-eyed" and "dark-haired," the queen is a fantasy of fairy aesthetics, not the racial phantasm dredged up from the bourgeois artistic unconscious. However, in the final lines, the speaker abdicates the voyeuristic control his or her position "behind a bush" affords to offer up a "whistl[ing] song." This gesture initiates an interaction that is born of the speaker's own, acknowledged desire and pitched at the register of social intercourse—flirtation, a not-too-invested game of equals.

Bennett carried her fine arts sensibility forward into her high renaissance work as one of its major foundations and an important instrument of ideological critique. Together with the resulting aesthetic of chiseled modernist control, the "art" poetry we have thus far examined suggests the direction of Bennett's full-blown claim to subcultural entitlement—her avant-garde voice—discussed later in this chapter. In stark contrast is the aesthetic of abandon to which Helene Johnson was drawn. Establishing lyric selfhood through lyric rapture, Johnson was pulled immediately into serious engagement with the explicit poetics of race; accordingly, her progress toward avant-garde expression occurs over an explicitly racial terrain from its very beginnings.

"My Race," from 1925, the first year of Johnson's published career, testifies in an odd way to the appeal of a rapturous voice for a renaissance woman poet who would speak directly of race.

Figure 8.1 Gwendolyn Bennett, untitled cover for *Crisis,* March 1924. (Beinecke Library, Yale University)

Ah my race,
Hungry race,
Throbbing and young—
Ah, my race,
Wonder race,
Sobbing with song—
Ah, my race,
Laughing race,
Careless in mirth—

Ah, my veiled
Unformed race,
Fumbling in birth.[24]

At this early stage, Johnson would seem to have only her abstract desire to speak to and for the race, without a clear subject position from which to do it. The result can only be a string of "Ahs"; the passionate/rapturous impulse expressed "from nowhere." By the time of "The Road," published the following year, Johnson has given her rapturous feeling the lyric medium of sustained metaphor and thereby begun the process of finding for herself a concrete positionality. On its face a more attenuated treatment of "her race," "The Road" actually goes much further (its vestigial "Ahs" notwithstanding) to bringing the race into focus than the abstract paean could do.

Ah, little road all whirry in the breeze,
A leaping clay hill lost among the trees,
The bleeding note of rapture streaming thrush
Caught in a drowsy hush
And stretched out in a single singing line of dusky song.
Ah little road, brown as my race is brown,
Your trodden beauty like our trodden pride,
Dust of the dust, they must not bruise you down.
Rise to one brimming golden, spilling cry![25]

As the race takes on concreteness, so does the speaker. Held to a definite metaphor, the race comes through as "like a road"—and by the same token, as defying our expectations for a road. Principally at issue is the idea that a road is the means to a destination, that it implies forward motion and future orientation. To the contrary, Johnson's poem conspicuously insists that we view the road as a stationary convergence of directionless, even ludic activity: a road "whirry in the breeze," "leaping" and "lost" in a "drowsy hush." The road has, in effect, been brought within the terms of lyric time; accordingly, the life of the race has been rendered a synchronic, lyric moment ("a single singing line of dusky song") in which all movement tends toward overflow ("bleeding," "brimming," and "spilling"). The exhortation of the final line brings this redefinition into full visibility in the same moment that the speaker herself comes into view. In the passionate call to passionate expression—"Rise to one brimming golden, spilling cry!"—we see the identification of the lyric woman poet and the race in their mutual rapture. Even more to the point, we see the way that rapture—a lyric "I"—has been implicit from the first line, calling our woman speaker into being.

"Fulfillment" builds on this dynamic with a more ambitious and particularized evocation of race and self. The opening stanza suggests the romantic voice associated with Edna St. Vincent Millay and (closer to home) Georgia Douglas Johnson:

To climb a hill that hungers for the sky,
 To dig my hands wrist deep in pregnant earth,
To watch a young bird, veering, learn to fly,
 To give a still, stark poem shining birth.[26]

The distinctiveness of "Fulfillment" starts to emerge in the subsequent stanza, as the Harlem topos of the street insinuates itself into the poem's giddy romantic vista:

To hear the rain drool, dimpling, down the drain
 And splash with a wet giggle in the street,
To ramble in the twilight after supper,
 And to count the pretty faces that you meet.

Johnson now hits her stride, giving her romantic rapture over entirely to the celebration of street life:

To ride to town on trolleys, crowded, teeming
 With joy and hurry and laughter and push and sweat—
Squeezed next a patent-leathered Negro dreaming
 Of a wrinkled river and a minnow net.

To buy a paper from a breathless boy,
 And read of kings and queens in foreign lands,
Hyperbole of romance and adventure,
 All for a penny the color of my hand.

At the center of Johnson's synthesis of Harlem and the romantic is a clear consciousness that, while the latter demands and cultivates an individualistic (if expansive) self, the former has a fundamentally collective structure—Harlem *is* its "pretty faces," the uniquely multicultural, rainbow-colored population of African Americans. On the face of it, Johnson has made the not insignificant gesture of "elevating" Harlem to the status of a traditionally "inspiring" subject for poetry. But as a woman of the renaissance, she has also begun the process by which she will finally achieve full access to the subculture she rightly feels is her own.

Taking herself away from the supper table and down to the street, there to be agent and not object, requires a sense of female self not built into Harlem poetics, which typically feature flaneurs like *Home to Harlem*'s Jake, visually sweeping the street for "sweet browns." Neither Jake nor "brown," Johnson's speaker hits the street armed with a selfhood derived from her stanza in nature, her romantic subjectivity. By the time she contemplates "a penny the color of [her] hand," she has achieved a truly remarkable identification of self with the world she would claim. Within the transaction this fourth stanza describes, this woman has gone beyond even the prerogative of observer-chronicler. In a final distancing of the commodity status her presence as a woman on the street raises, she asserts herself as a *buyer* in the marketplace—and not a buyer of fashion (the paradoxical buying of one's own self) but of a newspaper, vehicle of public discourse, her purchase "from a breathless boy" underscoring her potential power in this sphere. If the contents of the paper sound better than a women's novel ("hyperbole of romance and adventure"), that only serves to naturalize further the public entitlement of the female speaker, whose very skin, after all, is the color of currency.

Yet taken from another angle, "a penny the color of my hand" signals the imminent dissolution of self into the larger racial, urban body—just as did the collective human cloud of "joy and hurry and laughter and push and sweat." However desirable the Harlem matrix, the renaissance identity of the bourgeois female speaker is too fragile and hard-won to allow itself to disappear without a trace, hence the abrupt reversion to nature in the poem's final two stanzas, where we find a romantic subjectivity dialectically heightened by the journey to Harlem.

> To lean against a strong tree's bosom, sentient
> And hushed before the silent prayer it breathes,
> To melt the still snow with my seething body
> And kiss the warm earth tremulous underneath.
>
> Ah, life, to let your stabbing beauty pierce me
> And wound me like we did the studded Christ,
> To grapple with you, loving you too fiercely,
> And to die bleeding—consummate with Life.

The culminating crucifixion lacks any obvious preparation in the foregoing stanzas, except in the (rather trivial) sense that being "pierced" by "stabbing beauty" offers a "climax" to the experience of "Life." But if we attend to the drama of subjectivity the poem has unfolded until now, the advent of Christian masochism serves nicely to negotiate the impasse between the (bourgeois) bounded self and the (Harlem) collective self. As the extension of romantic subjectivity Johnson clearly intends it to be, crucifixion annihilates the boundaries of self by way of an apotheosis of self. And in its powerful presence within the poetics of African American rhetoric generally and renaissance women's poetry in particular, Christianity lets this speaker's selfhood come to rest within black tradition—if not quite yet on the streets of Harlem.

Bennett and Johnson in the Avant-garde

Feminine identity and male prerogative were key categories in the development of both Bennett's and Johnson's poetic subcultural entitlement—their sense of a place in the avant-garde. Johnson rode the rhetorical passion peculiarly available to feminine speakers to finally touch down square in the middle of an urban space and poetics more or less cordoned off as male territory. Bennett effectively shored up a genteel femininity with the distance and delicacy of her specifically imagist aesthetic and her generally modernist aestheticism. But she also took quickly to the masculine liberty of directing culture, in her own way orchestrating the renaissance as consciously as Wallace Thurman himself.

Bennett's relation to the avant-garde needs to be seen in the context of her renaissance activities as a whole, which involve her equally in establishment and fringe cultural circles. Bennett produced several signature cover illustrations for *Crisis* in the high renaissance years, and one of her first poems, "To Usward," officially served to honor Jessie Redmon Fauset at the famous Civic Club dinner that launched the renaissance. Less well known is the fact that Bennett was one of the two or three people to suggest the idea of the dinner itself to Charles Johnson.[27] Bennett was among the editorial collective that produced the de facto manifesto of the Harlem avant-garde, *FIRE!!*; she also served as guest editor for the second issue (of a total of three) of *Black Opals*, the ambitious art journal of the Philadelphia New Negroes. The invitation was testimony to her prestige: her editorial staff included Jessie Redmon Fauset, and contributors (aside from the young Philadelphians the journal was intended to showcase) included Alain Locke and Langston Hughes.[28] Thus, *Black Opals* was conspicuously a cross-generational venture, and the choice of Bennett as guest editor may well reflect specifically on the ability she cultivated to orchestrate the divergent voices of the renaissance. In fact, Bennett made a public renaissance ideal of such orchestration in her role as *Opportunity* columnist.

Through "The Ebony Flute," a literary news column that ran in *Opportunity* from August 1926 through May 1928, Bennett created for herself a truly singular subcultural voice. The only column of its kind in the renaissance public sphere, "Ebony Flute" was a miscellaneous collection of publication announcements, marriages, journeys, works in progress, and so forth. Its coherence derived from the voice of Bennett herself. Though she took no part in the cultivation of high-profile "personality" characteristic of self-consciously "modern" writers like those of *The Messenger*, Bennett made her presence felt through the paradoxically self-effacing role of speaking the renaissance. The renaissance took Harlem as its symbolic, affective locus, but the majority of people for whom the movement was a matter of active and intense interest lived elsewhere, as evidenced by the many New Negro "little magazines" scattered around the country, and the national readership of the New York–based journals. As an identifiable and ongoing cultural event, the renaissance had to be visibly and explicitly constructed—not simply interpreted but built up out of social and cultural bits gathered from around the United States and the world. Under these circumstances, a column of the "lighter side" of literary life takes on the status of cultural exoskeleton to lend shape and ontological status to what would otherwise be amorphous or invisible. Presiding over this subcultural materialization of the renaissance was the unobtrusive but distinctly enthusiastic voice of Bennett. It was Bennett's occasionally whimsical, deliberately inclusive voice that brought the renaissance into being for her readers, her stream of associations that served as its connecting tissue—quite explicitly so, her favorite segue being "which reminds me that. . . ." Moreover, the fact of the column as an identifiable center to renaissance life had the self-perpetuating effect of prompting newsy letters from itinerant renaissance celebrities, which, when they appeared in print addressed to her, testified to Bennett's personal force.

Just months after the first installment of "The Ebony Flute," *Opportunity* presented a second column, "The Dark Tower," written by Countee Cullen. Their mirror relation was reflected in their distinctive, identical graphics; not surprisingly, there is evidence that the two were intended to be complementary.[29] In this light, Bennett's inclusivity seems even more pointed: while Cullen chose just two or three topics each month and subjected them to close critical analysis and, often, ringing judgments, Bennett went out of her way to channel local political-aesthetic debates into a greater vision of racial progress, in a manner clearly suggesting the weight of real "race work." The pointedness of this strategy is evident in the comparison between Cullen's review and Bennett's counterreview of *Meek Mose*, a "Comedy of Negro Life" from 1928. Cullen pans it as "a wooden, amateurish play in which at intervals, apparently mathematically conceived, spirituals are indulged in for no good reason whatever, except that the action is on the wane."[30] In the subsequent month's "Ebony Flute," Bennett brings *Meek Mose* back before the public in order to refocus their attention.

> to us the play in itself and its success or failure was unimportant. We were more concerned with the fact that here had arrived the day when the theatre goers of Broadway were willing to attend seriously to the things that Negroes had to say about their own lives.[31]

Having made her point, Bennett goes on to specifically invert Cullen's complaint that the veteran actors of *Meek Mose* "do not fit a new day and time and, more to the point, a new play." Bennett celebrates the fact that actors "who were in essence the spirit of the old school in Negro acting . . . were taking a leading part in the new movement towards true Negro expression upon the American stage." Her next line is surely to be taken as a mischievous parting shot: "So . . . de sun do move. . . ." [original ellipses].

Not a mushy avoidance of conflict, Bennett's vision of racial progress seems more an assertion of faith in the force of her own enthusiastic chronicling to hold together all manner of contradictory things. The role of renaissance columnist and the Bennett persona as it had developed by 1926 dialectically produced in each other a certain subcultural ideal, for which Bennett took personal responsibility: one of inclusivity, with the obligation to orchestrate inclusivity's inevitible plurality.

Like "Ebony Flute" itself, Bennett's best-known poems take the renaissance as their subject, and with the same strong drive to bring it into being in its greatest possible multiplicity. This is evident from the early days of the commemorative poem she wrote for the historic Civic Club dinner. But as this text reveals, the "us" of "To Usward" is first and foremost the younger Negro artists and the ideal of inclusivity, Bennett's positioned response to her perception of antagonism (or, at least, interference) from the elder Negro leadership. "To Usward" includes a direct plea for tolerance:

If any have a song to sing
That's different from the rest,
Oh let them sing
Before the urgency of Youth's behest!
For some of us have songs to sing
Of jungle heat and fires,
And some of us are solemn grown
With pitiful desires,
And there are those who feel the pull
Of seas beneath the skies,
And some there be who want to croon
Of Negro lullabies.[32]

In the context of the politicized aesthetic debates of even these early days of the renaissance, Bennett seems here quite pointedly to defend artistic youth against appropriation to any preexisting racial agendas.

Yet the interest of this poem lies less in its call for artistic freedom and tolerance than in the strategies of Bennett's self-designation—from the very start of her career and the renaissance—as the voice of unity. The explicit imperative to transcendence—directed to herself *and* the movement—weaves itself into the rhetorical traces of her situatedness as a woman poet and her impulse toward avant-garde identity. The central metaphor, which frames the poem at beginning and end, draws directly on the lyric structure we have seen as core to public feminine self-construction in the renaissance. "To Usward" begins,

Let us be still
As ginger jars are still
Upon a Chinese shelf.
And let us be contained
By entities of Self. . . .

Having invoked the self-sufficiency, protective privacy, and fullness out of time so fundamental to contemporaneous African American women's poetry, Bennett goes on to merge this feminine selfhood into the very definition of renaissance artistry.

Not still with lethargy and sloth,
But quiet with the pushing of our growth.
Not self-contained with smug identity
But conscious of the strength in entity.

But if the ginger jars serve to root the new generation's art in the feminine tradition out of which Bennett herself emerges, they likewise gesture forward to Bennett's own avant-garde telos. To begin with, they echo a key trope of international modernism: Imagism's dense and luminous "oriental" object. But in the discursive context of a well-developed and ideologically purposive Africanist poetics, we might well ask, Why "ginger jars . . . / Upon a Chinese shelf"? Why not a metaphor of Africa to articulate the call "to usward," not least because Africa was as rich a vein of modernist meaning as China?[33]

In fact, Bennett's ginger jars displace not just Africa but China itself, substituting for the essential exoticism of the non-Western "homeland" (one's own or another's) the mediated encounter with heritage that city life provides: not the diffuse mystery of China, then, but the dusty shelf in Chinatown; not a soul-threatening encounter with the Other but a foray into the quietly receptive downtown herb shop. The struggle to locate and define African heritage and African American identity, particularly intense in this first flowering of a racially distinct aesthetic (as the Harlem renaissance understood itself), takes on particular contours for those who embrace the urban context in which the struggle takes place—that is, those of an avant-garde renaissance sensibility. In Bennett's poem, urban life provides access to concretely situated and embodied sites of culture into whose mystery transcendent, peripatetic urban subjects—modern artists—enter voluntarily, as an act of will (*Let us be* like ginger jars).[34] "Us"—we—are, of course, African American artists, but in the context of Bennett's displacement of African for Chinese exoticism, necessity goes out of the racial marking. However paradoxical this outcome, given the occasion of the poem, it captures the peculiar felicity of life in Harlem, where the norm is black and, wandering the streets free from the gaze that fixes one's otherness, the black artist glimpses the (flaneurial) promise of modern urban transcendence. For Harlemite urban artists, exoticism, Chinese or African, is (or might be) a matter of voluntary association. Importantly, Bennett invokes an artistic community who do choose such association; just as importantly, they do so as moderns whose aesthetic appropriations proceed from the freedom in identity conferred upon them by the urban space of Harlem. Bennett's ginger jars isolate the utopian moment of modernity and aesthetic endeavor as such, channeling the poem toward avant-garde affiliation even as they implicate the avant-garde in the feminine literary selfhood of lyric plenitude.

Written one year after "To Usward," "Song" takes Bennett significantly further in the development of her aesthetic politics. Aside from its titular self-designation, "Song" 's highly focused sense of actively orchestrating African American art may explain why Alain Locke placed it in the "Music" rather than the "Poetry" section of his landmark 1925 anthology, *The New Negro: Voices of the Harlem Renaissance*. The poem foregrounds its status as a performative act

I am weaving a song of waters,
Shaken from firm, brown limbs,
Or heads thrown back in irreverent mirth.
My song has the lush sweetness
Of moist, dark lips

Where hymns keep company
With old forgotten banjo songs.
Abandon tells you
That I sing the heart of a race
While sadness whispers
That I am the cry of a soul. . . .[35]

Even as she takes the "weaving" function to herself, the speaker renders the impulse an intrinsic part of African American cultural life: "moist dark lips" are home to modern Christian "hymns" as well as secular, antebellum "old forgotten banjo songs." Weaving, or orchestrating, racial culture puts her not so much above as immersed within the race, and the test of her cultural authenticity is in the African American reader's weaving response, in which the feeling of "Abandon tells you / That I sing the heart of a race / While [the feeling of] sadness whispers / That I am the cry of a soul." As the second stanza shifts to dialect, the speaker recedes behind a vernacular vision seemingly conjured up by the first stanza interactions of speaker and audience.

A-shoutin' in de ole camp-meetin' place,
A-strummin' o' de ole banjo.
Singin' in de moonlight,
Sobbin' in de dark.
Singin', sobbin', strummin' slow . . .
Singin' slow; sobbin' low.
Strummin', strummin', strummin' slow . . .

When the speaker returns to the fore in stanza three, it is to assert the power of Art to orchestrate culture in a more inclusive mode than folk expression could do:

Words are bright bugles
That make the shining for my song,
And mothers hold brown babes
To dark, warm breasts
To make my singing sad.

In clearly distinguishing between her song and the human life it celebrates, the speaker gives mothers and words their full due. At the same time, she reminds us of her own integrative task, performed with the sanction of the people, but out of her own power as an artist.

The concluding stanza is devoted to the general power of art with a specific focus on its effects within African American cultural life. Bennett wrests the Brown Girl, icon of renaissance artistry, from the disembodied gaze of her usual bourgeois viewer and sets her before a woman of the street: "A dancing girl with swaying hips / Sets mad the queen in a harlot's eye." What happens when contemporary art is not just for artists? The short answer for what we see here is racial—and feminine—pride. At the more complicated level of aesthetic politics, Bennett has effectively revealed what the bourgeois context of reception manages more or less successfully to obscure: the dangerous proximity to the harlot—and not just to the queen—of African American artistry's central icon. Given a viewer of her own class, the Brown Girl loses much of her transhistorical aura, but for a good cause, as we see the (African) queen take hold of the "lost" and generally unspeakable woman. More precisely, we see this woman gain access to what art has to offer. Bennett thus displays a supreme faith in art's redemptive power, a utopian dimension of modernism not often acknowledged in the (ostensibly) cynical renaissance avant-garde. And perhaps she forces an even more important avant-garde contradiction by actually crossing class lines to stage the redemption.

In the high renaissance year of 1927, Bennett circled back on the Brown Girl in what we might well see as an obligatory paean to this most essential figure of renaissance aesthetics. "To a Dark Girl" seems more or less to conform to its generic type, rendering the historical body of the race through the admiring scrutiny of her bourgeois explainer.

I love you for your brownness,
And the rounded darkness of your breast;
I love you for the breaking sadness in your voice
And shadows where your wayward eyelids rest.

Something of old forgotten queens
Lurks in the lithe abandon of your walk,
And something of the shackled slave
Sobs in the rhythm of your talk.

But if this speaker engages in the usual projections, she also manages finally to suggest that the "dark girl" might herself be the subject of history:

Oh, little brown girl, born for sorrow's mate,
Keep all you have of queenliness,
Forgetting that you once were slave,
And let your full lips laugh at Fate!

In thus granting the Brown Girl an unmediated relation to fate here in this most critical context of bourgeois African American self-understanding, Bennett gestures toward the sort of democratic decentering that constitutes her chief contribution to renaissance poetry.

A MERE SEVENTEEN AT THE official launch of the Renaissance, Helene Johnson came of age in the Harlem milieu and even more than Gwendolyn Bennett, wrestled fully with the avant-garde speech she perhaps misrecognized as her birthright. Moreover, she came closest to creating within it a space for feminine subjectivity and cultural authority. Precursor to "A Missionary Brings a Young Native to America" (chapter 6) is the exemplary

"Magalu," in which Johnson deliberately overrides the conventional boundaries of primitivist femininity. "Magalu," an individual person with a name, has neither the fetishized body nor the "barbaric dance" of Brown Girl convention; hence, no voyeuristic thrill drives the poem. Indeed, we are fully halfway through its twenty-four free verse lines before Magalu herself appears. Preceding her entrance is a lush but finally not exoticized junglescape.

Summer comes.
The ziczac hovers
'Round the greedy-mouthed crocodile.
A vulture bears away a foolish jackal.
The flamingo is a dash of pink
Against dark green mangroves,
Her slender legs rivaling her slim neck.
The laughing lake gurgles delicious music in its throat
And lulls to sleep the lazy lizard,
A nebulous being on a sun-scorched rock.[36]

The busy calm of this scene derives as much as anything from the particularity with which it is rendered; Africa is not a psychological state or a phantasm but a place, with seasons and inhabitants. When we finally encounter Magalu, we understand her, too, to be an inhabitant, distinguished by her darkness and pursuing her own individual purposes.

In such a place,
In this pulsing riotous gasp of color,
I met Magalu, dark as a tree at night,
Eager-lipped, listening to a man with a white collar
And a small black book with a cross on it.

Dangerously close to losing herself to this missionary, Magalu is yet tempted at the level of her own "eager" intellect. The speaker addresses her accordingly:

Oh Magalu, come! Take my hand and I will read you poetry,
Chromatic words,
Seraphic symphonies,
Fill up your throat with laughter and your heart with song.
Do not let him lure you from your laughing waters,
Lulling lakes, lissome winds.
Would you sell the colors of your sunset and the fragrance
Of your flowers, and the passionate wonder of your forest
For a creed that will not let you dance?

The speaker engages in a struggle with the missionary for the heart and mind of Magalu by pitting her book of poems against his book of pieties. Once unleashed, her "chromatic words" and "seraphic symphonies" infiltrate the meaning of the jungle, bringing it into an articulate aesthetic order to present to Magalu—in the "*colors* of your sunset" and the "*lulling* lakes, *lissome* winds." The poem assumes Magalu's sentience, her susceptibility to cognitive appeals (whether of an aesthetic or theological nature). But perhaps more fundamentally disruptive of her conventional Brown Girl status is Magalu's very separateness from the jungle she inhabits: not the embodiment of African culture (and hardly embodied at all), not the feminized symbol of the passive land, "Magalu" pulls the Brown Girl free from the heavily freighted meanings that typically subsume her. The revised Brown Girl who emerges is likewise distinct from the ideological dichotomy of ascetic white religion and lush black poetry. Magalu has the prerogative to choose between them—and embedded in that choice is the power to "sell," and even to "sell out." Johnson here extends to this most objectified figure of renaissance femininity, the African native, the redemptive possibility which she (like Bennett, in her own way) finds native to the city street: atomistic modern identity, the boundaries of which provide—or, at least, promise—an empowering distance from gender, race, and history itself.

Central to Johnson's work was the performance of this kind of rescue—from objectification, as in the case of the Brown Girl, or from obscurity, as in the several poems she devoted to celebrating the man in the (Harlem) street in her high-renaissance years of 1926 and 1927. And somewhere in the variety of speaking positions these poems afforded her, Johnson came into an identity which was feminine, urban, and quintessentially avant-garde.

"Bottled" is Johnson's best-known poem, published first in the premier journal of urbanity, *Vanity Fair*, for which it got considerable attention in literary circles both inside and outside Harlem.[37] It is the only one of Johnson's poems to utilize an explicitly male voice, but one imagines that its success stems not from the gender of the speaker per se, but from the exuberant sense of urban mastery his gender affords him. Having once captured that sense "as a man," Johnson will work to appropriate it to feminine terms.

"Bottled" may be seen as an extended encounter with racial heritage against the backdrop of urban Harlem, with which the speaker is strongly identified. In its central focus, "Bottled" turns the redemptive light of African heritage on an unappreciated man on the street, while giving considerable space to its speaker, whose vernacular voice renders him a full-blown character and whose musing, peripatetic relation to the city provides the structure of the poem. Strikingly, for a poem of the renaissance, the continuity of Harlem and Africa is never assumed; in fact, their disjunction constitutes the poem's central tension. Such skepticism regarding Africa is at least as common among the avant-garde as the converse embrace of primitivism. Not just ornery refusal to glorify the ancestry, the distanced relation to Africa was necessary to a certain avant-garde investment in modern identity, however ambivalent. Hence, Africa appears in the very first stanza of "Bottled," but as an anthropological oddity.

Upstairs on the third floor
Of the 135th Street library
In Harlem, I saw a little
Bottle of sand, brown sand
Just like the kids make pies
Out of down at the beach.
But the label said: "This
Sand was taken from the Sahara desert."
Imagine that! The Sahara desert!
Some bozo's been all the way to Africa to get some sand.

The speaker's diction ("some bozo") ensures his identity as a city dweller, just as the fact that Africa is contained in a remote ("third floor") library exhibit ensures that Harlem is a space separable, at some level, from racial heritage.

When, in the next stanza, we come to the man who constitutes the visual focus of the poem, the spectacle he creates on the street enters the poem as intentionally analogous to the bottle of sand—arcane, remote, not of Harlem, but for Harlem's amusement.

And yesterday on Seventh Avenue
I saw a darky dressed fit to kill
In yellow gloves and swallow tail coat
And swirling a cane. And everyone
Was laughing at him. Me too,
At first, till I saw his face
When he stopped to hear a
Organ grinder grind out some jazz.
Boy! You should a seen that darky's face!
It just shone. Gee he was happy!
And he began to dance. No
Charleston or Black Bottom for him.
No sir. He danced just as dignified
And slow. No, not slow either.
Dignified and *proud*! You couldn't
Call it slow, not with all the
Cuttin' up he did. You would a died to see him.

As the stanza progresses, the generational difference that has seemed to define this man—unaware of contemporary popular dances, happy in dandy's clothes, his very happiness seemingly anachronistic and minstrel-like—is replaced by a historical difference going beyond the space of a generation to racial ancestry. His dance, when it comes, is "dignified / And slow. No, not slow either./Dignified and *proud*!" At this point, the speaker has become the privileged audience for the man's essential self, as well as its articulator—at the same time that he must insist on his own character and generational distance from what he sees. In the clash of these two aims, we are confronted with the possibility that what he "sees" is, in fact, a youthful urban fantasy of Africa projected onto the old man. In the next stanza,

> The crowd kept yellin' but he didn't hear,
> Just kept on dancin' and twirlin' that cane
> And yellin' out loud every once in a while.
> I know the crowd thought he was coo-coo.
> But say, I was where I could see his face,
> And somehow, I could see him dancin' in a jungle,
> A real honest-to-cripe jungle, and he wouldn't have on them
> Trick clothes—those yaller shoes and yaller gloves
> And swallow-tail coat. He wouldn't have on nothing.
> And he wouldn't be carrying no cane.
> He'd be carrying a spear with a sharp fine point
> Like the bayonets we had "over there."
> And the end of it would be dipped in some kind of
> Hoo-doo poison. And he'd be dancin' black and naked and gleaming.
> And he'd have rings in his ears and on his nose
> And bracelets and necklaces of elephants' teeth.

As the fantasy becomes increasingly visual and ornate, a series of primitivist clichés, we get a glimpse of what motivates it.

> Gee, I bet he'd be beautiful then all right.
> No one would laugh at him then, I bet.
> Say! That man that took that sand from the Sahara desert
> And put it in a little bottle on a shelf in the library,
> That's what they done to this shine, ain't it? Bottled him.
> Trick shoes, trick coat, trick cane, trick everything—all glass—
> But inside—
> Gee, that poor shine!

Even as it seems to establish his perfect sympathy, the conclusion deliberately asserts the young speaker's impassable distance from the problems of "that poor shine."

A second poem from the same year imagines the same scenario, but with a feminine speaker/observer—and somewhere in the gender transition the rich, variegated terrain of Harlem fades away, leaving only speaker and object where there was a whole world. Given the centrality of the world of Harlem to Johnson's poetics, its disappearance warrants the suspicion that critical stakes are afoot in this poem. "Sonnet to a Negro in Harlem" attempts to embed a feminine presence on the street through an implicitly heterosexual framework. But adopting heterosexuality as a framework within which to speak as a subcultural bard apparently problematizes the value of the street itself.

"Sonnet to a Negro in Harlem," as its title suggests, makes a declaration of love to an anonymous and, perhaps more important, a generalized man of the race. More accurately termed a protolove poem, "Sonnet" channels its submerged love through the purest expression of appreciation. The subject of this paean is an exotic, but, unlike the Brown Girl, whose links to primitivism arise unbidden—and largely unnoticed—by her for the benefit of her bourgeois spectator, this "Negro" wears his primitivism as a self-conscious mantle of defiance:

> You are disdainful and magnificent—
> Your perfect body and your pompous gait,
> Your dark eyes flashing solemnly with hate,
> Small wonder that you are incompetent
> To imitate those whom you so despise—
> Your shoulders towering high above the throng,
> Your head thrown back in rich, barbaric song,
> Palm trees and mangoes stretched before your eyes.[38]

Most obviously, gender accounts for the man's difference, specifically, the masculine burden of exclusion from the white capitalist enterprise. Johnson deploys the long-standing African American critique of white capitalist greed in service to the imperative of masculine self-worth, as the poem concludes.

> Let others toil and sweat for labor's sake
> And wring from grasping hands their meed of gold.
> Why urge ahead your supercilious feet?
> Scorn will efface each footprint that you make.
> I love your laughter arrogant and bold
> You are too splendid for this city street!

Registered through her empathy with the disenfranchised black man, the speaker sees the city as the degraded territory of capitalist strife—a striking contrast to the celebration with which we have seen her female personae take to the very same turf. This divide would seem to reflect the classic gender dichotomy of male production, here prohibited, and female consumption, presumed to be easy. But in fact, the class difference between speaker and "Negro" overrides the gender difference in this case, perhaps willfully so: her privilege as a bourgeois intellectual (including the fact that *her* exoticism *makes* her money) affords her modern transcendence. By contrast, his greater economic vulnerability keeps him tied to regimented wage work, which, in fact, he *cannot* afford to despise, and for which his exoticism is a hindrance. But this celebration of the man's class defiance—this assertion of class empathy—functions implicitly to shore up the speaker's precarious claim to the street as a woman. The "Negro" is lordly, king of the street but not a part of it, and the street itself fails to offer him refuge, either as a general site of pleasure and variety or as a special black world standing between the individual African American and the capitalism of downtown (as epitomized by McKay's *Home to Harlem*). With no hint of a larger racial community, this man is isolated as no other figures we have seen in Johnson's poetry.

The key to so significant a departure from her usual depiction of Harlem life lies not in the man himself, however, but in the ontological needs of the speaker who addresses him. In isolating the male, the speaker comes into being as the one to recognize the true worth of this princely exotic, scorned by the world. Her identity—and his—are thus anchored in her necessary perception. In their intimate mutual interdependence, they are like lovers, but in her singularity and disembodiment (for the "Negro" of her admiring gaze does not physicalize her as a mere woman by gazing back) the speaker emerges as transcendent and authoritative poet of the race. This gendered dynamic of identification and desire crystallizes around the issue of urban alienation. The man's entitlement to ease on the street, as a man, is as much assumed as the female speaker's awkwardness. In letting this "magnificent" African bear the burden of alienation for both of them—and in particular for the alienation displaced from her to him—she transforms alienation itself from a mark of outsiderhood to a core component of racial authenticity *and* racially specific masculinity. To the extent that her displacement of alienation is successful, she is free of it; to the extent that her femininity inevitably draws alienation back to her, it returns dialectically transformed as a mark of inclusivity.

In their identification and difference, in their mutual need, the speaker and object of "Sonnet" are protolovers. "Poem," Johnson's most ambitious claim to avant-garde identity, is also grounded within this heterosexual framework. But the work of making a place for herself really begins in earnest when she melds heterosexual identity—by itself, a potentially hazardous basis for artistic authority—with vernacular diction. Contrary to what we might expect, Johnson's vernacular did not function to identify her with a specific—more racially "authentic"—class. Just the reverse, vernacular diction tapped into the potential for class transcendence implicit in modernity. With the voice of a slangy urbanite, Johnson could glide lightly across femininity *and* the street, heterosexuality *and* autonomy. Most significant for her contribution to avant-garde representation, she (like Bennett in her own way) could close the gap between racial authenticity and artistic authority.

Published alongside "Sonnet" in Countee Cullen's landmark anthology, *Caroling Dusk*, "Poem" emanates from the extraordinary rhetorical situation of a female modern watching a male vaudeville performer in a popular Harlem theater.

Little brown boy,
Slim, dark, big-eyed,
Crooning love songs to your banjo
Down at the Lafayette—

Gee, boy, I love the way you hold your head,
High sort of and a bit to one side,
Like a prince, a jazz prince. And I love
Your eyes flashing, and your hands,
And your patent-leathered feet,
And your shoulders jerking the jig-wa.
And I love your teeth flashing,
And the way your hair shines in the spotlight
Like it was the real stuff.
Gee, brown boy, I loves you all over.
I'm glad I'm a jig. I'm glad I can
Understand your dancin' and your
Singin', and feel all the happiness
And joy and don't care in you.
Gee, boy, when you sing, I can close my ears
And hear tom toms just as plain.
Listen to me, will you, what do I know
About tom toms? But I like the word, sort of,
Don't you? It belongs to us.
Gee, boy, I love the way you hold your head,
And the way you sing, and dance,
And everything.
Say, I think you're wonderful. You're
Allright with me,
You are.[39]

Johnson has, in effect, seized the means of avant-garde cultural production: her female speaker claims the right of the public space, the right of the specularizing gaze, and the power of cultural/racial definition. But what this appropriation entails is the transformation of the discursive apparatus itself, a transformation that points the way out of the impasse facing the avant-garde Harlem intellectual (delineated in chapter 6): his class distance, which slips easily into modernist exoticization or self-irony, and his generational embattlement, which necessitates modernist iconoclasm targeted at women. "Poem" radically restructures the Brown Girl paradigm: the "girl," first of all, has become a "boy"; the "barbaric dance," a theatrical number; the distant bourgeois viewer, a concretely situated, social equal (the Lafayette being the popular nightspot for ordinary Harlemites); and the "essential" race itself, a race under construction.

After briefly introducing us to the "little brown boy," the poem's speaker intrudes herself fully upon the space of the poem by force of her speech. The voice that says "Gee, boy," "the real stuff," "Listen to me, will you," "Say," and "You're / Allright with me" emanates from a modern girl, a "sheba,"[40] even. At this point, vernacular speech comes into focus as a marker that specifically overrides the class (and the race) of the speaker in favor of an identity that is generational only. We feel strongly her modernness and her youth without having much sense of the very vexed question of her class (vexed, since indeed she *is* a woman in a public place). According to historian Paula Fass, classlessness was the whole point of the American youth culture that emerged in the 1920s: the slanginess of self-conscious youth let nation and generation subsume the situatedness of class and race beneath a democratizing (and consumable) style.[41] Faced with the challenge of putting an African American woman into the public terrain of Harlem, Johnson avails herself of this national modernness to transcend the unsatisfying choice between degradation (for the working-class woman) and the threat of degradation (for the bourgeois woman). Socially situated, Johnson's sheba yet escapes such sexual definition and, from her seat in the darkened theatre, even bypasses embodiment.

As possessor of the gaze, "Poem" 's speaker takes no liberties outside her contractual relationship of audience to performer; having paid the price of a ticket, she has public sanction to look appraisingly at a man, as well as the tacit invitation of this man in particular. While the immediate benefit of this situation may be the protection it affords the female viewer, it also stands as a critique of the artist/viewer who helps himself voyeuristically to the fortuitous siting of his object, whether in a cabaret, in a forest glade, or through the window of a church.

But the theatrical context also authorizes the speaker's racial pronouncements. Whereas the image of a woman—and the Brown Girl in particular—is always already saturated with publicness by virtue of being in public circulation, this man needs to be literally placed on a theatrical stage to carry the same charge and thereby underwrite the speaker's cultural authority to ponder the meaning of race through his performance. But since their encounter is thus staged across a vaudevillian space, still strongly tied to minstrelsy, that performance is forcibly seen in light of a theatrical tradition that calls the very idea of racial authenticity into question. The speaker finds her brown boy "crooning . . . to [his] banjo" but simultaneously holding his head "Like a prince, a jazz prince." His teeth and eyes "flash," as do his "patent-leathered feet"; his shoulders "jerk," while his "hair shines in the spotlight / Like it was the real stuff." But she can "close [her] ears / And hear tom toms" in his singing. Rather than let even this trope of "Africa" stand, she topples its essentialist implications—and restores the tom toms to their rightful importance.

> Listen to me, will you, what do I know
> About tom toms? But I like the word, sort of,
> Don't you? It belongs to us.

Far from an unconscious cultural reservoir manifested in the more "primitive" members of the race, the true meaning of "Africa" is the possibility it offers for social solidarity and the collective construction of an enabling culture.

As this last point suggests, the theatrical context also makes African American culture-building the business of ordinary African Americans—

not merely an elite literary exercise of translating the unspoiled peasant to the world. Using the "African-ness" of a vaguely minstrel performance as the starting point for a construction of race puts the African American quest for racial self-definition squarely in mainstream culture, a suggestion buoyed by the mainstream modernness of the speaker herself. Moreover, the mainstream context preserves the possibility of a claim to American identity, an explicitly held value of Harlem discourse generally.

But what of the fact that this avant-garde paean to the race is also a suppressed love poem? The speaker says "I love" no less than five times, in an insistent chorus that holds its own against the racial message. In fact, the two are closely tied in their dynamics and finally inextricable in the ideological visions they project. Sitting in the audience, the speaker is part of a cultural collective—a remarkable female participant in the life of Harlem—and also unique in her recognition of the boy. Buried in her description is the strong implication that she sees something through the very ordinariness of his performance, something that makes her "glad [she's] a jig." That something is, in fact, the complex racial identity we have been examining. Her ability to "understand [his] dancin' and [his] / Singin', and [to] feel all the happiness / And joy and don't care in [him]" is both cause and effect of her love. Though attenuated, the "love" in this poem provides a structuring relation of mutually constituting uniqueness for the players: she sees the prince in him, and that very vision sets *her* apart. Conventional love and the theatrical context save both boy and girl from objectification and essentialism, paradoxically rescuing them for individuality. Through her privileged articulation of the boy's individual essence, the girl gains cultural authority. But the essence she articulates is clearly her own as well as his; they have in common this complex, urban, African, American way of being—and becoming. The avant-garde project of establishing independent racial self-definition emerges here as necessarily a function of self-implication and even affect. Love, not as a private indulgence but as a public embrace of an embodied cultural ethos, is finally the enabling condition for Johnson's feminization of the Harlem Renaissance avant-garde.

At this point, we seem ironically to have come full circle to Jessie Redmon Fauset and the values driving *There Is Confusion* (chapter 7). That "public love" (or, "love in public") could signify both discursive extremes, of women's constraint and women's freedom within renaissance subcultural identity, suggests the tremendous creativity with which women writers responded to their cultural imperatives, as well as the sobering power of the imperatives themselves.

Afterword

> The power of the metropolitan development is not to be denied. The excitements and challenges of its intricate processes of liberation and alienation, contact and strangeness, stimulation and standardization, are still powerfully available. But it should no longer be possible to present these specific and traceable processes as if they were universals, not only in history but as it were above and beyond it.
>
> Raymond Williams, *The Politics of Modernism*

My original interest in modernist women love poets was probably motivated by a form of what Carla Kaplan has identified as feminist "heroics": a critic's fantasy, in which "misunderstood, abandoned, neglected women" (lost writers) are "finally rescued and released by their stronger, bolder daughters" (contemporary feminists).[1] I chose Millay, Taggard, Parker, Bennett, and Johnson precisely for the challenge they presented to all the categories of significance—literary and political—with which I was familiar. Relying at least partly on the sheer heft of historical detail, I set about dignifying my women (on both literary *and* political grounds) by casting their writing within the framework of literary "negotiation." My idea was to show the complex tensions that structured even the most apparently quiescent text and writerly consciousness. My point would be that we should respect these women's *negotiations* because they did not enjoy our freedom from contradiction.

But the more I particularized my subjects—the more I inscribed their radical difference from me—the stronger my impulse to identify with them. Doubtless there was a touch of the feminist colonizer about all this ("recuperative readings may be at least as attached to self-representation as to a recovery of 'the other' "), and perhaps just the ordinary emotional investment that comes of putting years of intellectual work in a given body of material. But critical narcissism does not absolutely preclude the possibility of historical insight (we can not but believe this), and I would like at this time to suggest the way in which my late-twentieth-century "identification" with these early-twentieth-century women writers may not be wholly devoid of historical justification.

The phrase "making love modern" is meant to capture a complex of factors—a total *situation*—which culminates in a certain kind of literary production. Making love modern, as they do, firmly enmeshes the writers of this study in issues of publicity, identity, national culture, and subcultural value, the interactions of which take shape within the intimate/public genre of love poetry. I can only hope the forgoing chapters testify to the value of articulating this process for feminist literary criticism. But might the paradigm for subjectivity that emerges from attention to the making of modern love also have some contemporary explanatory force?

Implicit to the way this book has looked at literary production is a dual notion that (1) love poetry generates concretely accessible "moments" of identity by configuring self-other relations within historically specific discourses and (2) such moments are *defined by tensions* among and within the discourses they involve. I want to suggest that the kind of subjectivity this vision supports may be quintessentially modern and, more specifically, that it may be rooted in the imperatives of consumer capitalism. Dependent as it is on an ideology of personal style, omnivorous and in perpetual flux, consumer capitalism spawns the strong investment in "identity" and the cultivation of "personhood." But if identity feeds directly into the economic regime, it just as clearly provides a strong base of resistance to it.

This first, foundational tension of modern life raises the possibility that "tension" may not be a simple matter of ambivalence toward competing values but a means for *generating irony* with which to insulate the self from fully inhabiting any value in particular. The machinery of modern selfhood I have identified in this study imposes ironic distance—or produces opportunities to secure it, depending on your point of view: publicity makes of the self a luminous commodity for circulation in the marketplace; subculture provides for ardent belonging (to the margin) premised on an equally ardent self-exclusion (from the center); love proclaims a unique world in the language of convention, a refuge defined first and foremost by that which lies just outside of its domain; and love poetry expresses a private selfhood on the strength of public consumption, if not approval. All of these discursive structures pull the subjects they interpellate in at least two directions at once. When those subjects are women, the opportunities for such tension may be especially bountiful. Women, as I have argued, are caught between subjectivity and iconicity in the marginal subculture, are more luminous and more widely circulated than men, and are more defined by (and confined to) the paradoxes of love. In the broadest sense, they are expected to be moderns and be "modernity," too.

If women are more defined by tensions, it would follow that they also have special access to irony. Of course, such a gendering of "irony" flies in the face of some key tenets of high modernism. Indeed, one virtue of the model of subjectivity I am here proposing is the opportunity it offers to revisit the New Critical chestnuts of "tension" and "irony" to see them, not as proof of a transcendent work of art, but as the mark of a highly overdetermined artist. For the high male modernist, the *irony of transcendence* served first to establish his distance from his own art and finally to keep him at a safe remove from mass cultural sentiment and vulgarity. By contrast to this apparently simple and definitive gesture, the example of the "low female modern" suggests an *irony of embeddedness* deriving from a whole social matrix of tensions, to which there is no "outside" and no end. If the imperative for autonomous selfhood pertains in both cases, it does so on very different terms and with different degrees of subjective awareness.

The foregoing should remind us of the historicity of *style*, even that most transparent of styles, irony. When we engage in some of our most characteristically *contemporary* American behaviors—the insistence on first names among commercially involved strangers, casual-dress Fridays, and all other studied refusals of formality; self-deprecating humor, "black" humor, and humor itself as a dominant aesthetic; the tireless camping of our own, emotionally invested cultural past (fifties culture, and now seventies culture); the self-conscious vernacularisms of elite university professors—and when we think about the extent to which these gestures give us our sense of who we are, we might also reflect on where they *place* us. Nervously situated in the overlapping liminal spaces of our own lives in the marketplace, we are subjectivities born of tension. Rather than multiple and fragmented, perhaps we find ourselves buoyed up by the contradictions that let us imagine—or assert—our autonomy from the economic order that, more than ever, defines us.

Notes

Introduction

1. In some cases, this image seems to bring out a will to pathologize (or otherwise diminish), rather than celebrate. I am thinking in particular of *The Moderns*, whose characters range from historical caricature (of Stein and Hemingway) to anachronistically noirish triviality.

2. The critical revision of literary modernism has been dramatic, with feminist scholars leading the charge. See Sandra M. Gilbert and Susan Gubar's massive three-volume study, *No Man's Land: The Place of the Woman Writer in the Twentieth Century* (New Haven: Yale University Press, 1987–1994); Shari Benstock, *Women of the Left Bank: Paris 1900–1940* (Austin: University of Texas Press, 1986); Gillian Hanscombe and Virginia L. Smyers, *Writing for Their Lives: The Modernist Women, 1920–1940* (Boston: Northeastern University Press, 1987); Gloria T. Hull, *Color, Sex, and Poetry: Three Women Writers of the Harlem Renaissance* (Bloomington: Indiana University Press, 1987); Hazel V. Carby, "The Quicksands of Representation: Rethinking Black Cultural Politics" in *Reconstructing Womanhood: The Emergence of the Afro-American Woman Novelist* (New York: Oxford University Press, 1987); Suzanne Clark, *Sentimental Modernism: Women Writers and the Revolution of the Word* (Bloomington: Indiana University Press, 1991); Ann duCille, *The Coupling Convention: Sex, Text, and Tradition in Black Women's Fiction* (New York: Oxford University Press, 1993); Deborah McDowell, "Undercover: Passing and Other Disguises" in *The Changing Same: Black Women's Literature, Criticism, and Theory* (Bloomington: Indiana University Press, 1995) 61–97; Cheryl A. Wall, *Women of the Harlem Renaissance* (Chicago: University of Chicago Press, 1987); Michael North, *The Dialect of Modernism: Race, Language and Twentieth Century Literature* (New York: Oxford University Press, 1994); and Wayne Koestenbaum, *Double Talk: The Erotics of Male Literary Collaboration* (New York: Routledge, 1989).

3. *The Gender of Modernity* (Cambridge: Harvard University Press, 1995) 13.

4. Williams echoes Rita Felski on this point: "It is impossible to develop a modern cultural sociology unless we can find ways of discussing such formations which both acknowledge the terms in which they saw themselves and would wish to be presented, and at the same time enable us to analyze these terms and their general social

and cultural significance'' (''The Bloomsbury Fraction,'' in *Problems in Materialism and Culture* [New York: Verso, 1980] (152).

5. See Ken Gelder and Sarah Thornton, eds., *The Subcultures Reader* (New York: Routledge, 1997).

6. Ibid., ''General Introduction,'' 4.

7. Williams's article also discusses the Godwin Circle, whom he identifies as ''not a fraction, a break from an upper class [, but] an emergent sector of a still relatively subordinate class, the smaller independent commercial bourgeoisie'' (158).

8. In the case of Harlem, artistic marginality is most present to the avant-garde; the cultural establishment focuses its sense of marginality on racial subordination.

9. Williams's whole cultural-group enterprise, in fact, is driven by the promise of insights into class history (155).

10. Williams notes such metropolitan power as key to modernism itself:

> [The metropolis] was the place where new social and economic and cultural relations, beyond both city and nation in their older senses, were beginning to be formed: a distinct historical phase which was in fact to be extended, in the second half of the twentieth century, at least potentially, to the whole world. . . .
>
> [T]he facts of increasing mobility and social diversity, passing through a continuing dominance of certain metropolitan centres and a related unevenness of all other social and cultural development, led to a major expansion of metropolitan forms of perception, both internal and imposed. (*The Politics of Modernism: Against the New Conformists* [New York: Verso, 1989] 44, 46)

Ann Douglas colorfully describes the case of New York in particular:

> Modern American culture, with its mongrel markings, its extremes of formalism and commerciality, of avant-garde innovation and media smarts, of sheer elation and hard-core despair, is unimaginable without New York City. New York, as Ford Madox Ford suggested, might or might not be America, but in the 1920s the city was cornering, expanding, and reinventing the nation's cultural market, and it summoned a far-flung generation to its service. (*Terrible Honesty: Mongrel Manhattan in the 1920s* [New York: Farrar, Straus, and Giroux, 1995] 13)

11. The Russian-Negro connection tended to focus on the Moscow Art Theater tours (with never a mention of the vibrant Yiddish theater scene in New York). See, for example, W. Jackson, ''The Theatre—Drama,'' *The Messenger* (June 1923) 746–747.

12. Carroll Smith-Rosenberg, *Disorderly Conduct: Visions of Gender in Victorian America* (New York: Oxford University Press, 1985); Elizabeth Ammons, ''The New Woman as Cultural Symbol and Social Reality: Six Women Writers' Perspectives'' in 1915: *The Cultural Moment; The New Politics, the New Woman, the New Psychology, the New Art and the New Theatre in America*, ed. Adele Heller and Lois Rudnick (New Brunswick, N.J.: Rutgers University Press, 1991) 82–97; Felski focuses on continental Europe (*The Gender of Modernity* [Cambridge: Harvard University Press, 1995]), and Ann Ardis takes up the case of the New Woman in England (*New Women, New Novels: Feminism and Early Modernism* [New Brunswick, N.J.: Rutgers University Press, 1990]).

13. See Paula Fass, *The Damned and the Beautiful: American Youth in the 1920s* (New York: Oxford University Press, 1977).

14. Rita Felski, *The Gender of Modernity*, 13.

15. The presumed "ahistoricity" of sentimental life is a central topic in Clark, *Sentimental Modernism*.

16. The phrase is Kaja Silverman's ("*Histoire d'O*: The Construction of a Female Subject" in *Pleasure and Danger: Exploring Female Sexuality*, ed. Carol Vance [New York: Routledge, 1984] 320–349).

Chapter 1

1. Suzanne Clark notes that "Millay had grown so hugely popular by the late 1920's that her kitchen was featured in Ladies' Home Journal" (*Sentimental Modernism: Women Writers and the Revolution of the Word* [Bloomington: Indiana University Press, 1991] 34). Clark's assessment of Millay is premised on this very popularity, which was "risky" because of its association with the sentimental, "a term of invective" for the high modernists and the new critics who canonized them (34–35). Clark reads Millay's work as creating a community of women readers on the basis of the scorned (but popular) values of sentiment (*Sentimental Modernism*, 67–96).

2. *Edna St. Vincent Millay and Her Times* (Chicago: University of Chicago Press, 1936) 70. Atkins's book remains an authoritative and informative work.

3. "Renascence" had caused a significant stir among the cognoscenti when, in 1912, she entered it (under the name of E. Vincent Millay) in the prestigious Lyric Year poetry contest (Norman A. Brittin, Edna St. Vincent Millay, revised ed. [Boston: Twayne, 1982] 21; 25–26).

4. Edmund Wilson, *The Shores of Light: A Literary Chronicle of the Twenties and Thirties* (New York: Farrar, Straus, and Young, 1952) 751.

5. Gerald Early, "Introduction," in *My Soul's High Song: The Collected Writings of Countee Cullen, Voice of the Harlem Renaissance* (New York: Doubleday, 1991) 20. Margaret Perry traces profound affinities to Millay in Cullen's work (*A Bio-Bibliography of Countee P. Cullen, 1903–1946* [Westport, Conn.: Greenwood Press, 1971] 42–49), and Alan R. Shucard cites evidence that Cullen was actually faulted by his contemporaries for being too exclusively influenced by Millay (*Countee Cullen* [Boston: Twayne, 1984] 89).

6. Atkins cites as followers Mary Austin, Edith Sitwell, Max Eastman, Max Bodenheim, Rose O'Neill, Virginia Moore, Louis Untermeyer, and Louise Bogan and then goes on: "Of course, I am naming only poets of originality, who did more than make a blurred carbon copy of the original. In addition, carbon copies enough were made and printed. It would be a thankless task to count them" (76). Consistent with the critical lens of her time, Atkins' sense of Millay's literary influence does not extend beyond white—i.e., same-race—writers. Her list might well have included Helene Johnson and Georgia Douglas Johnson, as well as Countee Cullen.

7. Ellen Kay Trimberger, "Introduction," in *Intimate Warriors: Portraits of a Modern Marriage; Selected Works by Neith Boyce and Hutchins Hapgood* (New York: Feminist Press, 1991) 8.

8. Adele Heller and Lois Rudnick, eds., 1915: *The Cultural Moment; The New Politics, the New Woman, the New Psychology, the New Art, and the New Theatre in America* (New Brunswick, N.J.: Rutgers University Press, 1991) treats bohemian theater extensively; see Adele Heller, "The New Theatre" (217–232); Mary C. Henderson, "Against Broadway: The Rise of the Art Theatre in America (1900–1920)" (233–

249; and Robert K. Sarlos, "Jig Cook and Susan Glaspell: Rule Makers and Rule Breakers" (250–260). The book also includes reprinted plays of the Provincetown Players and many photographs of participants and productions.

9. Brittin, *Millay*, 1.

10. Allen Churchill, *The Improper Bohemians: A Re-Creation of Greenwich Village in Its Heyday* (New York: E. P. Dutton, 1959) 262; Edmund Wilson, *I Thought of Daisy* (New York: Farrar, Straus and Giroux, 1967) 107–125.

11. Malcolm Cowley, *Exile's Return: A Literary Odyssey of the 1920's* (1934; New York: Penguin Books, 1979) 69.

12. Churchill, *Improper Bohemians*, 84–176; Albert Parry, *Garrets and Pretenders: A History of Bohemianism in America* (New York: Dover, 1933) 267–315; Carolyn F. Ware, *Greenwich Village, 1920–1930: A Comment on American Civilization in the Post-War Years* (Boston: Riverside Press, 1935) 261.

13. Ware, *Greenwich Village*, 235–263.

14. Parry, *Garrets*, 277–279, see n. 9.

15. Floyd Dell, *King Arthur's Socks and Other Village Plays* (New York: Knopf, 1922).

16. Parry, *Garrets*, 307.

17. Ware, *Greenwich Village*, 111–112.

18. The Jewish immigrants to the east of the Village, meanwhile, served as an important point of idealism for the more radically political bohemians, especially in the teens, when association with the Industrial Workers of the World (the IWW, or Wobblies) made the labor movement an immediate and key bohemian cause. See Lola Ridge, *The Ghetto and Other Poems* (New York: Huebsch, 1918); the journal Masses (discussed briefly in chapter 2 of this text) and its 1920s successor, *New Masses*; Mike Gold, *Jews without Money* (1926; New York: Avon, 1965), an autobiographical work by a radical Villager who actually hailed from the Jewish Lower East Side; and Hutchins Hapgood, *The Spirit of the Ghetto*, ed. Moses Rischin (1902; Cambridge: Harvard University Press, 1967), arguably a precursor text by a founding bohemian. On radical politics in the Village, see Eugene E. Leach, "The Radicals of *The Masses*," in Heller and Rudnick, *1915*, 27–47.

19. In this light, Village anarchist and waiter Hippolyte Havel's famous remark, "Bohemia is a state of mind, it has no boundaries," takes on an ominous ambiguity (Churchill, *Improper Bohemians*, 35).

20. The prime example in Dell's *Love in Greenwich Village* (New York: George H. Doran, 1926) is "Phantom Adventure" (77–98).

21. Churchill, *Improper Bohemians*, 310; Daniel Aaron, *Writers on the Left* (1961; New York: Oxford University Press, 1977) 86; Leach, "Radicals," 29–30.

22. Douglas Clayton, *Floyd Dell: The Life and Times of an American Rebel* (Chicago: Ivan R. Dee, 1994) 85–88.

23. Floyd Dell, "The Rise of Greenwich Village," in *Love in Greenwich Village*, 18.

24. Ibid., 24. Dell rounds out his description with a fictionalized Polly Holladay, a popular Village restaurateur aptly rendered as a mother figure in the triad of women (24).

25. "Philistia" appears on "The Map of Bohemia: From the Explorations of Gelett Burgess, 1896," reprinted as frontispiece in Parry, *Garrets*.

26. Millay married Eugen Boissevain in 1923 (Brittin, *Millay*, 53–54).

27. Parry, *Garrets*, 307–310. Of Guido Bruno, Parry (*Garrets*) reports that he was a career "foreigner": "To some he said he was an Italian, to others he represented

himself as a Serbian, to a few he boasted of his early life as an Austrian officer." We might note "Guido's Garret," then, as the grotesque, if logical, outcome of the peculiar Village dynamics of enterprise, anticapitalism, artistry, xenophobia, and (in Parry's phrase) "the listless worship of foreign mysticism" (308).

28. Dell, *Love in Greenwich Village*, 134. Cf. his description of Millay in an anonymously published essay of 1924.

> When she is reading her poetry, she will seem to the awed spectator a fragile little girl. . . . When she is picnicking in the country she will be . . . an Irish 'newsy.' When she is meeting the bourgeoisie in its lairs, she is likely to be a highly artificial and very affected young lady with an exaggerated Vassar accent and abominably overdone manners. . . . A New England nun; a chorus girl on holiday; the Botticelli Venus of the Uffizi gallery. . . . She is all of these and more ("Edna St. Vincent Millay," *The Literary Spotlight*, ed. John Farrar [New York: George H. Doran, 1924] 77).

29. Those close to Millay would have recognized the echo of Pat with "Vincent," with which Millay signed her personal correspondence and even her poetry before she became famous. Indeed, her initial Village splash, "Renascence," came under this pretense of masculine identity (Brittin, *Millay*, 25).

30. See, for example, "The Button," "A Piece of Slag," and "The Ex-Villager's Confession" in Dell, *Love in Greenwich Village* (101–119; 203–238; 239–254).

31. See chapter 2 of this text for an exploration of this ideological formation through Genevieve Taggard's poetry.

32. Dell, *Love in Greenwich Village*, 33. Ware (*Greenwich Village*) suggests a communal ethos for the Villagers: "According to all testimony, many of its members constituted a fairly close group, eating together, criticizing each other's work, and, though intensely individualistic, feeling a common bond holding them together against the world" (241).

33. The "Paul" character appears repeatedly in the collection and seems to be a figure for Dell himself. No other character is treated with the same degree of irony, and no other male character gets "left for art." See "The Rise of Greenwich Village" (35–44), "The Kitten and the Masterpiece" (47–73), "A Piece of Slag" (203–235), and "The Fall of Greenwich Village" (295–321).

34. The explicit message of Dell's "A Piece of Slag" (*Love in Greenwich Village*, 203–235).

35. As the quote suggests, Fried's essay argues that Millay exercises control in the Free Love milieu through the use of genre, specifically the traditional sonnet ("Andromeda Unbound: Gender & Genre in Millay's Sonnets." *Twentieth Century Literature* 32[1] [Spring 1986]: 1–22).

36. Edmund Wilson, *I Thought of Daisy*, 125.

37. Millay, *A Few Figs from Thistles* (New York: Harper & Brothers, 1920) 10–11.

38. Ibid., 14–15.

39. Montefiore's argument is that Millay uses the love experience (to which the lover is a prop) for self-dramatization (*Feminism and Poetry* [London: Pandora, 1987] 124–125). Wilson's remark, taken in the context of his discourse on Millay as a whole, suggests a certain pique at being unable to detect himself in Millay's verses (*Shores of Light*, 755; quoted in Montefiore, *Feminism and Poetry*, 118).

40. See, for example, Beatrice Forbes-Robertson Hale, "Women in Transition," in *Sex in Civilization*, ed. V. G. Calverton and S. D. Schmalhusen (New York: Ma-

caulay, 1929); Gladys H. Groves and Robert A. Ross, *The Married Woman: A Practical Guide to Happy Marriage* (New York: World, 1936) 7; Phyllis Blanchard and Carolyn Manasses, *New Girls for Old* (New York: Macauley, 1930) 6; Havelock Ellis, *Studies in the Psychology of Sex*, vol. 2 (Philadelphia: F. A. Davis Company, 1925) 547.

41. Millay, *Second April* (New York: Mitchell Kennerly, 1921) 32.

42. See Jane Stanborough, "Edna St. Vincent Millay and the Language of Vulnerability," in *Shakespeare's Sisters: Feminist Essays on Women Poets*, ed. Sandra M. Gilbert and Susan Gubar (Bloomington: Indiana University Press, 1979) 183–199, for the counterargument that Millay's poems reveal her vulnerability despite her efforts at its repression.

43. Millay, *Second April*, 17–19.

44. Kathleen Millay's one published novel, *Against the Wall* (New York: Macaulay, 1929), is a bitter and acrimonious autobiographical narrative of life in New York and at a fictionalized Vassar (where, again, Edna had already made an indelible mark).

45. Millay, "To Kathleen," in *Figs*, 24.

Chapter 2

1. Eastman used the phrase to title his memoir of the period. While he devoted equal attention to both of its terms, love and revolution remain effectively separate, sometimes even competing interests in his account of Village life (*Love and Revolution: My Journey through an Epoch* [New York: Random House, 1964]). Taggard, the more serious-minded idealist, sought a synthesis of the two.

2. William Drake, *The First Wave: Women Poets in America, 1915–1945* (New York: Macmillan, 1987) 174. See chapter 7, "The Quest for an Alternative Vision," for critical-biographical discussion of Taggard's life and work based on Drake's archival research.

3. Genevieve Taggard, *May Days: An Anthology of Verse from Masses-Liberator* (New York: Boni and Liveright, 1926).

4. Quoted in Eugene E. Leach, "The Radicals of *The Masses*," in 1915: *The Cultural Moment: The New Politics, the New Woman, the New Psychology, the New Art, and the New Theatre in America*, ed. Adele Heller and Lois Rudnick (New Brunswick, N.J.: Rutgers University Press, 1991) 27.

5. Taggard, "Her Massive Sandal," *Measure* (April 1924) no. 38, 11–13. Taggard produced a sustained study of a woman's writing in the context of her womanly circumstances with her critical biography of Emily Dickinson (*The Life and Mind of Emily Dickinson* [New York: Knopf, 1930]), a work of intense and highly invested psychological scrutiny.

6. Quoted in Drake, *The First Wave*, 174.

7. Robert L. Wolf is the author of *After Disillusion* (New York: Seltzer, 1923).

8. Drake identifies Taggard's marriage as the watershed of her career, "plung[ing] her into her own unique and lonely crisis of female power in relation to men." Of the time following the birth of her child, he says that "the next few years were a kind of hell from which she emerged only slowly" (*The First Wave*, 174, 176).

9. Letter to Herbst, 5 December 1922, quoted in Drake, *The First Wave*, 177.

10. "Taggard, If You Are a Man," *Measure* (July 1924): 12.

11. Drake, *The First Wave*, 177.

12. For a discussion of the relationship between gender and romantic transcendence, see Margaret Homans, *Women Writers and Poetic Identity: Dorothy Words-*

worth, Emily Bronte, and Emily Dickinson (Princeton, N.J.: Princeton University Press, 1980). The classic articulation of male transcendence versus female immanence is Simone de Beauvoir, *The Second Sex*, trans. H. M. Parshley (New York: Vintage, 1952).

13. Elinor Langer, *Josephine Herbst* (New York: Warner Books, 1983) 72.

14. Malcom Cowley is remarkable for his insight on this score, laying out the full extent to which bohemia participated in the large shift to consumerism (*Exile's Return: A Literary Odyssey of the 1920's* [1934; New York: Penguin, 1976] esp. 62–63).

15. Historian Lary May cites statistics such as a 55 percent voter turnout in 1920 down from 95 percent in the 1890s and a decline in church and voluntary organizations. Moreover, Christian sermonizing shifted from an emphasis on social duty to personal fulfillment, while sex took the place once given over to civic duty in the movies (*Screening Out the Past: The Birth of Mass Culture and the Motion Picture Industry* [New York: Oxford University Press, 1980] 202, 211–212).

16. On the dissemination of Freud, see Sanford Gifford, "The American Reception of Psychoanalysis, 1908–1922" in Heller and Rudnick, *1915*, 128–145. For sources on the sociocultural dynamics of the 1920s, see Stuart Ewen, *Captains of Consciousness: Advertising and the Social Roots of the Consumer Culture* (New York: McGraw-Hill, 1976); and Paula Fass, *The Damned and the Beautiful: American Youth in the 1920s* (Oxford: Oxford University Press, 1977). For the relationship among women, feminism, and sexuality in the era, see Nancy Cott, *The Grounding of Modern Feminism* (New Haven: Yale University Press, 1987); Lisa Duggan, "The Social Enforcement of Heterosexuality and Lesbian Resistance in the 1920s," in *Class, Race, and Sex: The Dynamics of Control*, ed. Amy Swerdlow and Hanna Lessinger (Boston: G. K. Hall, 1983) 75–80; Christina Simmons, "Companionate Marriage and the Lesbian Threat," *Frontiers* 4: 3 (Fall 1979): 54–59; Rayna Rapp and Ellen Ross, "The Twenties' Backlash: Compulsory Heterosexuality, the Consumer Family, and the Waning of Feminism," in Swerdlow and Lessinger, *Class, Race, and Sex*, 93–107; and Carroll Smith-Rosenberg, "The New Woman as Androgyne: Social Disorder and Gender Crisis, 1870 to 1936," in *Disorderly Conduct: Visions of Gender in Victorian America* (New York: A. A. Knopf, 1985) 245–349.

17. For contemporaneous examples of sexology, see V. F. Calverton and S. D. Schmalhusen, ed. *Sex in Civilization* (New York: Macaulay, 1929); Havelock Ellis, *Studies in the Psychology of Sex*, vols. 1 and 2 (Philadelphia: F. A. Davis Company, 1925); Margaret Sanger, *Woman and the New Race* (New York: Blue Ribbon Books, 1920).

18. Smith-Rosenberg, *Disorderly Conduct*, 280–283. Malcolm Cowley includes "the idea of psychological adjustment" in his list of bohemian principles and comes to the same basic conclusion as Smith-Rosenberg: "The implication [of psychological and other therapies] . . . is . . . that the environment itself need not be altered. That explains why most radicals who became converted to psychoanalysis or glands or Gurdjieff gradually abandoned their political radicalism" (*Exile's Return*, 61).

19. Elizabeth Ammons notes that by 1910 there were only thirty-three jobs in the U.S. Census that could not list at least one woman employee ("The New Woman as Cultural Symbol and Social Reality: Six Women Writers' Perspectives," in Heller and Rudnick, *1915*, 82).

20. Cott, *Grounding*, 7; Duggan, "Social Enforcement," 78; Ewen, *Captains of Consciousness*, 159–160; Rapp and Ross, *The Twenties' Backlash*, 93. An illuminating

document in this context is the collection of essays solicited by *The Nation* in 1926 from seventeen professional women (Taggard and several other Villagers among them) regarding the psychological origins of their "modern point of view" (see discussion in chapter 3).

21. Fass, *The Damned*, 22.

22. Duggan, "Social Enforcement," 79; Ewen, "The Family as Ground For Business Enterprise" (131–138) and "Consumption and the Ideal of the New Woman" (159–176), in *Captains of Consciousness*; Roland Marchand, "Apostles of Modernity" (1–24) and "Keeping the Audience in Focus" (52–87), in *Advertising the American Dream: Making Way for Modernity, 1920–1940* (Berkeley: University of California Press, 1985); Rapp and Ross, "The Twenties' Backlash," 93. As we shall see in the chapters on the Harlem Renaissance, the move to privatize middle-class African American women was also strongly motivated by a eugenic imperative to uplift the race by raising middle-class children.

23. As biographer Anne Cheney describes it, Dell took on the task of "freeing" Millay from "the enchanted garden of childhood" [a reference to her lesbian relationships in college] in which she was "trapped" (*Millay in Greenwich Village* [University, Ala.: University of Alabama Press, 1975] 64). Cheney seems quite comfortable with Dell's analysis: in a breathtaking denial of lesbianism *as* sexuality, she asserts that "without Dell's intrusion, Millay might never have understood the necessity of physical love for a deep spiritual union" (65).

24. Smith-Rosenberg, *Disorderly Conduct*, 280–281.

25. Judge Ben B. Lindsey and Wainwright Evens, *The Companionate Marriage* (Garden City, N.Y.: Garden City Publishing, 1929).

26. Historians cite a significant increase in the rate of marriage in the 1920s and a drop in the age for first marriages (see, for example, Cott, *Grounding*, 145).

27. Significantly, archetypal Villager Floyd Dell eventually produced his own contribution to the field of sexology with *Love in the Machine Age: A Psychological Study of the Transition from Patriarchal Society* (New York: Farrar, 1930). This second *Love*, a sweeping study of sexuality and civilization, allies itself with the implicit conservatism typically characterizing sexology; like so many similar works, it justifies the exceedingly normative cast it gives to heterosexual monogamy by recourse to the self-evidently "neutral" developmental category of "sexual maturity." While this work represents an ostensible reversal of Dell's earlier bohemian radicalism, it may also be taken as evidence of the ease with which unstable Village gender "equality" resolved itself into traditional male dominance.

28. George Chauncy, "Street Culture and Gay Male Identity in Early Twentieth-Century New York," lecture, Northwestern University, 31 May 1991. Significantly, Taggard's close friend Josephine Herbst, a writer whose life before and during this period parallels Taggard's own in many ways, did not act on what were presumably repressed lesbian desires until the thirties, and even then she apparently told almost no one (Langer, *Josephine Herbst*, 141; see n. 24).

29. See, for example, Maxwell Bodenheim, *A Virtuous Girl* (New York: Horace Liveright, 1930); Stephen Vincent Benet, *Young People's Pride* (New York: Henry Holt, 1922).

30. See chapter 5 for further discussion of this idea.

31. Ellen Key, *Love and Marriage* (1911; New York: Source Book Press, 1970) 92.

32. Hutchins Hapgood, *The Story of a Lover* (New York: Boni & Liveright, 1919), quoted in Robert E. Humphrey, *Children of Fantasy: The First Rebels of Greenwich Village* (New York: John Wiley, 1978) 74.

33. Floyd Dell, *Women as World Builders: Studies in Modern Feminism* (Chicago: Forbes, 1913) 19–20.

34. Quoted in Elaine Showalter, ed. *These Modern Women: Autobiographical Essays from the Twenties* (New York: Feminist Press, 1989) 63.

35. "Ice Age" was published in the first number of *The Measure* and subsequently collected in *For Eager Lovers* (New York: Thomas Seltzer, 1922) 55–62.

36. Edmund Wilson, "A Poet of the Pacific," in *The Shores of Light: A Literary Chronicle of the Twenties and Thirties* (New York: Farrar, Straus and Young, 1952) 348.

37. As Drake put it, "She believed she had actually experienced an ideal, alternative way of life, so never stopped fighting for it" (*The First Wave*, 172). Taggard entitled her late-life collection of poetry *Origin: Hawaii* (Honolulu: Honolulu Star-Bulletin, 1947).

38. Taggard, "Doomsday Morning," in *Words for the Chisel* (New York: Alfred A. Knopf, 1926) 45.

39. In its Marxian analysis, "Doomsday Morning" anticipates Taggard's definitive move to the left in the early thirties. See, for example, her *Calling Western Union* (New York: Harper, 1936).

40. Taggard, *For Eager Lovers*, 10.

41. Taggard, *Words for the Chisel*, 64.

Chapter 3

1. Havelock Ellis, *Studies in the Psychology of Sex*, vol. 1 (Philadelphia: F. A. Davis Company, 1925) 522.

2. Sandra M. Gilbert and Susan Gubar, *No Man's Land*, vol. 1: *The War of the Words* (New Haven: Yale University Press, 1988) 156. See also Gilbert and Gubar, eds., "The Female Imagination and the Modernist Aesthetic," special issue of *Women's Studies* 13: 1–2 (1986).

3. Gilbert and Gubar, *War of the Words*, 172.

4. Taggard, *For Eager Lovers* (New York: Thomas Seltzer, 1922) 26–27.

5. Taggard, *Words for the Chisel* (New York: Alfred A. Knopf, 1926) 46.

6. In fact, the poem was orginally published as "Desert Woman Remembers Her Reasons" (*Measure* 21 [November 1922]: 8).

7. Taggard, *Words for the Chisel*, 39.

8. William Drake, *First Wave: Women Poets in America, 1915–1945* (New York: Macmillan, 1987) 174. Moreover, given that Wolf was committed to an mental institution in 1931, he may well have suffered mental illness during the period of his marriage to Taggard.

9. Taggard, *Words for the Chisel*, 50.

10. Taggard, *For Eager Lovers*, 12.

11. Ibid., 34.

12. Taggard, *Words for the Chisel*, 34.

13. Taggard, *For Eager Lovers*, 47.

14. Ibid., 16.

15. See "Evening Love-of-Self," "Detail," "To Mr. Maunder Maunder, Professional Poet," "The Synonym (to a Romantic)," "Melodrama: or the Duel in the Morning Dew," and "Called Divine" in Taggard, *Not Mine to Finish: Poems 1928–1934* (New York: Harper & Brothers, 1934).

16. Elaine Showalter, ed., *These Modern Women: Autobiographical Essays from the Twenties* (New York: Feminist Press, 1989) 67–68.

17. Taggard, *Not Mine to Finish* 83, 85.

Chapter 4

1. Though I describe middle-brow culture in terms of its material production—as a phenomenon of New York journals, many of which had national circulation and, therefore, national influence—the values it propounds are not unrelated to the pragmatist reconciliation called for by native modernist cultural critics like Van Wyck Brooks. Lamenting the American dichotomy of highbrow and lowbrow as the fallout from "our" Puritan heritage, Brooks looked to an experientially grounded synthesis of the airy, cultured idealism he associated with the elite University and the crass economic "self-assertion" of the commercial world (" 'Highbrow' and 'Lowbrow,' " *America's Coming of Age* [1915], in *Three Essays on America* [New York: E. P. Dutton, 1934] 15–35). I discuss further the connections between popular modernism and its modernist intellectual milieu in my account of Parker's poetics (chapter 5).

2. Parker stopped going to school at the age of fourteen for unknown reasons (Marion Meade, *Dorothy Parker: What Fresh Hell Is This?* [New York: Villard Books, 1988] 27).

3. Ibid., 33–45 and passim.

4. Among them, Harpo Marx, Jascha Heifetz, Helen Hayes, and Tallulah Bankhead (James R. Gaines, *Wit's End: Days and Nights of the Algonquin Round Table* [New York: Harcount Brace Iovanovich, 1977] 94, 58, 30, 53).

5. The list presented here reflects Gaines's judgment of which Round Tablers formed the essential core.

6. Among the women who might have approached Parker's status was Neysa McMein, a commercial painter and salon-keeper remembered chiefly for working silently at her easel while the Round Table banter roared all around her. She was also known for attaching herself to famous men (Gaines, *Wit's End*, 58, 56; Meade, *Dorothy Parker*, 80). Though a more or less regular member, novelist Edna Ferber was explicitly scorned by much of the Round Table for writing "potboilers." F. P. A. respected and befriended her, however, and she is consequently a presence in his columns (Gaines, *wit's End*, 60; Meade, *Dorothy Parker*, 75–76).

7. Margaret Case Harriman states that

> when the ladies began to move in on the Round Table, Aleck Woollcott balked a little. Woman's place was in the home, he announced sternly when George Kaufman brought his wife Beatrice to lunch, and when Ruth Hale took to appearing regularly with or without her husband, Heywood Broun. Whenever Edna Ferber wandered in Woollcott made a point of addressing her peevishly as Fannie Hurst—a popular writer for whose style the Round Tablers felt something less than reverence.

Nevertheless, Harriman insists, "the relations of the sexes at the Round Table remained amiable and mutually respectful" (*The Vicious Circle: The Story of the Algonquin Round Table* [New York: Rinehart, 1951] 47, 143).

8. Another factor that must surely have exacerbated Parker's situation was the Thanotopsis Inside Straight Club, an exclusively male, poker-playing wing of the Round Table (Gaines, *Wit's End*, 54–56).

9. Gaines, *Wit's End*, 81.

10. Ibid. Gaines asserts that the Round Table actresses were "sympathetic" to the cause. Harriman, by contrast, claims that the Round Table women as a whole "remained cool" toward the endeavor (*Vicious Circle*, (139). The point holds, in either case.

11. Gaines, *Wit's End*, 81; see also Meade, *Dorothy Parker*, 40, 46, 249.

12. Dorothy Parker, "The First Hundred Plays Are the Hardest," in *Vanity Fair: A Cavalcade of the 1920s and 1930s*, ed. Cleveland Amory and Frederic Bradlee (New York: Viking, 1960) 35.

13. Sally Ashley, *F. P. A.: The Life and Times of Franklin Pierce Adams* (New York: Beaufort Books, 1986) 55–56. Ashley notes that F. P. A. took the general idea for his column from Chicago columnist BLT, "although he was determined to stamp his own personality on the technique in a way that BLT—who served more as editor and observer than participant—didn't." F. P. A.'s innovation was to make "the column . . . like a real conversation. It was an unusual concept, [and] he wasn't able to fashion it overnight" (56).

14. Ibid., 69–71.

15. Barbara W. Grossman, *Funny Woman: The Life and Times of Fanny Brice* (Bloomington: Indiana University Press, 1992) 166.

16. Admittedly, the New York sophisticates also got some help from groups such as the Anti–Stage Jew Ridicule Committee in Chicago, the Anti-Defamation League of B'nai B'rith, and the Associated Rabbis of America, all of whom worked to eliminate Jewish caricatures from the vaudeville stage (Grossman, *Funny Woman*, 110).

17. It should be no great surprise that biographies of each of these figures all note encounters with anti-Semitism and the strategic personal negotiations they necessitated. (Indeed, the Round Table itself was apparently not free of such incidents; see Leslie Frewin, *The Late Mrs. Dorothy Parker* [New York: Macmillan, 1986] 17.) Generally, the Round Table Jews came from third-generation German families who valued at least a certain degree of Americanization in their children. The arrival of vast numbers of Russian Jews at the turn of the century only exacerbated this tendency, as the long-standing German-Americans moved to put distance between themselves and the "immigrant hordes." See, for example, Ashley, *F. P. A.*; Malcolm Goldstein, *George S. Kaufman: His Life, His Theater* (New York: Oxford University Press, 1979); and Frewin.

18. Lola Ridge, *The Ghetto and Other Poems* (New York: Huebsch, 1918) and John Dos Passos, *Manhattan Transfer* ([1925] Boston: Houghton Mifflin, 1953) 11; 400.

19. Mary V. Dearborn discusses Yezierska's self-presentation (and her self-understanding as a Jewish woman) at length through an analysis of her formative affair with John Dewey, WASP "father of modern education," in *Love in the Promised Land: The Story of Anzia Yezierska and John Dewey* (New York: The Free Press, 1988). See chapter 5 of this text for further discussion of Yezierska.

20. Carol B. Schoen traces Yezierska's participation in the "New York literary scene" from 1921 to about 1926 (*Anzia Yezierska* [Boston: Twayne, 1970] 29, 36). She specifically notes her "fashionable uptown address" and her "dining with [major literary figures] at the Algonquin, the famed center for the literati, [where] she could . . . gossip about writing and feel herself an accepted American author" (61).

21. This idea is implicit or explicit in the following sources: Daniel Lieberfeld, "Here under False Pretenses: The Marx Brothers Crash the Gates," paper presented at the 1995 Modern Language Association Convention, Chicago; Gerald Mast, "The Neurotic Jew as American Clown," *Jewish Wry: Essays on Jewish Humor*, ed. Sarah

Blacher Cohen (Bloomington: Indiana University Press, 1987) 125–140; Robert Leslie Liebman, "Rabbis or Rakes, Schlemiels or Supermen?" *Literature Film Quarterly* 12:3 (1984): 195–201; Scott Haas, "The Marx Brothers, Jews, and My Four-Year-Old Daughter," *Cineaste* 19: 2–3 (1992): 48–49; Jay Boyer, "The Schlemiezel: Black Humor and the Shtetl Tradition," in *Semites and Stereotypes: Characteristics of Jewish Humor*, ed. Ziv Avner and Anat Zajdman (Westport, Conn.: Greenwood Press, 1993) 3–12. Boyer traces a *schlimiezel* tradition, which he characterizes as "a new notion of American manhood, American man as *Homo incapacitus*" (11).

22. Neal Gabler, in *An Empire of Their Own: How the Jews Invented Hollywood* (New York: Crown, 1988), makes a parallel argument for the modern (and modernizing) film industry, noting that many of Hollywood's founders were recent immigrants.

> By making a "shadow" America, one which idealized every old glorifying bromide about the country, the Hollywood Jews created a powerful cluster of images and ideas—so powerful that, in a sense, they colonized the American imagination. . . . Ultimately, American values came to be defined largely by the movies the Jews made. Ultimately, by creating their idealized America on the screen, the Jews reinvented the country in the image of their fiction. (6–7).

23. Gaines, *Wit's End*, 80.

24. See Ernest Boyd, *H. L. Mencken* (New York: Robert H. McBride, 1925) 16; and Sara Mayfield, *The Constant Circle: H. L. Mencken and His Friends* (New York: Delacorte Press, 1968) 42, 79, for the midtown journalists' relations with the Village. There were exceptions to Round Table quietism: Parker and Robert Benchley (like so many writers of the day) marched in defense of Sacco and Vanzetti, while Heywood Broun made of them a cause célèbre as early as 1925 in his New York *World* column. Broun's left political leanings culminated in his 1930 Socialist party candidacy for Congress (in Gaines's contemptuous account), running from "Manhattan's silk-stocking district . . . with his Rose Room friends in various supporting roles" (Gaines, *Wit's End*, 172–173; 222).

25. Lary May, "Revitalization: Douglas Fairbanks, Mary Pickford, and the New Personality, 1914–1918," in *Screening Out the Past: The Birth of Mass Culture and the Motion Picture Industry* (New York: Oxford University Press, 1980) 96–146. In particular, Mary Pickford and Douglas Fairbanks, ensconced in their Pickfair estate, came to be the premier symbol of the happy consumer marriage. See also Mary P. Ryan, "The Projection of a New Womanhood: The Movie Moderns in the 1920's," in *Our American Sisters: Women in American Life and Thought*, ed. Jean E. Friedman and William G. Shade (Boston: Allyn and Bacon, 1976) 366–384.

26. Meade, *Dorothy Parker*, 175.

27. Anita Loos, *But Gentlemen Marry Brunettes* (New York: Boni & Liveright, 1928) 41–43; original spelling.

28. Dr. Alvin Barach, a psychoanalyst who treated several Round Tablers in the late twenties, considered the group to be neurotically interdependent and obsessed with maintaining a group fantasy (Gaines, *Wit's End*, 116). I take the liberty of translating this judgment into the (nonpathologizing) terms of subcultural dynamics.

29. Important here, again, is the precedent set by the early F. P. A. column, which, for all its high-culture references, was the most popular item in a distinctly nonelite newspaper, the *New York Evening Mail*, whose front page was dominated by sports news (Ashley, *F. P. A.*, 86). Also important is *Vanity Fair*, which

> was pleased to take for granted the fact that its readers were cultured people, or at least people susceptible to so being—and, to prove the point, published modern art as if people were already initiated to it, which most of them were not, and was also not averse, on occasion, to publishing a piece entirely in French. If a few readers did not understand French, it was the editor's opinion that they should—and, more important, would—ask somebody who did. (Cleveland Amory, "Introduction—A Fair Kept," in Amory and Bradlee, *Vanity Fair*, 7)

30. Gaines, *Wit's End*, 116; Anita Loos, *A Girl Like I* (New York: Viking Press, 1966) 147–148.

31. Quoted in Gaines, *Wit's End*, xi.

32. Gaines, *Wit's End*, 29, 40, 47.

33. F. P. A., entry for 12 January 1921, *The Diary of Our Own Samuel Pepys*, vol. 1, *1911–1925* (New York: Simon and Schuster, 1935) 275.

34. Ibid., 339.

35. Ibid., 306.

36. Gaines, (*Wit's End*, 30–32) and Meade (*Dorothy Parker*, 83) both describe Parker's humorous "Eddie" stories as a regular feature of her Round Table discourse.

37. Note that the drawing room comedy (of which George Kaufman and Marc Connelly were masters) dominated the Broadway stage at this time (Gaines, *Wit's End*, 39–46). Chapter 5 discusses the significant role of manners (as decorum) in Parker's poetics.

38. See, for example, Parker's 1927 review of pulp novelist Elinor Glyn's *It*:

> Even those far, far better informed than I must work a bit over the opening sentence of Madame Glyn's foreword to her novel. "This is not," she says, drawing her emeralds warmly about her, "the story of the moving picture entitled, *It*, but a full character study of the story *It*, which the people in the picture read and discuss." I could go mad, in a nice way, straining to figure that out. . . . After all, what more could one ask than a character study of a story? ("Madame Glyn Lectures on 'It,' with Illustrations," *The Portable Dorothy Parker* [New York: Penguin, 1986] 465)

See also the entry for Monday, January 5, in "The Diary of Our Own Samuel Pepys": "Miss Edwards very good [in the play under review], albeit she should not say 'laws' when she means 'law,' and Mr. Peacock should learn correctly the words in 'When Britain Really Ruled the Waves,' nor should he say 'intwallectual' " (*Pepys*, 240).

39. Gaines, *Wit's End*, 84.

40. Gaines, *Wit's End*, 34.

41. This was the milieu from which F. Scott Fitzgerald, also part of the writer-millionaire circuit, drew the material for *The Great Gatsby* (Meade, *Dorothy Parker*, 113, 186–187).

42. Ibid., 115; Gaines, *Wit's End*, 128–136.

43. Meade, *Dorothy Parker*, 194–195.

44. May, *Screening Out the Past*, 197. May goes on to suggest that public investment in persons and lives perceived as rich but innocuous did much to mitigate class tensions in the twenties, specifically labor unrest.

45. As a scriptwriter in Hollywood in the 1930s, Parker was an anti-Fascist activist, a U.S. Communist party fellow traveler, and an organizer for the Screen

Writer's Guild. Upon her death in 1967, she left her estate to Dr. Martin Luther King Jr. (whom she had never met). In the early years, Parker's political expressions were largely confined to an overwhelming and sentimental devotion to animals, mostly stray dogs (Meade, *Dorothy Parker,* 252–258, 410).

46. May, *Screening Out the Past,* 200–236.

47. See n. 29.

48. Loos, *A Girl Like I,* 145.

49. Benchley, "The Brow-Elevation in Humor," in *Love Conquers All* (New York: Henry Holt, 1922) 303–306; Amory and Bradlee, *Vanity Fair,* 88.

50. Paula Fass, *The Damned and the Beautiful: American Youth in the 1920s* (Oxford: Oxford University Press, 1977) 357. May argues that youth culture itself was a powerful force for the leveling of class distinctions (*Screening Out the Past,* 114–115).

51. A particularly dramatic example is the collectively scripted *The 49'ers,* a musical revue which closed after only fifteen performances because it simply made no sense to anyone but its Round Table writers. Gaines accounts for this flop by speculating that it was produced in "a giddy haze of alcohol" (*Wit's End,* 74). The point, finally, is that the Round Tablers saw fit to produce the show, and it seems fair to read this incident as suggestive of the reinforcement they derived by flaunting the private character of their own wit.

52. Roland Marchand, *Advertising the American Dream: Making Way for Modernity, 1920–1940* (Berkeley: University of California Press, 1985) 51.

53. Benchley, "The Real Public Enemies," in *No Poems, or Around the World Backwards and Sideways* (New York: Harper & Brothers, 1932) 315–316. Benchley's film shorts of the thirties and forties—most famously, "How to Sleep" (1935)—continue the theme of befuddled modern man.

54. F. P. A., *Column Book of F. P. A.* (Garden City, N.Y.: Doubleday, Doran, 1928) 8.

55. F. P. A., *Pepys,* 317.

56. Hannah Arendt, "The Jew as Pariah" (1959), quoted in Liebman, "Rabbis or Rakes," 195–201.

57. See Lieberfeld, "Here under False Pretenses"; Haas, "The Marx Brothers," 48–49; Mast, "The Neurotic Jew," 125–140.

58. Boyer, "*Schlemiezel,*" 6. As his title suggests, Boyer concludes that the contemporary American male protagonist is best described as a hybrid of the traditional *schlemiel* and *schlimazl.*

59. Benchley, "Eddie Cantor and 'Yes, We Have No Bananas,'" *Life* (July 26, 1923), reprinted in *Benchley at the Theatre: Dramatic Criticism, 1920–1940,* ed. Charles Getchell (Ipswich, Mass.: Ipswich Press, 1985) 33.

60. On the decline of vaudeville as a viable mode of entertainment, see, for example, Alexander Bakshy, "Vaudeville Must Be Saved," *The Nation* 129:3342 (July 24, 1929): 98, 100; and Rob Wagner, "Smart-Crackers and Cheese," *Rob Wagner's Script* 2:5 (September 14, 1929) 1–2, 32, both reprinted in *Selected Vaudeville Criticism,* ed. Anthony Slide (Metuchen, N.J.: Scarecrow Press, 1988).

61. Benchley "Harpo, Groucho, Chico, Zeppo and Karl," *Life* (November 16, 1928), in *Benchley at the Theatre,* 87.

62. Gaines, *Wit's End,* 47; emphasis mine.

63. F. P. A., Entries for January 24, 1921; March 4, 1921; June 13, 1921; October 9, 1922 (*Pepys,* 276, 278, 285, 355).

64. F. P. A., *Column Book,* 158.

65. F. P. A., *Overset* (Garden City, N.Y.: Doubleday, Page, 1922) 7.
66. F. P. A., *Half a Loaf* (Garden City, N.Y.: Doubleday, Page, 1927).
67. Benchley, "Matinees—Wednesdays and Saturdays," in *No Poems,* 328.
68. Marchand, *Advertising,* 71.
69. Ibid., 70.
70. Meade, *Dorothy Parker,* 68.
71. Ibid., 67–71; Gaines, *Wit's End,* 36–38.
72. Parker, *Sunset Gun* (New York: Boni & Liveright, 1928) 23.
73. Meade, *Dorothy Parker,* 120–122, 129, 135.
74. Ibid., 130, 220.
75. Parker, "Such a Pretty Little Picture," *Smart Set* (December 1922): 76.
76. Parker so names him in her introduction to *The Most of S. J. Perelman* (New York: Simon and Schuster, 1958) xii.
77. I refer to Alan Rudolf and his interesting and historically careful film depiction of *Mrs. Parker and the Vicious Circle* (1994).
78. Quoted in Gaines, *Wit's End,* 39.
79. Marchand, *Advertising,* passim. Carroll Smith-Rosenberg and Nancy Cott each discuss women and women's domestic work as the subject of early-twentieth-century scientific scrutiny (Smith-Rosenberg, "The New Woman as Androgyne: Social Disorder and Gender Crisis, 1870–1936," in *Disorderly Conduct: Visions of Gender in Victorian America* [New York: Oxford University Press, 1985] 245–297; and Nancy Cott, "Modern Times," in *The Grounding of Modern Feminism* [New Haven: Yale University Press, 1987] 145–174).
80. Marchand, *Advertising,* 13; see also 9–13, 106–110, 208–217, and 335–363.
81. See, for example, Benchley, *Pluck and Luck* (New York: Henry Holt, 1925) especially "How One Woman Kept the Budget from the Door" (231–233).
82. See, for example, F. P. A., *Pepys,* 357.
83. Henriette Rousseau [Dorothy Rothschild], "Women: A Hate Song," *Vanity Fair* (August 1916): 61. Crowninshield advised Parker (then Rothschild) to publish under a pseudonym, given the content of the poem (Meade, *Dorothy Parker,* 37).
84. Meade, *Dorothy Parker,* 37.
85. See chapter 2.
86. See n. 88 for examples of modern love.
87. Coeducation became a middle-class ideal in the twenties (Fass, *The Damned,* 13); while working class women had been a significant presence in industry for a long time, the new boom in office work gave working-and middle-class women expanded employment opportunities as well as highly visible participation in the "modern" world represented by business (May, *Screening Out the Past,* 201; Ryan, "Projection," passim).
88. For examples of Modern Love and the war of the sexes, see Ring Lardner, *The Love Nest* (1926); James Thurber's illustrations in *The New Yorker* beginning in 1927 and his sexology parody, with E. B. White, *Is Sex Necessary*? (1929); Edna Ferber, "That's Marriage," in *Cheerful by Request* (New York: Doubleday, Page, 1918), 143–180; "Fish" (cartoons) in *Vanity Fair,* e.g., "Is Love a Failure? A Serio-Tragic Comedy" (May 1915): 43, and "The Popularity of Divorce in Our Best Society: If Your Wife Ever Begins Acting in Any One of These Roles in Your Domestic Drama—Call in Your Lawyer," *Vanity Fair* (September 1920): 44; Reginald Birch, "The Husband's Union" (cartoon) *Vanity Fair* (May 1915): 53; Nancy Boyd [Modern Love pseudonym of Edna St. Vincent Millay], *Distressing Dialogues* (New York: Harper & Brothers, 1924); Anita Loos, "The Force of Heredity, and Nella; A Modern

Fable with a Telling Moral for Eugenists," *Vanity Fair* (February 1915): 42, *Gentlemen Prefer Blondes* (New York: Boni & Liveright, 1925), and *But Gentlemen Marry Brunettes* (New York: Boni & Liveright, 1928); and F. P. A.'s syndicated columns in the *New York Tribune* and the *World* collected in F. P. A. *So There!* (New York: Doubleday Doran, 1923).

89. *Vanity Fair* (January 1915): 39 and (April 1915): 49.

90. See discussion of Gilbert and Gubar's *War of the Words* in chapter 3. The seminal analysis of the cultural defense against the New Woman is Smith-Rosenberg (*Disorderly Conduct*, 245–297), while Fass examines the flapper as a locus of cultural anxiety (*The Damned*, 22–25).

91. Fitzgerald was as much the authoritative voice of twenties youth culture for his contemporaries as he would be for subsequent generations of literary critics. As an enactment of Modern Love, his writing was important, though, for our purposes, idiosyncratic; while sophistication was well thematized in his works, it was not characteristic of their style. His depictions of love had tragic overtones, which were, moreover, a function of his use of complex and sympathetic protagonists. However much it may have suited the more mature observers of *Vanity Fair* and the Round Table, the ironic distance implied by Modern Love discourse was apparently inappropriate to the self-expression of a generation that took itself seriously.

92. F. Scott Fitzgerald, "Bernice Bobs Her Hair," in *The Stories of F. Scott Fitzgerald* (New York: Macmillan, 1986) 43.

93. The degree to which heterosociality and sophistication-as-humor were inextricable may be seen in the *Ladies' Home Journal*'s brief attempt in 1920 to provide its female readers with something "to help the conversation along at dinner." Generally, the *Journal* worked to create a dense and serene world of women and children. The sudden intrusion of a page of jokes is jarring at several levels. First, humor and sophistication are completely out of place in the unruffled self-sufficiency of this world. Accordingly, the jokes themselves are aimed entirely at the male outsiders, usually at the expense of the females. Finally, the fact of the jokes' appearance at all—the sudden apparent necessity for dignified and self-respecting homemakers to entertain their apparently restless husbands at dinner—speaks to the new imperative for heterosexual recreation as the mark of a successful marriage (see Jay E. House, "Out of the Frying Pan," *Ladies' Home Journal* 37 [1] [January 1920]: 4).

94. Cf. "women's magazines," such as *Ladies' Home Journal* and *Redbook*, and men's journals such as *The Detroit Athletic Club News* (where Benchley was a regular contributor). *Vanity Fair*'s inaugural editorial statement made explicit the self-conscious nature of the magazine's invitation to women readers to partake of what would otherwise be men's material: "For women we intend to do something in a noble and missionary spirit, something which, so far as we can observe, has never before been done for them by an American magazine. We mean to make frequent appeals to their intellects." ("In Vanity Fair," *Vanity Fair* [March 1914], reprinted in Amory and Bradlee, *Vanity Fair*, 13).

95. In fact, much advertising in the teens and twenties was initially and sometimes even ultimately indistinguishable from the actual fiction featured by the magazine itself (Marchand, *Advertising*, 103–104).

96. "A Word about Debutantes," *Vanity Fair* (January 1915): 15.

97. See, for example, "Leaves from the Diary of a Young Man of Fashion" (May 1915): 21; "What Women Like in a Man, Stray Leaves from the Diary of a Modern Don Juan" (November 1915): 33; "Fete Galante: A Pantomime with Words, Composed, through Our Staff Medium, by the Spirit of Paul Verlaine" (July 1920): 29;

"A Deuced Close Shave: Explaining for the First Time, the Sudden Marriage of a Famous New York Debutante" (November 1920): 39.

98. F. P. A., "Half Minutes with the Best Authors," *Vanity Fair* (August 1920): 21.

99. Their uneasiness may emanate specifically from the loss of the woman as the heterosexualizing mediation in their own relationship. The full articulation of this argument is Eve Kosofsky Sedgwick, *Between Men: English Literature and Male Homosocial Desire* (New York: Columbia University Press, 1985).

100. Sander L. Gilman, "Salome, Syphilis, Sarah Bernhardt and the 'Modern Jewess,' " *The German Quarterly* 66:2 (Spring 1993): 203.

101. Judging from the evidence Frewin presents, it would seem that this loathing came (ironically enough) at least partly from her sense of Henry Rothschild's own anti-Semitism. Though, as an adult, he earned a degree in Talmudic studies, he practiced no religion, married first a Protestant and then a fanatical Catholic (who sent Dorothy to a convent school), and (typically for second-or third-generation Germans) looked down on the recent wave of Eastern European Jewish immigrants (Frewin, *The Late Mrs. Dorothy Parker*, 3; Meade, *Dorothy Parker*, 10–11). Meade has a different version of Parker's relationship to her father, describing him as a warm and loving parent whom Parker lived with and nursed through a final illness—though Meade notes that as an adult, Parker regularly implied she had had a "gothic" childhood under a cruel father (28–29). Meade's account also does not suggest that Parker had an ethnically based hatred of her family.

102. Frank Crane, *New York Journal American* (December 12, 1920), quoted in Schoen, *Anzia Yezierska*, 36.

103. Paula E. Hyman, *Gender and Assimilation in Modern Jewish History* (Seattle: University of Washington Press, 1995) 137.

104. Round Tabler Edna Ferber, by contrast, was "inordinately proud of being a Jew," though we should note she made that public declaration in the thirties (in response to the rise of Fascism). More to the point, she was never a figure of New Womanhood (see Edna Ferber, *A Peculiar Treasure* [1938; Garden City, N.Y.: Doubleday, 1960] 8).

105. Loos, *A Girl Like I*, 130.

Chapter 5

1. Sharon Cameron, *Lyric Time: Dickinson and the Limits of Genre* (Baltimore: Johns Hopkins University Press, 1979) 23.

2. David Lindley, *Lyric* (New York: Methuen, 1985) 3. Lindley here paraphrases Johnathan Culler in "Apostrophe," *The Pursuit of Signs* (London: Routledge & Kegan Paul, 1981).

3. According to contemporary observer Ruth Goodman Goetz, "[Dorothy Parker] and Fanny Brice . . . were the queens of the town. They divided New York between them" (quoted in Marion Meade, *Dorothy Parker: What Fresh Hell Is This?* [New York: Villard Books, 1988] 225).

4. Barbara Grossman, *Funny Woman: The Life and Times of Fanny Brice* (Bloomington: Indiana University Press, 1991) passim; see especially 66–67 and 102. It was apparently her pronounced ethnicity that later prevented Brice from making the transition to the modern medium of film; national audiences found her "too New York" (179).

5. The paradigm case would be Rose Pastor Stokes, whose success story is literally identical with her love story—that is, her marriage to old-millionaire William Phelps Stokes. Mary V. Dearborn quotes Stokes's announcement to friends Yezierska and Minnie Zunser: " 'Children, listen to me. I am going to be married to the millionaire Stokes. Riches and poverty, Jew and Christian will be united. Here is an indication of the new era' " (*Love in the Promised Land: The Story of Anzia Yezierska and John Dewey* [New York: The Free Press, 1988] 69).

6. All of these men were apparently redactions of John Dewey, the actual "father of modern education," with whom Yezierska had a brief but formative affair in 1917–1918. See Dearborn for a comprehensive analysis of this relationship in the context of Dewey's and Yezierska's respective careers.

7. "Though Anzia Yezierska made America the subject of her fiction—America as promised land, America as the land where promises are broken—she never saw herself as an American. She chose to remain a 'Russian Jewess,' defined by her past" (Dearborn, *Love in the Promised Land,* 33).

8. Quoted in Grossman, *Funny Woman,* 60–61, from a series of interviews that ran in *Cosmopolitan* in 1936.

9. Grossman, *Funny Woman,* 125.

10. Ibid., 168.

11. Walter Frank, *Our America,* 188, quoted in Walter Benn Michaels, *Our America: Nativism, Modernism, and Pluralism* (Durham, N.C.: Duke University Press, 1995) 136.

12. Grossman, *Funny Woman,* 133–151.

13. *Life* (October 14, 1926): 23; reprinted in Anthony Slide, ed., *Selected Vaudeville Criticism* (Metuchen, N.J.: Scarecrow Press, 1988) 41.

14. Grossman, *Funny Woman,* 149.

15. See n. 101, chapter 4.

16. Meade, *Dorothy Parker,* 125. As Meade surmises, "[Parker] preferred tall, slim, cinematically beautiful blonds. Rice was a dour six-foot, red-haired, bespectabled Jew. . . . He must have reminded her of a childhood she had no wish to recall."

17. Frewin, *The Late Mrs. Dorothy Parker,* 23.

18. Meade, *Dorothy Parker,* 40. In fairness, it should also be noted that Round Table subculture included a low-key but occasionally outspoken abhorrence of racial injustice. In this light, see Parker's short story, "Arrangement in Black and White," in *The Portable Dorothy Parker* (New York: Penguin, 1986) 19–23.

19. Frewin, *The Late Mrs. Dorothy Parker,* 19.

20. Robert E. Drennan, *The Algonquin Wits* (Secaucus, N.J.: Citadel Press, 1977) 122. Interestingly, the parallel quality of their careers continues to this day: neither of them has been admitted fully to the literary critical canon of serious writers, but both have such a secure following among general readers that their works have never gone out of print.

21. Frewin, *The Late Mrs. Dorothy Parker,* 19–21.

22. See Iris Marion Young on the structural exclusion of women (associated with "the particular, private realm of needs and desires") from the liberal public sphere ("the universal, public realm of sovereignty and the state") in *Justice and the Politics of Difference* (Princeton, N.J.: Princeton University Press, 1990) 107–108.

23. John Brenkman ("Aesthetics of Male Fantasy," in *Culture and Domination* [Ithaca, N.Y.: Cornell University Press, 1987] 184–227) and Niklas Luhmann ("Romantic Love," in *Love as Passion: The Codification of Intimacy,* trans. Jeremy Gaines

and Doris L. Jones [Cambridge: Harvard University Press, 1986] 134–144) have argued that modern individuality itself is dependent on romantic love.

24. Roland Barthes, *A Lover's Discourse: Fragments*, trans. Richard Howard (New York: Farrar, Straus and Giroux, 1978) 52, 35, 26, 34. In the first passage, Barthes is citing Goethe's *The Sorrows of Young Werther*, Ur-text of romantic love (my italics).

25. Luhmann, *Love as Passion*, 138, 142.

26. Jan Montefiore, *Feminism and Poetry* (London: Pandora, 1987) 98.

27. Brenkman, *Culture and Domination*, 219.

28. Genevieve Taggard makes a structurally similar use of tertiary figures to level the dyadic hierarchy and even to eradicate gender difference within it (see chapter 3).

29. Indeed, the break from nineteenth-century True Love to an urbane assumption of serial lovers has just this profound structural consequence for a woman love poet, providing options not available to public love precursors like Christina Rossetti and Elizabeth Barrett Browning.

30. John Stuart Mill, quoted in *Princeton Encyclopedia of Poetry and Poetics*, ed. Alex Preminger (Princeton, N.J.: Princeton University Press, 1974) 461.

31. Parker, *Enough Rope* (New York: Boni & Liveright, 1926) 56.

32. William Congreve, *The Way of the World* [1700] in *British Dramatists from Dryden to Sheridan*, ed. George H. Nettleton and Arthur E. Case, revised by George Winchester Stone Jr. (Carbondale: Southern Illinois University Press, 1969) 335.

33. Parker, *Enough Rope*, 54.

34. Casey Nelson Blake, *Beloved Community: The Cultural Criticism of Randolph Bourne, Van Wyck Brooks, Waldo Frank, & Lewis Mumford* (Chapel Hill: University of North Carolina Press, 1990) 2. Blake cites communitarian thinking in "figures as diverse as Edward Bellamy, Josiah Royce, Jane Addams, Charles Horton Cooley, and Mary Parker Follett" and in European social scientists Max Weber, Émile Durkheim, and Ferdinand Tonnies (4).

35. Other relevant points from the "young Americans" include the definition of the intellectual as bridging ethnic folk culture and university high culture (Blake, *Beloved Community*, 119–120) and the idea of the Jew, specifically, the Zionist, as exemplar of the modern ideal, combining strong cultural identity (difference) with perfect commitment to the American nation-state (unity) (see Randolph Bourne, "The Jew and Trans-National America," *War and the Intellectuals: Essays by Randolph Bourne, 1915–1919*, ed. Carl Resek [New York: Harper Torchbooks, 1964] 124–133).

36. Parker, *Enough Rope*, 32.

37. Iris Marion Young's notion of a specifically urban sense of community may be relevant here, in particular, her argument that such community demands only partial and overlapping identifications and so avoids the reactionary fantasy of sameness plaguing other models of community (*Justice*, 238–239).

38. See Jessica Benjamin, *The Bonds of Love: Psychoanalysis, Feminism, and the Problem of Domination* (New York: Pantheon, 1988) for the groundbreaking discussion of intersubjectivity and power relations which informs this point. On the presumption of a fully "sophisticated" audience for popular modernism more generally, see chapter 4.

39. Parker, *Enough Rope*, 68.

40. Ibid., 82.

41. Ibid., 59.

42. Ibid., 11.

43. See Leo Bersani, "Sexuality and Esthetics," in *The Freudian Body* (New York: Columbia University Press, 1986) for a discussion of erotic-aesthetic multiplicity as the liberatory antithesis of Oedipal fixation.

44. Parker, *Enough Rope*, 26.

45. Ibid., 16.

46. See for example "Epitaph," "The Satin Dress," "The White Lady," and "Resume," in *Enough Rope*, 20, 23, 39, 61; "Thought for a Sunshiny Morning," "Swan Song," and "Coda," in *Sunset Gun*, 38, 44, 75; and "Cherry White" in *Death and Taxes* (New York: Viking, 1931) 19.

47. Consistent with the genre, Parker's biographers Marion Meade and the earlier John Keats (*You Might as Well Live: The Life and Times of Dorothy Parker* [New York: Paragon House Publishers, 1970]) assume the directly autobiographical nature of Parker's writing.

48. Meade, *Dorothy Parker*, 56.

Chapter 6

1. Raymond R. Patterson, "Helene Johnson," and Walter C. Daniel and Sandra Y. Govan, "Gwendolyn Bennett," *Dictionary of Literary Biography*, vol. 51 (Detroit: Gale Research, 1987) 164, 3; Gloria T. Hull, *Color, Sex, and Poetry: Three Women Writers of the Harlem Renaissance* (Bloomington: Indiana University Press, 1987) 13.

2. Ann duCille, *The Coupling Convention: Sex, Text, and Tradition in Black Women's Fiction* (New York: Oxford University Press, 1993) 69.

3. Hull has asserted that "Johnson's work most reflects the qualities commonly designated as characteristic of the Renaissance" (*Color, Sex, and Poetry*, 13).

4. W. E. B. DuBois, "The Younger Literary Movement," Crisis (February 1924): 161.

5. Countee Cullen, "The League of Youth," *Crisis* (August 1923): 167.

6. Alain Locke, "The New Negro," in *The New Negro: Voices of the Harlem Renaissance*, ed. Alain Locke (1925; New York: Macmillan, 1992) 7.

7. Wallace Thurman, *Infants of the Spring* (1932; Boston: Northeastern University Press, 1992) 61–62.

8. George S. Schuyler, "Shafts and Darts," *Messenger* (January 1926): 9.

9. Most prominently, Houston Baker has argued for a definition of modernism specific to this development, one that displaces the traditional view of the Harlem Renaissance as a poor cousin to High (i.e., white) Modernism, with a recognition of the 1920s "renaissance" as building on a modernist rhetorical project inaugurated in 1895 by Booker T. Washington (*Modernism and the Harlem Renaissance* [Chicago: University of Chicago Press, 1987]).

10. See George Hutchinson, *The Harlem Renaissance in Black and White* (Cambridge: Harvard University Press, 1995) for a discussion of renaissance discourse in the context of its many complex, external affiliations.

11. Indeed, by 1933, he condemns the renaissance as nothing but the artificial creation of white patronage (W. E. B. Du Bois, "The Negro College," *A Reader*, ed. Meyer Weinberg [New York: Harper, 1970], quoted in Ralph D. Story, "Patronage and the Harlem Renaissance: You Get What You Pay For," *College Language Association Journal* 32[3]: 284–295).

12. One might see the promotion of male artists to the exclusion of women simply as a means of protesting the seriousness of the new renaissance as against the charge of mere faddishness. For example, in his editorial "Some Perils of the 'Renaissance' "

(marking perhaps his first use of the term), Charles Johnson worries that "zeal to catch the flood tide has exposed many immaturities" but concludes his piece with the reassuring recitation of contrastingly solid artistic successes—all of which are by men (*Opportunity* [March 1927]: 68). Georgia Douglas Johnson, who had enjoyed the status of great Negro poet (along with Countee Cullen and Langston Hughes), suffered the demotion to great Negro *woman* poet in many public citations—when she was mentioned at all. See, for example, Charlotte E. Taussig, "The New Negro as Revealed in His Poetry," *Opportunity* (April 1927): 108.

13. Or to *resist* the obligation to bring it about. My characterization of the contemporaneous Harlem intellectual climate is meant to include such renegade figures as Wallace Thurman, whose model of intergenerational conflict over the question of art and racial responsibility (fictionally described in *Infants of the Spring* [1932]), assumes the cultural framework of a definable (if undefined) movement.

14. See Hull's introduction, "Color, Sex, and Poetry in the Harlem Renaissance," *Color, Sex, and Poetry*, 1–31.

15. Chidi Ikonné, *From Du Bois to Van Vechten: The Early New Negro Literature, 1903–1926* (Westport, Conn.: Greenwood Press, 1981) 113.

16. Interestingly, both of the latter two features—though for different journals—were written by the same commentator, Eugene Gordon; for examples, see "Outstanding Negro Newspapers of 1925," *Opportunity* (December 1925): 358–361 and "The Month's Best Editorial," *The Messenger* (March 1927): 74.

17. Charles S. Johnson, "The 'Charleston,' " *Opportunity* (July 1926): 208–209.

18. Cleveland G. Allen, "Our Young Artists," *Opportunity* (August 1923): 25.

19. Charles Johnson, "Racial Humor and Propaganda," *Opportunity* (August 1923): 218.

20. Zona Gale, "Bronze," *Opportunity* (August 1923): 218. Gale's statement concurs to such a degree with the general drift of *Opportunity* rhetoric that it seems safe to assume at least a tacit editorial endorsement of its sentiments.

21. *Opportunity* (December 1928): 385.

22. W. E. B. DuBois, *Crisis* (October 1923): 248–249.

23. For a compelling analysis of the mechanisms of national identification and desire for gender-and race-marked subjects see Lauren Berlant, "National Brands/National Body: *Imitation of Life*," in *The Phantom Public Sphere*, ed. Bruce Robbins (Minneapolis: University of Minnesota Press, 1993) 173–208.

24. See, for example, "The Theatre—Drama," *Messenger* (June 1923): 746; [Charles S. Johnson], "An Opportunity for Negro Writers," *Opportunity* (September 1924): 258. Harlem journals also printed and cited white critics to this effect; see Carl Van Doren, "The Younger Generation of Negro Writers" and Alain Locke, "Max Rheinhardt Reads the Negro's Dramatic Horoscope," *Opportunity* (May 1924): 144–145, 146; [Charles S. Johnson], editorial, *Opportunity* (May 1925): 130.

25. The "Exalting Negro Womanhood" feature was announced in January 1924 (7) and ran regularly until the *Messenger* ceased publication in 1928.

26. "Exalting Negro Womanhood," *Messenger* (January 1924): 7.

27. For a cogent account of the psychoanalytic logic of the class-mapped body, see Peter Stallybrass and Allon White, *The Politics and Poetics of Transgression* (London: Methuen, 1986).

28. Anna Julia Cooper, *A Voice from the South; by a Black Woman of the South* (New York: Negro Universities Press, 1969) 31 [emphasis in the original]. In her landmark history, *When and Where I Enter: The Impact of Black Women on Race and Sex in America* (New York: William Morrow, 1984), Paula Giddings suggests that

African American women came into prominence as activists in the late nineteenth century in response to a power vacuum in male leadership (83).

29. Montgomery Gregory, "The Spirit of Phyllis [*sic*] Wheatley," *Opportunity* (June 1924): 181; Eunice Roberta Hunton, "A Story about Northern Negroes," *Opportunity* (April 1924): 11.

30. Eunice Roberta Hunton, "The Spirit of Phyllis [*sic*] Wheatley," *Opportunity* (April 1924): 11.

31. Countee Cullen, "The Dark Tower," *Opportunity* (March 1928): 90.

32. Critic Montgomery Gregory identifies this necessary cultural figure in Jean Toomer's mystical portraits. Reviewing *Cane*, he says, "Toomer appreciates as an artist the surpassing beauty, both physical and spiritual, of the Negro woman's eyes. Visitors from foreign lands have frequently pointed out this unique glory of our women. Is it any wonder? For do not their eyes express from mysterious depths the majesty of lost empires, the pathos of a woman's lot in slavery, and the spirit of a resurgent race?" (*Opportunity* [January 1924]: 374).

33. See, for example, Eunice Roberta Hunton, "Replica," *Opportunity* (September 1924): 276; and Louis L. Redding, "A Florida Sunday," *Opportunity* (October 1925): 302–303. Examples of white writers exoticizing their African American subjects are, of course, legion, but interestingly, many of these writers were praised and occasionally even reprinted by the Harlem press; for example, see Elizabeth Coatsworth, "A Negress on Sixth Avenue," *Opportunity* (April 1924): 114; [Charles S. Johnson], "New Pattern in the Literature about the Negro," *Opportunity* (June 1925): 164.

34. Eunice Roberta Hunton, "Digression (To Three Companions in Adventure on a Spring Night)," *Opportunity* (December 1923): 359.

35. Nella Larsen, *Quicksand and Passing* (New Brunswick, N.J.: Rutgers University Press, 1988) 59.

36. Alain Locke, *The New Negro* (1925; New York: Atheneum, 1992) 9.

37. George Schuyler, "The Negro-Art Hokum," *The Nation* (June 16, 1926): 662–663.

38. George Hutchinson, "Mediating 'Race' and 'Nation': The Cultural Politics of *The Messenger*," *African American Review* 8:4 (Winter 1994): 531–548.

39. "Who's Who" in *The Messenger* begins in December 1922 (545) and runs for several months into 1923.

40. Interestingly, however, Du Bois's rhetorical style in his *Crisis* writings becomes progressively "modern" over the course of the decade.

41. George S. Schuyler and Theophilus Lewis, "Shafts and Darts," *The Messenger* (January 1925): 35, 36.

42. As may already be evident, Schuyler was strongly influenced by H. L. Mencken. For an exploration of Mencken's relation to Schuyler and other renaissance writers, see Charles Scruggs, *The Sage in Harlem: H. L. Mencken and the Black Writers of the 1920s* (Baltimore: Johns Hopkins University Press, 1984).

43. Schuyler actually titled his autobiography *Black and Conservative* (New Rochelle, N.Y.: Arlington House, 1966).

44. Chandler Owen's articles ran in the March through April issues of 1923.

45. In *Black and Conservative*, Schuyler refers to "Davy Carr" as "a series of 'inside' stories on Washington's Negro society" (159), the scare quotes confirming its highly fictionalized feel despite the label of "true" it bears.

46. See, for example, Schuyler's one-act play *The Yellow Peril*, in *The Messenger*

(January 1925): 28–31. Conversely, note Schuyler's praise for prostitute Amber Lee's memoir *The Woman I Am*, for her revelation of the truth of women's social power (December 1925): 398.

47. Helene Johnson, "Futility," *Opportunity* (August 1926): 259.

48. Male writers also made use of the parlor-alley trope, though less frequently and to different ends. See, for example, Eugene Gordon's "Rootbound," *Opportunity* (September 1926): 279–283; 299.

49. Dorothy West, "Hannah Byde," *The Messenger* (July 1926): 197; ellipses in the original.

50. Anita Scott Coleman, "Silk Stockings," *The Messenger* (August 1926): 230.

51. I take my definition of *avant-garde* largely from Renato Poggioli, *The Theory of the Avant-Garde* (Cambridge: Harvard University Press, 1968).

52. Langston Hughes, *The Big Sea* (1940; New York: Hill and Wang, 1993) 235–236.

53. Du Bois did not, in fact, review *FIRE!!* for the *Crisis*.

54. My thanks to Mathew Roberts for these references in particular and for his general insights into the avant-garde dimensions of *FIRE!!*

55. Cary Wintz, *Black Culture and the Harlem Renaissance* (Houston: Rice University Press, 1988) 88.

56. Again, *Infants of the Spring* confirms the Younger Artists' impatience with the celebration of Africa in the scene in which Dr. Parkes, the character modeled on renaissance impresario Alain Locke, admonishes the assembled young artists to look to their African roots (235–242).

57. Theophilus Lewis, "Souls of Black Folk," *The Messenger* (June 1925): 230.

58. Umberto Boccioni, Carlo Carra, Luigi Rossolo, et al. "Futurist Painting: Technical Manifesto 1910," in *Futurist Manifestos*, ed. Umbro Appollonio (New York: Viking Press, 1973) 30–31.

59. A term from Jazz-Age Slang, *Sheba* refers to "a beautiful, often flirtations young woman" (editor's note in Nella Larsen, *Quicksand and Passing*, ed. Deborah E. McDowell, p. 245).

60. Langston Hughes described Thurman as "a strange kind of fellow, who liked to drink gin, but *didn't* like to drink gin; who liked being a Negro, but felt it a great handicap; who adored bohemianism, but thought it wrong to be a bohemian. . . . Once I told him if I could feel as bad as he did *all* the time, I would surely produce wonderful books. But he said you had to know how to *write*, as well as how to feel bad" (*The Big Sea*, 238).

61. David Levering Lewis, *When Harlem Was in Vogue* (New York: Oxford University Press, 1979) 202–203.

62. Hurston appears in *Infants of the Spring* as Sweetie Mae Carr, the "short story writer, more noted for her ribald wit and personal effervescence than for any actual literary work" (229).

63. Charles Johnson announces *Ebony Flute* in the August 1926 issue of *Opportunity* (241).

64. On *Salome* as a cultural phenomenon, see Elaine Showalter, *Sexual Anarchy: Gender and Culture at the Fin de Siècle* (New York: Viking, 1990) 149–156.

65. Esther Fulks Scott, "Negroes As Actors in Serious Plays," *Opportunity* August 1923:20.

66. Ironic in this light is John Corbin's *New York Times* review which absolves Salome of ever "suggest[ing] the Negress," but finds Sidney Kirkpatrick in the role

of Herod "not so much moral and religious" as expressive of "the savage heart of darkness, of fetich-worship and devil-fears." "[W]hen he is stirred to the depths," says Corbin, "it is the spirit of the jungle that finds utterance." reprinted in *New York Times Theatre Reviews, 1920–1970,* vol. 1 (New York: New York Times and Arno Press, 1971):1.

67. Thanks to Kathy Hickok for pointing out this detail.

Chapter 7

1. "Performance" has been much discussed in recent theory, most prominently in the works of Judith Butler (*Gender Trouble* [New York: Routledge, 1990] and *Bodies That Matter* [New York: Routledge, 1993]). In this essay, I am explicitly setting out to evolve an historically specific understanding of the term, an aim I believe is well-served by my proceeding inductively.

2. *The Messenger* (December 1923): 924.

3. See, for example, Lovett Fort-Whiteman, "Theatre—Drama—Music," *The Messenger* (November 1917): 29; "Drama," *The Messenger* (April 1923): 671; Esther Fulks Scott, "Negroes as Actors in Serious Plays," *Opportunity* (August 1923): 20–23; Rogier Didier [review of Dixie to Broadway], *Opportunity* (November 1924): 346; W. E. B. DuBois, "The Negro and the American Stage," *The Crisis* (June 1924): 54; Raymond O'Neil, "The Negro in Dramatic Art," *The Crisis* (February 1924): 155–157; and Theophilus Lewis, "Theatre," *The Messenger* (January 1925): 380. For critical discussions of the history and special place of drama in the Harlem Renaissance, see Elizabeth Brown-Guillory, *Their Place on Stage: Black Women Playwrights in America* (Westport, Conn.: Greenwood Press, 1988) 2–3; and Henry Louis Gates Jr., "A Tragedy of Negro Life," in *Mule Bone: A Comedy of Negro Life,* ed. George Houston Bass and Henry Louis Gates Jr. (New York: HarperCollins, 1991) 15–17.

4. In fact, the women of *The Crisis* cover illustrations were often noted for their accomplishments and/or named as prominent individuals. For example, the note on the cover woman of August 1926 reads, "A Bachelor of Music from Oberlin"; for September 1925, "A portrait in colors of Miss Ada Gaines, who played the part of Ethiopia in the pageant in Los Angeles."

5. In an astute analysis of rhetorical dynamics in *Incidents in the Life of a Slave Girl,* Carla Kaplan argues convincingly for the compulsory and constrained nature of Jacobs's writing—that is, her public self-assertion—as against the critical tendency to see this writing as inherently a space of liberation ("Narrative Contracts and Emancipatory Readers: *Incidents in the Life of Slave Girl,*" *Yale Journal of Criticism* 6[1]: 93–119).

6. The tendency to denigrate Fauset and other renaissance writers of the so-called genteel school has increasingly given way to more sympathetic and careful analyses. See, for example, Deborah E. McDowell, "Introduction," in Nella Larsen, *Quicksand and Passing,* (New Brunswick, N.J.: Rutgers University Press, 1988) ix–xxxv; and "Introduction: Regulating Midwives," in Jessie Redmon Fauset, *Plum Bun* (Boston: Beacon Press, 1990) ix–xxxiii; Hazel Carby, "The Quicksands of Representation," in *Reconstructing Womanhood: The Emergence of the Afro-American Woman Novelist* (New York: Oxford University Press, 1987) 163–175; Thadious Davis, "Foreword," in Jessie Redmon Fauset, *There Is Confusion* (Boston: Northeastern University Press,

1989) v–xxvi; and, most recently, Ann duCille, "The Bourgeois, Wedding Bell Blues of Jessie Fauset and Nella Larsen," in *The Coupling Convention: Sex, Text, and Tradition in Black Women's Fiction* (New York: Oxford University Press, 1993) 86–109.

7. Ottie B. Graham, *Holiday, The Crisis* (May 1923): 12.

8. See Jo A. Tanner's fascinating study of the African American actress in the early twentieth century, *Dusky Maidens: The Odyssey of the Early Black Dramatic Actress* (Westport, Conn.: Greenwood Press, 1992).

9. With this play title, the echo of "Margot Cotell" with William Wells Brown's "Clotel" intensifies. Graham's use of this literary legacy merits close attention, but for the moment we may simply note the dignifying effect of an allusion to the literary tradition of genteel African American womanhood on what might otherwise be a moment of degrading or merely ironic masquerade for Margot.

10. Mamie Elaine Francis, "Souls for Gasoline," *The Messenger* (April 1925): 176.

11. The significance of the geographical move is likely complex, but to start with, we may point to the distinctness—even uniqueness—of New Orleans culture, such that leaving it for Washington (and later New York) might be something like entering mainstream America in its full racial dynamics.

12. Lewis A. Erenberg notes the popularity in postwar New York of hula dances, Egyptian dances, South Sea Island dances—significantly, for our purposes, all exotic and racially "ambiguous" displays (*Steppin' Out: New York Nightlife and the Transformation of American Culture, 1890–1930* [Westport, Conn.: Greenwood Press, 1981] 224–226).

13. The description of Anderson as "neurotic" identifies him with the psychoanalytic discourse commonly used in this period for naming whites' relations to blacks—another important determinant for black women's performative context.

14. Fauset, *There Is Confusion*, 10.

15. We should note, though, that Joanna (in a much more explicit way than Margot) is subject to a species of "blaming the victim": the very performance that is her racial duty will be cast increasingly as selfish indulgence.

16. I would argue that the "yellow and white faces" of this passage are meant, in accordance with the convention of the time, to suggest the variety of African American people, rather than the multiracial rainbow of our own conventions.

17. "The Dance of the Nations" appears to be of the ubiquitous period genre, the "pageant."

18. Moreover, this incident is the first of several in which Joanna learns from the street what she will ultimately perform on the stage.

19. The class-specific nature of this valuation of Peter's musical career is greatly underscored by the genre of music he plays: ragtime—surely an instance of "showing them us" if there ever was one.

20. In fact, it is this willingness to close off heterosexual relationship from the public light of day that allows Maggie to be married to the gambler Neal for months without ever knowing anything of his professional life.

21. See, for example, Fauset, *There is Confusion*, 150–153.

22. For alternative (though not conflicting) discussions of clothes in Fauset, see duCille, *Coupling Convention*, 93–102, and Mary Jane Lupton, "Clothes and Closure in Three Novels by Black Women," *Black American Literature Forum* 20:4 (Winter 1986): 409–421.

23. Ann duCille argues rightly that Fauset is quite sympathetic to her working-

class women characters, critical accusations of elitism to the contrary (*Coupling Conventions,* 93).

Chapter 8

1. Maureen Honey, *Shadowed Dreams: Women's Poetry of the Harlem Renaissance* (New Brunswick, N.J.: Rutgers University Press, 1989) 1–8.

2. Gloria T. Hull, *Color, Sex, and Poetry* (Bloomington: Indiana University Press, 1987) 14.

3. Sharon Cameron's observations on Emily Dickinson's lyrics are interesting in this context: Cameron argues that "all of Dickinson's poems fight temporality with a vengeance," saying, "All action, these poems seem to insist, and consequently all narrative and story on whose shoulders action is carried, leads to ending, leads to death" (*Lyric Time: Dickinson and the Limits of Genre* [Baltimore: Johns Hopkins University Press, 1979] 203).

4. In this light, note Houston A. Baker Jr.'s reading of Gaston Bachelard's The Poetics of Space (1964): "the poetic image for Bachelard is a means of liberation from a reductive dialectics of order. The poetic image disrupts, exaggerates, transgresses, transforms. Its unpredictability makes us aware of possibilities of freedom" (*Workings of the Spirit: The Poetics of Afro-American Women's Writing* [Chicago: University of Chicago Press, 1991] 70).

5. Marion Grace Conover, "Comments," *Saturday Evening Quill* (June 1928): 64. The *Saturday Evening Quill* was the journal of a literary club by the same name, which comprised the Boston outpost of the renaissance. Helene Johnson got her start there, as did Dorothy West (Abby Arthur Johnson and Ronald Maberry Johnson, *Propaganda and Aesthetics: The Literary Politics of Afro-American Magazines in the Twentieth Century* [Amherst: University of Massachusetts Press, 1979] 92–93).

6. In the interest of avoiding misappropriation of Baker's argument, I must note that *Workings of the Spirit* (and Baker's work generally) very explicitly takes those works that engage what Baker calls vernacular modes as the true African American cultural tradition. Bourgeois identity and style, under discussion here, fall distinctly outside Baker's purview. My implicit contention, however, is that bourgeois writers do participate in the African American literary tradition, even to the point of engaging many of the same issues and with similar strategies as their vernacular counterparts.

7. Not even Hagar, the slave whose enforced surrogate motherhood made her a primary and enduring figure of African American women's Christian experience, is a presence in the poetry of the time. On Hagar and the history of black women's experience in the church generally, see Delores S. Williams. *Sisters in the Wilderness: The Challenge of Womanist God-Talk* (Maryknoll, N.Y.: Orbis Books, 1993).

8. Alice Dunbar-Nelson, "Of Old St. Augustine," *Opportunity* (June 1925): 216.

9. Kimberly Rae Connor, *Conversions and Visions in the Writings of African-American Women* (Knoxville: University of Tennessee Press, 1994) 14; my italics.

10. Connor's argument is consistent with Lawrence W. Levine's landmark 1977 study *Black Culture and Black Consciousness: Afro-American Folk Thought from Slavery to Freedom,* in which, discussing the earlier spirituals, he argues, "The religious music of the slaves is almost devoid of feelings of depravity or unworthiness, but is rather, as I have tried to show, pervaded by a sense of change, transcendence, ultimate justice, and personal worth" ([New York: Oxford University Press] 39).

11. Dora Lawrence Houston, "Preference," *Opportunity* (June 1925): 164.

12. Jessie Redmon Fauset, "Rain Fugue," Crisis (August 1924): 155.

13. Most prominent in this mode are Georgia Douglas Johnson's poems for *The Crisis*. See "Armageddon" (March 1925): 231; "Escape" (May 1925): 15; "Companion" (August 1925): 180; and "Finality" (September 1926): 247.

14. Gwendolyn Bennett, "Street Lamps in Early Spring," *Opportunity* (May 1926): 152.

15. Langston Hughes, *The Weary Blues* (New York: Knopf, 1926) 19.

16. Helene Johnson, "Night," *Opportunity* (January 1926): 23.

17. Helene Johnson, "What Do I Care for Morning," in *Caroling Dusk: An Anthology of Verse by Negro Poets*, ed. Countee Cullen (New York: Harper Brothers, 1927) 216.

18. This intellectual tradition includes such major works as W. E. B. Du Bois, *Souls of Black Folk* (1903) and Pauline Hopkins, *Of One Blood* (1901).

19. Importantly, as the renaissance wore on, the equation of African American race with youth reversed the terms of the earlier rhetoric, all the while keeping the values intact but adding the crucial emphasis on color and pleasure.

20. Gwendolyn Bennett, "Moon Tonight," in *Gypsy* (Cincinnati: October 1926): 13.

21. Gwendolyn Bennett, "Purgation," *Opportunity* (February 1925): 56.

22. Gwendolyn Bennett, "Wind," *Opportunity* (November 1924): 335.

23. Gwendolyn Bennett, "Fantasy," in *Caroling Dusk*, 158.

24. Helene Johnson, "My Race," in *Caroling Dusk*, 221.

25. Helene Johnson, "The Road," *Opportunity* (July 1926): 221.

26. Helene Johnson, "Fulfillment," *Opportunity* (June 1926): 194.

27. Hull, *Color, Sex, and Poetry*, 6.

28. Johnson and Johnson, *Propaganda and Aesthetics*, 89–90.

29. For example, they divided the labor of eulogizing Florence Mills and Clarissa Scott Delaney, who both died in the fall of 1927. My characterization of the columns refers mostly to their first year or so of existence, after which they lose their prominent graphics and much of their column space (especially "Ebony Flute").

30. Countee Cullan, "The Dark Tower," *Opportunity* (March 1928): 90.

31. Gwendolyn Bennett, "The Ebony Flute," *Opportunity* (April 1928): 122.

32. Gwendolyn Bennett, "To Usward," *Crisis* (May 1924): 19.

33. Michael North's *The Dialect of Modernism: Race, Language and Twentieth Century Literature* (New York: Oxford University Press, 1994) thoroughly explores the largely buried function of Africa (and African America) for the high modernists.

34. I allude here to the flaneurial tradition inaugurated by Charles Baudelaire ("The Painter of Modern Life" [1845]) and theorized by Walter Benjamin (*Charles Baudelaire or the Lyric Poet of High Capitalism* [London: New Left Books, 1969). For state-of-the-art flaneurial scholarship, see Keith Tester, ed., *The Flaneur* (New York: Routledge, 1994).

35. Gwendolyn Bennett, "Song," in *The New Negro*, ed. Alain Locke (1925; New York: Atheneum, 1992) 225.

36. Helene Johnson, "Magalu," in *Caroling Dusk*, 223–224.

37. Helene Johnson, "Bottled," *Vanity Fair* (May 1927):76.

38. Helene Johnson, "Sonnet to a Negro in Harlem," in *Caroling Dusk*, 217.

39. Helene Johnson, "Poem," in *Caroling Dusk*, 218–219.

40. See n. 59, chapter 6.

41. Paula Fass, *The Damned and the Beautiful: American Youth in the 1920s* (New York: Oxford University Press, 1977).

Afterword

1. Carla Kaplan, *The Erotics of Talk: Women's Writing and Feminist Paradigms* (New York: Oxford University Press, 1996) 25.
2. Ibid., 33.

Bibliography

Aaron, Daniel. *Writers on the Left*. New York: Oxford University Press, 1977.

Adams, Franklin Pierce [F. P. A.]. *Column Book of F. P. A.* Garden City, N.Y.: Doubleday, Doran, 1928.

———. *The Diary of Our Own Samuel Pepys*, vol. 1, 1911–1925. New York: Simon and Schuster, 1935.

———. *Half a Loaf*. Garden City, N.Y.: Doubleday, Page, 1927.

———. "Half Minutes with the Best Authors." *Vanity Fair* (August 1920): 21.

———. *Overset*. Garden City, N.Y.: Doubleday, Page, 1922.

———. *So There!* New York: Doubleday Doran, 1923.

Allen, Cleveland G. "Our Young Artists," *Opportunity* (August 1923): 25.

Ammons, Elizabeth. "The New Woman as Cultural Symbol and Social Reality: Six Women Writers' Perspectives." In Heller and Rudnick, *1915*, pp. 82–97.

Amory, Cleveland, and Frederic Bradlee, Eds. *Vanity Fair: A Cavalcade of the 1920's and 1930's*. New York: Viking, 1960.

Ardis, Ann. *New Women, New Novels: Feminism and Early Modernism*. New Brunswick, N.J.: Rutgers University Press, 1990.

Ashley, Sally. F. P. A.: *The Life and Times of Franklin Pierce Adams*. New York: Beaufort Books, 1986.

Atkins, Elizabeth. *Edna St. Vincent Millay and Her Times*. Chicago: University of Chicago Press, 1936.

Baker, Houston A., Jr. *Modernism and the Harlem Renaissance*. Chicago: University of Chicago Press, 1987.

———. *Workings of the Spirit: The Poetics of Afro-American Women's Writing*. Chicago: University of Chicago Press, 1991.

Barthes, Roland. *A Lover's Discourse: Fragments*. Trans. Richard Howard. New York: Farrar, Straus and Giroux, 1978.

Benchley, Robert. *Benchley at the Theatre: Dramatic Criticism, 1920–1940*. Ed. Charles Getchell. Ipswich, Mass.: Ipswich Press, 1985.

———. *Love Conquers All*. New York: Henry Holt, 1922.

———. *No Poems, or Around the World Backwards and Sideways*. New York: Harper & Brothers, 1932.

———. *Pluck and Luck.* New York: Henry Holt, 1925.

Benet, Stephen Vincent. *Young People's Pride.* New York: Henry Holt, 1922.

Benjamin, Jessica. *The Bonds of Love: Psychoanalysis, Feminism, and the Problem of Domination.* New York: Pantheon, 1988.

Benjamin, Walter. *Charles Baudelaire, or the Lyric Poet of High Capitalism.* London: New Left Books, 1969.

Bennett, Gwendolyn. "Ebony Flute." *Opportunity* (April 1928): 122.

———. "Fantasy." In Countee Cullen, ed., *Caroling Dusk.*

———. "Street Lamps in Early Spring." *Opportunity* (May 1926): 152.

———. "Moon Tonight." *Gypsy* (Cincinnati) (October 1926): 13.

———. "Purgation." *Opportunity* (February 1925): 56.

———. "Song." In Locke, ed., *The New Negro.*

———. "To Usward." *The Crisis* (May 1924): 19.

———. "Wind." *Opportunity* (November 1924): 335.

Benstock, Shari. *Women of the Left Bank: Paris 1900–1940.* Austin: University of Texas Press, 1986.

Berlant, Lauren. "National Brands/National Body: *Imitation of Life.*" In *The Phantom Public Sphere.* Ed. Bruce Robbins. University of Minnesota Press, 1993, pp. 173–208.

Bersani, Leo. *The Freudian Body.* New York: Columbia University Press, 1986.

Blake, Casey Nelson. *Beloved Community: The Cultural Criticism of Randolph Bourne, Van Wyck Brooks, Waldo Frank, and Lewis Mumford.* Chapel Hill: University of North Carolina Press, 1990.

Blanchard, Phyllis, and Carolyn Manasses. *New Girls for Old.* New York: Macauley, 1930.

Boccioni, Umberto, Carlo Carra, Luigi Rossola, et al. "Futurist Painting: Technical Manifesto 1910." *In Futurist Manifestos.* Ed. Umbro Appollonio. New York: Viking, 1973, pp. 30–31.

Bodenheim, Maxwell. *A Virtuous Girl.* New York: Horace Liveright, 1930.

Bourne, Randolph. "The Jew and Trans-National America." In *War and the Intellectuals: Essays by Randolph Bourne,* 1915–1919. Ed. Carl Resek. New York: Harper Torchbooks, 1964.

Boyd, Ernest. *H. L. Mencken.* New York: Robert H. McBride, 1925.

Boyer, Jay. "The *Schlemiezel*: Black Humor and the *Shtetl* Tradition." In *Semites and Stereotypes: Characteristics of Jewish Humor.* Ed. Avner Ziv and Anat Zajdman. Westport, Conn.: Greenwood Press, 1993, pp. 3–12.

Brackett, Charles. *Entirely Surrounded.* New York: Alfred A. Knopf, 1934.

Brenkman, John. *Culture and Domination.* Ithaca, N.Y.: Cornell University Press, 1987.

Brittin, Norman A. *Edna St. Vincent Millay,* Rev. Ed. Boston: Twayne, 1982.

Brooks, Van Wyck. *Three Essays on America.* New York: E. P. Dutton, 1934.

Brown-Guillory, Elizabeth. *Their Place on Stage: Black Women Playwrights in America.* Westport, Conn.: Greenwood Press, 1988.

Butler, Judith. *Bodies That Matter: On the Discursive Limits of "Sex."* New York: Routledge, 1993.

———. *Gender Trouble: Feminism and the Subversion of Identity.* New York: Routledge, 1990.

Calverton, V. F., and S. D. Schmalhusen, Eds. *Sex in Civilization.* New York: Macaulay, 1929.

Cameron, Sharon. *Lyric Time: Dickinson and the Limits of Genre*. Baltimore: Johns Hopkins University Press, 1979.

Carby, Hazel V. *Reconstructing Womanhood: The Emergence of the Afro-American Woman Novelist*. New York: Oxford University Press, 1987.

Chauncy, George. "Street Culture and Gay Male Identity in Early-Twentieth-Century New York." Lecture. Northwestern University, 31 May 1991.

Cheney, Anne. *Millay in Greenwich Village*. University, Ala.: University of Alabama Press, 1975.

Churchill, Allen. *The Improper Bohemians: A Re-Creation of Greenwich Village in Its Heyday*. New York: E. P. Dutton, 1959.

Clark, Suzanne. *Sentimental Modernism: Women Writers and the Revolution of the Word*. Bloomington: Indiana University Press, 1991.

Clayton, Douglas. *Floyd Dell: The Life and Times of an American Rebel*. Chicago: Ivan R. Dee, 1994.

Coatsworth, Elizabeth. "A Negress on Sixth Avenue." *Opportunity* (April 1924): 114.

Coleman, Anita Scott. "Silk Stockings." *Messenger* (August 1926): 230.

Congreve, William. *The Way of the World*. In *British Dramatists from Dryden to Sheridan*. Ed. George H. Nettleton and Arthur E. Case; Rev. George Winchester Stone Jr. Carbondale: Southern Illinois University Press, 1969.

Connor, Kimberly Rae. *Conversions and Visions in the Writings of African-American Women*. Knoxville: University of Tennessee Press, 1994.

Conover, Mary Grace. "Comment." *Saturday Evening Quill* (June 1928): 64.

Cooper, Anna Julia. *A Voice from the South: By a Black Woman of the South*. New York: Negro Universities Press, 1969.

Corbin, John. "Salome" [review]. *New York Times Theatre Reviews, 1920–1970*, vol. 1. New York: *New York Times* and Arno Press, 1971.

Cott, Nancy. *The Grounding of Modern Feminism*. New Haven, Conn.: Yale University Press, 1987.

Cowley, Malcolm. *Exile's Return: A Literary Odyssey of the 1920's*. New York: Penguin Books, 1979.

Cullen, Countee. *Caroling Dusk: An Anthology of Verse by Negro Poets*. New York: Harper Brothers, 1927.

———. "The Dark Tower." *Opportunity* (March 1928): 90.

———. "The League of Youth." *Crisis* (August 1923): 167.

Daniel, Walter C., and Sandra Y. Govan. "Gwendolyn Bennett." In *Dictionary of Literary Biography*, vol. 51. Detroit: Gale Research, 1987, pp. 3–10.

Davis, Thadious. "Foreword." In Jessie Redmon Fauset, *There Is Confusion*, pp. v–xxvi.

Dearborn, Mary V. *Love in the Promised Land: The Story of Anzia Yezierska and John Dewey*. New York: Free Press, 1988.

De Beauvoir, Simone. *The Second Sex*. Trans. H. M. Parshley. New York: Vintage, 1952.

Dell, Floyd. "Edna St. Vincent Millay." *The Literary Spotlight*, Ed. John Farrar. New York: George H. Doran, 1924, p. 77.

———. *King Arthur's Socks and Other Village Plays*. New York: Knopf, 1922.

———. *Love in Greenwich Village*. New York: George H. Doran, 1926.

———. *Love in the Machine Age: A Psychological Study of the Transition from Patriarchal Society*. New York: Farrar, 1930.

———. *Woman as World Builders: Studies in Modern Feminism.* Chicago: Forbes, 1913.

Didier, Rogier. [Review of Dixie to Broadway.] *Opportunity* (November 1924): 346.

Dos Passos, John, *Manhattan Transfer* (1925). Boston: Houghton Mifflin, 1953.

Douglas, Ann. *Terrible Honesty: Mongrel Manhattan in the 1920s.* New York: Farrar, Straus, and Giroux, 1995.

Drake, William. *The First Wave: Women Poets in America,* 1915–1945. New York: Macmillan, 1987.

"Drama." *The Messenger* (April 1923): 671.

Drennan, Robert M. *The Algonquin Wits.* Secaucus, N.J.: Citadel Press, 1977.

Du Bois, W. E. B. *Darkwater: Voices from within the Veil.* New York: Schocken Books, 1969.

———. Editorial. *Crisis* (October 1923): 248–249.

———. "The Negro and the American Stage." *Crisis* (June 1924): 54.

———. "The Younger Literary Movement." *Crisis* (February 1924): 161.

duCille, Ann. *The Coupling Convention: Sex, Text, and Tradition in Black Women's Fiction.* New York: Oxford University Press, 1993.

Duggan, Lisa. "The Social Enforcement of Heterosexuality and Lesbian Resistance in the 1920's." In Swerdlow and Lessinger, *Class, Race, and Sex,* pp. 75–80.

Dunbar-Nelson, Alice. "Of Old[,] St. Augustine." *Opportunity* (June 1925): 216.

Early, Gerald, Ed. *My Soul's High Song: The Collected Writings of Countee Cullen, Voice of the Harlem Renaissance.* New York: Doubleday, 1991.

Eastman, Max. *Love and Revolution: My Journey through an Epoch.* New York: Random House, 1964.

Ellis, Havelock. *Studies in the Psychology of Sex,* vol. 2. Philadelphia: F. A. Davis Company, 1925.

Erenberg, Lewis A. *Steppin' Out: New York Nightlife and the Transformation of American Culture,* 1890–1930. Westport, Conn: Greenwood Press, 1981.

Ewen, Stuart. *Captains of Consciousness: Advertising and the Social Roots of the Consumer Culture.* New York: McGraw-Hill, 1976.

"Exalting Negro Womanhood." *Messenger* (January 1924): 7.

Fass, Paula. *The Damned and the Beautiful: American Youth in the 1920s.* New York: Oxford University Press, 1977.

Fauset, Jessie Redmon. "Rain Fugue." *Crisis* (August 1924): 155.

———. *There Is Confusion.* Boston: Northeastern University Press, 1989.

Felski, Rita. *The Gender of Modernity.* Cambridge: Harvard University Press, 1995.

Ferber, Edna. *Cheerful by Request.* New York: Doubleday, Page, 1918.

———. *A Peculiar Treasure.* Garden City, N.Y.: Doubleday, 1960.

Fitzgerald, F. Scott. "Bernice Bobs Her Hair." In *The Stories of F. Scott Fitzgerald.* New York: Macmillan, 1986, pp. 39–60.

Fort-Whiteman, Lovett. "Theatre-Drama-Music." *The Messenger* (November 1917): 29.

Francis, Mamie Elaine. "Souls for Gasoline." *The Messenger* (April 1925): 176.

Frewin, Leslie. *The Late Mrs. Dorothy Parker.* New York: Macmillan, 1986.

Fried, Debra. "Andromeda Unbound: Gender & Genre in Millay's Sonnets." *Twentieth Century Literature* 32 (Spring 1986): 1–22.

Gabler, Neal. *An Empire of Their Own: How the Jews Invented Hollywood.* New York: Crown, 1988.

Gaines, James R. *Wit's End: Days and Nights of the Algonquin Round Table.* New York: Harcourt Brace Jovanovich, 1977.

Gale, Zona. "Bronze." *Opportunity* (August 1923): 218.

Gates, Henry Louis Jr. "A Tragedy of Negro Life." *In Mule Bone: A Comedy of Negro Life*. Ed. George Houston Bass and Henry Louis Gates Jr. New York: HarperCollins, 1991.

Gelder, Ken, and Sarah Thornton, Eds. *The Subcultures Reader*. New York: Routledge, 1997.

Giddings, Paula. *When and Where I Enter: The Impact of Black Women on Race and Sex in America*. New York: William Morrow, 1984.

Gifford, Sanford. "The American Reception of Psychoanalysis, 1908–1922." In Heller and Rudnick, *1915*, 128–145.

Gilbert, Sandra M., and Susan Gubar. "The Female Imagination and the Modernist Aesthetic." Special issue *Women's Studies* 13 (1–2) (1986).

———. *No Man's Land: The Place of the Woman Writer in the Twentieth Century*. 3 Vols. New Haven, Conn. Yale University Press, 1987–1994.

Gilman, Sander L. "Salome, Syphilis, Sarah Bernhardt and the 'Modern Jewess.' " *German Quarterly* 66(2) (Spring 1993): 203.

Gold, Mike. *Jews without Money*. New York: Avon, 1965.

Goldstein, Malcolm. *George S. Kaufman: His Life, His Theater*. New York: Oxford University Press, 1979.

Gordon, Eugene. "The Month's Best Editorial (Selected from the American Negro Press)." *The Messenger* (March 1927): 74.

———. "Outstanding Negro Newspapers of 1925." *Opportunity* (December 1925): 358–361.

———. "Rootbound." *Opportunity* (September 1926): 279–284; 299.

Graham, Ottie B. "Holiday." *The Crisis* (May 1923): 12.

Gregory, Montgomery. [review of Cane]. *Opportunity* (January 1924): 374.

———. "The Spirit of Phyllis Wheatley." *Opportunity* (June 1924): 184.

Grossman, Barbara W. *Funny Woman: The Life and Times of Fanny Brice*. Bloomington: Indiana University Press, 1992.

Groves, Gladys H., and Robert A. Ross. *The Married Woman: A Practical Guide to Happy Marriage*. New York: World, 1936.

Haas, Scott. "The Marx Brothers, Jews, and My Four-Year-Old Daughter." *Cineaste* 19(2–3) (1992): 48–49.

Hale, Beatrice Forbes-Robertson. "Women in Transition." *Sex in Civilization*, Ed. V. G. Calverton and S. D. Schmalhusen. New York: Macauley, 1929.

Hanscombe, Gillian, and Virginia L. Smyers. *Writing for Their Lives: The Modernist Women, 1920–1940*. Boston: Northeastern University Press, 1987.

Hapgood, Hutchins. *The Spirit of the Ghetto*. Ed. Moses Rischin. Cambridge: Harvard University Press, 1967.

———. *The Story of a Lover*. New York: Boni and Liveright, 1919.

Harriman, Margaret Case. *The Vicious Circle: The Story of the Algonquin Round Table*. New York: Rinehart, 1951.

Heller, Adele. "The New Theatre," in Heller and Rudnick, eds., *1915*, pp. 217–232.

Heller, Adele, and Lois Rudnick, Eds. *1915: The Cultural Moment; The New Politics, the New Woman, the New Psychology, the New Art and the New Theatre in America*. New Brunswick, N.J.: Rutgers University Press, 1991.

Henderson, Mae. "Speaking in Tongues: Dialogics, Dialectics and the Black Woman Writer's Literary Tradition." In *Colonial Discourse and Post-Colonial Theory*. Ed. Patrick Williams and Laura Chrisman. New York: Columbia University Press, 1994, pp. 257–267.

Henderson, Mary C. "Against Broadway: The Rise of the Art Theatre in America (1900–1920) in Heller and Rudnick, *1915*, pp. 233–249.

Homans, Margaret. *Women Writers and Poetic Identity: Dorothy Wordsworth, Emily Bronte, and Emily Dickinson*. Princeton, N.J.: Princeton University Press, 1980.

Honey, Maureen. *Shadowed Dreams: Women's Poetry of the Harlem Renaissance*. New Brunswick, N.J.: Rutgers University Press, 1989.

House, Jay E. "Out of the Frying Pan." *Ladies Home Journal* (January 1920): 4.

Houston, Dora Lawrence. "Preference." *Opportunity* (June 1925): 164.

Hughes, Langston. *The Big Sea*. New York: Hill and Wang, 1993.

———. *The Weary Blues*. New York: Knopf, 1926.

Hull, Gloria T. *Color, Sex, and Poetry: Three Women Writers of the Harlem Renaissance*. Bloomington: Indiana University Press, 1987.

Humphrey, Robert E. *Children of Fantasy: The First Rebels of Greenwich Village*. New York: John Wiley, 1978.

Hunton, Eunice Roberta. "Digression." *Opportunity* (December 1923): 359; 381.

———. "Replica." *Opportunity* (September 1924): 276.

———. "A Story about Northern Negroes." *Opportunity* (April 1924): 11.

Hutchinson, George. *The Harlem Renaissance in Black and White*. Cambridge: Harvard University Press, 1995.

———. "Mediating 'Race' and 'Nation': The Cultural Politics of *The Messenger*." *African American Review* 8(4) (Winter 1994): 531–548.

Hyman, Paula E. *Gender and Assimilation in Modern Jewish History*. Seattle: University of Washington Press, 1995.

Ikonné, Chidi. *From DuBois to Van Vechten: The Early New Negro Literature, 1903–1926*. Westport, Conn.: Greenwood Press, 1981.

Jackson, W. "The Theatre—Drama." *The Messenger* (June 1923): 746–747.

Johnson, Abby Arthur, and Ronald Maberry Johnson. *Propaganda and Aesthetics: The Literary Politics of Afro-American Magazines in the Twentieth Century*. Amherst: University of Massachusetts Press, 1979.

Johnson, Charles. "The Charleston." *Opportunity* (July 1926): 208–209.

———. Editorial. *Opportunity* (May 1925): 130.

———. "New Pattern in the Literature about the Negro." *Opportunity* (June 1925): 164.

———. "An Opportunity for Negro Writers." *Opportunity* (September 1924): 258.

———. "Racial Humor and Propaganda." *Opportunity* (August 1923): 218.

———. "Some Perils of the 'Renaissance.' " *Opportunity* (March 1927): 68.

Johnson, Georgia Douglas. "Armageddon." *The Crisis* (March 1925): 231.

———. "Companion." *The Crisis* (August 1925): 180.

———. "Escape." *The Crisis* (May 1925): 15.

———. "Finality." *The Crisis* (September 1926): 247.

Johnson, Helene. "Bottled." *Vanity Fair* (May 1927):76.

———. "Futility." *Opportunity* (August 1926): 259.

———. "Fulfillment." *Opportunity* (June 1926): 194.

———. "Magalu." In Countee Cullen, ed., *Caroling Dusk*, pp. 223–224.

———. "My Race." *Opportunity* (June 1925).

———. "Poem." In Countee Cullen, ed., *Caroling Dusk*, pp. 218–219.

———. "Night." *Opportunity* (January 1926): 23.

———. "The Road." In Countee Cullen, ed., *Caroling Dusk*, p. 221.

———. "Sonnet to a Negro in Harlem." In Countee Cullen, ed., *Caroling Dusk*, p. 217.

———. "What Do I Care for Morning?" In Countee Cullen, *Caroling Dusk*, p. 216.

Kaplan, Carla. *The Erotics of Talk: Women's Writing and Feminist Paradigms*. New York: Oxford University Press, 1996.

———. "Narrative Contracts and Emancipatory Readers: *Incidents in the Life of Slave Girl*." *Yale Journal of Criticism* 6 (1): 93–119.

Keats, John. *You Might as Well Live: The Life and Times of Dorothy Parker*. New York: Paragon House, 1970.

Key, Ellen. *Love and Marriage*. New York: Source Book Press, 1970.

Koestenbaum, Wayne. *Double Talk: The Erotics of Male Literary Collaboration*. New York: Routledge, 1989.

Langer, Elinor. *Josephine Herbst*. New York: Warner Books, 1983.

Larsen, Nella. *Quicksand and Passing*. Ed. Deborah McDowell. New Brunswick, N.J.: Rutgers University Press, 1988.

Leach, Eugene E. "The Radicals of the *The Masses*." In Heller and Rudnick, *1915*, pp. 27–47.

Levine, Lawrence W. *Black Culture and Black Consciousness: Afro-American Folk Thought from Slavery To Freedom*. New York: Oxford University Press, 1977.

Lewis, David Levering. *When Harlem Was in Vogue*. New York: Oxford University Press, 1979.

Lewis, Theophilus. "Souls of Black Folk." *The Messenger* (May 1925): 195; (June 1925): 230.

———. "Theatre." *The Messenger* (January 1925): 380.

Lieberfeld, Daniel. "Here under False Pretences: The Marx Brothers Crash the Gates." Paper presented at the Modern Language Association Annual Convention, December 1995.

Liebman, Robert Leslie. "Rabbis or Rakes, Schlemiels or Supermen?" *Literature Film Quarterly* 12(3) (1984): 195–201.

Lindley, David. *Lyric*. New York: Methuen, 1985.

Lindsey, Judge Ben B., and Wainwright Evens. *The Companionate Marriage*. Garden City, N.Y.: Garden City Publishing, 1929.

Locke, Alain. "Max Rheinhardt Reads the Negro's Dramatic Horoscope." *Opportunity* (May 1924): 146.

———, Ed. *The New Negro: Voices of the Harlem Renaissance*. New York: Macmillan, 1992.

Loos, Anita. *But Gentlemen Marry Brunettes*. New York: Boni & Liveright, 1928.

———. "The Force of Heredity, and Nella; A Modern Fable with a Telling Moral for Eugenists." *Vanity Fair* (February 1915): 42.

———. *Gentlemen Prefer Blondes*. New York: Boni & Liveright, 1925.

———. *A Girl Like I*. New York: Viking, 1966.

Luhmann, Niklas. *Love as Passion: The Codification of Intimacy*. Trans. Jeremy Gaines and Doris L. Jones. Cambridge: Harvard University Press, 1986.

Lupton, Mary Jane. "Clothes and Closure in Three Novels by Black Women." *Black American Literature Forum* 20 (Winter 1986): 409–421.

McDowell, Deborah. *The Changing Same: Black Women's Literature, Criticism, and Theory*. Bloomington: Indiana University Press, 1995.

———. "Introduction." In Larsen, *Quicksand and Passing*, pp. ix–xxxv.

———. "Introduction: Regulating Midwives." In Jessie Redmon Fauset, *Plum Bun*. Boston: Beacon Press, 1990, pp. ix–xxiii.

Marchand, Roland. *Advertising the American Dream: Making Way for Modernity, 1920–1940*. Berkeley: University of California Press, 1985.

Mast, Gerald. "The Neurotic Jew as American Clown." In *Jewish Wry: Essays on Jewish Humor*, Ed. Sarah Blacher Cohen. Bloomington: Indiana University Press, 1987, pp. 125–140.

May, Lary. *Screening Out the Past: The Birth of Mass Culture and the Motion Picture Industry*. New York: Oxford University Press, 1980.

Mayfield, Sara. *The Constant Circle: H. L. Mencken and His Friends*. New York: Delacorte Press, 1968.

Meade, Marion. *Dorothy Parker: What Fresh Hell Is This?* New York: Villard Books, 1987.

Michaels, Walter Benn. *Our America: Nativism, Modernism, and Pluralism*. Durham, N.C.: Duke University Press, 1995.

Millay, Edna St. Vincent [Nancy Boyd]. *Distressing Dialogues*. New York: Harper & Brothers, 1924.

———. *A Few Figs from Thistles*. New York: Harper & Brothers, 1920.

———. *Renascence*. New York: Harper & Brothers, 1917.

———. *Second April*. New York: Mitchell Kennerly, 1921.

Millay, Kathleen. *Against the Wall*. New York: Macaulay, 1929.

Montefiore, Jan. *Feminism and Poetry*. London: Pandora, 1987.

Morton, Patricia. *Disfigured Images: The Historical Assault on Afro-American Women*. Westport, Conn.: Greenwood Press, 1991.

Newton, Esther. "The Mythic Mannish Lesbian: Radclyffe Hall and the New Woman." In *The Lesbian Issue: Essays from Signs*. Ed. Estelle B. Freeman, Barbara C. Gelpi, Susan L. Johnson, and Kathleen M. Weston. Chicago: University of Chicago Press, 1985, pp. 7–25.

North, Michael. *The Dialect of Modernism: Race, Language and Twentieth Century Literature*. New York: Oxford University Press, 1994.

O'Neil, Raymond. "The Negro in Dramatic Art." *The Crisis* (February 1924): 155–157.

Parker, Dorothy. *Death and Taxes*. New York: Viking, 1931.

———. *Enough Rope*. New York: Boni & Liveright, 1926.

———. "The First Hundred Plays Are the Hardest." In Amory and Bradlee, eds., *Vanity Fair*, pp. 34–35.

———. "Introduction." In *The Most of S. J. Perelman*. New York: Simon and Schuster, 1958, pp. xi–xiv.

———. *The Portable Dorothy Parker*. New York: Penguin, 1986.

———. "Such a Pretty Little Picture." *The Smart Set* (December 1922).

———. *Sunset Gun*. New York: Boni & Liveright, 1928.

———. [Rousseau, Henriette]. "Women: A Hate Song." *Vanity Fair* (August 1916): 61.

Parry, Albert. *Garrets and Pretenders: A History of Bohemianism in America*. New York: Dover, 1933.

Patterson, Raymond R. "Helene Johnson." In *Dictionary of Literary Biography*, vol. 51. Detroit: Gale Research, 1987.

Perry, Margaret. *A Bio-Bibliography of Countee P. Cullen, 1903–1946*. Westport, Conn.: Greenwood Press, 1971.

Poggioli, Renato. *The Theory of the Avant-Garde*. Cambridge: Harvard University Press, 1968.

Preminger, Alex, Ed. *Princeton Encyclopedia of Poetry and Poetics*. Enlarged edition. Princeton, N.J.: Princeton University Press, 1974.

Ransom, F. B. "Manufacturing Toilet Articles: A Big Negro Business." *Messenger* (December 1923): 937.

Rapp, Rayna, and Ellen Ross. "The Twenties' Backlash: Compulsory Heterosexuality, the Consumer Family, and the Waning of Feminism." In Swerdlow and Lessinger, *Class, Race, and Sex*, pp. 93–107.

Redding, Louis L. "A Florida Sunday." *Opportunity* (October 1925): 302–303.

Ridge, Lola. *The Ghetto and Other Poems*. New York: Huebsch, 1918.

Rudolf, Alan. *Mrs. Parker and the Vicious Circle*. [film] 1994.

Ryan, Mary P. "The Projection of a New Womanhood: The Movie Moderns in the 1920's." In *Our American Sisters: Women in American Life and Thought*, 2d edition. Ed. Jean E. Friedman and William G. Shade. Boston: Allyn and Bacon, 1980, pp. 366–384.

Sanger, Margaret. *Woman and the New Race*. New York: Blue Ribbon Books, 1920.

Sarlos, Robert K. "Jig Cook and Susan Glaspell: Rule Makers and Rule Breakers," in Heller and Rudnick, eds., *1915*, pp. 250–260.

Schoen, Carol B. *Anzia Yezierska*. Boston: Twayne, 1970.

Schuyler, George. *Black and Conservative*. New Rochelle, N.Y.: Arlington House, 1966.

———. "The Negro-Art Hokum." *The Nation* (June 16, 1926): 662–663.

———. [review of Amber Lee, *The Woman I Am*]. *Messenger* (December 1925): 398.

———. "Shafts and Darts." *Messenger* (January 1926): 9; (January 1925): 35–36.

———. *The Yellow Peril*. *Messenger* (January 1925): 28–31.

Scott, Esther Fulks. "Negroes as Actors in Serious Plays." *Opportunity* (August 1923): 20–23.

Scruggs, Charles. *The Sage in Harlem: H. L. Mencken and the Black Writers of the 1920s*. Baltimore: Johns Hopkins University Press, 1984.

Sedgwick, Eve Kosofsky. *Between Men: English Literature and Male Homosocial Desire*. New York: Columbia University Press, 1985.

Showalter, Elaine. *Sexual Anarchy: Gender and Culture at the Fin de Siècle*. New York: Viking, 1990.

———, Ed. *These Modern Women: Autobiographical Essays from the Twenties*. New York: Feminist Press, 1989.

Shucard, Alan R. *Countee Cullen*. Boston: Twayne, 1984.

Silverman, Kaja. "*Histoire d'O*: The Construction of a Female Subject." In *Pleasure and Danger: Exploring Female Sexuality*. Ed. Carole S. Vance. New York: Routledge, 1984, pp. 320–349.

Simmons, Christina. "Companionate Marriage and the Lesbian Threat." *Frontiers* 4 (Fall 1979): 54–59.

Slide, Anthony, Ed. *Selected Vaudeville Criticism*. Metuchen, N.J.: Scarecrow Press, 1988.

Smith-Rosenberg, Carroll. *Disorderly Conduct: Visions of Gender in Victorian America*. New York: Oxford University Press, 1985.

Stallybrass, Peter, and Allon White. *The Politics and Poetics of Transgression*. London: Methuen, 1986.

Stanborough, Jane. "Edna St. Vincent Millay and the Language of Vulnerability." In *Shakespeare's Sisters: Feminist Essays on Woman Poets*, Ed. Sandra M. Gilbert and Susan Gubar. Bloomington: Indiana University Press, 1979, pp. 183–199.

Story, Ralph D. "Patronage and the Harlem Renaissance: You Get What You Pay For." *College Language Association Journal* 32(3): 284–295.

Swerdlow, Amy, and Hanna Lessinger, Eds. *Class, Race, and Sex: The Dynamics of Control*. Boston: G. K. Hall, 1983.

Taggard, Genevieve. *Calling Western Union*. New York: Harper, 1936.

———. "Desert Woman Remembers Her Reasons." *Measure* 21 (November 1922): 8.

———. *For Eager Lovers*. New York: Thomas Seltzer, 1922.

———. "Her Massive Sandal." *Measure* 38 (April 1924): 11–13.

———. "If You Are a Man." *Measure* 41 (July 1924): 12–14.

———. *The Life and Mind of Emily Dickinson*. New York: Knopf, 1930.

———, Ed. *May Days: An Anthology of Verse from Masses-Liberator*. New York: Boni & Liveright, 1926.

———. *Not Mine to Finish: Poems, 1928–1934*. New York: Harper & Brothers, 1934.

———. *Origin: Hawaii*. Honolulu: Honolulu Star-Bulletin, 1947.

———. *Words for the Chisel*. New York: Alfred A. Knopf, 1926.

Tanner, Jo A. *Dusky Maidens: The Odyssey of the Early Black Dramatic Actress*. Westport, Conn.: Greenwood Press, 1992.

Taussig, Charlotte E. "The New Negro as Revealed in His Poetry." *Opportunity* (April 1927): 108.

"The Theatre—Drama." *Messenger* (June 1923): 746.

Tester, Keith, Ed. *The Flaneur*. New York: Routledge, 1994.

Thurman, Wallace. *FIRE!!: Devoted to Younger Negro Artists*. New York: 1926.

———. *Harlem: A Forum of Negro Life*. New York: 1928.

———. *Infants of the Spring*. Boston: Northeastern University Press, 1992.

Trimberger, Ellen Kay, Ed. *Intimate Warriors: Portraits of a Modern Marriage. Selected Works by Neith Boyce and Hutchins Hapgood*. New York: Feminist Press, 1991.

Van Doren, Carl. "The Younger Generation of Negro Writers." *Opportunity* (May 1924): 144–145.

Wall, Cheryl A. *Women of the Harlem Renaissance*. Bloomington: Indiana University Press, 1995.

Ware, Carolyn F. *Greenwich Village, 1920–1930: A Comment on American Civilization in the Post-War Years*. Boston: Riverside Press, 1935.

West, Dorothy. "Hannah Byde." *Messenger* (July 1926): 197–199.

Williams, Delores S. *Sisters in the Wilderness: The Challenge of Womanist God-Talk*. Maryknoll, N.Y.: Orbis Books, 1993.

Williams, Raymond. *The Politics of Modernism: Against the New Conformists*. New York: Verso, 1989.

———. *Problems in Materialism and Culture*. New York: Verso, 1980.

Wilson, Edmund. *I Thought of Daisy*. New York: Farrar, Straus, and Giroux, 1967.

———. *The Shores of Light: A Literary Chronicle of the Twenties and Thirties*. New York: Farrar, Straus, and Young, 1952.

Wintz, Cary. *Black Culture and the Harlem Renaissance*. Houston: Rice University Press, 1988.

Wolf, Robert L. *After Disillusion*. New York: Seltzer, 1923.

"A Word about Debutantes." *Vanity Fair* (January 1915): 15.

Young, Iris Marion. *Justice and the Politics of Difference*. Princeton, N.J.: Princeton University Press, 1990.

Index